America Now

Short Readings from Recent Periodicals

America Now

Short Readings from Recent Periodicals

TENTH EDITION

EDITED BY

Robert Atwan

Series Editor, *The Best American Essays*

EXERCISES PREPARED WITH THE ASSISTANCE OF

Valerie Duff-Strautmann

Mallory Moore

Bedford/St. Martin's   Boston • New York

For Bedford/St. Martin's

Developmental Editor: Christina Gerogiannis
Production Editor: Annette Pagliaro Sweeney
Production Supervisor: Samuel Jones
Executive Marketing Manager: Molly Parke
Editorial Assistant: Amanda Legee
Copy Editor: Steven M. Patterson
Permissions Managers: Kalina K. Ingham and Martha Friedman
Senior Art Director: Anna Palchik
Text Design: Dutton & Sherman Design
Cover Design: Marine Miller
Cover Photo: Newsand at bookstore © Steve Hamblin/Alamy
Composition: Cenveo® Publisher Services
Printing and Binding: RR Donnelley and Sons

President, Bedford/St. Martin's: Denise B. Wydra
Presidents, Macmillan Higher Education: Joan E. Feinberg and Tom Scotty
Editor in Chief: Karen S. Henry
Director of Marketing: Karen R. Soeltz
Production Director: Susan W. Brown
Associate Production Director: Elise S. Kaiser
Managing Editor: Elizabeth M. Schaaf

Manufactured in the United States of America.

1   2   3   4   5   6   16   15   14   13

For information, write: Bedford/St. Martin's, 75 Arlington Street, Boston, MA 02116 (617-399-4000)

ISBN 978-1-4576-1593-1 (Student Edition)
ISBN 978-1-4576-3639-4 (High School Edition)
ISBN 978-1-4576-1595-5 (Instructor's Edition)

Acknowledgments

Ahmad, Meher, "My Homeland Security Journey" from *The Progressive*, May 2012. Copyright © 2012 by Meher Ahmad. Reprinted with permission of The Progressive, Inc. www.progressive .org. All rights reserved.

Ajmani, Tim, "Compensation for College Athletes?" *The Corsair*, Pensacola State College, April 25, 2012. Reprinted by permission of the author.

Acknowledgments and copyrights are continued at the back of the book on pages 359–61, which constitute an extension of the copyright page. It is a violation of the law to reproduce these selections by any means whatsoever without the written permission of the copyright holder.

At the time of publication all Internet URLs published in this text were found to accurately link to their intended Web site. If you do find a broken link, please forward the information to alegee@bedfordstmartins.com so that it can be corrected for the next printing.

About the Editor

Robert Atwan is the series editor of the annual *Best American Essays*, which he founded in 1985. His essays, reviews, and critical articles have appeared in the *New York Times*, the *Los Angeles Times*, the *Atlantic Monthly, Iowa Review, Denver Quarterly, Kenyon Review, River Teeth*, and many other publications. For Bedford/St. Martin's, he has also edited *Ten on Ten: Major Essayists on Recurring Themes* (1992), *Our Times*, Fifth Edition (1998), and *Convergences*, Third Edition (2009). He has coedited (with Jon Roberts) *Left, Right, and Center: Voices from Across the Political Spectrum* (1996), and is coeditor with Donald McQuade of *The Writer's Presence*, Seventh Edition (2012). He lives in New York City.

Preface for Instructors

People write for many reasons, but one of the most compelling is to express their views on matters of current public interest. Browse any Web site, newsstand, or library magazine rack and you'll find an abundance of articles and opinion pieces responding to current issues and events. Too frequently, students see the writing they do in a composition class as having little connection with real-world problems and issues. *America Now*, with its provocative professional and student writing — all very current opinion essays drawn from a range of periodicals — shows students that by writing on the important issues of today, they can influence campus and public discourse and truly make a difference.

The tenth edition of *America Now* offers a generous sampling of timely and provocative material. *America Now* is designed to immerse introductory writing students in the give-and-take of public dialogue and to stimulate thinking, discussion, and composition. Its overriding instructional principle — which guides everything from the choice of readings and topics to the design of questions — is that participation in informed discussion will help generate and enrich student writing.

America Now encourages its users to view reading, thinking, discussion, and writing as closely interrelated activities. It assumes that (1) attentive reading and reflection will lead to informed discussion; (2) participation in open and informed discussion will result in a broadening of viewpoints; (3) an awareness of different viewpoints will stimulate further reflection and renewed discussion; and (4) this process in turn will lead to thoughtful papers.

The book's general introduction, "The Persuasive Writer: Expressing Opinions with Clarity, Confidence, and Civility," takes the student through these interrelated processes and offers some useful guidelines for engaging in productive discussion that will lead to effective essays. Three annotated student essays serve as models of persuasive opinion writing. Instructors may also find helpful my essay "Writing and the Art of Discussion," which can be found in the instructor's manual.

New to This Edition

Following is a brief overview of the tenth edition of *America Now*. For a more in-depth description of the book, see "Using *America Now*" beginning on page ix of this preface.

Forty-six readings, 3 visual texts, and 12 e-Pages — all new and *very* current. Drawn from more than 36 recent periodicals, including 12 student newspapers, each reading not only is new to this edition but also has appeared within a year or two of the book's publication. With half of its selections published in 2012, *America Now* is the most current short essay reader available. Some of the readings you will find in the tenth edition are by best-selling authors Barbara Ehrenreich and John Ehrenreich on the economy, actor Ashton Kutcher on romance in the digital age, noted writer Thomas Chatterton Williams on multiracial identity, and *Friday Night Lights* author Buzz Bissinger on the future of college football.

Nine new issues of current interest — and lively visuals. Nine of the twelve thematic chapters have been updated to reflect the changing interests of students over the past two years. Sure to spark lively discussion and writing, these new topics include the state of marriage today, communicating through social media (and what we gain and lose), college sports, higher education, the American prison system, and the economy. In a new chapter on consumer culture, we ask the question: Is *everything* for sale?

New "casebook" chapter. The book's final chapter, "Debating Climate Change: How Scientific Is the Evidence?" contains seven selections that focus on one of today's most widely discussed issues. The expanded chapter, which also includes a debate between experts on the topic, can be used by instructors who want to set up classroom panels or forums for extended discussion and writing.

E-Pages for every chapter take advantage of what the Web can do. Twelve online selections, including videos and interactive graphics, extend the print book and offer new ways to master key composition skills. And every e-Page is supported by interesting, useful editorial apparatus and questions that students can complete online. For example, Harvard University's "Project Implicit" in the chapter on racial and ethnic identity lets students test themselves for biases they may not have been aware of — and participate in ongoing research at the same time. Presidential campaign commercials, from both our recent and distant past, in the chapter on American consumerism will provoke discussion and writing about how even those elected to our highest office market themselves. For a complete list of these e-Pages, see the book's table of contents. You and your students can access these collected selections at the book companion site for *America Now* at bedfordstmartins.com /americanow/epages. Students receive access automatically with the purchase of a new book. If the activation code printed in the inside cover of the student edition is revealed, it might be expired. Students can purchase access at the book companion site. Instructors don't need an access code; they can access the e-Pages at the book companion site. They can also use the free tools accompanying the e-Pages to upload a syllabus, readings, and assignments to share with the class.

Using *America Now*

Professional and Student Writing from a Wide Variety of Sources

The book's selections by professional writers are drawn from recent periodicals, ranging from specialized journals such as *Chronicle of Higher Education* to influential general magazines such as *Harper's Bazaar, Esquire,* and *The Atlantic*. As would be expected in a collection that focuses heavily on social trends and current events, *America Now* features several newspapers and news-oriented magazines: the *Boston Globe,* the *New York Times,* and the *Washington Post*. With its additional emphasis on public discourse, this collection also draws on some of America's leading political magazines, including *Mother Jones, The Nation, The Weekly Standard,* and *The Progressive*. Also represented are magazines that appeal primarily to specialized audiences, such as *Ploughshares, Wired,* and *GOOD*. In general, the selections illustrate the variety of personal, informative, and persuasive writing encountered daily by millions of Americans. The readings are kept short (many under three pages, and some no longer than a page) to hold student interest and to serve as models for the student's own writing. To introduce a more in-depth approach to various topics, the book includes a few longer essays, especially in the final chapters.

America Now also features twelve published student selections from print and online college newspapers and, in two cases, a professional magazine. These recent works reveal student writers confronting in a public forum the same topics and issues that challenge some of our leading social critics and commentators, and they show how student writers can enter into and influence public discussion. In this way, the student selections in *America Now* — complemented by Student Writer at Work interviews — encourage students to see writing as a form of personal and public empowerment. This edition includes 10 brief, inspiring interviews in which student authors in the book explain how — and why — they express their opinions in writing. In addition, the book contains four examples of student writing for a classroom assignment.

To highlight models of persuasive writing, each chapter contains an annotated section of a student paper labeled "Looking Closely." The comments point out some of the most effective strategies of the student writers in the book and offer advice for stating a main point, shaping arguments, presenting examples and evidence, using quotations, recommending a course of action, and more.

Timely Topics for Discussion and Debate

Student essays not only make up a large percentage of the readings in this book, but also shape the volume's contents. As we monitored the broad spectrum of online college newspapers — and reviewed several hundred student essays — we gradually found the most commonly discussed campus issues and topics. Issues such as those mentioned on page vii of this preface have provoked so much recent student response that they could have resulted in several single-topic collections. Many college papers do not restrict themselves to news items and editorial opinion but make room for personal essays as well. Some popular student topics are sports, technology, ethnic and racial identity, and consumerism, all of which are reflected in the book's table of contents.

To facilitate group discussion and in-class work, *America Now* features eleven bite-sized units and one in-depth "casebook" chapter at the end. These focused chapters permit instructors to cover a broad range of themes and issues in a single semester. Each can be conveniently handled in one or two class periods. In general, the chapters move from accessible, personal topics (for example, names, marriage, and social media) to more public and controversial issues (violence, the economy, and climate change), thus accommodating instructors who prefer to start with personal writing and gradually progress to exposition, analysis, and argument.

Since composition courses naturally emphasize issues revolving around language and the construction of meaning, *America Now* also includes a number of selections designed to encourage students to examine the powerful influence of words and symbols.

The Visual Expression of Opinion

Reflecting the growing presence of advertising in public discussion, among the book's images are opinion advertisements (or "op-ads"). These pieces, which focus on racial profiling and immigration, encourage students to uncover the visual and verbal strategies of various advocacy groups trying to influence the consciousness and ideology of large audiences.

Because we live in an increasingly visual culture, the book's introduction offers a section on expressing opinions visually — with striking examples from photojournalism, cartoons, and opinion advertisements. Another assortment of visual selections, titled "America Then," provides students with historical perspectives on "America Now." These images show that many of the issues we deal with today have roots in the past. They include the first map that named America, a 1940s telegram from jazz legend Louis Armstrong to his manager, and a magazine quiz from the 1950s asking, "Are You Ready for Marriage?"

The Instructional Apparatus: Before, During, and After Reading

To help promote reflection and discussion, the book includes a prereading assignment for each main selection. The questions in "Before You Read" provide students with the opportunity to explore a few of the avenues that lead to fruitful discussion and interesting papers. A full description of the advantages gained by linking reading, writing, and classroom discussion can be found in my introduction to the instructor's manual.

The apparatus of *America Now* supports both discussion-based instruction and more individualized approaches to reading and writing. Taking into account the increasing diversity of students (especially the growing number of speakers for whom English is not their first language) in today's writing programs, the apparatus offers extensive help with college-level vocabulary and features a "Words to Learn" list preceding each selection. This vocabulary list with brief definitions will allow students to spot ahead of time some of the words they may find difficult; encountering the word later in context will help lock it in memory. It's unrealistic, however, to think students will acquire a fluent knowledge of new words by memorizing a list. Therefore, the apparatus following each selection includes additional exercises under the headings "Vocabulary/ Using a Dictionary" and "Responding to Words in Context." These sets of questions introduce students to prefixes, suffixes, connotations, denotations, tone, and etymology.

Along with the discussion of vocabulary, other incrementally structured questions follow individual selections. "Discussing Main Point and Meaning" and "Examining Sentences, Paragraphs, and Organization" questions help to guide students step by step through the reading process, culminating in the set of "Thinking Critically" questions. As instructors well know, beginning students can sometimes be too trusting of what they see in print, especially in textbooks. Therefore, the "Thinking Critically" questions invite students to take a more skeptical attitude toward their reading and to form the habit of challenging a selection from both analytical and experiential points of view. The selection apparatus concludes with "Writing Activities," which emphasize freewriting exercises and collaborative projects.

In addition to the selection apparatus, *America Now* contains end-of-chapter questions designed to stimulate further discussion and writing. The chapter apparatus approaches the reading material from topical and thematic angles, with an emphasis on group discussion. The introductory comments to each chapter highlight the main discussion points and the way selections are linked together. These points and linkages are then reintroduced at the end of the chapter through three sets of interlocking study questions and tasks: (1) a suggested topic for discussion, (2) questions and ideas to help students prepare for class discussion, and (3) several writing assignments that ask students to move from discussion to composition — that is, to develop papers out of the ideas and opinions expressed in class discussion and debate. Instructors with highly diverse writing classes may find "Topics for Cross-Cultural Discussion" a convenient way to encourage an exchange of perspectives and experiences that could also generate ideas for writing. Located on the book's Web site (bedfordstmartins.com/americanow) are ESL and Developmental Quizzes that test vocabulary and comprehension skills. Electronic scoring, which can be monitored by instructors, offers immediate feedback.

Lastly, e-Pages for every chapter bring *America Now* online and engage students with media that can't be covered in a traditional book. Every e-Page features a video, interactive graphic, or other visual, and the selections are supported by headnotes, "Before You Explore" questions, and three question sets labeled "Respond," "Act," and "Connect" — encouraging your students to think critically and respond thoughtfully to multimodal texts.

Acknowledgments

While putting together the tenth edition of *America Now,* I was fortunate to receive the assistance of many talented individuals. I am enormously grateful to Valerie Duff-Strautmann, Mallory Moore, and Beth

Castrodale, who contributed to the book's instructional apparatus and Instructor's Manual, bringing to the task valuable classroom experience at all levels of composition instruction. Gregory Atwan was responsible for researching and authoring the apparatus for the e-Pages, which are an essential part of this new edition. Liz deBeer of Rutgers University contributed a helpful essay in the Instructor's Manual on designing student panels ("Forming Forums"), along with advice on using the book's apparatus in both developmental and mainstream composition classes.

To revise a text is to entertain numerous questions: What kind of selections work best in class? What types of questions are most helpful? How can reading, writing, and discussion be most effectively intertwined? This edition profited immensely from the following instructors who generously took the time to respond to the ninth edition: Eva Norinne K. Betjemann, Norwalk Community College; Melanie Burdick, Washburn University; Richard Flinn, Naval Academy Preparatory School; Jay Gordon, Youngstown State University; Ann Jennings, Rustburg High School; Elizabeth Pirie, Diablo Valley College; Vicki Lynn Samson, Western Kentucky University; Bobbi Jo Scott, Patriot High School; Kimberly Swensen, Westerville North High School; and Patricia Vandever, Charlottesville High School.

I'd also like to acknowledge instructors who have reviewed previous editions, and whose ideas and suggestions continue to inform the book: Kim M. Baker, Roger Williams University; Kevin Ball, Youngstown State University; Deborah Biorn, St. Cloud State University; Joan Blankmann, Northern Virginia Community College; Diane Bosco, Suffolk County Community College; Melanie N. Burdick, University of Missouri–Kansas City; Mikel Cole, University of Houston–Downtown; Danielle Davis, Pasadena City College; Darren DeFrain, Wichita State University; Kaye Falconer, Bakersfield College; Steven Florzcyk, the State University of New York–New Paltz; Nancy Freiman, Milwaukee Area Technical College; Andrea Germanos, Saint Augustine College; Jay L. Gordon, Youngstown State University; Kim Halpern, Pulaski Technical College; Jessica Harvey, Alexandria Technical College; Chris Hayes, University of Georgia; Sharon Jaffee, Santa Monica College; Patricia W. Julius, Michigan State University; Jessica Heather Lourey, Alexandria Technical College; Brian Ludlow, Alfred University; Sherry Manis, Foothill College; Terry Meier, Bakersfield College; Melody Nightingale, Santa Monica College; Kimme Nuckles, Baker College; Michael Orlando, Bergen Community College; Thomas W. Pittman, Youngstown State University; Marty Price, Mississippi State University; David Pryor, University of the Incarnate Word; Hubert C. Pulley, Georgia Southern University; Sherry Robertson, Pulaski Technical College; Lynn Sabas, Saint Augustine College; Vicki Lynn Samson, Western Kentucky University and Bowling

Green Community College; Jennifer Satterlee, Parkland College; Wendy Scott, Buffalo State College; Andrea D. Shanklin, Howard Community College; Ann Spurlock, Mississippi State University; Linda Weiner, the University of Akron; Frances Whitney, Bakersfield College; Richard A. Williams, Youngstown State University; and Martha Anne Yeager-Tobar, Cerritos College.

Other people helped in various ways. I'm indebted to Barbara Gross of Rutgers University, Newark, for her excellent work in helping to design the Instructor's Manual for the first edition. Two good friends, Charles O'Neill and the late Jack Roberts, both of St. Thomas Aquinas College, went over my early plans for the book and offered many useful suggestions.

As always, it was a pleasure to work with the superb staff at Bedford/ St. Martin's. Jane Helms and Ellen Thibault, my editors on earlier editions, shaped the book in lasting ways. I also am indebted to my developmental editor, Christina Gerogiannis. As usual, Christina provided excellent guidance and numerous suggestions, while doing her utmost best to keep a book that depends on so many moving parts and timely material on its remarkably tight schedule. Christina is also responsible for the student interviews that are such an important feature of this edition. Amanda Legee, editorial assistant, contacted the students profiled in the book and worked energetically on the book's Web site and Instructor's Manual. Kalina Ingham and Martha Friedman managed text and art permissions under a tight schedule. Annette Pagliaro Sweeney guided the book through production with patience and care, staying on top of many details, and Elizabeth Schaaf managed the production process with great attentiveness. I was fortunate to receive the careful copyediting of Steven M. Patterson. Senior new media editor Kimberly Hampton deserves warm thanks for her work, as does executive marketing manager Molly Parke.

I am grateful to Charles H. Christensen, the retired president of Bedford/St. Martin's, for his generous help and thoughtful suggestions throughout the life of this book. Finally, I especially want to thank Macmillan Higher Education's co-president, Joan E. Feinberg, who conceived the idea for *America Now* and who continues to follow it closely through its various editions, for her deep and abiding interest in college composition. It is a great pleasure and privilege to work with her.

Robert Atwan

You Get More Digital Choices for *America Now*

America Now doesn't stop with a book. Online, you'll find both free and affordable premium resources to help students get even more out of the book and your course. You'll also find convenient instructor resources, such as downloadable sample syllabi, classroom activities, and even a nationwide community of teachers. To learn more about or order any of the products below, contact your Bedford/St. Martin's sales representative, e-mail sales support (sales_support@bfwpub.com), or visit the Web site at bedfordstmartins.com.

e-Pages for America Now

E-Pages for *America Now* take full advantage of what the Web can do for your classroom. A thoughtfully curated collection of videos, interactive graphics, and full-color visuals connect conversations in the print text to the Web with assignments that students can complete online. For a complete list of e-Pages, please see the table of contents on page xvii. For access, visit bedfordstmartins.com/americanow/epages. Note: Students receive access to e-Pages automatically with the purchase of a new book.

Student Site for America Now

bedfordstmartins.com/americanow

Send students to free and open resources, choose flexible premium resources to supplement your print text, or upgrade to an expanding collection of innovative digital content.

Free and open resources for America Now provide students with easy-to-access reference materials, visual tutorials, and support for working with sources.

- ESL & Developmental Quizzes for every reading in the book
- 3 free tutorials from *ix visual exercises* by Cheryl Ball and Kristin Arola
- *TopLinks* with reliable online sources
- *The Bedford Bibliographer*: a tool for collecting source information and making a bibliography in MLA, APA, and *Chicago* styles

VideoCentral is a growing collection of videos for the writing class that captures real-world, academic, and student writers talking about how and why they write. *VideoCentral* can be packaged for free with *America Now*. An activation code is required. To order *VideoCentral* packaged with the print book, use ISBN 1-4576-3649-2 or 978-1-4576-3649-3.

Re:Writing Plus gathers all of Bedford/St. Martin's' premium digital content for composition into one online collection. It includes hundreds of model documents, the first ever peer review game, and *VideoCentral*. *Re:Writing Plus* can be purchased separately or packaged with the print book at a significant discount. An activation code is required. To order *Re:Writing Plus* packaged with *America Now*, use ISBN 1-4576-3652-2 or 978-1-4576-3652-3.

i-series

Add more value to your text by choosing one of the following tutorial series, free when packaged with *America Now*. This popular series presents multimedia tutorials in a flexible format — because there are things you can't do in a book. To learn more about package options or any of the products below, contact your Bedford/St. Martin's sales representative or visit bedfordstmartins.com.

ix visualizing composition 2.0 (available online) helps students put into practice key rhetorical and visual concepts. To order *ix visualizing composition* packaged with the print book, use ISBN 1-4576-3648-4 or 978-1-4576-3648-6.

i-claim: visualizing argument 2.0 (available online) shows students how to analyze and compose arguments in words, images, and sounds with 6 tutorials, an illustrated glossary, and over 70 multimedia arguments. To order *i-claim: visualizing argument* packaged with the print book, use ISBN 1-4576-3651-4 or 978-1-4576-3651-6.

i-cite: visualizing sources (available online as part of *Re:Writing Plus*) brings research to life through an animated introduction, four tutorials, and hands-on source practice. To order *i-cite: visualizing sources* packaged with the print book, use ISBN 1-4576-3654-9 or 978-1-4576-3654-7.

Instructor Resources

You have a lot to do in your course. Bedford/St. Martin's wants to make it easy for you to find the support you need — and to get it quickly.

The Instructor's Manual for *America Now* is available bound into the Instructor's Edition and as a PDF that can be downloaded from bedfordstmartins.com/americanow. In addition to chapter overviews and teaching tips, the Instructor's Manual includes sample syllabi and suggestions for classroom activities.

Teaching Central (bedfordstmartins.com/teachingcentral) offers the entire list of Bedford/St. Martin's print and online professional resources in one place. You'll find landmark reference works, source-books on pedagogical issues, award-winning collections, and practical advice for the classroom — all free for instructors.

Bits (bedfordbits.com) collects creative ideas for teaching a range of composition topics in an easily searchable blog. A community of teachers — leading scholars, authors, and editors — discuss revision, research, grammar and style, technology, peer review, and much more. Take, use, adapt, and pass the ideas around. Then, come back to the site to comment or share your own suggestion.

Contents

Preface for Instructors vii

The Persuasive Writer: Expressing Opinions with Clarity, Confidence, and Civility 1

What is *America Now*? 1

Participating in Class Discussion: Six Basic Rules 3

What Are Opinions? 4

How Do We Form Opinions? 7

From Discussion to Writing 9

The Practice of Writing 11

What Is "Correct English"? 12

Writing as a Public Activity 13

How to Support Opinions 15

Writing for the Classroom: Three Annotated Student Essays 16

 Indicates online content. Go to
bedfordstmartins.com/americanow/epages

xvii

Expressing an Opinion Based on Personal Experience Alone 17

    KATI MATHER (Wheaton College), **The Many Paths to Success—With or Without a College Education** 17

Expressing an Opinion in Response to an Opposing Opinion 21

    CANDACE ROSE RARDON (University of Virginia), **Not-So-Great Expectations** 22

Expressing an Opinion with Reference to Reading and Research 27

    MILOS KOSIC (Northwest Community College), **How to Approach a Different Culture?** 27

The Visual Expression of Opinion 31

    Photography 32

        JOE ROSENTHAL, **Flag Raising at Iwo Jima** (Photograph) 32
        THOMAS E. FRANKLIN, **Three Firefighters Raising the Flag** (Photograph) 33
        ALAN DIAZ, **Elián González** 34

    Political Cartoons 35

        DOUG MARLETTE, **When It's Too Late to Warn Iran** (Cartoon) 37
        ED FISCHER, **It's Only until We End Terrorism** (Cartoon) 39
        JACK ZIEGLER, **Stem Cells** (Cartoon) 40

    Opinion Ads 41

        ACLU, **The Man on the Left** (Advertisement) 42

Writing as Empowerment 45

1

What's in a Name? 47

Does it matter to you if someone's first name is Leszczynska? Would that be the same to you as Luke or David? . . . An online columnist summarizes some recent psychological research showing that people tend to prefer others with easily pronounceable names . . . Reaching the Mexican border, a four-year-old girl must remember the right name to tell the guards . . . A University of Maryland student finds the name of the local pro-football team inappropriate and offensive . . . How did two vast continents in the Western Hemisphere wind up with the name *America*? It all starts with a map . . . Online, the Baby Name Voyager offers a guided tour through naming trends over the years.

DAVE MOSHER, **Easily Pronounced Names May Make People More Likable** [*Wired Science*, February 24, 2012] 49

SSA.GOV, **Top 10 Baby Names for 2011** 51
   Top 10 Baby Names of the 1970s 51

MARIA VENEGAS, **The Devil's Spine** [*Ploughshares*, Spring 2012] 54

STUDENT ESSAY: GREG NASIF, **Washington, Yea! Redskins, Boo!** [*The Diamondback*, The University of Maryland, October 13, 2011] 58
   LOOKING CLOSELY: Using Examples 61
   STUDENT WRITER AT WORK: Greg Nasif 63

AMERICA THEN . . . 1507: **Who Named America?** 65

[e] e-PAGE: **The Baby Name Voyager**

2

Relationships Today: Is Marriage in Decline? 69

Do young American couples still aspire to a married life or does our society today discourage marriage and the ideals of a love that lasts forever? Are someone's chances of getting married today considerably less than those of their parents years ago? A university alumni magazine examines the ways marriage has changed over the past fifty years and why it is declining . . . Biologists once thought that a common Midwest creature was the symbol of a happy monogamous life, but a columnist reports on new research proving that even the prairie vole is sexually unfaithful . . . A University of California student doubts that newly proposed legislation to stem the tide of divorce by permitting "temporary marriage" will be effective . . . In 1950, anxious young women could take a "quiz" to find out if they were "ready" for marriage . . . An interactive singles map shows what's happening where.

AJA GABEL, **The Marriage Crisis** [*University of Virginia Magazine*, Summer 2012] 71

SPOTLIGHT ON RESEARCH
   KAYT SUKEL, **Rethinking Monogamy** [*Big Think*, June 3, 2012] 78
   ALEXANDER G. OPHIR, STEVEN M. PHELPS, ANNA BESS SORIN, JERRY O. WOLFF, **Social but Not Genetic Monogamy Is Associated with Greater Breeding Success in Prairie Voles (excerpt)** [*Animal Behaviour*, 2008] 79

STUDENT ESSAY: NATALIE RIVERA, **Could Temporary Marriages Reduce the Alarming Rate of Divorce?** [*Daily Sundial*, California State University, Northridge, May 6, 2012] 80

LOOKING CLOSELY: Effective Openings: Establishing a Clear Context for an Argument 84

AMERICA THEN. . . 1950: **Are You Ready for Marriage?** 85

e e-PAGE: **The Interactive Singles Map of the United States**

3

Communicating through Social Media: What Do We Gain? What Do We Lose? 89

Are e-mail, Facebook, Twitter, and other kinds of social media altering traditional forms of communication? Are they seriously limiting the way people interact conversationally? Is communicating digitally now preferable to face-to-face conversation? A writer and editor worries about how the new social media will "alter our emotional experience of connection" with others . . . In our digital age, argues a noted young actor, are we losing our ability to truly communicate? . . . "A previous generation was referred to as Gen X," a Virginia Tech columnist maintains, but the way "our generation is socializing, it ought to be known as Generation teXt" . . . What's "humblebragging," and what does it say about us?

CHRISTINE ROSEN, **Electronic Intimacy** [*Wilson Quarterly*, Spring 2012] 91

ASHTON KUTCHER, **Has Texting Killed Romance?** [*Harper's Bazaar*, January 2011] 99

REBECCA ARMENDARIZ, **Chat History** [*GOOD*, September 2011] 102

STUDENT ESSAY: SHAWN GHUMAN, **Is Technology Destroying Social Bonds?** [*Collegiate Times*, Virginia Tech, February 22, 2012] 110

LOOKING CLOSELY: Including the Reader 113

STUDENT WRITER AT WORK: Shawn Ghuman 114

e e-PAGE: **Hashtag Humblebrag**

4

How Important Are Racial and Ethnic Identity?   117

Do you see yourself as representative of a racial or ethnic group? How important is it to your sense of identity to belong to this particular group? How do you identify yourself if, like a growing number of Americans, you belong to more than one group? A decade after the 9/11 attacks, one of the nation's most prominent essayists reflects on how in airports everywhere everyone now has an "identity" problem . . . A Pakistani American college student describes how it feels to always be detained by airport security . . . With more and more people claiming multiple identities, a noted author wonders if biracial Americans with African ancestry, like himself, have an ethical obligation to identify as black . . . An advertisement for the American Indian College Fund stresses the importance of tribal colleges for preserving Native American identity . . . An online research study measures how we see each other.

PICO IYER, **The Terminal Check** [*Granta*, #116, Summer 2011]   **119**

STUDENT ESSAY: MEHER AHMAD, **My Homeland Security Journey**
   [*The Progressive*, May 2012]   **124**
   LOOKING CLOSELY: Varying Sentences   **129**
   STUDENT WRITER AT WORK: Meher Ahmad   **130**

THOMAS CHATTERTON WILLIAMS, **As Black as We Wish to Be** [*New York Times*, March 18, 2012]   **132**

ADVERTISEMENT: **Think Indian** [American Indian College Fund, 2012]   **137**

e e-PAGE: **Project Implicit**

5

The American Consumer: Is Everything for Sale?   143

Has consumption grown out of control? Has shopping become not a practical necessity but a genuine addiction? Is everything for sale? A prominent political philosopher argues that we need a "public debate about where markets belong — and where they don't" . . . "Get to the mall and knock yourselves out," says a historian who believes that spending is good for the economy, and for the planet . . . Two community college students engage in a debate common during the holiday season: Are we an overly materialistic society? . . . An ad for one of the first automobiles suggests a trend toward what the American economist Thorstein Veblen called "conspicuous consumption" . . . A treasure trove of televised presidential campaign ads over the years shows what's changed—and what hasn't.

MICHAEL J. SANDEL, **What Isn't for Sale?** [*The Atlantic*, April 2012] 145

JAMES LIVINGSTON, **Americans, Thou Shalt Shop and Spend for the Planet**
[*Wired*, December 2011] 153

STUDENT DEBATE
Is the Holiday Season Too Materialistic? [AMEL SALEH, Yes] [*The Glacier*,
Moraine Valley Community College, December 2011] 157
Is the Holiday Season Too Materialistic? [LAUREN SMITH, No] [*The Glacier*,
Moraine Valley Community College, December 2011] 158
LOOKING CLOSELY: Supplying Evidence 161

AMERICA THEN . . . 1899: **The Powerful Theory of Conspicuous Consumption** 162

e e-PAGE: **The Living Room Candidate**

6

College Sports: Is It Time to Change the Game? 167

What should be done about the many scandals, financial and otherwise, that have plagued college sports? Is it time to start paying college athletes? Or are more extreme measures needed? The author of *Friday Night Lights* offers a bold solution to the problems facing college athletics, and football in particular: to ban this sport altogether at the college level. Why? "[B]ecause college football has no academic purpose" . . . A journalist argues that such a ban would be "paternalistic and shortsighted" and proposes more modest reforms . . . A student at Pensacola State College agrees that it's time to start paying student athletes—and also to stop placing so much blame on them for the recent sports scandals . . . A scene from a videotaped debate seconds Bissinger's argument for banning college football.

BUZZ BISSINGER, **Why College Football Should Be Banned** [*Wall Street Journal*, May 8, 2012] **169**

MEGAN GREENWELL, **Do College Sports Affect Students' Grades? A Defense of the NCAA** [*GOOD*, January 3, 2012] **173**

STUDENT ESSAY: TIM AJMANI, **Compensation for College Athletes?** [*The Corsair*, Pensacola State College, April 25, 2012] **177**
  LOOKING CLOSELY: The Art of Argument: Anticipating Opposition **180**
  STUDENT WRITER AT WORK: Tim Ajmani **182**

[e] e-PAGE: **Should College Football Be Banned?**

Is Society Becoming Less Violent? 185

If you regularly watch the evening news, you most likely think the world is a violent place — with warfare, civil insurrections, murder, and terrorism a constant feature. Yet, in a provocative study a noted neuroscientist claims that human beings are far less violent today than in the past and that violent acts are declining everywhere . . . Although he doesn't question the study's statistics, an Ashland University student in Ohio believes there may be holes in the claim that violence is declining . . . It certainly doesn't seem that way, suggests a noted author and activist, on the streets of Chicago, Detroit, New Orleans, Baltimore, and many other American cities devastated by poverty and crime . . . Do video games contribute to this violence? A Philadelphia columnist claims that violent video games may actually be therapeutic and decrease aggressive impulses . . . After hearing counter arguments and reviewing numerous studies, a recent Supreme Court decision concluded that censoring video game violence did not justify the infringement of free expression . . . An interactive quiz invites you to test your gun law IQ.

STEVEN PINKER, **Violence Vanquished** [*Wall Street Journal*, September 24, 2011] **187**

STUDENT ESSAY: JACOB EWING, **Steven Pinker and the Question of Violence** [Ashland University, April 27, 2012] **195**
  LOOKING CLOSELY: Effective Endings **200**
  STUDENT WRITER AT WORK: Jacob Ewing **201**
ALEX KOTLOWITZ, **Defusing Violence** [*The Rotarian*, February 2012] **202**

ANNETTE JOHN-HALL, **Using Video Games to Reduce Violence** [*Philadelphia Inquirer*, February 3, 2012] 208

SPOTLIGHT ON LAW AND SOCIETY: ROBERT ATWAN, **Can the State Prohibit the Sale of Violent Video Games to Minors?** [U.S. Supreme Court, *Brown v. Entertainment Merchants Association*, June 27, 2011] 211

e-PAGE: **Test Your Gun Law IQ**

8

The American Language Today: How Is It Changing? 215

What are some of the factors currently transforming our language? How is technology altering the way we write, spell, and express ourselves in general? Is it risky to let our casual texting styles carry over into our professional or academic writing? How much, for example, does spelling matter? Very much so, suggests a humanities professor who doesn't want to seem a "nit-picker" but finds it hard to tolerate "egregious misspellings" . . . Not so much, maintains another college professor who argues that the way we write is changing and so must our spelling . . . A journalist wonders if anyone can send a message today without using an exclamation point . . . Our "politically correct" society is making us overcautious about which words we can and cannot use, says a University of Hawai'i student . . . How did Americans convey instant messages long before the smart phone? . . . A video from Google asks, on the Web, do spelling and grammar matter?

OPPOSING VIEWS: **Does Spelling Count?** 217
 MIKITA BROTTMAN, **Spelling Matters** [*The Chronicle of Higher Education*, January 15, 2012] 217
 ANNE TRUBEK, **Use Your Own Words** [*Wired*, February 2012] 220

CHRISTOPHER MUTHER, **We Get the Point!** [*Boston Globe*, April 26, 2012] 224

STUDENT ESSAY: SHAYNA DIAMOND, **Words Are What We Make of Them** [*Ka Leo*, University of Hawai'i at Manoa, February 5, 2012] 229
 LOOKING CLOSELY: Establishing Your Main Point 233
 STUDENT WRITER AT WORK: Shayna Diamond 234

AMERICA THEN . . . 1844–2006: **The Telegram** 236

:e e-PAGE: **On the Web, Do Spelling and Grammar Matter?**

9

Education: Does College Still Matter? 241

Given the rising cost of college, is it really the best choice for everyone? And should those who pursue higher education choose majors that will provide the most financial bang for the tuition buck? Or is emphasizing the economic benefits of college selling short the intellectual satisfactions? Maintaining that a college education continues to be valuable, both economically and intellectually, for all citizens, one professor says it also gives students "the precious chance to think and reflect before life engulfs them" . . . But another professor says we need to face the fact that college isn't for everyone and do a better job of creating alternatives to it . . . A financial-advice columnist says a college education is still worth it—as long as students consider potential majors' job prospects and avoid taking on too much debt . . . Yet a student at Santa Monica College urges potential college attendees not to let financial concerns discourage them from pursuing a degree . . . A look into a virtual classroom of a nonprofit academy sheds light on a growing educational trend.

ANDREW DELBANCO, **Three Reasons College Still Matters** [*Boston Globe Magazine*, March 4, 2012] 243

ALEX TABARROK, **Tuning In to Dropping Out** [*The Chronicle Review*, March 9, 2012] 249

MICHELLE SINGLETARY, **Not All College Majors Are Created Equal** [*Washington Post*, January 14, 2012] 254

STUDENT ESSAY: MARIA DIMERA, **A College Degree Is a Worthy Achievement** [*The Corsair*, Santa Monica College, October 8, 2011] 258
　LOOKING CLOSELY: Moving from General to Specific 262
　STUDENT WRITER AT WORK: Maria Dimera 263

:e e-PAGE: **Khan Academy: "172,799,250 Lessons Delivered"**

The Economy: Are We Making Progress? 265

Have disparities in opportunities and wealth across income groups brought us to the point of class warfare? Or are lower- and middle-class Americans actually making more progress than we've been led to believe? And what about the Occupy movement? Has it sparked any lasting and meaningful changes? A journalist says the notion that all Americans have an equal opportunity to succeed has become a "dangerous lie...More than anything else, class now determines Americans' fates"...In contrast, a public policy analyst and an economist argue that "[o]ver the past three decades, growth in the U.S. economy has produced considerable...improvement in material well-being for both the middle class and the poor"...Examining the impact of the Occupy movement, two writers contend that "[w]hat started as a diffuse protest against economic injustice became a vast experiment in class building"...A student at Clark University explains why she also believes the Occupy movement is having lasting, positive effects... *The New York Times* asks its readers, "What's Your Economic Outlook?"

STEPHEN MARCHE, **We Are Not All Created Equal** [*Esquire*, January 2012]   267

BRUCE D. MEYER AND JAMES X. SULLIVAN, **American Mobility** [*Commentary Magazine*, March 2012]   271

BARBARA EHRENREICH AND JOHN EHRENREICH, **The Making of the 99%** [*The Nation*, December 14, 2011]   279

STUDENT ESSAY: BREANNA LEMBITZ, **A Taste of Freedom: What I Got at Occupy Wall Street** [*The Progressive*, February 2012]   287
LOOKING CLOSELY: Using Concrete Language   295
STUDENT WRITER AT WORK: Breanna Lembitz   296

e-PAGE: **What's Your Economic Outlook?**

Can We Shrink Our Growing Prison Population?   299

The United States now has the highest incarceration rate in the developed world. How did we get to this point? And what have the consequences been for the prison population and the larger society? Can anything be done to address the problem? A criminal-justice expert explores the reasons for the growth of the U.S. prison population and suggests ways to reduce recidivism and, perhaps, incarceration . . . A journalist examines the perverse incentives that make certain communities dependent on prisons . . . A student at American River College urges her state to reduce prison spending so that it can improve its funding of education . . . A Web broadcast explores the booming business of private prisons.

JOAN PETERSILIA, **Beyond the Prison Bubble** [*Wilson Quarterly*, Winter 2011]   301

CHRISTOPHER GLAZEK, **Raise the Crime Rate (excerpt)** [*n + 1*, Winter 2012]   310

STUDENT ESSAY: KAREN THOMAS, **Misplaced Priorities: It's Time to Invest in Schools, Not Prisons** [*American River Current*, American River College, June 2, 2011]   314
> LOOKING CLOSELY: Effective Persuasion: Recommending a Course of Action   317
> STUDENT WRITER AT WORK: Karen Thomas   318

 e-PAGE: **The Private Prison Problem**

Debating Climate Change: How Scientific Is the Evidence?   321

Are concerns about climate change justified or pure panic mongering? Can differing views on the issue be attributed to differing levels of education or opposing political and economic interests, or is something more complicated going on? And assuming that human activity is posing a serious threat to the

environment, what can be done? A journalist for a liberal magazine and two con-
tributors to a conservative publication come to different conclusions about the
reasons for, and possible value of, climate change skepticism . . . Taking it as a
given that climate change exists, a journalist asks what, if anything, the average
citizen can do about it. Buying organic cotton sheets certainly isn't enough, she
concludes . . . A political analyst criticizes "global warmists" for kicking up a "climate panic" . . . A student at Glendale Community College describes one academic's even more dire view: that solutions to climate change may be far beyond our
reach . . . While a popular scientist's 1985 alert about global warming attracted
limited attention, a 2012 "Climate Impacts Day" involved people from around the
world. An organization devoted to the issue invites visitors to "connect the dots."

OPPOSING VIEWS: **Is Climate Change Real?**   323
   CHRIS MOONEY, **We Can't Handle the Truth** [*Mother Jones*, May/June 2011]   323
   JOSEPH BOTTUM AND WILLIAM ANDERSON, **Unchanging Science** [*Weekly
      Standard*, November 28, 2011]   333

SARAH LASKOW, **Debunking "Green Living": Combatting Climate Change
   Requires Lifestyle Changes, Not Organic Products** [*GOOD*, May 12, 2012]   341

MONA CHAREN, **Cuddly Symbols Not Cooperating in Climate Change Panic**
   [Townhall.com, June 14, 2012]   344

STUDENT ESSAY: TATEVIK MANUCHARYAN, **Professor Lectures on Dangers of
   Climate Change** [*El Vaquero*, Glendale Community College, April 4, 2012]   348
   LOOKING CLOSELY: Integrating Quotations   352
   STUDENT WRITER AT WORK: Tatevik Manucharyan   354

AMERICA THEN . . . 1985: **The Warming of the World**   355

e-PAGE: **Connect the Dots**

Index   363

America Now

Short Readings from Recent Periodicals

The Persuasive Writer
Expressing Opinions with Clarity, Confidence, and Civility

It is not possible to extricate yourself from the questions in which your age is involved.

— Ralph Waldo Emerson, "The Fortune of the Republic" (1878)

What Is *America Now*?

America Now collects very recent essays and articles that have been carefully selected to encourage reading, provoke discussion, and stimulate writing. The philosophy behind the book is that interesting, effective writing originates in public dialogue. The book's primary purpose is to help students proceed from class discussions of reading assignments to the production of complete essays that reflect an engaged participation in those discussions.

The selections in *America Now* come from two main sources — from popular, mainstream periodicals and from college newspapers available on the Internet. Written by journalists and columnists, public figures and activists, as well as by professors and students from all over the country, the selections illustrate the types of material read by millions of Americans every day. In addition to magazine and newspaper writing, the book features a number of recent opinion advertisements (what I call "op-ads" for short). These familiar forms of "social marketing" are often sponsored by corporations or nonprofit organizations and advocacy groups to promote policies, programs, and ideas such as gun control, family planning, literacy, civil rights, or conservation. Such advertising texts allow the reader to pinpoint and discuss specific techniques of verbal and visual persuasion that are critical in the formation of public opinion.

I have gathered the selections into twelve units that cover today's most widely discussed issues and topics: social media, racial identity, college sports, consumption and marketing, environmentalism, and so on. As you respond to the readings in your discussion and writing, you will be actively taking part in some of the major controversies of our time. Although I have tried in this new edition of *America Now* to represent as many viewpoints as possible on a variety of controversial topics, it's not possible in a collection of this scope to include under each topic either a full spectrum of opinion or a universally satisfying balance of opposing opinions. For some featured topics, an entire book would be required to represent the full range of opinion; for others, a rigid procon, either-or format could distort the issue and perhaps overly polarize students' responses to it. Selections within a unit usually illustrate the most commonly held opinions on a topic so that readers will get a reasonably good sense of how the issue has been framed and the public discourse and debate it has generated. But if a single opinion isn't immediately or explicitly balanced by an opposite opinion, or if a view seems unusually idiosyncratic, that in no way implies that it is somehow editorially favored or endorsed. Be assured that questions following *every* selection will encourage you to analyze and critically challenge whatever opinion or perspective is expressed in that selection.

Participation is the key to this collection. I encourage you to view reading and writing as a form of participation. I hope you will read the selections attentively, think about them carefully, be willing to discuss them in class, and use what you've learned from your reading and discussion as the basis for your papers. If you do these things, you will develop three skills necessary for successful work in college and beyond: the ability to read critically, to discuss topics intelligently, and to write persuasively. These skills are also sorely needed in our daily lives as citizens. A vital democracy depends on them. The reason democracy is hard, said the Czech author and statesman Václav Havel, is that it requires the participation of everyone.

America Now invites you to see reading, discussion, and writing as closely related activities. As you read a selection, imagine that you have entered into a discussion with the author. Take notes as you read. Question the selection. Challenge its point of view or its evidence. Compare your experience with the author's. Consider how different economic classes or other groups are likely to respond. Remember, just because something appears in a newspaper or book doesn't make it true or accurate.

Form the habit of challenging what you read. Don't be persuaded by an opinion simply because it appears in print or because you believe you should accept it. Trust your own observations and experiences. Though logicians never say so, personal experiences and keen observations often form the basis of our most convincing arguments.

Participating in Class Discussion: Six Basic Rules

Discussion is a learned activity. It requires a variety of essential skills: speaking, listening, thinking, and preparing. The following six basic rules are vital to healthy and productive discussion.

1. **Take an active speaking role.** Good discussion demands that everyone participates, not (as so often happens) just a vocal few. Many students remain detached from discussion because they are afraid to speak in a group. This fear is quite common — psychological surveys show that speaking in front of a group is one of our worst fears. It helps to remember that most people will be more interested in *what* you say than in how you say it. Once you get over the initial fear of speaking in public, your confidence will improve with practice.

2. **Listen attentively.** No one who doesn't listen attentively can participate in group discussion. Just think of how many senseless arguments you've had because either you or the person with whom you were talking completely misunderstood what was said. A good listener not only hears what someone is saying but also understands *why* he or she is saying it. Listening carefully also leads to good questions, and when interesting questions begin to emerge, you know good discussion has truly begun.

3. **Examine all sides of an issue.** Good discussion requires that we be patient with complexity. Difficult problems rarely have obvious and simple solutions, nor can they be easily summarized in popular slogans. Complex issues demand to be turned over in our minds so that we can see them from a variety of angles. Group discussion broadens our perspective and deepens our insight into difficult issues and ideas.

4. **Suspend judgment.** To fully explore ideas and issues, you need to be open-minded and tolerant of other opinions, even when they contradict your own. Remember, a discussion is not a debate. Its primary purpose is communication, not competition. The goal of group discussion should be to open up a topic so that everyone is exposed to a spectrum of attitudes. Suspending judgment does not mean you shouldn't hold a strong belief or opinion about an issue; it means that you should be receptive to rival beliefs or opinions. An opinion formed without an awareness of other points of view — one that has

continued

not been tested against contrary ideas — is not a strong opinion but merely a stubborn one.

5. **Avoid abusive or insulting language.** Free and open discussion occurs only when we respect the beliefs and opinions of others. If we speak in ways that fail to show respect for differing viewpoints — if we resort to name-calling or use demeaning and malicious expressions, for example — not only do we embarrass ourselves, but we also close off the possibility for an intelligent and productive exchange of ideas. Some popular radio and television talk shows are poor models of discussion: Shouting insults and engaging in hate speech are usually the last resort of those who have little to say.

6. **Be prepared.** Discussion is not merely random conversation. It demands a certain degree of preparation and focus. To participate in class discussion, you must consider assigned topics beforehand and read whatever is required. Develop the habit of reading with pen in hand, underlining key points, and jotting down questions, impressions, and ideas in your notebook. The notes you bring to class will be an invaluable aid.

When your class discusses a selection, be especially attentive to what others think of it. It's always surprising how two people can read the same article and reach two entirely different interpretations. Observe the range of opinion. Try to understand why and how people arrive at different conclusions. Do some seem to miss the point? Do some distort the author's ideas? Have someone's comments forced you to rethink the selection? Keep a record of the discussion in your notebook. Then, when you begin to draft your paper, consider your essay as an extension of both your imaginary conversation with the author and the actual class discussion. If you've taken detailed notes of your own and the class's opinions about the selection, you should have more than enough information to get started.

What Are Opinions?

One of the primary aims of *America Now* is to help you learn through models and instructional material how to express your opinions in a persuasive, reasonable, civil, and productive fashion. But before we look at effective ways of expressing opinion, let's first consider opinions in general: What are they? Where do they come from?

When we say we have an opinion about something, we usually mean that we have come to a conclusion that something appears true or seems to be valid. But when we express an opinion about something, we are not claiming we are 100 percent certain that something is so. Opinion does not imply certainty and, in fact, is accompanied by some degree of doubt and skepticism. As a result, opinions are most likely to be found in those areas of thought and discussion where our judgments are uncertain. Because human beings know so few things for certain, much of what we believe, or discuss and debate, falls into various realms of probability or possibility. These we call opinions.

Journalists often make a distinction between fact and opinion. Facts can be confirmed and verified and therefore do not involve opinions. We ordinarily don't have opinions about facts, but we can and often do have opinions about the interpretation of facts. For example, it makes no sense to argue whether Washington, D.C., is the capital of the United States since it's an undisputed fact that it is. It's a matter of record and can be established with certainty. Thus, we don't say we have an opinion that Washington, D.C., is the nation's capital; we know for a fact that it is. But it would be legitimate to form an opinion about whether that city is the best location for the U.S. capital and whether it should permanently remain the capital. In other words:

- *Washington, D.C., is the capital of the United States of America* is a statement of fact.
- *Washington, D.C., is too poorly located to be the capital of a vast nation* is a statement of opinion.

Further, simply not knowing whether something is a fact does not necessarily make it a matter of opinion. For example, if we don't know the capital of Brazil, that doesn't mean we are then free to form an opinion about what Brazilian city it might be. The capital of Brazil is a verifiable fact and can be identified with absolute certainty. There is no conflicting public opinion about which city is Brazil's capital. The answer is not up for grabs. These examples, however, present relatively simple, readily agreed-upon facts. In real-life disputes, a fact is not always so readily distinguished from an opinion; people argue all the time about whether something is a fact. It's therefore a good idea at the outset of any discussion or argument to try to arrive at a mutual agreement of the facts that are known or knowable and those that could be called into question. Debates over abortion, for example, often hinge on biological facts about embryonic development that are themselves disputed by medical experts.

An opinion almost always exists in the climate of other, conflicting opinions. In discourse, we refer to this overall context of competing opinions as public controversy. Every age has its controversies. At any given time, the public is divided on a great number of topics about which it holds a variety of different opinions. Often the controversy is reduced to two opposing positions; for example, we are asked whether we are pro-life or pro-choice; for or against government health care; in favor of or opposed to same-sex marriage; and so on. This book includes many such controversies and covers multiple opinions. One sure way of knowing that something is a matter of opinion is that the public is divided on the topic. We often experience these divisions firsthand as we mature and increasingly come into contact with those who disagree with our opinions.

Some opinions are deeply held — so deeply, in fact, that those who hold them refuse to see them as opinions. For some people on certain issues there can be no difference of opinion; they possess the Truth, and all who differ hold erroneous opinions. This frequently happens in some controversies, where one side in a dispute is so confident of the truth of its position that it cannot see its own point of view as one of several possible points of view. For example, someone may feel so certain that marriage can exist only between a man and a woman that he or she cannot acknowledge the possibility of another position. If one side cannot recognize the existence of a different opinion, cannot entertain or tolerate it, argues not with the correctness of another's perspective but denies the possibility that there can legitimately be another perspective, then discussion and debate become all but impossible.

To be open and productive, public discussion depends on the capacity of all involved to view their own positions, no matter how cherished, as opinions that can be subject to opposition. There is nothing wrong with possessing a strong conviction, nor with believing our position is the better one, nor with attempting to convince others of our point of view. What is argumentatively wrong and what prevents or restricts free and open discussion is twofold: (1) the failure to recognize our own belief or position as an opinion that could be mistaken; and (2) the refusal to acknowledge the possibility that another's opinion could be correct.

Is one person's opinion as good as another's? Of course not. Although we may believe that everyone has a right to an opinion, we certainly wouldn't ask our mail carrier to diagnose the cause of persistent heartburn or determine whether a swollen gland could be a serious medical problem. In such instances, we respect the opinion of a trained physician. And even when we consult a physician, in serious matters we often seek second and even third opinions just to be sure. An auto mechanic is in a better position to evaluate a used car than someone who's never repaired a car; a lawyer's opinion on whether a contract is valid is more reliable than that belonging to someone who doesn't understand the legal nature of contracts. If an airline manufacturer wants to test a new cockpit instrument design, it solicits opinions from experienced pilots, not passengers. This seems obvious, and yet people continually are persuaded by those who can claim little expert knowledge on a subject or issue: For example, how valuable or trustworthy is the opinion of a celebrity who is paid to endorse a product?

When expressing or evaluating an opinion, we need to consider the extent of our or another person's knowledge about a particular subject. Will anyone take our opinion seriously? On what authority do we base our position? Why do we take someone else's opinion as valuable or trustworthy? What is the source of the opinion? How reliable is it? How biased? One of the first Americans to study the effects of public opinion, Walter Lippmann, wrote in 1925, "It is often very illuminating, therefore, to ask yourself how you get at the facts on which you base your opinion. Who actually saw, heard, felt, counted, named the thing, about which you have an opinion?" Is your opinion, he went on to ask, based on something you heard from someone who heard it from someone else, who in turn heard it from someone else?

How Do We Form Opinions?

How can we possibly have reasonable opinions on all the issues of the day? One of the strains of living in a democracy that encourages a diversity of perspectives is that every responsible citizen is expected to have informed opinions on practically every public question. What do you think about the death penalty? About dependency on foreign oil? About the way the media cover the news? About the extent of racial discrimination? Certainly no one person possesses inside information or access to reliable data on every topic that becomes part of public controversy. Still, many people, by the time they are able to vote, have formed numerous opinions. Where do these opinions come from?

Although social scientists and psychologists have been studying opinion formation for decades, the sources of opinion are multiple and constantly shifting, and individuals differ so widely in experience, cultural background, and temperament that efforts to identify and classify the various ways opinion is formed are bound to be tentative and incomplete. What follows is a brief, though realistic, attempt to list some of the practical ways that Americans come by the opinions they hold.

1. *Inherited opinions.* These are opinions we derive from earliest childhood — transmitted via family, culture, traditions, customs, regions, social institutions, or religion. For example, young people may identify themselves as either Democrats or Republicans because of their family affiliations. Although these opinions may change as we mature, they are often ingrained. The more traditional the culture or society, the more likely the opinions that grow out of early childhood will be retained and passed on to the next generation.

2. Involuntary opinions. These are opinions that we have not culturally and socially inherited or consciously adopted but that come to us through direct or indirect forms of indoctrination. They could be the customs of a cult or the propaganda of an ideology. Brainwashing is an extreme example of how one acquires opinions involuntarily. A more familiar example is the constant reiteration of advertising messages: We come to possess a favorable opinion of a product not because we've ever used it or know anything about it but because we have been "bombarded" by marketing to think positively about it.

3. Adaptive opinions. Many opinions grow out of our willingness — or even eagerness — to adapt to the prevailing views of particular groups, subgroups, or institutions to which we belong or desire to belong. As many learn, it's easier to follow the path of least resistance than to run counter to it. Moreover, acting out of self-interest, people often adapt their opinions to conform to the views of bosses or authority figures, or they prefer to succumb to peer pressure rather than oppose it. An employee finds himself accepting or agreeing with an opinion because a job or career depends on it; a student may adapt her opinions to suit those of a professor in the hope of receiving a better grade; a professor may tailor his opinions in conformity with the prevailing beliefs of colleagues. Adaptive opinions are often weakly held and readily changed, depending on circumstances. But over time they can become habitual and turn into convictions.

4. Concealed opinions. In some groups in which particular opinions dominate, certain individuals may not share the prevailing attitudes, but rather than adapt or "rock the boat," they keep their opinions to themselves. They may do this merely to avoid conflict or out of much more serious concerns — such as a fear of ostracism, ridicule, retaliation, or job loss. A common example is seen in the person who by day quietly goes along with the opinions of a group of colleagues but at night freely exchanges "honest" opinions with a group of friends. Some individuals find diaries and journals to be an effective way to express concealed opinions, and many today find online chat rooms a space where they can anonymously "be themselves."

5. Linked opinions. Many opinions are closely linked to other opinions. Unlike adaptive opinions, which are usually stimulated by convenience and an incentive to conform, these are opinions we derive from an enthusiastic and dedicated affiliation with certain groups, institutions, or parties. For example, it's not uncommon for someone to agree with every position his or her political party endorses — this phenomenon is usually called "following a party line." Linked opinions may not be well thought out on every narrow issue: Someone may decide to be a Republican or a Democrat or a Green or a Libertarian for a few specific reasons — a position on war, cultural values, the environment, civil liberties, and so forth — and then go along with, even to the point of strenuously defending, all of the other positions the party espouses because they are all part of its political platform or system of beliefs. In other words, once we accept opinions A and B, we are more likely to accept C and D, and so on down the chain. As Ralph Waldo Emerson succinctly put it, "If I know your sect, I anticipate your argument."

6. Considered opinions. These are opinions we have formed as a result of firsthand experience, reading, discussion and debate, or independent thinking and reasoning. These opinions are formed from direct knowledge and often from exposure and consideration of other opinions. Wide reading on a subject and exposure to diverse views help ensure that our opinions are based on solid information and tested against competing opinions. One simple way to judge whether your opinion is carefully thought out is to list your reasons for holding it. Some people who express opinions on a topic are not able to offer a single reason for why they have those opinions. Of course, reasons don't necessarily make an opinion correct, but people who can support their opinions with one or more reasons are more persuasive than those who cannot provide any reasons for their beliefs (see "How to Support Opinions," p. 15).

This list is not exhaustive. Nor are the sources and types above mutually exclusive; the opinions of any individual may derive from all six sources or represent a mixture of several. As you learn to express your opinions effectively, you will find it useful to question yourself about the origins and development of those opinions. By tracing the process that led to the formation of our present opinions, we can better understand ourselves — our convictions, our inconsistencies, our biases, and our blind spots.

From Discussion to Writing

As this book amply demonstrates, we live in a world of conflicting opinions. Each of us over time has inherited, adopted, and gradually formed many opinions on a variety of topics. Of course, there are also a good number of public issues or questions about which we have not formed opinions or have undecided attitudes. In many public debates, members have unequal shares at stake. Eighteen-year-olds, for example, are much more likely to become impassioned over the government reviving a military draft or a state raising the legal age for driving than they would over Medicare cuts or Social Security issues. Some public questions personally affect us more than others.

Thus, not all the issues covered in this book will at first make an equal impact on everyone. But whether you take a particular interest in a given topic or not, this book invites you to share in the spirit of public controversy. Many students, once introduced to the opposing sides of a debate or the multiple positions taken toward a public issue, will begin to take a closer look at the merits of different opinions. Once we start evaluating these opinions, once we begin stepping into the shoes of others and learning what's at stake in certain positions, we often find ourselves becoming involved with the issue and may even come to see ourselves as participants. After all, we are all part of the public, and to a certain extent all questions affect us: Ask the eighteen-year-old if he or she will be equipped to deal with the medical and financial needs of elderly parents, and an issue that appears to affect only those near retirement will seem much closer to home.

As mentioned earlier, *America Now* is designed to stimulate discussion and writing grounded in response to a variety of public issues. A key to using this book is to think about discussion and writing not as separate activities but as interrelated processes. In discussion, we hear other opinions and formulate our own; in writing, we express our opinions in the context of other opinions. Both discussion and writing require articulation and deliberation. Both require an aptitude for listening carefully to others. Discussion stimulates writing, and writing in turn stimulates further discussion.

Group discussion stimulates and enhances your writing in several important ways. First, it supplies you with ideas. Let's say that you are participating in a discussion on the importance of ethnic identity (see selections in Chapter 4). One of your classmates mentions some of the problems a mixed ethnic background can cause. But suppose you also come from a mixed background, and when you think about it, you believe that your mixed heritage has given you more advantages than disadvantages. Hearing her viewpoint may inspire you to express your differing perspective on the issue. Your perspective could lead to an interesting personal essay.

Suppose you now start writing that essay. You don't need to start from scratch and stare at a blank piece of paper or computer screen for hours. Discussion has already given you a few good leads. First, you have your classmate's opinions and attitudes to quote or summarize. You can begin your paper by explaining that some people view a divided ethnic identity as a psychological burden. You might expand on your classmate's opinion by bringing in additional information from other student comments or from your reading to show how people often focus on only the negative side of mixed identities. You can then explain your own perspective on this topic. Of course, you will need to give several examples showing *why* a mixed background has been an advantage for you. The end result can be a first-rate essay, one that takes other opinions into account and demonstrates a clearly established point of view. It is personal, and yet it takes a position that goes beyond one individual's experiences.

Whatever the topic, your writing will benefit from reading and discussion, activities that will give your essays a clear purpose or goal. In that way, your papers will resemble the selections found in this book: They will be a *response* to the opinions, attitudes, experiences, issues, ideas, and proposals that inform current public discourse. This is why most writers write; this is what most newspapers and magazines publish; this is what most people read. *America Now* consists entirely of such writing. I hope you will read the selections with enjoyment, discuss the issues with an open mind, and write about the topics with purpose and enthusiasm.

The Practice of Writing

Suppose you wanted to learn to play the guitar. What would you do first? Would you run to the library and read a lot of books on music? Would you then read some instructional books on guitar playing? Might you try to memorize all the chord positions? Then would you get sheet music for songs you liked and memorize them? After all that, if someone handed you an electric guitar, would you immediately be able to play like Jimi Hendrix or Eric Clapton?

I don't think you would begin that way. You probably would start out by strumming the guitar, getting the feel of it, trying to pick out something familiar. You probably would want to take lessons from someone who knows how to play. And you would practice, practice, practice. Every now and then your instruction book would come in handy. It would give you basic information on frets, notes, and chord positions, for example. You might need to refer to that information constantly in the beginning. But knowing the chords is not the same as knowing how to manipulate your fingers correctly to produce the right sounds. You need to be able to *play* the chords, not just know them.

Learning to read and write well is not that much different. Even though instructional books can give you a great deal of advice and information, the only way anyone really learns to read and write is through constant practice. The only problem, of course, is that nobody likes practice. If we did, we would all be good at just about everything. Most of us, however, want to acquire a skill quickly and easily. We don't want to take lesson after lesson. We want to pick up the instrument and sound like a professional in ten minutes.

Wouldn't it be a wonderful world if that could happen? Wouldn't it be great to be born with a gigantic vocabulary so that we instantly knew the meaning of every word we saw or heard? We would never have to go through the slow process of consulting a dictionary whenever we stumbled across an unfamiliar word. But, unfortunately, life is not so easy. To succeed at anything worthwhile requires patience and dedication. Watch a young figure skater trying to perfect her skills and you will see patience and dedication at work; or watch an accident victim learning how to maneuver a wheelchair so that he can begin again an independent existence; or observe a new American struggling to learn English. None of these skills are quickly or easily acquired. Like building a vocabulary, they all take time and effort. They all require practice. And they require something even more important: the willingness to make mistakes. Can someone learn to skate without taking a spill? Or learn a new language without mispronouncing a word?

What Is "Correct English"?

One part of the writing process may seem more difficult than others — correct English. Yes, nearly all of what you read will be written in relatively correct English. Or it's probably more accurate to say "corrected" English, because most published writing is revised or "corrected" several times before it appears in print. Even skilled professional writers make mistakes that require correction.

Most native speakers don't actually *talk* in "correct" English. There are numerous regional patterns and dialects. As the Chinese American novelist Amy Tan says, there are "many Englishes." What we usually consider correct English is a set of guidelines developed over time to help standardize written expression. This standardization — like any agreed-upon standards such as weights and measures — is a matter of use and convenience. Suppose you went to a vegetable stand and asked for a pound of peppers and the storekeeper gave you a half pound but charged you for a full one. When you complained, he said, "But that's what *I* call a pound." Life would be very frustrating if everyone had a different set of standards: Imagine what would happen if some states used a red light to signal "go" and a green one for "stop." Languages are not that different. In all cultures, languages — especially written languages — have gradually developed certain general rules and principles to make communication as clear and efficient as possible.

You probably already have a guidebook or handbook that systematically sets out certain rules of English grammar, punctuation, and spelling. Like our guitar instruction book, these handbooks serve a very practical purpose. Most writers — even experienced authors — need to consult them periodically. Beginning writers may need to rely on them far more regularly. But just as we don't learn how to play chords by merely memorizing finger positions, we don't learn how to write by memorizing the rules of grammar or punctuation.

Writing is an activity, a process. Learning how to do it — like learning to ride a bike or prepare a tasty stew — requires *doing* it. Correct English is not something that comes first. We don't need to know the rules perfectly before we can begin to write. As in any activity, corrections are part of the learning process. You fall off the bike and get on again, trying to "correct" your balance this time. You sample the stew and "correct" the seasoning. You draft a paper about the neighborhood you live in, and as you (or a classmate or instructor) read it over, you notice that certain words and expressions could stand some improvement. And step by step, sentence by sentence, you begin to write better.

Writing as a Public Activity

Many people have the wrong idea about writing. They view writing as a very private act. They picture the writer sitting all alone and staring into space waiting for ideas to come. They think that ideas come from "deep" within and reach expression only after they have been fully articulated inside the writer's head.

These images are part of a myth about creative writing and, like most myths, are sometimes true. A few poets, novelists, and essayists do write in total isolation and search deep inside themselves for thoughts and stories. But most writers have far more contact with public life. This is especially true of people who write regularly for magazines, newspapers, and professional journals. These writers work within a lively social atmosphere in which issues and ideas are often intensely discussed and debated. Nearly all the selections in this book illustrate this type of writing.

As you work on your own papers, remember that writing is very much a public activity. It is rarely performed alone in an "ivory tower." Writers don't always have the time, the desire, the opportunity, or the luxury to be all alone. They may be writing in a newsroom with clacking keyboards and noise all around them; they may be writing at a kitchen table, trying to feed several children at the same time; they may be texting on subways or buses. The great English novelist D. H. Lawrence (1885–1930) grew up in a small impoverished coal miner's cottage with no place for privacy. It proved to be an enabling experience. Throughout his life, he could write wherever he happened to be; it didn't matter how many people or how much commotion surrounded him.

There are more important ways in which writing is a public activity. Writing is often a response to public events. Most of the articles you encounter every day in newspapers and magazines respond directly to timely or important issues and ideas, topics that people are currently talking about. Writers report on these topics, supply information about them, and discuss and debate the differing viewpoints. The units in this book all represent topics now regularly discussed on college campuses and in the national media. In fact, all of the topics were chosen because they emerged so frequently in college newspapers.

When a columnist decides to write on a topic like airport security measures that threaten individual privacy, she willingly enters an ongoing public discussion about the issue. She hasn't just made up the topic. She knows that it is a serious issue, and she is aware that a wide variety of opinions have been expressed about it. She has not read everything on the subject but usually knows enough about the different arguments to state her own position or attitude persuasively. In fact, what helps make her writing persuasive is that she takes into account the opinions of others. Her own essay, then, becomes a part of the continuing debate and discussion, one that you in turn may want to join.

Such issues are not only matters for formal and impersonal debate. They also invite us to share our *personal* experiences. Many of the selections in this book show how writers participate in the discussion of issues by drawing on their experiences. For example, the essay by Christine Rosen, "Electronic Intimacy," is based largely on the author's personal observations and experience, though the topic — how the new social media affect relationships today — is one widely discussed and debated by countless Americans. You will find that nearly every unit of *America Now* contains a selection that illustrates how you can use your personal experiences to discuss and debate a public issue.

Writing is public in yet another way. Practically all published writing is reviewed, edited, and re-edited by different people before it goes to press. The author of a magazine article has most likely discussed the topic at length with colleagues and publishing professionals and may have asked friends or experts in the field to look over his or her piece. By the time you see the article in a magazine, it has gone through numerous readings and probably quite a few revisions. Although the article is credited to a particular author, it was no doubt read and worked on by others who helped with suggestions and improvements. As a beginning writer, you need to remember that most of what you read in newspapers, magazines, and books has gone through a writing process that involves the collective efforts of several people besides the author. Students usually don't have that advantage and should not feel discouraged when their own writing doesn't measure up to the professionally edited materials they are reading for a course.

How to Support Opinions

In everyday life, we express many opinions, ranging from (as the chapters in this collection indicate) weighty issues such as race relations or the environment to personal matters such as our Facebook profile. In conversation, we often express our opinions as assertions. An assertion is merely an opinionated claim — usually of our likes or dislikes, agreements or disagreements — that is not supported by evidence or reasons. For example, "*Amnesty for illegal immigrants is a poor idea*" is merely an assertion about public policy — it states an opinion, but it offers no reason or reasons why anyone should accept it.

When entering public discussion and debate, we have an obligation to support our opinions. Simple assertions — "*Men are better at math than women*" — may be provocative and stimulate heated debate, but the discussion will go nowhere unless reasons and evidence are offered to support the claim. The following methods are among the most common ways you can support your opinions.

1. **Experts and authority.** You support your claim that the earth is growing warmer by citing one of the world's leading climatologists; you support your opinion that a regular diet of certain vegetables can drastically reduce the risk of colon cancer by citing medical authorities.

2. **Statistics.** You support the view that your state needs tougher drunk driving laws by citing statistics that show that fatalities from drunk driving have increased 20 percent in the past two years; you support the claim that Americans now prefer smaller, more fuel-efficient cars by citing surveys that reveal a 30 percent drop in SUV and truck sales over the past six months.

3. **Examples.** You support your opinion that magazine advertising is becoming increasingly pornographic by describing several recent instances from different periodicals; you defend your claim that women can be top-ranked chess players by identifying several women who are. Note that when using examples to prove your point, you will almost always require several; one example will seldom convince anyone.

4. **Personal experience.** Although you may not be an expert or authority in any area, your personal experience can count as evidence in support of an opinion. Suppose you claim that the campus parking

continued

facilities are inadequate for commuting students, and, a commuter yourself, you document the difficulties you have every day with parking. Such personal knowledge, assuming it is not false or exaggerated, would plausibly support your position. Many reporters back up their coverage with their eyewitness testimony.

5. **Possible consequences.** You defend an opinion that space exploration is necessary by arguing that it could lead to the discovery of much-needed new energy resources; you support an opinion that expanding the rights of gun ownership is a mistake by arguing that it will result in more crime and gun-related deaths.

These are only a few of the ways opinions can be supported, but they are among the most significant. Note that providing support for an opinion does not automatically make it true or valid; someone will invariably counter your expert with an opposing expert, discover conflicting statistical data, produce counterexamples, or offer personal testimony that contradicts your own. Still, once you've offered legitimate reasons for what you think, you have made a big leap from "mere opinion" to "informed opinion."

Writing for the Classroom: Three Annotated Student Essays

The following three student essays perfectly characterize the kind of writing that *America Now* features and examines. The essays will provide you with effective models of how to express an opinion on a public issue in a concise and convincing manner. Each essay demonstrates the way a writer responds to a public concern — in this case, the stereotyping of others. Each essay also embodies the principles of productive discussion outlined throughout this introduction. In fact, these three essays were especially commissioned from student writers to perform a double service: The essays show writers clearly expressing opinions on a timely topic that personally matters to them and, at the same time, demonstrate how arguments can be shaped to advance the possibility of further discussion instead of ending it.

These three essays also feature three different approaches to the topic of stereotyping. Each essay reflects a different use of source material: The first essay uses none; the second responds directly to a recent controversial magazine article; and the third relies on reading material that supports a thesis. Thus, students can observe three distinct and common methods of learning to write for the classroom:

1. expressing an opinion based on personal experience alone
2. expressing an opinion in response to an opposing opinion
3. expressing an opinion with reference to reading and research

Although there are many other approaches to classroom writing (too many to be fully represented in an introduction), these three should provide first-year students with accessible and effective models for the types of writing they will most likely be required to do in connection with the assignments in *America Now*.

Each essay is annotated to help you focus on some of the most effective means of expressing an opinion. First, read through each essay and consider the points the writer is making. Then return to the essay and analyze more closely the key parts highlighted for examination. This process is designed to help you see how writers construct arguments to support their opinions. It is an analytical process you should begin to put into practice on your own as you read and explore the many issues in this collection. A detailed explanation of the highlighted passages follows each selection.

Expressing an Opinion Based on Personal Experience Alone

The first essay, Kati Mather's "The Many Paths to Success — With or Without a College Education," expresses an opinion that is based almost entirely on personal experience and reflection. In her argument that Americans have grown so predisposed to a college education that they dismiss other forms of education as inferior, Mather shows how this common attitude can lead to unfair stereotypes. Her essay cites no formal evidence or outside sources — no research, studies, quotations, other opinions, or assigned readings. Instead, she relies on her own educational experience and the conclusions she draws from it to support her position.

Kati Mather wrote "The Many Paths to Success — With or Without a College Education" when she was a senior at Wheaton College in Massachusetts, majoring in English and Italian studies.

Kati Mather

The Many Paths to Success — With or Without a College Education

1
Opens with personal perspective

<u>I always knew I would go to college. When I was younger, higher education was not a particular dream of mine, but I understood that it was the expected path.</u> (1)

1

Even as children, many of us are so thoroughly groomed for college that declining the opportunity is unacceptable. Although I speak as someone who could afford such an assumption, even my peers without the same economic advantages went to college. Education is important, but I believe our common expectations — that everyone can and should go to college, and that a college education is necessary to succeed — and the stigmas attached to those who forgo higher education, are false and unfair.

In the past, only certain fortunate people could attain a college education. But over time, America modernized its approach to education, beginning with compulsory high school attendance in most states, and then evolving into a system with numerous options for higher learning. (2) Choices for post-secondary education today are overwhelming, and — with full- and part-time programs offered by community colleges, state universities, and private institutions — accessibility is not the issue it once was. In our frenzy to adhere to the American dream, which means, among other things, that everyone is entitled to an education, the schooling system has become too focused on the social expectations that come with a college education. It is normally considered to be the gateway to higher income and an upwardly mobile career. But we would all be better served if the system were instead focused on learning, and on what learning means to the individual.

It is admirable that we are committed to education in this country, but not everyone should be expected to take the college track. Vocational education, for instance, seems to be increasingly a thing of the past, which is regrettable because careers that do not require a college degree are as vital as those that do. If vocational schooling were more widely presented as an option — and one that everyone should take the time to consider — we would not be so quick to stereotype those who do not attend traditional academic institutions. Specialized labor such as construction, plumbing, and automobile repair are crucial to a healthy, functioning society. (3) While a college education can be a wonderful thing to possess, we need people to aspire to other forms of education, which include both vocational schooling and learning skills on the job. Those careers (and there are many others) are as important as teaching, accounting, and medicine.

Despite the developments in our educational system that make college more accessible, financial constraints

2
Establishes main
point early

3
Supports main
point

2

3

4

exist for many — as do family pressures and expectations, intellectual limitations, and a host of other obstacles. Those obstacles warrant neither individual criticism nor far-reaching stereotypes. For example, a handful of students from my high school took an extra year or two to graduate, and I sadly assumed that they would not be as successful as those who graduated on time. I did not stop to consider their situations, or that they might simply be on a different path in life than I was. Looking back, it was unfair to stereotype others in this way. Many of them are hard-working and fulfilled individuals today. There is no law that says everyone has to finish high school and go to college to be successful. Many famous actors, musicians, artists, and professional athletes will freely admit that they never finished high school or college, and these are people we admire, who could very well be making more money in a year than an entire graduating class combined. (4) Plus, we applaud their talent and the fact that they chose their own paths. But banking on a paying career in the arts or sports is not a safe bet, which is why it is so important to open all practical avenues to young people and to respect the choices they make.

4
Provides examples of alternatives to college

We should focus on this diversity instead of perpetuating the belief that everyone should pursue a formal college education and that those who do not are somehow inadequate. There are, of course, essential skills learned in college that remain useful throughout life, even for those who do not pursue high-powered careers. As a student myself, I will readily admit that a college education plays an important role in a successful life. The skills we have the opportunity to learn in college are important to "real" life, and some of these can be used no matter what our career path. (5) Among other things, I've learned how to interact with different people, how to live on my own, how to accept rejection, how to articulate what I want to say, and how to write. Writing is one of the most useful skills taught in college because written communication is necessary in so many different aspects of life.

5

5
Offers balanced view of alternatives

I hope that my college education will lead to success and upward mobility in my career. But I can also allow that, once out of college, most students want to find a job that relates to their studies. In these hard times, however, that may not always be the case. I know from my own experience that other jobs — including those that do not require a college education — can be meaningful to anyone with the will to

6

work and contribute. I'm grateful for the opportunities I've had that led to my college education, and though I do think we have grown too rigid in our thinking about the role of education, I also think we have the chance to change our attitudes and approaches for everyone's benefit.

The widespread belief that everyone must go to college to be a success, and that everyone *can* go to college, is not wholly true. Of course, many people will benefit greatly from a quality education, and a quality education is more accessible today than ever before. But college is not the only option. (6) Hard-working people who do not take that path can still be enormously successful, and we should not think otherwise. We can all disprove stereotypes. There are countless accomplished people who are not formally educated.

7

6
Closes by summa-rizing position

This country offers many roads to success, but we must remember that embracing diversity is essential to all of us. While I will not deny that my education has helped me along my chosen path, I firmly believe that, had I taken a different one, it too would have enabled me to make a valuable contribution to our society.

8

Comments

The following comments correspond to the numbered annotations that appear in the margins of Kati Mather's essay.

1. Opens with personal perspective. Mather begins her essay with an effective opening sentence that at once identifies her background and establishes the personal tone and perspective she will take throughout. The word *always* suggests that she personally had no doubts about attending college and knew it was expected of her since childhood. Thus, she is not someone who opted to skip college, and she is writing from that perspective. As a reader, you may want to consider how this perspective affects your response to arguments against attending college; for example, would you be more persuaded if the same argument had been advanced by someone who decided against a college education?

2. Establishes main point early. Mather states the main point of her essay at the end of paragraph 1. She clearly says that the "common expectations" that everyone should attend college and that only those who do so will succeed are "false and unfair." She points out that those who don't attend college are stigmatized. These general statements allow her to introduce the issue of stereotyping in the body of her essay.

3. Supports main point. Although Mather does not offer statistical evidence supporting her assumption that a college education is today considered a necessity, she backs up that belief with a brief history of how the increasing accessibility of higher education in the United States has evolved to the point that a college degree now appears to be a universal entitlement.

4. Provides examples of alternatives to college. In paragraph 3, Mather introduces the subject of vocational education as an alternative to college. She believes that vocational training is not sufficiently presented to students as an option, even though such skills are as "vital" to society as are traditional college degrees. If more students carefully considered vocational schooling, she maintains, we would in general be less inclined to "stereotype" those who decide not to attend college. In paragraph 4, she acknowledges how she personally failed to consider the different situations and options faced by other students from her high school class.

5. Offers balanced view of alternatives. In paragraph 5, Mather shows that she is attempting to take a balanced view of various educational options. She thus avoids a common tendency when forming a comparison — to make one thing either superior or inferior to the other. At this point in the argument, some writers might have decided to put down or criticize a college education, arguing that vocational training is even better than a college degree. By stating how important college can be to those who choose to attend, Mather resists that simplistic tactic and strengthens her contention that we need to assess all of our educational options fairly, without overvaluing some and undervaluing others.

6. Closes by summarizing position. In her concluding paragraphs, Mather summarizes her position, claiming that "college is not the only option" and reminding readers that many successful careers were forged without a college degree. Her essay returns to a personal note: Had she decided not to attend college, she would still be a valuable member of society.

Expressing an Opinion in Response to an Opposing Opinion

Candace Rose Rardon's essay "Not-So-Great Expectations" tackles the difficult and sensitive question of differences in gender. Like Mather, Rardon draws from personal experience in her argument, but rather than responding to a general climate of opinion, she is writing in direct contradiction to another writer — in this case, the late columnist Christopher Hitchens, whose essay "Why Women Aren't Funny" proposes a sense-of-humor gap between the sexes. This forces Rardon to structure her argument in relation to Hitchens's essay, to cite the essay verbatim, to concede points to him, and to distance herself from another writer with roughly the same position as her own. In doing so, Rardon crafts an argument — that women can be just as funny as men — that is both personal and engaged with an open dialogue.

Candace Rose Rardon graduated Phi Beta Kappa from the University of Virginia with a BA in English language and literature.

Candace Rose Rardon

Not-So-Great Expectations

We've all no doubt heard or used the idiom, "She can't take a joke," to describe that particularly sensitive soul in our circle of friends. In his 2007 *Vanity Fair* article "Why Women Aren't Funny," Christopher Hitchens takes this expression two steps further in his discussion of women and humor: women often don't get the joke, and they certainly can't make one. (1) As a female and thus a part of the gender of "inferior funniness," as Hitchens so graciously puts it, I was appalled by his argument and immediately went on the defensive. Although I'm no comedian and would never describe myself as "funny," I have plenty of girlfriends who make me laugh til my sides hurt; they defy the blanket statements abounding in Hitchens's article.

But I wasn't the only one to question his argument. Just over a year later, Alessandra Stanley wrote a countering article for *Vanity Fair* titled, "Who Says Women Aren't Funny?" (2) Stanley asserts that, not only are they funny, women — now more than ever — possess established, widely embraced careers "dishing out the jokes with a side of sexy." To me, the underlying issue stemming from this pair of articles is a question of expectations — both of *who* and *what* is funny. To near any solution in this debate of women and humor, we must begin by raising these expectations. For starters, what *is* actually expected of men and women? If, as Stanley writes, "society has different expectations for women," what are these divergent requirements? For Hitchens, there is a lot of pressure riding on a man's ability to make a woman laugh. Women don't feel this pressure, he says, because "they already appeal to men, if you catch my drift." If I'm catching Hitchens's drift, a woman's physical attractiveness is analogous to a man's sense of humor

1

2

1
Cites opposing view concisely

2
Additional response expands discourse

as a necessary component in impressing the opposite sex. According to Hitchens, it seems to be all about what one has to offer. If a woman is attractive, there is no need for her to be funny or intelligent. Moreover, Hitchens even suggests a combination of qualities actually becomes "threatening to men if [women] appear too bright."

3
Extra examples broaden scope of argument

At this point, I can't help but think of the pilot episode of *Sex and the City*, (3) in which Miranda Hobbes brings up this exact point to her date, Skipper Johnston: "Women either fall into one of two categories: beautiful and boring, or homely and interesting. Is that what you're saying to me?" Despite Skipper's resounding "no" for an answer, it's clear Miranda has a point. Society has conditioned us into this mindset. Society has set the bar low for women — in my opinion, much lower than what women are capable of offering. This is an idea reinforced by Patricia Marx, an American humorist, former writer for *Saturday Night Live*, and one of the first two women writers on *The Harvard Lampoon*. As quoted in Stanley's article, Marx speculates, "Maybe pretty women weren't funny before because they had no reason to be funny. There was no point to it — people already liked you." Thus, if women are not expected to be funny, why should they be?

3

To take the question of expectations another step further, Hitchens cites a recent study from the Stanford University School of Medicine analyzing the different ways men and women process humor based on their responses to seventy black-and-white cartoons. Dr. Allan L. Reiss, who led the research team, explains, "Women appeared to have less expectation of a reward, which in this case was the punch line of the cartoon. So when they got to the joke's punch line, they were more pleased about it." These lower expectations translate into higher standards for what's funny. Can these women be blamed? Just because the women in the study submitted the cartoons to a higher level of analysis and scrutiny than men, that does not qualify them as unfunny and even "backward in generating" humor, as Hitchens asserts.

4

4
Challenges the meaning of statistics

(4) The study essentially points out that men and women have very different expectations when it comes to what they deem funny. Dr. Reiss continues, "The differences can help account for the fact that men gravitate more to one-liners and slapstick while women tend to use humor more in narrative form and stories." Or, as Hitchens puts it, "Men will laugh at almost anything, often precisely because it is — or they are — extremely stupid. Women aren't like that."

So with that in mind, I have to ask: Would a woman even   5
want to make a man laugh? A brief look at TV shows geared
primarily towards a male audience answers my question.
Spike TV, a network designed for young adult males, features shows with humor that is often crude, immature, and
just childish — not exactly the qualities any woman I know
is racing to embody. Instead, women often want to make
men laugh for the same reasons they'd want to make anyone,
male or female, laugh — to reach common ground, establish
familiarity, and build friendship. Slapstick and one-liners by
their nature do not achieve those goals. Even in relationships
between the two sexes, men don't usually try to make women
laugh through slapstick; rather, such humor is culturally
perceived as a way of fostering camaraderie between males.
Essentially, Hitchens's argument is flawed here because none
of this means women aren't funny. The sense of narrative in
women's humor, as pointed out by the Stanford study, is simply a different idea of what is funny. It actually makes sense
that women are deemed "not funny" by male counterparts
such as Hitchens. If Hitchens believes women generally fall
short in the humor department, and that we do so because
women are slower to laugh at slapstick and one-liners, then
making a man laugh is a quality I wouldn't even want.

Whenever I'm faced with a problem, I always have to   6
ask, <u>is there a concrete solution?</u> In other words, <u>are there</u>
<u>any expectations for change? Can you indeed change your</u>
<u>sense of humor?</u> (5) A quick search through Amazon.com
reveals scores of books that seem to think so, such as Jon
Macks's *How to Be Funny* (Simon and Schuster, 2003) or
Steve Allen's *How to Be Funny: Discovering the Comic You*
(Prometheus Books, 1998) and *Make 'Em Laugh* (Prometheus Books, 1993). But where does our sense of humor
come from in the first place? Can you develop this ability
to crack a joke, or is it something we're born with? Hitchens agrees with the latter idea, writing that Mother Nature
has equipped "many fellows with very little armament for
the struggle" of impressing women. Stanley, though, seems
to feel "the nature-versus-nurture argument also extends to
humor," asserting that our sense of humor is often predetermined by our culture and society. I find some truth in
both of these arguments. While the Stanford study points
out the innate differences in each gender's responses to
humor, our society has also conditioned these differences
and continues to reinforce our expectations of each sex.
Changing these expectations will be no easy task.

5
*Places debate in
larger context*

Finally, the question of women and humor is not about whether a woman can be attractive and funny, as Stanley's point seems to be. In fact, I find the photographs that accompany her article, portraying female comedians in seductive, alluring poses, to be just as demeaning as Hitchens's generalizations. It's about looking past stereotypes and gender lines and raising our expectations for all parties involved. I've known plenty of funny females and an equal number of not-so-funny guys. And I refuse to accept low expectations — of *who* is funny and *what* is funny.

7

6
Ends on an appropriate punch line

If Hitchens still wants to insist women aren't funny, well . . . *the joke's on him.* (6)

8

Comments

The following comments correspond to the numbered annotations that appear in the margins of Candace Rose Rardon's essay.

1. Cites opposing view concisely. Rardon is obliged to quote Hitchens's essay, but instead of a long block quotation articulating his position as a whole, she begins by citing the title and the phrase "inferior funniness," which gets at the gist of her antagonist's argument without burdening the reader with too much outside material. This concision allows Rardon to move straight into her own points. Notice how this argument is immediately personal: Rardon declares that she was "appalled" by Hitchens's position when she came across it, and that her immediate reaction was that she had "plenty of girlfriends who make me laugh til my sides hurt."

2. Additional response expands discourse. Toward the middle of paragraph 2, Rardon quotes Alessandra Stanley's response to Hitchens's article. Adding another voice more or less on her side helps frame the debate and contextualizes Rardon's essay within an already existing exchange of opinions. But Rardon does not buy into Stanley's argument wholesale; she announces that she'll try to probe a larger question — "*who* and *what* is funny." Rardon sets us up to expect an essay not only about genetic differences between the sexes but also about the nature of humor itself, and what we laugh at.

3. Extra examples broaden scope of argument. In paragraph 3, Rardon brings in two other sources to back up her view that "society has set the bar low for women — in my opinion, much lower than what women are capable of offering." The first is the HBO series *Sex and the City*, and the second (also cited by Stanley) is humorist Patricia Marx.

These very divergent sources of information — a hit television show and a print humor writer — help broaden the scope of the argument beyond the simple manufacture of one-liners. The appeal to *Sex and the City* especially offers Rardon's readers a familiar voice in doubting the dichotomy between attractive women and intelligent women.

4. Challenges the meaning of statistics. In paragraph 4, Rardon attacks what would appear to be a strong plank in Hitchens's argument: a Stanford study seeming to indicate that men are more likely than women are to appreciate the punch lines of one-line jokes. Rardon employs an interesting tactic here: Instead of casting doubt on the data or the reasoning of the study as manifested in Hitchens's piece, she challenges her opponent's very conception of humor. Rardon asserts that the sort of simpleminded jokes Hitchens alludes to aren't true humor, and asks rhetorically, "Would a woman even want to make a man laugh?" The Stanford study doesn't prove, Rardon argues, that women are less funny than men, but simply that women possess "a different idea of what is funny." In paragraph 5, Rardon sketches her own delineation of the purposes of humor: "to reach common ground, establish familiarity, and build friendship." Is this an agreed-upon definition? Or is Rardon arguing for the supremity of this definition?

5. Places debate in larger context. Rardon goes on to place the Hitchens-Stanley debate in the context of the age-old argument of nature versus nurture. If it's true that men and women have different senses of humor, are their genes or cultural conditioning to blame? Rardon says she sees truth in both sides but offers a strong admonition that cultural stereotypes about women are often firm and hard to crack. Even Stanley's article in defense of female funniness, Rardon points out, features photographs of female comedians in alluring poses, a reinforcement of gender roles that Rardon finds "just as demeaning as Hitchens's generalizations." By reminding us about the difficulty of overcoming preconceptions about gender, Rardon underlines the significance of an issue that might otherwise seem trivial to some readers.

6. Ends on an appropriate punch line. Rardon ends with a punch line: "If Hitchens still wants to insist women aren't funny," she writes, "well . . . *the joke's on him.*" This isn't the only time the tone of Rardon's essay is humorous. What is the importance of a female writer making a few jokes in a piece defending the joke-making ability of women? More important, how should an author approaching this difficult topic balance the impulse to take a wry look at the subject — and even to crack a joke here and there — and the desire to afford it the seriousness and gravity it merits? How do you think Rardon achieves this balance?

Expressing an Opinion with Reference to Reading and Research

Our third example shows a student writer responding to an assignment that asks him not only to consider the issue of stereotyping from a personal perspective but also to refer to relevant readings found in the library or on the Internet. In "How to Approach a Different Culture?," Milos Kosic uses the highly popular 2006 movie *Borat* and his physical resemblance to the central character (played by Sacha Baron Cohen) as a way to make Americans aware of how easily and unfairly they can stereotype people from other cultures. Most fans of the film are unaware of its subtitle: *Cultural Learnings of America for Make Benefit Glorious Nation of Kazakhstan.*

To lend support to some of his points, Kosic quotes from two essays he found while doing research. At the end of the essay, he provides a "Works Cited" list to indicate the precise sources of his quotations.

Milos Kosic has studied journalism at Northwest Community College in Powell, Wyoming, and English at City College of New York.

Milos Kosic
How to Approach a Different Culture?

1
Opens with a specific moment

<u>Joss said that I look like Borat the second time we met.</u> (1) It was a hot summer morning, and a group of us were out eating breakfast when he let the comment slip. Joss, who hadn't yet bothered to remember my name, was visiting from out of town. We share a group of friends, and at that moment all of them laughed, shaking their heads up and down, yes, yes, and they turned to me to observe the similarities more closely. To make his joke complete, Joss raised his palm and enthusiastically added in a high-pitched impression of Borat, "High five!"

I didn't really care because, honestly, what Joss said was not far from the truth. With the exception of a few style differences between us — namely, moustache and haircut — my face pretty much resembles Borat's. In fact, it is so obvious that even one of my professors couldn't manage to keep it to himself, making the observation

1

2

once in front of the whole class and leaving me blushing. This time, at breakfast, I didn't blush. I was a good sport about the joke and hoped only that Joss would soon move on to a new topic of conversation.

But he didn't. He started asking me questions about Kazakhstan. He wanted to know if we sleep with our sisters there. Do we eat dogs? (2) These questions were ridiculous for many reasons, not least of which is the fact that I am not from Kazakhstan. I'm from Serbia, which is not even geographically close to Kazakhstan, but for Joss it didn't make a difference. He gleefully asked, "Are all the women in Serbia fat?" He mentioned a famously large American actress and exclaimed, "She must have been from Serbia!" I stopped listening when he asked how much he could buy a Serbian girl for. I put my head down and prayed really, really hard that he hadn't seen the first season of *24*, in which a bunch of Serbian terrorists attempt to assassinate an African-American presidential candidate. The last thing I needed was to feel like my safety was compromised just because of my nationality.

2
Increases dramatic tensions

3

It had happened once already, a year ago, while I was getting a haircut. One of the waiting customers was complaining loudly about Orthodox Christianity, the primary religion in Serbia, connecting it with Islamic terrorism. As the barber's scissors danced around my head, I suddenly remembered a friend of my mother's, who, after hearing that I was studying in the U.S., asked my parents, "Why did you send him right into enemy hands?"

4

Well, at that moment, I felt like I was in the enemy's hands. I felt an undeniable need to belong, to hide who I was and where I was from. In his essay, "Leave Your Name at the Border," Manuel Muñoz describes this feeling, shared by many immigrants, as the "corrosive effect of assimilation . . . needing and wanting to belong, . . . seeing from the outside and wondering how to get in and then, once inside, realizing there are always those still on the fringe." (3) But then the barber chimed in, saying in his western, cowboy's accent, "I don't have anything against the Orthodox." I relaxed for a moment and responded, "Huh, good for me that you don't." But as I turned to the customer, I realized that I may have made a mistake.

5

3
Supports idea with quotation

Now that I had exposed my identity to "the enemy," I expected a couple of harsh words, or at least a dirty look, but it was not so dramatic. With a sudden change in demeanor, the customer was eager to hear more about

6

Serbia, telling me about his army experiences abroad. I was the first Serb that he had met. His obvious embarrassment made me uncomfortable.

4

Approaches issue
with open tone
of voice

Both my interaction in the barbershop and the one   7
with Joss remind me that I am always on the outside. (4)
Dinaw Mengestu discusses his experience as an immigrant in his essay, "Home at Last." He is "simply . . . Ethiopian, without the necessary 'from' that serves as the final assurance of [his] identity and origin." Mengestu explains his cultural dilemma as follows: It "had less to do with the idea that I was from Ethiopia and more to do with the fact that I was not from America." I can identify with Mengestu's situation.

Since I've come to the U.S., I've been called a Russian,   8
a Communist, and a Texan. I have been asked all kinds of questions from "Do you eat Pez in your country?" to "Do you have electricity there?" Even though my professors and American friends usually assume that those kinds of earnest questions bother me, they don't. It's quite interesting, actually, to hear people thinking about my background as something completely different from their own, a life with candles instead of electric light and with a Chihuahua on my lunch plate.

I feel almost sad when I reveal that none of that is true.   9
Many of us try to find something to identify with, but there have been so many racial and cultural mixtures throughout time that now it is almost impossible to define yourself as a member of one particular group. I grew up eating at McDonald's and watching *The Simpsons*. My shelves were overwhelmed with Harry Potter and Stephen King books, CDs of Creedence, Led Zeppelin, and The Rolling Stones.

5

Establishes a
broad identity

My favorite show as a kid was *Baywatch*. Yes, *Baywatch*. (5)
I even collected *Baywatch* sticky cards and filled a whole album. So even though I may identify myself as a reader, fast food enthusiast, or classic rock fan, others may see me as something else entirely.

I could have told Joss all of these things, but, of course,   10
he wouldn't want to know any of this; it would mean his joke was pointless. I guess it is because of people like Joss that the cousins and friends of Manuel Muñoz felt that traditional Mexican names — or "nombres del rancho" — "were names that stood as barriers to a complete embrace of an American identity, simply because their pronunciations required a slip into Spanish, the otherness that assimilation was supposed to erase."

Maybe changing "Milos" would make things easier for   11
me, too, but I don't want to do that. I don't want to become
Miles or Mike so that I can chum up with someone who
judges me by my name or my nationality. My name is not
only a word but part of my identity. Rather than "redefine"
myself, as Mengestu puts it, I choose to believe that "there
is room here for us all." Aside from the obvious fact that
he should avoid using Hollywood movies — and satires,
no less — as reliable sources, Joss should try to learn about
other cultures instead of ridiculing them. I am sure he
would be surprised by the interesting things he might hear.
For example, did you know that in Mongolia it is offensive
to touch the back of someone's head? Or that Japanese people never make fun of another person? They simply don't
see a good reason for doing it, even if you happen to look
like Borat.

6
*Demonstrates
source of
quotations*

Works Cited (6)

Mengestu, Dinaw. "Home at Last." *Open City*. Winter 2008.
Print.

Muñoz, Manuel. "Leave Your Name at the Border." *New
York Times*. New York Times, 1 Aug. 2007. Web. 1 Aug.
2007.

Comments

The following comments correspond to the numbered annotations
that appear in the margins of Milos Kosic's essay.

1. Opens with a specific moment. Writing often grows out of our
responses to the opinions and comments of others. Note that Kosic
begins his essay with a concrete reference to joking remarks made by
an acquaintance. The jokes deal with the writer's resemblance to the
central character of the film *Borat*, a physical resemblance that Kosic
concedes in paragraph 2 isn't "far from the truth." In his opening paragraphs, Kosic deftly lays out the scene and introduces an element of
dramatic tension. You should observe that he begins not with general
statements about cultural differences and stereotyping, but instead
with a highly specific moment.

2. Increases dramatic tensions. In paragraphs 3 and 4, Kosic
increases the dramatic tension of the scene by showing how Joss keeps
joking instead of moving on to new conversational topics. Kosic lets us
see the stereotypical views some Americans may have about other
cultures, indicating that Joss even confuses one country (Serbia) for

another (Kazakhstan). By the end of paragraph 4, we learn of the personal dangers Kosic feels as a result of stereotyping, and in paragraph 5 he expands on this feeling of danger, again using specific characters and incidents.

3. Supports idea with quotation. Note how Kosic reinforces his feeling of cultural conflict by introducing a quotation from Manuel Muñoz's "Leave Your Name at the Border." You should observe how Kosic uses ellipses (. . .) to indicate that he is citing not the entire passage but only the parts relevant to his point. The ellipses point out that some text is omitted.

4. Approaches issue with open tone of voice. Kosic ties both anecdotes together with a reference to Dinaw Mengestu's essay "Home at Last." Kosic's experiences in America — like Mengestu's — have reinforced his sense that he is an outsider — a nonnative individual in a culture unwilling to extend itself and learn more about the outside world. Note that Kosic responds not with anger toward those who frighten him or ask him silly, stereotypical questions but rather with an understanding that accepts the fact that they have no idea what his cultural background is like, that they consider it "something completely different from their own." Throughout the essay, he does not express anger, sarcasm, or disgust toward those who use stereotypes but instead is approachable and open to further discussion. As a quick exercise, try rewriting paragraph 8 in an angry tone of voice.

5. Establishes a broad identity. In paragraph 9, Kosic illustrates how much American popular culture he absorbed while growing up in Serbia: McDonald's, Stephen King, Led Zeppelin, and so on. These specific examples help persuade his readers that he cannot be defined by a single non-American identity.

6. Demonstrates source of quotations. To show his reliance on source material for his essay, Kosic adds a "Works Cited" list. This list, arranged in alphabetical order by the authors' last names (not in the order that the citations appeared in the essay), allows readers to find the works he cites.

The Visual Expression of Opinion

Public opinions are expressed in a variety of ways, not only in familiar verbal forms such as persuasive essays, magazine articles, or newspaper columns. In newspapers and magazines, opinions are often expressed through photography, political cartoons, and paid opinion advertisements (or op-ads). Let's briefly look at these three main sources of visual opinion.

Photography

At first glance, a photograph may not seem to express an opinion. Photography is often considered an "objective" medium: Isn't the photographer simply taking a picture of what is actually there? But on reflection and careful examination, we can see that photographs can express subjective views or editorial opinions in many different ways.

1. A photograph can be deliberately set up or "staged" to support a position, point of view, or cause. For example, though not exactly staged, the renowned World War II photograph of U.S. combat troops triumphantly raising the American flag at Iwo Jima on the morning of February 23, 1945, was in fact a reenactment. After a first flag-raising was photographed, the military command considered the flag too small to be symbolically effective (though other reasons are also cited), so it was replaced with a much larger one and the event reshot. The 2006 Clint Eastwood film *Flags of Our Fathers* depicts the reenactment and the photo's immediate effect on reviving a war-weary public's patriotism. The picture's meaning was also more symbolic than actual, as the fighting on the island went on for many days after the flag was raised. Three of the six

"Flag Raising at Iwo Jima," taken by combat photographer Joe Rosenthal on February 23, 1945.

Americans who helped raise the famed second flag were killed before the fighting ended. The photograph, which was also cropped, is considered the most reproduced image in photographic history.

2. A photographer can deliberately echo or visually refer to a well-known image to produce a political or emotional effect. Observe how the now-famous photograph of firefighters raising a tattered American flag in the wreckage of 9/11 instantly calls to mind the heroism of the Iwo Jima marines.

© Associated Press Photo/Thomas E. Franklin/The Record (Bergen County, NJ).

"Three Firefighters Raising the Flag," taken by Thomas E. Franklin, staff photographer for *The Record* (Bergen County, NJ), on September 11, 2001.

3. A photographer can shoot a picture at such an angle or from a particular perspective to dramatize a situation, to make someone look less or more important, or to suggest imminent danger. A memorable photograph taken in 2000 of Cuban refugee Elián González, for example, made it appear that the boy, who was actually in no danger whatsoever, was about to be shot. (See photo below.)

© Alan Diaz/AP Photo.

4. A photographer can catch a prominent figure in an unflattering position or embarrassing moment, or in a flattering and lofty fashion. Newspaper or magazine editors can then decide based on their political or cultural attitudes whether to show a political figure in an awkward or a commanding light.

5. A photograph can be cropped, doctored, or digitally altered to show something that did not happen. For example, a photo of a young John Kerry was inserted into a 1972 Jane Fonda rally to show misleadingly Kerry's association with Fonda's anti–Vietnam War activism. Dartmouth College has created a Web site that features a gallery of doctored news photos. (See http://www.fourandsix.com/photo-tampering-history.)

6. A photograph can be taken out of context or captioned in a way that is misleading.

These are only some of the ways the print and online media can use photographs for editorial purposes. Although most reputable news sources go to great lengths to verify the authenticity of photographs, especially those that come from outside sources, and enforce stiff penalties on photographers who manipulate their pictures, some experts in the field maintain that doctoring is far more common in the media than the public believes.

"We can no longer afford to accept news photography as factual data," claims Adrian E. Hanft III, a graphic designer, in an August 2006 photography blog. "If we are realistic," he continues, "we will come to the conclusion that much of the photography in the news is fake — or at least touched up to better tell the story. It is relatively simple to doctor a photo and everybody knows it. The fact that the term 'Photoshop it' is a part of the English vernacular shows just how accustomed to fake photography we have become. The interesting thing is that in the face of the massive amounts of doctored photos, most people still expect photos in the news to be unaltered. I think this has something to do with a human desire for photographs to be true. We know the cover photo of Teri Hatcher (of "Desperate Housewives" fame) is touched-up but we don't question it because we *want* her to look like that. Likewise when we see news stories that confirm our beliefs we want them to be true. As photo manipulation becomes easier and easier, there is an increase in the demand for photographs that confirm what people want to believe. The market responds by flooding the world with 'fake' photography. Today people can believe almost anything they want and point to photography that 'proves' their beliefs."

Political Cartoons

The art of American political cartoons goes back to the eighteenth century; Benjamin Franklin was allegedly responsible for one of the nation's earliest cartoons. Almost from the start, political cartoonists developed what would become their favored techniques and conventions. Because cartoonists hoped to achieve an immediate intellectual and emotional impact, usually with imagery and a brief written message, they soon realized that exaggeration worked better than subtlety and that readily identified symbols were more quickly comprehended than nuanced or unusual imagery. The political cartoon is rarely ambiguous — it takes a decided position that frequently displays enemies negatively and friends positively. Rarely does a political cartoonist muddy the waters by introducing a mixed message or entertaining an opposing view. A cartoonist, unlike a columnist, cannot construct a detailed argument to support a position, so the strokes applied are often broad and obvious.

The humorous impact of most political cartoons depends on a combination of elements. Let's look at three relatively recent cartoons and examine the role of **context, iconography, exaggeration, irony, caricature, symbol,** and **caption**. Please note that the following cartoons are included for illustrative purposes only. They were not selected for their political and social opinions or for their artistic skill but primarily because they conveniently demonstrate the major elements and techniques of the political cartoon. Many other recent cartoons could just as easily have been selected.

First, a note about **context**. Chances are that if you don't know the political situation the cartoonist refers to, you won't "get" the cartoon's intended message. So it's important to remember that the cartoon's meaning depends on previously received information, usually from standard news sources. In other words, most cartoonists expect their audience to know a little something about the news story the cartoon refers to. Unlike the essayist, the cartoonist works in a tightly compressed verbal and visual medium in which it is unusually difficult to summarize the political context or the background the audience requires for full comprehension. This is one reason that cartoonists often work with material from headlining stories that readers are likely to be familiar with. In many cases, the audience needs to supply its own information to grasp the cartoon's full meaning.

Let's examine the context of the 2006 cartoon "When It's Too Late to Warn Iran." The cartoonist expects his audience to know that the United Nations has been criticized for its soft handling of Iran's nuclear weapons program by continually issuing warnings without taking more concrete action. So the spoken words in the cartoon are presumably by the head of the UN, and the cartoon's message is that even after Iran uses its nuclear weaponry, the UN will *still* be issuing ultimatums. The cartoon thus satirizes the UN as powerless and ineffectual in the face of nuclear threat. Note how much political context the audience is asked to supply and how much information it needs to infer. Ask yourself: If you knew nothing of Iran's plans and the UN's involvement, would you be able to understand the cartoon at all? Also, imagine that you saw the cartoon without the spoken comment: How would you interpret the imagery?

The image is unambiguous: The United Nations building is rocketing upward as a result of a nuclear explosion, torn away from its New York City site. Note the elements of **iconography**. Iconography is the use of shorthand images that immediately suggest an incident, idea, era, institution, and so on. Such images are intended to reflect immediately and clearly what they stand for. For example, a teenager with a pack of cigarettes rolled up inside the sleeve of his T-shirt is iconographic of the 1950s; a cap and gown indicates an academic; a briefcase represents a businessperson or a public official; a devil is traditionally represented with horns and a pitchfork. In this cartoon, the mushroom cloud represents

"When It's Too Late to Warn Iran," by *U.S. News & World Report* cartoonist Doug Marlette, published on September 25, 2006.

a nuclear explosion and the building represents the institution of the United Nations, which is labeled on the side in case someone doesn't recognize its familiar architecture. The cartoonist doesn't use a caption but instead includes the conventional dialogue balloon to indicate that someone is speaking. The speaker isn't pictured or identified but is clearly inside the building.

Note, too, the cartoon's use of **exaggeration** and unrealistic depiction: Does anyone imagine that — outside of a comic strip — a nuclear blast would send an entire building skyward and totally intact, and that we could hear a single human voice? We are, of course, not expected to understand the events literally. Nor are we even to assume that Iran *will* attack the United States. The overall effect is to call attention to the weakness of the UN by showing it to be all talk and no action.

To "get" the cartoon's full meaning is to understand its clever use of **visual irony**. Although it's a large literary subject, irony can be understood simply as a contrast between what appears to be expressed and what is actually being expressed. The contrast is often humorous and could be sarcastic, as when someone says after you've done something especially dumb, "Nice work!" What appears to be expressed (verbally) in the cartoon is that the ineffectual United Nations is issuing yet again another "last warning." What is actually expressed (visually) is that this statement truly and literally is — now that the United Nations has been completely destroyed — the institution's "last warning."

Let's turn to another cartoon, this one of former president George W. Bush, which demonstrates a cartoonist's use of **caricature** and **symbol**. Caricature is the artistic rendering of someone's physical features in an exaggerated manner for quick recognition. Depending on their political perspective, cartoonists can use caricature for purposes of quick identification or as a way to demean, stereotype, or satirize someone. Throughout his presidency Bush was portrayed by political cartoonists as a goofy-looking individual with large, protruding ears.

The political context of the cartoon is readily understood: After the terrorist attacks of 9/11, President Bush advanced policies in the name of security that many Americans considered serious violations of civil rights and liberties. To visually reinforce the powers the president assumed, the cartoonist depicts him not as a president but as a king. Note the regal symbols of throne, crown, robe, and scepter. Note, too, the dangling pair of binoculars that symbolize government spying.

Now to a third cartoon that illustrates another common feature of the cartoonist's stock-in-trade: the succinct combination of topical issues. In this case, the cartoonist's humor covers two national debates — the

"It's Only until We End Terrorism," by syndicated cartoonist Ed Fischer.

use of stem-cell research and the oil crisis. Like the anti–United Nations cartoon, this one also relies heavily on iconography, in the image of the instantly recognized Capitol building in Washington, D.C. The architecture dominates the cartoon and dwarfs the unidentified male figures carrying briefcases, who might be members of Congress or lobbyists. The Capitol architecture lends the scene an aura of dignity and stateliness that is undercut by the cynical remark of the caption, which suggests that conservative pieties over the sacredness of stem cells would be easily set aside if the cells yielded crude oil. In other words, economic interests and profits would "of course" trump religious and ethical positions. The casually expressed remark suggests that the speaker would in no way protect stem cells from scientific use if they could help our oil supply.

Note that this cartoon depends almost entirely on its **caption** for its effect. There is nothing intrinsic to the overall drawing that links it to the caption. If there were no caption and you were invited to supply one, you might come up with any one of thousands of remarks on any number of topics or issues. The main function of the image is to set the remark in a

"Of course it would be a different story entirely if we could extract crude oil from stem cells."

"Stem Cells," by *New Yorker* cartoonist Jack Ziegler, published on August 7–14, 2006.

political context. The remark then can be read as a satirical comment on how our current government works — on profits, not principles.

The relationship between the Capitol building and the caption does, however, suggest an ironic incongruity. The imposing image of the U.S. Capitol — like the UN in the cartoon on page 37, one of the world's most significant political buildings — would seem more in keeping with a principled rather than an unprincipled comment. Thus, the overall image adds to the satire by making us aware of the separation between how a revered political institution should perform and how it actually does. For example, consider how the level of satire would be reduced if the cartoonist used the same caption but instead portrayed two research scientists in a medical laboratory.

Opinion Ads

Most of the ads we see and hear daily try to persuade us to buy consumer goods like cars, cosmetics, and cereal. Yet advertising does more than promote consumer products. Every day we also encounter numerous ads that promote not things but opinions. These opinion advertisements (op-ads) may take a variety of forms — political commercials, direct mail from advocacy groups seeking contributions, posters and billboards, or paid newspaper and magazine announcements. Sometimes the ads are released by political parties and affiliated organizations, sometimes by large corporations hoping to influence policy, and sometimes by public advocacy groups such as Amnesty International, the National Association for the Advancement of Colored People, the National Rifle Association, or — as we see on page 42 — the American Civil Liberties Union (ACLU).

This selection represents only one of hundreds of such opinion ads readers come across regularly in newspapers and magazines. To examine carefully its verbal and visual techniques — whether you agree with its message or not — will help you better understand the essentials of rhetorical persuasion.

At the center of the ad (which appeared in many magazines in 2000), we see two photographs. The man on the left nearly everyone will recognize as Martin Luther King Jr. The other photo will be familiar to many Americans, especially older ones, but may not be recognized by all — it is the convicted California mass murderer, Charles Manson. The ad's headline refers only to "the man on the left" and "the man on the right." According to the headline, then, King, one of the nation's most outstanding leaders, "is 75 times more likely to be stopped by the police while driving" than one of the nation's most horrific murderers. The headline and photos are intended to attract our attention. The image of King also powerfully suggests that the issue of civil rights is still alive. (The ad's creators expect us to set aside the facts that King has been dead for decades and Manson has never been released from prison. So there is no possibility that the particular man on the left "is" more likely to be subjected to a police search than the particular man on the right. Thus, the ad's central statement cannot be taken as literally true.)

Why doesn't the headline say "Martin Luther King is 75 times more likely to be stopped by the police while driving than Charles Manson"?

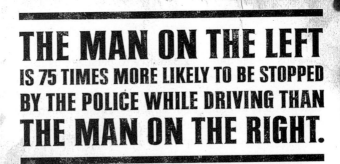

"The Man on the Left," an opinion advertisement that was part of the ACLU's 2000 campaign against racial profiling.

Why does the ad deliberately not identify each photo? One reason may be that the ACLU is counting on King's iconographic status; he needs no identification. But what about Manson: Did you instantly recognize him? Why doesn't the ACLU balance the photos by portraying John F. Kennedy, another American icon, on the right? The main point of the ad would not be at all affected if Kennedy were on the right because the central issue is that African American drivers are more likely to be stopped than whites. Nor would the ad's message be affected if the photo on the right were simply of an anonymous, clean-shaven, white male. So, given the message, any white male could have been used instead of Manson. Why portray Manson?

Featuring Manson drives home the point that the system of stopping drivers based on their skin color is totally indiscriminate and doesn't take status, character, or virtue into account. The ACLU wants to surprise, even shock, its audience into realizing that the U.S. criminal justice system would stop and search one of America's most honored public figures while giving a free pass to one of the nation's most reviled convicts. Analyzing the ad in this way, however, raises an uncomfortable issue. If you don't recognize Manson (who was convicted in 1971 and has rarely been seen since his sentencing) and are still surprised or shocked by the headline, is it then because of the way he looks — the long hair, full beard, and glaring eyes? Does he look suspicious? If you think so, are you also engaging in a kind of "profiling," allowing yourself to think the man on the right ought to be stopped simply because he fits some kind of stereotype — a "hippie," a homeless person, a mentally ill individual? Here's a good question to ask about a visual image presented in a way that assumes you know what or who it is: What are the unintended consequences if you don't know it? In this case, what happens to the ad's message if you don't recognize either figure from the 1960s?

Besides the visual argument outlined above, the ad also expresses in smaller print a verbal argument. In print advertising, this element usually contains the ad's central argument and is known as body copy, body text, or simply text to distinguish it from the headline, illustrations, and other visuals. The argument is essentially that "humiliating and illegal searches are violations of the Constitution and must be fought." The text does not state why or how racial profiling (a term not used in the ad) violates the Constitution. In other words, it assumes our assent and offers no reasons why we must be legally concerned about the issue. There is no mention of which part of the Constitution the police violate, nor is any relevant phrase of the Constitution quoted directly.

The argument depends wholly on statistical evidence that a dispro-portionate percentage of certain drivers are stopped by the police. Note that the headline and the body of the text appear to cite two different sets of statistics: The headline claims that someone like King "is 75 times more likely to be stopped" than a white person, while the text reads that "in Florida 80% of those stopped and searched were black and His-panic, while they constituted only 5% of all drivers." These two statistics are offered with no attribution of sources (Who gathered them? Is the source reliable?) nor any dates (Are they recent?). We might also wonder why only Florida is mentioned. The ad also introduces an ambiguity by mentioning the Florida statistic because we are then led to wonder what the statistic in the headline refers to. Is it only in Florida that the man on the left "is 75 times more likely to be stopped"? Or does that number rep-resent a national figure? And is the number also meant to represent His-panics, or does the "75" in the headline refer only to African Americans as represented by King? To question these numbers and their manner of presentation is not to dispute their accuracy or the seriousness of the issue, but only to demonstrate the necessity of responding to statistical evidence cautiously before giving our assent to an argument.

Nearly all opinion ads (and most ads in general) are action oriented. The purpose of persuasion is to produce a change in opinion or attitude that will produce social or political action. This ad, like most opinion ads, encourages a twofold action: (1) It asks the reader to assent to an opinion (in this case, that our Constitution is being violated); and (2) it asks directly for the reader's support, which could mean both to encour-age the work of the ACLU and to assist it with donations. Note the text's final words: "Help us defend your rights. Support the ACLU." Because ads must work in such a compressed verbal format, some of the words we need to pay special attention to are pronouns. A reader may wonder why the final words didn't say, "Help us defend the rights of African Ameri-cans and Hispanics" (or "people of color"), since the ad never claimed that the rights of any other group were being violated. But "your rights" is intentionally all-inclusive: It stands for you, the reader, and everyone else. In a highly abbreviated way, the ad implies that whenever anyone's constitutional rights are violated, everyone's rights are violated.

The ad contains an extra visual feature that may take a while to notice or comprehend. The ad isn't just a page in a magazine; it's designed to look like the sort of wanted poster the police and FBI display to help catch criminals or the kind often seen in pictures of the old West ("Wanted — Dead or Alive"). Note the discoloration from weather and the nails attaching it to what appears to be a wooden surface. Why did the designer do this? Why take the ad's image to another dimension? And how does imagining the ad as a wanted poster affect its overall argument and our response? The ACLU's intention, it seems, is to enforce the image of criminalization. One photo is of an actual psychopathic criminal, so the wanted poster image makes sense in its depiction of Manson (though he is already in prison). But why would King, one of the greatest Americans, appear on a wanted poster? The general effect appears to be that in the eyes of the highway police who are profiling black drivers, even someone as distinguished as King would be considered a criminal. The effect and implication of the wanted poster ramp up the visual rhetoric and contribute to the shock value of the advertisement.

Writing as Empowerment

Writing is one of the most powerful means of producing social and political change. Through their four widely disseminated gospels, the first-century evangelists helped propagate Christianity throughout the world; the writings of Adam Smith and Karl Marx determined the economic systems of many nations for well over a century; Thomas Jefferson's Declaration of Independence became a model for countless colonial liberationists; the carefully crafted speeches of Martin Luther King Jr. and the books and essays of numerous feminists altered twentieth-century consciousness. In the long run, many believe, "The pen is mightier than the sword."

Empowerment does not mean instant success. It does not mean that your opinion or point of view will suddenly prevail. It does mean, however, that you have made your voice heard, that you have given your opinions wider circulation, that you have made yourself and your position a little more visible. And sometimes you get results: A newspaper prints your letter; a university committee adopts your suggestion; people visit your Web site. Throughout this collection, you will encounter writing specifically intended to inform and influence a wide community.

Such influence is not restricted to professional authors and political experts. This collection features a large number of student writers who are actively involved with the same current topics and issues that engage the attention of professionals — the environment, racial and ethnic identity, gender differences, media bias, and so on. The student selections, all of them previously published and written for a variety of reasons, are meant to be an integral part of each unit, to be read in conjunction with the professional essays, and to be criticized and analyzed on an equal footing.

What's in a Name?

"What's in a name?" asks Shakespeare's Juliet: "That which we call a rose/ by any other word would smell as sweet." Yet not everyone has agreed with Juliet's widely quoted remark. For a large number of Americans, names are a matter of vital importance. Names can suggest family origins, social status, racial and ethnic identity, and religious affiliation. Some names are legally owned under trademarks and their unauthorized use subject to enormous fines.

Is it fair to judge people by their names? Many would think not, but it appears that people often do let names affect their attitude. In "Easily Pronounced Names May Make People More Likable," Dave Mosher cites recent research that indicates the "more pronounceable a person's name is, the more likely people are to favor them." The idea behind this research is that the human brain "favors information that's easy to read." But as the following selection demonstrates, "likability" is merely a minor issue in certain situations. In a short autobiographical essay, "The Devil's

Dave Mosher is a science journalist and self-proclaimed Web nerd who regularly contributes to Wired Science *and manages* Wired Science Blogs. *His freelancing credits include* National Geographic News, Scientific American, *and* Popular Mechanics. *He holds a BS in biology and a BA in journalism from Ohio State University.*

Spine," Maria Venegas recalls her struggle as a four-year-old to remember the name she is told to use when asked by guards at the Mexican border.

You don't have to be a sports fan to realize how many teams are identified by nicknames, some of which may be mysterious, others appropriate, and still others racist and offensive. In a casually written, blog-style essay, "Washington, Yea! Redskins, Boo!" University of Maryland history major Greg Nasif uses humor to raise some serious points about racial stereotypes.

In "America Then," we take a step back some five hundred years and look at the peculiar way we became "Americans." Who named us? Answer: It's someone whose name in all probability you never heard of.

Finally, the e-Page for this chapter, "The Baby Name Voyager," lets you explore naming trends in America since the 1880s—and come to conclusions about why some rise in popularity and some fall.

Dave Mosher

Easily Pronounced Names May Make People More Likable

[*Wired Science*, February 24, 2012]

BEFORE YOU READ

What factors come into play when making judgments about someone? Do you think your ability to pronounce a name has a bearing on your opinions? What conclusions might you come to about someone if his or her name is hard to pronounce?

WORDS TO LEARN

inadvisable (para. 1): not recommended (adj)

delinquent (para. 6): guilty of inappropriate behavior (adj)

quantify (para. 8): to determine an amount (verb)

context (para. 8): circumstances around a situation (noun)

solely (para. 10): exclusively (adv)

pedigree (para. 13): record (usually refers to lineage) (noun)

correlation (para. 13): similarity between two things (noun)

competent (para. 15): qualified (adj)

1 Though it might seem impossible, and certainly inadvisable, to judge a person by their name, a new study suggests our brains try anyway.

2 The more pronounceable a person's name is, the more likely people are to favor them.

> The more pronounceable a person's name is, the more likely people are to favor them.

3 "When we can process a piece of information more easily, when it's easier to comprehend, we come to like it more," said psychologist Adam Alter of New York University and co-author of a *Journal of Experimental Social Psychology* study published in December.

4 Fluency, the idea that the brain favors information that's easy to use, dates back to the 1960s, when researchers found that people most liked images of Chinese characters if they'd seen them many times before.

5 Researchers since then have explored other roles that names play, how they affect our judgment and to what degree.

Studies have shown, for example, that people can partly predict a 6
person's income and education using only their first name. Childhood
is perhaps the richest area for name research: Boys with girls' names are
more likely to be suspended from school. And the less popular a name is,
the more likely a child is to be delinquent.

In 2005, Alter and his colleagues explored how pronounceability of 7
company names affects their performance in the stock market. Stripped
of all obvious influences, they found companies with simpler names
and ticker symbols traded better than the stocks of more difficult-to-
pronounce companies.

"The effect is often very, very hard to quantify because so much 8
depends on context, but it's there and measurable," Alter said. "You can't
avoid it."

But how much does pronunciation guide our perceptions of people? 9
To find out, Alter and colleagues Simon Laham and Peter Koval of the
University of Melbourne carried out five studies.

In the first, they asked 19 female and 16 male college students to 10
rank 50 surnames according to their ease or difficulty of pronunciation,
and according to how much they liked or disliked them. In the second,
they had 17 females and 7 male students vote for hypothetical political
candidates solely on the basis of their names. In the third, they asked 55
female and 19 male students to vote on candidates about whom they
knew both names and some political positions.

Altogether the researchers found that a name's pronounceability, 11
regardless of length or seeming foreignness, mattered most in determining likability. Ease of pronunciation accounted for about 40 percent of
off-the-cuff likability.

"These settings were pretty impoverished, of course. In the real 12
world, so many other things are going on that play a role," Alter said.

In the latter studies, Alter's team wanted to get a better sense of 13
name-pronunciation effects outside the lab. They collected the names
of 500 randomly selected lawyers, which undergraduates then rated for
pronounceability and likability. When the researchers compared their
tastes against the lawyers' academic pedigrees, average salaries and corporate positions, they found a small but noticeable correlation.

With other variables eliminated, about 1.5 percent of a lawyer's suc- 14
cess — at least in this study — seemed to rest on the pronounceability of
his or her name.

"Obviously that's a lot smaller than 40 percent, and we don't know 15
which lawyer is most competent, which is clearly going to matter the
most," Alter said. "But the name still matters."

Alter has already been influenced by his own work. If and when he   16
has children, he said, he plans to keep their names simple.

Citation: "The name-pronunciation effect: Why people like Mr. Smith more than Mr. Colquhoun. " By Simon M. Lahama, Peter Kovala and Adam L. Alter. Journal of Experimental Social Psychology, published online Dec. 9, 2011. DOI: 10. 1016/j.jesp. 2011.12.002

ALL IN A NAME

Top 10 Baby Names for 2011

Rank	Male name	Female name
1	Jacob	Sophia
2	Mason	Isabella
3	William	Emma
4	Jayden	Olivia
5	Noah	Ava
6	Michael	Emily
7	Ethan	Abigail
8	Alexander	Madison
9	Aiden	Mia
10	Daniel	Chloe

The top baby names for 2011, according to the Social Security Administration.

Top 10 Baby Names of the 1970s

Rank	Male name	Female name
1	Michael	Jennifer
2	Christopher	Amy
3	Jason	Melissa
4	David	Michelle
5	James	Kimberly
6	John	Lisa
7	Robert	Angela
8	Brian	Heather
9	William	Stephanie
10	Matthew	Nicole

The top baby names of the 1970s, according to the Social Security Administration.

VOCABULARY/USING A DICTIONARY

1. The word *surname* (para. 10) refers to a family name, or last name—a name that connects several people. If you didn't know that already, how might you have guessed its meaning by breaking down the parts of the word?
2. What is the definition of *comprehend* (para. 3)? What are some synonyms for *comprehend*?
3. What is the etymology of the word *income* (para. 6), and what is its modern meaning?

RESPONDING TO WORDS IN CONTEXT

1. The verb *pronounce* can be modified and become other parts of speech. Identify a few modifications of *pronounce* used in this essay and add some of your own.
2. *Fluency* is defined as "the idea that the brain favors information that's easy to use" (para. 4). When you look up *fluency* in the dictionary, what definition do you find?
3. The word *influence* comes up in paragraph 7 and in paragraph 16. How do the uses of the word differ in each sentence?

DISCUSSING MAIN POINT AND MEANING

1. According to the author, studies of which age group provide the richest information to support the correlation between name pronounceability and life consequences?
2. Ease of name pronunciation can sway whether or not a person is found "likable." When Alter applied that information to other areas of research, what did he discover?
3. Are you surprised that "studies have shown, for example, that people can partly predict a person's income and education using only their first name" (para. 6)? How do you understand that statement based on Mosher's argument here?

EXAMINING SENTENCES, PARAGRAPHS, AND ORGANIZATION

1. What is the effect of having a series of very short paragraphs in this essay?
2. What is the effect of the final paragraph on the essay? How would the essay be different if it ended on the penultimate paragraph?
3. Paragraph 4 refers to a study done in the 1960s. Why does Mosher include that information? What effect does it have on your understanding of this essay?

THINKING CRITICALLY

1. Although he wants to make the case that pronounceability of names affects our perceptions, Mosher does not want to suggest that

pronounceability is the only influence on how we react to others. What other things influence how we perceive others?

2. Mosher includes data from Alter's studies in paragraph 10. Do you think that data adds anything important to his essay? What does it add?

3. Does this essay give you any ideas about which names are more or less desirable? Explain.

WRITING ACTIVITIES

1. Create a survey that mimics Alter's research in some way. For example, you might offer classmates a list of names and ask them to rate them or include information on why they prefer one name to another. In small groups, distribute the survey and ask participants to answer your questions/fill out your survey anonymously. Once you receive your data, try to interpret it in some way. Write a short paragraph that explains your conclusions.

2. In a short essay, consider why the ability to pronounce a name has an effect on one's opinion of someone. What do names tell us about someone?

3. As a class, choose two names (either first names or surnames). Under each one, write a list of that person's attributes as quickly as you can without stopping. Then read through what you've written and make a short note about *why* you assume that attribute corresponds with that name. Discuss the results of this writing exercise.

Maria Venegas

The Devil's Spine

[*Ploughshares*, Spring 2012]

BEFORE YOU READ

Ideas about identity are often formed when we are very small, before we can fully understand what's happening in the world around us. In this short essay, a name change colors a young girl's perception of her relationships and the foundation of her memories as she moves from one world into another.

WORDS TO LEARN

memorize (para. 1): to learn by heart (verb)

pale (para. 5): lacking color (adj)

wedge (para. 5): something having a triangular shape (noun)

void (para. 5): empty space (noun)

veer (para. 10): to change direction (verb)

evaporating (para. 11): disappearing (adj)

You have been sent for and now you must memorize a name. A new 1 name. A borrowed name. Nine thousand feet above sea level, the options are laid out before you: Get the name right and you see your parents again; get the name wrong and you never see them again. It's that simple. The bus you are traveling on snakes through the clouds, around the Devil's Spine, as it makes its way along the Sierra Madre Occidental mountain range.[1]

"What is your name?" A face emerges from the clouds and asks you. 2 It's a familiar face, a face that is so much like your mother's face, though her face has faded in your memory, the way plastic flowers tied to a cross and left on the side of the road fade in the sun.

"Maria de Jesus Venegas Robles," you respond. This is the one thing 3 you do know — your name. But it's the wrong answer. The bus jerks to the left and the force slams your body against the window.

---

[1] Sierra Madre Occidental mountain range (para. 1): Part of the Sierra Madre mountain system in Mexico, it runs through Mexico until it nears the U.S. border with Arizona.

Maria Venegas immigrated to Chicago from Zacatecas, Mexico, when she was four years old. Now a New Yorker, she recently finished her first book, Bulletproof Vest, *which was excerpted in* Granta *magazine and published in 2012.*

"When the men in green uniforms ask what your name is, you have   4
to say Maricela Salazar, or you will never see your parents again. Do you
understand?"

But you're only four years old, and you must look so yellow, so pale,   5
for you are handed a grapefruit wedge and instructed to suck on it. You
put it in your mouth, and the bittersweet juice runs down your chin and
neck as you repeat the name, over and over, like a prayer, like a wish. It's
only a name. But it's the one thing that might rescue you from the void
into which you slipped the day your parents vanished. The day they dropped you off at your grandmother's house and never returned. After that,
you asked anyone who came by her house if they had seen them. If your
grandmother took you to the corner store, the plaza, the bakery, the mercado, you asked anyone who greeted her if they had seen them. They all
gave you the same tight-lipped smile, or a pat on the head. Some handed
you a piece of hard candy, a chicle, or an ice cream cone — anything to
get your mind off of them — because everyone knew that your parents
had gone to the other side.

"What is your name?" The bus swerves right, and the sun comes at   6
you, a giant ball of fire smacking the window and diffusing.

"Maria de Jesus Venegas Robles," you respond, as ten thousand rays   7
of light flood the bus, blinding you. Once again, the options are laid
before you. Time is running out, and if you give the men in uniforms the
wrong answer, well . . .

Focus on the dust particles that are free-falling through the sun-   8
light and settling on your boney knee as you whisper the name like a
chant. Mari-cela Sala-zar. Concentrate on
the citrus scent that is lingering in the
air. Ma-ri-ce-la Sa-la-zar. It's the smell of
something green or orange, a respite from
the nausea that is already creeping in. An
ice cube dissolving on the tongue. ¿Qué
se pela por la panza? It's a riddle, but what

> It's a name you
> must slip into and
> wear like a second
> skin.

is it? It's only a name. A borrowed name. But it's a name you must slip
into and wear like a second skin, for on the other side of that name, your
parents are alive and waiting.

Though you believed them to be gone for good, ever since the day   9
that your grandmother took you back to your house. When you arrived,
you watched as she turned the skeleton key in the heavy wooden door and
pushed it open. It hit against the adobe wall with a crashing blow. Everything was in place. La Virgen de Guadalupe still hung on the wall behind
the couch. In the kitchen, all the dishes were in the cupboard, the pile of
chopped wood sat in the corner, and the scent of the wood-burning oven

still lingered in the air. In their bedroom, the bed was made and the shutters were closed. Her floral printed dresses hung in the wardrobe next to his cowboy shirts, but they weren't there. They had seemingly slid through the cracks in the limestone floor and vanished. Never again did you ask about them.

The road curves right and the shadow of the mountain falls upon you as you recite the name. Maricela Salazar. It's been two years since they disappeared. Two years is not such a long time, though it's long enough. The road veers left and again you are swimming in the sunlight, while in the valley below, among the thorns and boulders, are rusted out cars and trucks that plunged into their dusty grave years ago. Inside, their passengers are still strapped in, still waiting to be rescued. But there is no escape from the Devil's Spine. He who plunges into its valley stays there forever and ever. Amen.   10

The bus emerges from the clouds and you are struggling to memorize the name, even as the memories of everything that came before this journey are evaporating. Try and grab two handfuls of the images that are already fading: the bougainvillea in your grandmother's courtyard, the sweet sting of a honey taco, the scent of the wood-burning oven, running barefoot through the cornfields, the flight of the blackbirds at sunset, the marching sound of an approaching rainstorm, and the scent of wet earth that lingers once the storm has passed. One day you will open your clutched fists to find you have nothing — no memory of the things that came before this passage — not even a bit of red dirt under your fingernails to remind you.   11

"What is your name?" a man in a green uniform asks when you reach the border.   12

"Maricela Salazar."   13

VOCABULARY/USING A DICTIONARY

1. Venegas uses the Spanish word *mercado* (para. 5) in her essay. What does it mean?
2. What is *bougainvillea* (para. 11)?
3. Venegas mentions two types of materials: *adobe* and *limestone* (para. 9). Describe them.

RESPONDING TO WORDS IN CONTEXT

1. What is the definition of the word *border* (para. 12)? What borders are being crossed at the end of this essay?
2. Venegas refers to people's *tight-lipped* smiles (para. 5). What does that mean? What feeling does it convey?
3. Define *respite* (para. 8). What would a respite be for the child narrator of this essay?

DISCUSSING MAIN POINT AND MEANING

1. How does Venegas point out differences between the two names presented in this essay? How are they different? How are they the same?
2. Is it important that the speaker in this essay is a young child rather than an adult? Why do you think Venegas writes from that perspective?
3. Where does Venegas's essay feel realistic and where does it seem to rely on metaphor or feel more like a dream? Why do you think Venegas sets up this duality between the real and unreal?

EXAMINING SENTENCES, PARAGRAPHS, AND ORGANIZATION

1. Why is the essay called "The Devil's Spine"? How is the title reflected in the essay?
2. Identify places in the essay where Venegas's verbs are in the imperative and say why you think she chooses this form.
3. Do you know what the sentence *¿Qué se pela por la panza?* (para. 8) means? What is the effect of including that sentence in this essay, along with other random words in Spanish?

THINKING CRITICALLY

1. What is the effect of the phrase *citrus scent* in paragraph 8? Why not just repeat *grapefruit* (para. 5)?
2. Is this story fiction or nonfiction? Does it make a difference to you if you read it one way or the other? Why or why not?
3. Venegas includes a sentence written in Spanish in paragraph 8. Why does she include that sentence, knowing that some readers will not understand it?

WRITING ACTIVITIES

1. Write about a memory, but put yourself in the third person. Is it easier to write a personal essay this way? How does your writing about yourself change from this perspective?
2. Are you simply the person you are, regardless of what you are called, or does your name create the person you are? With Venegas's essay in mind, write a short essay about how your name has or has not influenced you.
3. In pairs, perform an interview with your partner, asking questions about some element of his or her childhood. Once you have the answers, write a story about your interviewee based on the answers. Be sure you collect enough details in your interview to be able to ground your story in the senses, as Venegas does.

Greg Nasif (student essay)

Washington, Yea! Redskins, Boo!

[*The Diamondback*, The University of Maryland, October 13, 2011]

BEFORE YOU READ

Have you thought about the racial implications behind sports team names like the Redskins, Indians, or Chiefs? What do you think these names are trying to convey? Do you think they are appropriate for professional sports teams? Why or why not?

WORDS TO LEARN

monikers (para. 2): names (noun)

To all of my friends among the Washington Redskins faithful, I wish to convey my congratulations that your team is not God-awful this year. But I'm going to ruin your day by asking: Seriously, what the hell is a Redskin? 1

Sports nicknames generally convey certain qualities — creativity, relevance, competitiveness, ferocity, mystique — and many other things that don't describe a Redskin. That name isn't remotely relevant, there's no mystique, and the ferocity is based on an ancient stereotype. Society has moved on from promoting teams with racist monikers (81 percent of Native Americans are unoffended by their patronage in sports). But the Redskins have found innovative ways to be profoundly racist. They refused to integrate their team until buckling to federal pressure to do so in 1962. 2

> The ferocity is based on an ancient stereotype.

Meanwhile, other teams that use Native American mascots tend to narrow their identification. The Atlanta Braves (the Redskins' original nickname until they presumably determined it wasn't racist enough) use the term for a Native American warrior, which also happens to be a synonym for courage. The Florida State Seminoles represent a specific cultural aspect of Florida's history. The Kansas City Chiefs represent leadership, and are also a nod to a former mayor who helped spread 3

Greg Nasif graduated in 2012 from the University of Maryland, where he majored in U.S. history, with a minor in astronomy.

awareness of Native American culture in the Boy Scouts. There's your example of mystique.

Let's look at some other teams with outstanding names, beginning   4
with my hometown favorite, the New England Patriots. Our nation's fight for independence began in Massachusetts; the term 'patriot' is synonymous with the region, and it's easy to rally behind. If you disagree, you can go live in Russia. And who can forget the Patriots winning their first Super Bowl just months after the September 11 attacks, when Patriots' owner Robert Kraft held the Lombardi Trophy high and said, "We are all Patriots, and tonight, the Patriots are world champions!" Perfect.

What else is out there? The Dallas Cowboys have a good image going.   5
Cowboys are associated with fearlessness, boldness, and adventure. They are also historically linked to Texas. Well done. The name "Forty-niners" is a reference to the Gold Rush of 1849. It's an interesting choice, but I give more credit to the Pittsburgh Steelers, a nod to the industry that built their city. Steel also implies toughness, endurance . . . do I need to continue? It's steel.

As for the San Diego Chargers . . . charge up, bro! It's a weird pick,   6
but it works for the surfer bros. The Baltimore Ravens are named for Edgar Allan Poe's poem, "The Raven," as Poe lived in Baltimore for some time and is buried there. So that nickname is relevant, and the raven is a fierce creature. I also appreciate how they've incorporated the Maryland flag into their symbol. Still, they named a football team after a poem.

I'm generally not much a fan of using ferocious animals as mascots.   7
When St. Louis fans call their team the Rams, I remind them they are, in fact, humans. However, I give credit to Chicago for matching two of their teams (Bears and Cubs).

As a Super Bowl XLII attendant, I will always resent the Giants for   8
robbing my Patriots of a perfect 19–0 season. But I respect their name choice, a reference to a city that's larger than life. (Go to hell, Giants fans.)

A lot goes into naming a football team, and most of the sports teams   9
I've mentioned did a pretty good job picking their mascots. But Redskins, your team didn't. It's not cool, interesting, relevant, or competitive. Washington is our nation's capital, named for a man who led an unorganized military to victory over a much more powerful enemy, a general who could bloodlessly have become George I of the Kingdom of America, but chose instead to relinquish his power to the people.

I could write thirty of these columns about George Washington's   10
epic awesomeness. Our nation's capital is named for the man even King George III of England begrudgingly acknowledged as "the greatest man

who ever lived." Yet all the city's proud football team reminds us is that our nation was built upon stolen land and broken promises.

Good luck with the remainder of the season, Redskins fans. Just   11
know that for every generation its finest hour comes from breaking the cherished traditions of the past.

VOCABULARY/USING A DICTIONARY

1. Define the word *mystique* (para. 2).
2. What does the word *patriot* (para. 4) mean and what are the origins of the word?
3. Define *forty-niner* (para. 5).

RESPONDING TO WORDS IN CONTEXT

1. In the sentence, "It's a weird pick, but it works for the surfer bros" (para. 6), what kinds of connotations does the word *bros* have?
2. Nasif writes, "Our nation's capital is named for the man even King George III of England begrudgingly acknowledged as 'the greatest man who ever lived'" (para. 10). What does *begrudgingly* mean here?
3. When Nasif says, "The Dallas Cowboys have a good image going" in paragraph 5, what does he mean by *image*?

DISCUSSING MAIN POINT AND MEANING

1. What is Nasif's overall argument in this essay? Is his point clear? Why or why not?
2. What are Nasif's reasons for believing team names like Braves, Seminoles, and Chiefs are acceptable, but Redskins is not?
3. What are the author's thoughts on the Baltimore Ravens' team name?

EXAMINING SENTENCES, PARAGRAPHS, AND ORGANIZATION

1. What is the purpose of introducing George Washington and the history of Washington, D.C., in the second-to-last paragraph?
2. How are the essay's paragraphs arranged and formed? What would you say is the organizing principle? Do you think the organization is clear and focused?
3. Describe the tone of this essay. Is it appropriate to the subject matter? Why or why not?

THINKING CRITICALLY

1. In paragraph 10, Nasif states, "Yet all the city's proud football team reminds us is that our nation was built upon stolen land and broken promises." Do you believe this is what the Redskins' name represents? Why or why not? How does this statement compare to the statements Nasif made earlier regarding Washington's choice of name?

2. What bias does Nasif admit to in the essay, and how might that affect his analysis of team names? Do you think this bias is appropriate or acceptable in this essay? Why or why not?

3. Look back at the teams that Nasif determines have "outstanding names." Do you agree with his assessment of the team names? Explain why or why not.

WRITING ACTIVITIES

1. Consider Nasif's tone and use of humor in this essay. In your opinion, do they help or hurt his argument? Can a lighthearted tone ever successfully explain a serious topic? Why or why not?

2. Using Nasif's essay as a guide, write an essay that is in the form of an open letter to a group of people and makes an argument you think that group needs to hear. Use specific examples to support your argument.

3. In a short essay, take the opposite position of Nasif, and defend the use of the name Redskins. Even if you don't believe in it, think of ways to counter Nasif's claims and support the opposite argument.

LOOKING CLOSELY

Using Examples

In any discussion or debate, nothing is more persuasive than well-chosen examples. We often use examples to back up a generalization with concrete instances or to support a claim. The examples *show* what we mean. We can easily see the effective use of appropriate examples in "Washington, Yea! Redskins, Boo!," an essay by University of Maryland student Greg Nasif. Arguing that the name "Redskins" is stereotypical and inappropriate, Nasif assembles numerous examples of other sports teams to establish his point. Note that he isn't critical of all team names but cites those he feels are relevant to the team's image in one way or another.

1

A football team name that is relevant

Let's look at some other teams with outstanding names, beginning with my hometown favorite, the New England Patriots. Our nation's fight for independence began in Massachusetts; the term 'patriot' is synonymous with the region, and it's easy to rally behind. (1) If you disagree, you can go live in Russia. And who can forget the Patriots winning their first Super Bowl just months after the September 11 attacks, when Patriots' owner Robert Kraft held the Lombardi

Trophy high and said, "We are all Patriots, and tonight, the Patriots are world champions!" Perfect.

What else is out there? The Dallas Cowboys have a good image going. Cowboys are associated with fearlessness, boldness, and adventure. They are also historically linked to Texas. Well done. The name "Forty-niners" is a reference to the Gold Rush of 1849. It's an interesting choice, but I give more credit to the Pittsburgh Steelers, a nod to the industry that built their city. Steel also implies toughness, endurance . . . do I need to continue? It's steel. (2)

2
Strengthens his point by adding three more examples of relevant names

STUDENT WRITER AT WORK
Greg Nasif

R.A. What inspired you to write this essay? And publish it in your campus paper?

G.N. I love football, and many of my friends are Redskins fans. I enjoy stirring the pot, but I don't always enjoy being too serious about it; I saw this as an opportunity to combine humor, wit, and a dash of politics. The common evaluation of all the team names was the cream of the crop. To me, it was the kind of thing that would undoubtedly hook a reader in and keep them coming back. It's also something I think about frequently. How does a city take pride in itself? How does it manifest itself? Sports are a major part of that, perhaps the purest way a city identifies itself relative to other American cities, and I wanted to explore that.

R.A. What response have you received to this piece? Has the feedback you have received affected your views on the topic you wrote about?

G.N. Many of my friends didn't talk to me about it, which amused me. The comments appeared mixed; many people attacked me, many attacked my points, a few seemed to agree but express indifference, some even suggested their own new team names. The only thing you could say about the response was that it was voluminous: I started a conversation, and I'm very satisfied with that.

R.A. How long did it take for you to write this piece? Did you revise your work? What were your goals as you revised?

G.N. I was planning this column longer than most any other I had ever written — for over 6 months. I thought of it last spring but never thought of a time to print it. I finally saw my opportunity with the Redskins' early success last season. Initially I drafted the major points and comparisons, I cut many of them, and finally wrote the actual column in the two weeks before it ran. I generally brainstorm, outline, write, rewrite, edit with the ruthlessness of Attila the Hun, submit, request to change my submission, then remark to myself how shamefully little I edited.

R.A. Do you generally show your writing to friends before submitting it? Do you collaborate or bounce your ideas off others?

G.N. This is one topic I spoke about with many people, mostly friends. I had many discussions like the main comparisons in this piece, where I evaluated mascots and team names from each city. In terms of my writing, I generally find other people just want to tell me how to write in their own way and I don't often seek their discretion. However, I do have my dad review my articles, and I would say I take 20 percent of his suggestions.

R.A. What advice do you have for other student writers?

G.N. Write. Write even if no one will read it. Keep a journal. Write down everything that makes you laugh or cry. Realize that 90 percent of what you write might never be read by anyone but you. But it only takes one reader for it to matter, even if it is only you.

Also, brainstorm and outline. You'd be surprised how much better your writing is if you stack like phrases together and morph them into one stronger point. Think of your points like rain clouds: They are much stronger with a much richer center if they are bunched up as opposed to if they are scattered about. Better than making a light drizzle on a thousand people is just making it pour on twenty people. I'm talking buckets. Just make it rain and don't stop.

Who Named America?

When Christopher Columbus reached the shores of San Salvador on October 12, 1492, he incorrectly thought that he had achieved his commercial goal and successfully had proven to the Spanish royalty, who supported his mission, that a trade route to India could be found by sailing west across the Atlantic. He did not realize that he had instead reached a previously unknown part of the globe. Obviously, he was not the first to "discover" this region, since he encountered native populations everywhere he sailed. Many, many people had arrived at these lands long before he did. But, convinced that he had reached the outskirts of India, he knew what to call these people: Indians.

Most historians believe it was another Italian navigator, Amerigo Vespucci, who first realized that the world Columbus visited was actually a new world. Vespucci in 1501 reached what is now Brazil. In 1503 he wrote about his voyage and titled it, appropriately, *Mundus Novus* (*The New World*). When a German mapmaker named Martin Waldseemüller came across Vespucci's writings, he decided to place these newly discovered lands on the world map he was preparing in 1507. The mapmaker — acknowledging that Europe, Asia, and Africa had been widely explored but that this fourth new world remained both mysterious and unnamed — took the liberty of naming it. He wrote, "I do not see why anyone should rightly forbid naming it Amerigo, land of Americus as it were, after its discoverer Americus, a man of acute genius, or America, inasmuch as both Europa and Asia have received their names from women." So after turning the Italian name *Amerigo* into its Latin version *Americus* and then feminizing it to be consistent with the other continents, he inked the word *America* across the new lands, and the vast new world west of Europe received its permanent name.

In 2003, the only surviving copy of the Waldseemüller map was purchased by the Library of Congress, which claims in its information bulletin: "The map has been referred to in various circles as America's birth certificate and for good reason; it is the first document on which the name 'America' appears. It is also the first map to depict a separate and full Western Hemisphere and the first map to represent the Pacific

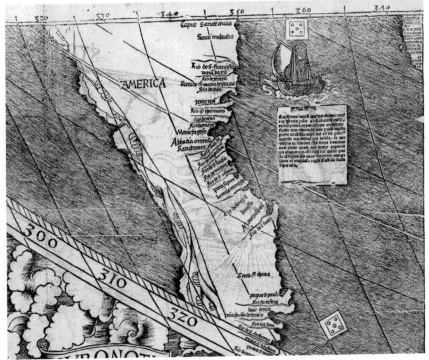

Detail from the first map of America.

Ocean as a separate body of water. The map, printed on twelve separate sheets, measures over 4 feet by 8 feet."

For a full and recent account of how America received its name and identity, interested readers should consult Toby Lester's informative study, *The Fourth Part of the World* (2009).

Discussing the Unit

SUGGESTED TOPIC FOR DISCUSSION

Each of these authors explores the importance and often the difficulty of choosing a name. What difficulties does each author encounter when choosing a name? How is it more or less difficult to name a person or a country rather than a sports team? After reading these essays, consider what choices are made when naming anyone or anything, and all that a name comes to stand for.

PREPARING FOR CLASS DISCUSSION

1. What sort of associations get caught up in a name, and why might one name be preferable to another? How do you sort through all of the factors and feelings that end up connected to a name?

2. We often think of names as solid, solitary, unchangeable. When are you sure a name "fits" its subject? Can a time or a country or a person take on many names and still be "named"? Consider examples of this from the essays in this chapter.

FROM DISCUSSION TO WRITING

1. How do we know when a name is "right"? Which arguments in this chapter were particularly compelling about when a name does or doesn't fit? Write an essay that explains why one discussion or story was more compelling than another.

2. What's the process of choosing a name? Compare the different reasons one might choose one name over another as outlined in this chapter. Does Mosher's essay have anything in common with Venegas's essay? Does the naming that happens in "America Then . . . 1507" share any similarity to the naming in "Washington, Yay! Redskins, Boo!"? Explain in a brief essay.

TOPICS FOR CROSS-CULTURAL DISCUSSION

1. Does gender or race play a part in how these authors approach the question of naming? How so? Cite examples from at least three of the essays you read in this chapter and explain how gender and race come into play in the discussion of names.

2. "Washington, Yay! Redskins, Boo!" points out the importance of respect for a particular ethnicity in the naming process. While "America Then . . . 1507" doesn't deal directly with the influence of ethnicity on naming, it is clear that the names considered for America were the names of Europeans (or a European's misrepresentation of the peoples found there). When Maria Venegas arrives illegally in the United States, she must adopt a more mainstream name in order to become American. What is lost when one ethnic group has control over the names of other people or things? What sort of damage is done, as suggested by these essays?

 This chapter continues online. Visit the e-Page at
bedfordstmartins.com/americanow/epages for an interactive visual assignment.

2

Relationships Today: Is Marriage in Decline?

Is marriage still a dominant institution in American life? Is it still the goal of young American couples to enter into matrimony, to love each other faithfully for the rest of their lives, and to raise a family? A large number of researchers in the social sciences have begun to doubt the appeal of marriage as a major aspiration of young people as we move further into the twenty-first century. In "The Marriage Crisis," Aja Gabel, a contributing writer for the University of Virginia alumni magazine, takes a close look at what researchers at that university are discovering about marriage today. In examining the ways marriage has changed over the past fifty years, she concludes that it has changed "because America has changed." "We can't return to the model of marriage from the mid-twentieth century," she adds, "because we no longer live in the culture or the economy that created it."

For many, a successful marriage depends on monogamy—the cultural practice, usually stipulated by law, of having only one spouse at a time. Monogamy has come to be defined in terms of sexual fidelity to one's spouse; in other words, a good marriage cannot tolerate sexual relationships with other partners, whether casual or serious. In our Spotlight on Research feature, columnist Kayt Sukel summarizes some recent research on a common Midwest creature that is often pointed to as "a poster child" of monogamous behavior, the prairie vole. Yet new genetic studies show, as Sukel reveals, that the prairie vole may be *socially* but not *sexually* monogamous. The new study suggests to Sukel that "We may be culturally and socially encouraged to be faithful, but it is unclear how much that sway really has over our biology."

The romantic ideal of remaining faithful to each other forever is made even harder to attain today by the rapid increase in opportunities for individuals to meet. There are numerous reasons behind any single divorce, but finding someone who appears to be a more suitable or attractive partner is often a leading cause of splitting up. So should couples entering into marriage agree to do so for a limited amount of time, say vow to remain faithful for ten, five, or two years? Responding to a recent legislative proposal in Mexico to grant limited marriage licenses, Natalie Rivera, a California State University student, considers carefully the implications of such legislation in "Could Temporary Marriages Reduce the Alarming Rate of Divorce?" Pointing out that marriage is still a valuable experience, Rivera believes that "Allowing couples to choose how long they should be married defeats the purpose of getting married at all."

In "America Then . . . 1950," you will sample a "thought-provoking quiz" in multiple-choice format designed to inform young women if they are "ready for marriage."

Finally, the e-Page for this chapter is an interactive singles map of the United States, inviting you to analyze the data for yourself.

Aja Gabel

The Marriage Crisis

[*University of Virginia Magazine,* Summer 2012]

BEFORE YOU READ

Do you think that people today are more or less inclined to get married than people of previous generations? What factors come into play when one is considering marriage in the twenty-first century?

WORDS TO LEARN

fidelity (para. 5): faithfulness (noun)
fertility (para. 13): the ability to pro-
    duce children (noun)
chronicle (para. 16): to record (verb)
inoculate (para. 17): to protect (verb)

plague (para. 21): to afflict or cause
    worry (verb)
reap (para. 26): to gather (verb)
innovate (para. 30): to do something
    in a new way (verb)

B rad Pitt and Angelina Jolie have made headlines for all sorts of reasons during their relationship, but their latest stint on the cover of gossip magazines was for something that shouldn't be all that shocking: their decision to marry. Why is it so gossip-worthy? For seven years, the pair had chosen to raise a family while unmarried. The personal relationships of rich and famous actors usually bear little resemblance to those of regular Americans, but in this case the couple's lifestyle reflects a larger trend.

Only about half of Americans are married now, down from 72 percent in 1960, according to census data. The age at which one first gets married has risen by six years since 1960, and now only 20 percent of Americans get married before the age of 30. The number of new marriages each year is declining at a slow but steady rate. Put simply, if you are an unmarried adult today, you face a lower chance of ever getting married, a longer wait and higher divorce rates if you do get married. The Pew Research Center recently found that about 40 percent of unmarried adults believe that marriage is becoming obsolete.

1

2

Aja Gabel is a fiction writer currently pursuing a PhD in literature and creative writing at the University of Houston. She lives and teaches in Houston, where she serves as a fiction editor at Gulf Coast literary journal. Her work can be found in the New England Review, the Southeast Review, and Bay City Review.

While marriage is in decline, unmarried cohabitation is on the   3
rise. Fifteen times the number of couples today live together outside of
marriage than in 1960. Almost half of cohabiting households include
children.

Why should we care about what may be a failing institution? Brad   4
Wilcox, UVA sociology professor and director of the National Marriage
Project, argues that the institution of marriage still symbolizes core val-
ues important to intimate relationships.

"Marriage conveys a sense of meaning, purpose, direction, and sta-   5
bility that tends to benefit adults and especially children. People who get
married have an expectation of sexual fidelity, and that fidelity tends to
engender a sense of trust and security," Wilcox says. "There is no kind of
similar solemn ritual marking the beginning of cohabitation."

Allison Pugh, also a UVA sociology professor, has a slightly different   6
take on it. She says that it isn't so much the institution of marriage that is
important, but rather how well a family cares for children, regardless of
its structure. Children need stability, nurturing, and love, but both married and unmarried parents can provide those things, Pugh says.

Is America having a "marriage crisis"? Certainly, the institution of   7
marriage is changing and it's worth taking a look at why and where it
might end up. It's a question that a number of researchers at U. Va. are
trying to answer by exploring the role of women in the workforce, emotional expectations for partnership, and marriage's benefits or costs to
individuals and families.

WHY HAS MARRIAGE DECLINED?

The answer depends on whom you ask, but almost every expert points   8
in part to the women's liberation movement of the late 1960s and '70s.
As more women earned college degrees, entered the workforce and
delayed motherhood, marriage became less necessary for their economic
survival.

UVA psychology professor Robert Emery says that, in the past,   9
people thought of marriage as "more of a businesslike relationship."
Women often received financial support from their husbands and women
often provided household and child-rearing labor. Marriage rates fell and
divorce rates rose when people started thinking less with their wallets
and more with their hearts.

"The notion today is that marriage is about love and love is about   10
personal fulfillment," Emery says. Mutual personal fulfillment is a complex and evolving goal, and, without the extra glue of financial interdependence, people who no longer feel fulfilled may more easily leave a
relationship.

Certainly, each marriage is different. A happy couple who married   11
in 1960 would likely stay married, even without the reinforcement of
economic disparity between men and women. But an unhappy couple
married in 2000 would be more likely to divorce than an unhappy couple
in 1960.

Marriage has changed because the relationship between the sexes   12
has changed, but that's not all. Amalia Miller, a UVA economics professor currently conducting research at the RAND Corp., has published a
study linking the use of the birth control pill at a young age to women's
earnings in later years. She found that women who had access to the pill
before the age of 21 in the 1960s not only had 8 percent higher wages
than their counterparts later on in their careers, but also ended up marrying higher-earning men.

"[Access to the pill] narrowed the gender wage gap," Miller says. "Part   13
of it was that the women were able to become mothers later, but part of it
was that they had more confidence and control over the timing of fertility."

Miller's research shows that women who have access to birth control   14
are more likely to attend and graduate from college. They can plan their
families and their careers. She found that women who delay motherhood
by one year increase their earnings by 9 percent on average.

"The pill as a form of technology gave a lot more control to women   15
in general," Miller says. As the pill allowed women to both control when
they became mothers and earn higher wages, the necessity for early
marriage — or marriage at all — became less compelling.

The availability of birth control is not the only social change that   16
has transformed marriage. Beginning in the 1970s, a more globalized
economy began changing the American job market with outsourcing
and layoffs. Gone are the days when one
could spend his or her entire career at a
single company. Greater job instability and
a more mobile workforce have changed the
way that we live. Pugh's research, chronicled
in her upcoming book, *The Tumbleweed
Society: Working and Caring in an Age of
Insecurity,* found that when either men or
women experience insecurity at work, they
tend to take it out on their partners at home.

> Greater job insta-
> bility and a more
> mobile workforce
> have changed the
> way that we live.

"Low expectations for loyalty at work inoculate them from feeling   17
betrayed at work. There's no such protection for them at home, however,"
Pugh says. "Instead, their high expectations — their sense that surely, at
least here, we can fight off the culture of insecurity — led them to see and
name betrayal, to feel outraged, to walk around wounded." Wilcox's work

also shows that people who suffer from job and financial instability are least likely to marry and more likely to divorce.

The earliest indicator of society's response to shifting ideas about marriage was a spike in the rate of divorce. Although the divorce rate has fallen since the 1980s, when it was at an all-time high, it is still twice as high as it was in 1960, currently hovering around 50 percent.   18

Emery says that from a psychological standpoint, the high divorce rate has partly caused the decline in marriages today. "It makes young people today less secure in the idea of committing to and being in a lasting marriage," Emery says. "Much of the rise in cohabitation as an alternative to marriage is actually an alternative to divorce. If you never make a commitment, you are never going to divorce."   19

MARRIAGE DIAGNOSTICS: COLLEGE COUNTS

For some sections of the population, there is no marriage crisis. If you are college educated, you are much more likely to be in a long-lasting, stable, happy marriage, and much less likely to divorce. Between the '70s and the '90s, the divorce rate among the college educated fell from 15 to 11 percent. In contrast, the divorce rate among those with only a high school education rose from 36 to 37 percent.   20

Wilcox sees evidence that marriage among the higher socio-economic classes is going strong, but about 70 percent of the country does not fall into that category. But is marriage the answer to the multitude of economic and societal problems that plague Americans in the lower socio-economic range? Is a more married America a better America?   21

In some cases, a drive to marry may cause more instability in the lives of children and parents. Pugh says that the way a family provides for children is more important than whether it is based upon a marriage. She puts particular emphasis on family transitions, when family structure changes with marriage, divorce, or remarriage.   22

"Family transition is what matters, not family structure," Pugh says. "If we get on the pro-marriage bandwagon, we send the wrong message, particularly to single mothers who are anxious about what has been termed 'father need.'" Pugh refers to single mothers who may not choose the best marriage partners because they feel pressure to provide a father for their children at any cost. Households like the one she describes may go through several different marriages, which only decreases family stability.   23

Emery is in the midst of research that addresses this question: Does marriage make people happy or do happy people marry more than unhappy people? He is comparing the marriage experiences of identical twins. He uses twins to control for genetic variables that might contribute   24 to unhappiness, so that he can study the environmental aspects of marriage and happiness.

Initial results suggest that marriage often does make people happy   25
and happy people are more likely to marry. "We know that a particularly happy marriage is associated with all sorts of psychological benefits: you are less depressed, less anxious, less likely to be in trouble with the law, less likely to be engaged in drinking or drug use, and you live longer," says Emery. "We're finding evidence that marriage is both a cause and an effect of happiness."

This doesn't necessarily mean that all people outside of marriages   26
are less happy than people in marriages. Emery is quick to point out that some married people exhibit negative psychological outcomes. Single people often reap benefits from their status as well. But most scholars agree that there is something about marriage that benefits a large portion of the population.

THE FUTURE OF MARRIAGE

In countries in northern Europe, marriage rates are even lower and   27
cohabitation rates are even higher than in the U.S. Sweden has one of the lowest rates of marriage in the world, and three times as many couples cohabit there as in America. There, cohabitation is quickly becoming the norm, as there are almost no government benefits favoring marriage and no taboos against unmarried cohabitation among religious or cultural institutions.

"We're not exactly moving to Sweden's model," Pugh says, "but I do   28
think we're making up new ways to be together. Maybe the way we're coming together has changed, but we still want to be together."

It turns out that people do want to be together, despite the declining   29
number of marriages. Of the 40 percent of people who agree that marriage is obsolete in the Pew Research Center study, half still want to wed.

"We're seeing people innovate culturally in response to massive social   30
changes, and some of those cultural innovations we should welcome. We should make the lives of young people easier and provide them with the support they need to be able to commit to each other for the long term, rather than have them invest all of their hopes in this institution that has not proven flexible enough to handle the demands of modern life," Pugh says. "Maybe we're asking too much of traditional forms of marriage to be able to absorb all these changes."

What about cohabitation? Like marriage, cohabitation has changed   31
in the last 50 years. These days, living together precedes more than half of all first marriages. The No. 1 reason couples say they live together is to learn more about their potential marriage partner.

Emery encourages his students to "go outside the notion of just   32
romantic marriage and think about arranging their marriages." He suggests that people consider not only how they feel, but also the logistical
considerations of a long-term partnership. Does a potential partner have
compatible values? Or the interpersonal skills to resolve conflict?

Wilcox says that there's no reason to give up hope for good, healthy   33
marriages, but that people should take it slow.

"[We are] focused so much on education and work. [We communi-   34
cate those values in the] kinds of messages we're giving to young adults,"
Wilcox says. "Yet when we're looking at what really predicts global happiness, it's our core relationships with family and friends — including
spouses — that tend to matter a lot more in our lives."

Marriage has changed because America has changed. We can't   35
return to the model of marriage from the mid-twentieth century because
we no longer live in the culture or the economy that created it. And some
would argue that we wouldn't want to return to it even if we could. Both
men and women have greater choice than they did 50 years ago not only
in regard to whom they marry, but also if they do and what kind of family
they want to build. And, if the experts agree on one thing, it is that these
choices are some of the most important we make for our own happiness.

VOCABULARY/USING A DICTIONARY

1. What does it mean if something is in *decline* (para. 3)?
2. What part of speech is *engender* (para. 5)? How is it defined?
3. What is the opposite of *disparity* (para. 11)?

RESPONDING TO WORDS IN CONTEXT

1. If America is having a "marriage crisis" (para. 7 and title), what is the state
   of the institution?
2. What is the difference between financial interdependence (para. 10) and
   independence?
3. What might women's liberation (para. 8) look like?

DISCUSSING MAIN POINT AND MEANING

1. What is happening to marriage rates in this country, according to Gabel?
   How do rising or falling numbers contribute to the idea of a "crisis"?
2. What has changed about why people get married, based on research
   that studies reasons for marriage in the 1960s versus today? What other
   changes between the 1960s and now are cited as having an effect on
   marriage?
3. In what ways are marriages and cohabitative relationships similar? In
   what ways are they different?

EXAMINING SENTENCES, PARAGRAPHS, AND ORGANIZATION

1. Even if you are unfamiliar with the relationship of Brad Pitt and Angelina Jolie, their situation is fairly well-described in paragraph 1 of this essay. Describe the way their choices appear to you, based on the first paragraph. Can you imagine something particularly gossip-worthy about them from what you read here?

2. Gabel writes that family building is an important part of why people get married. Where and how is that idea communicated in this essay?

3. Gabel cites several "experts" on marriage and other relationship structures throughout the essay. Is the quoted information incorporated successfully into the discussion? Where is it particularly effective?

THINKING CRITICALLY

1. Do you think marriage offers more stability to children than unmarried families, based on what you've read here? Explain your answer.

2. What do you think about the idea that some marriages work because they are centered around the more "businesslike" model of the past? What do you think helps hold marriages together?

3. Gabel's conclusion states "Marriage has changed because America has changed" (para. 35). In what ways might this be so? Are there other ways America has changed that aren't cited in this essay?

WRITING ACTIVITIES

1. Look at some of the gossip magazines similar to ones mentioned in this article. How many articles are about famous entertainers and their personal relationships? Do you think the articles you find reflect the experience of average Americans with their spouses or girlfriends/boyfriends? Why or why not?

2. Consider the idea of "family stability" (para. 23). In a brief essay, describe as many different family structures as you can imagine. Which ones are more stable and why? Use detailed examples, imagined or real, to support your position.

3. Research the ways in which people cohabitate and create families in Sweden, which Gabel says has "one of the lowest rates of marriage in the world." Is there anything you find in your research to explain their particular model? Can you find any information that indicates their structures are working well for the people who live there (family or social stability, economic benefits, and so on)? Write up a short report on your findings and your opinion of the way things work for the Swedes.

Spotlight on Research

Kayt Sukel
Rethinking Monogamy

[*Big Think*, June 3, 2012]

Among Kayt Sukel's writing credits are personal essays in the Washington Post, USA Today, *and the* Christian Science Monitor, *as well as articles for* The Atlantic, National Geographic Traveler, *and others. A regular blogger, she recently released her first book,* Dirty Minds: How Our Brains Influence Love, Sex and Relationships *(2012).*

Over the past few weeks, I've been hearing quite a bit about monogamy — especially within the context of human marriage and what is supposedly "natural." I use the quotes intentionally. Mostly because I'm so surprised that so many people are convinced that monogamy — heterosexual, human monogamy, in particular — is some type of biological default. 1

Science doesn't quite back up that notion. (Though, admittedly, it has not been studied as in-depth as many would have you believe.) 2

Let me explain. Only about 3% of mammalian species demonstrate monogamous behavior. 3%. That's a pretty paltry number. And those few animals that do exhibit monogamous behaviors only demonstrate what scientists call socially monogamous behavior. The modifier is important, and I'll get to that in a moment. 3

Prairie voles (*Microtus ochrogaster*) might well be the monogamy poster children. These small, furry rodents not only happily burrow underneath meadows in the American Midwest. Male and female prairie voles mate for life, working together to take care of pups. These animals are the model of choice for studying monogamy and pair-bonding behaviors — and when you see headlines touting the latest neurobiological research on monogamy, chances are there were a few prairie vole brains sacrificed to get those findings. 4

© Getty Images.

Neurochemicals like vasopressin, oxytocin, and dopamine have been ⁵ linked to forming strong monogamous bonds. And some have suggested that perhaps we can even create a love drug (or vaccine, depending on your particular frame of reference) using those chemicals to strengthen our relationships. Such pharmaceuticals could ensure that everyone is living within that expected monogamous default.

There's only one problem. Our monogamy poster children, those lovely ⁶ and talented prairie voles, are not sexually monogamous. Remember my use of *socially* above? While they do mate for life, and take quite good care of one another, they aren't above occasionally getting some side action. Yes, prairie voles cheat.

When Alexander Ophir, a researcher at Oklahoma State University, looked ⁷ at the genetic links between prairie vole pups and the Mom/Dad pair that was raising them, he found something interesting. Approximately 20% of those pups were not related to Mom's pair-bonded partner. Think of Ophir's study as the prairie vole equivalent of "You are not the father!" from the Maury Povich show. Out in the wild, outside controlled laboratory conditions, prairie voles, while devoted to their pair-bonded partners, are not sexually monogamous.

It may be time, especially given the way America has politicized the concept ⁸ of marriage, to rethink monogamy. Because just as prairie voles aren't as pure as the driven snow, there is also no biological evidence to suggest that human beings are naturally monogamous. We may be culturally and socially encouraged to be faithful, but it is unclear how much that sway really has over our biology.

Alexander G. Ophir, Department of Zoology, University of Florida
Steven M. Phelps, Department of Zoology, University of Florida
Anna Bess Sorin, Department of Biology, University of Memphis
Jerry O. Wolff, Department of Biological Sciences, St. Cloud State University

Social but Not Genetic Monogamy Is Associated with Greater Breeding Success in Prairie Voles (excerpt)

[Animal Behaviour, 2008]

Much attention has focused on distinguishing between social and genetic monogamy in avian taxa. However, surprisingly few studies have directly investigated this distinction among mammals. We investigated the genetic mating system of the prairie vole, *Microtus ochrogaster*, a popular model for mammalian monogamy and human attachment. We used space use patterns to define paired and single animals and assessed paternity using microsatellite loci. Prairie voles in this study engaged in significantly more extrapair fertilizations than predicted under genetic monogamy but fewer than predicted under random mating, demonstrating social but not genetic

continued

monogamy. Furthermore, we found that paired individuals were more likely to produce offspring than were unpaired individuals of either sex. This finding was true for both sexes and was attributable to differences in fertilization rates rather than litter sizes. Among mated individuals, however, faithful animals were no more successful than those that mated outside a pair. Taken together, our data demonstrate that paired prairie voles have greater breeding success than single voles, but such success is not contingent on mating exclusively with a social partner. If this species is to serve as a model for human love, our findings emphasize the need to distinguish between mammalian social attachment and sexual fidelity.

DRAWING CONCLUSIONS

1. What is the main purpose of Sukel's article? How does it differ from the main purpose of the scientific abstract used as its source?
2. What do you believe is Sukel's bias? Where does her bias make itself apparent in the article? Cite two specific quotes from the article to support your answer.
3. How does the tone in the scientific study differ from the tone in Sukel's article? How do the tones of the pieces reflect their respective purposes?

Natalie Rivera (student essay)

Could Temporary Marriages Reduce the Alarming Rate of Divorce?

[*Daily Sundial*, California State University, Northridge, May 6, 2012]

BEFORE YOU READ
Why do you think the divorce rate is so high in America? What are some solutions you can think of to lower the rate of divorce?

In September, Mexico City lawmakers proposed legislation that would allow couples to apply for temporary marriage licenses. Under the law couples would be able to choose the length of their marriage, starting at a minimum of two years, and would be able to renew their

Natalie Rivera is a student at California State University, Northridge, where she serves as Arts and Culture Editor for the school newspaper, The Daily Sundial.

licenses if they wished to be married longer. According to Assemblyman Leonoel Luna, who co-authored the bill, the short contract will slow down increasing divorce rates and free couples from the hassle of divorce.

Choosing how long to be married is like an easy way out of a life-long commitment; it is like doubting the marriage before it even starts. Stan Charnofsky, coordinator of the Family and Marriage Counseling program at California State University, Northridge, explains that some people would choose to partake in a temporary marriage because they do not want to be fully committed. According to Charnofsky, in our culture of advanced technology and quick means of communication, it is easier for people to find partners. They do not wish to lose this freedom and ruin the fun for themselves by being permanently tied down.   **2**

> It is like doubting the marriage before it even starts.

He also explains that the negative way people might view marriage may be a result of incidents that have happened to them. "I had an uncle who did joint physical custody for his children growing up, after he and his wife divorced," Charnofsky said. "When I spoke to his son, who was in his 40s at that time, I asked him if he would ever want to be married someday. He said he would for maybe 10 years and that 10 years would be a good marriage. I thought that maybe the way his family functioned had to do with the way he saw marriage."   **3**

Issues within families and staggering divorce rates can be the reason why people would be reluctant to take the long-term plunge. According to the National Vital Statistics Report, there were 3.4 divorces per 1,000 people as of 2010 in the United States. In Mexico, the divorce rate is 0.33 divorces per 1,000 people, according to nationmaster.com. These staggering divorce numbers may frighten someone out of fully committing to a marriage, but there are benefits that come with marriage that one cannot acquire otherwise. For instance, medical benefits allow you to make emergency decisions when your spouse is in critical care. These perks can be beneficial for someone who wishes to be involved in a loved one's life.   **4**

Some may criticize marriage as irrelevant in today's more progressive society because of the institution's long connection with patriarchy and gender inequality. Charnofsky explained that marriage in the western world served to uphold society's gender roles and economy — to obtain more land for knights in medieval times who fought for a wife — and that marriage was not considered as an act of love until the 1700s. Years before, there was "pair bonding," which categorized women as mothers and nurturers and the men as protectors.   **5**

Though marriage started off in this patriarchal way it still can offer something valuable to today's society.   **6**

Bryan and John Rodriquez-Saringo are a gay couple attending CSUN   7
who have been in a domestic partnership since last April. John is a political
science major and Bryan a linguistics major. They consider each other as
their husbands, but cannot legally marry. Though they are both young, they
wish to marry someday because of what marriage offers them as a couple.

"We want that option." John said. "It will make us secure in some   8
ways a domestic partnership can't. If something were to happen to Bryan,
I would have more say if I'm married to him, than just being in a domestic partnership." John and Bryan said that they both grew up wanting to
get married and that "even just the word 'married' means more than a
domestic partnership."

Allowing couples to choose how long they should be married defeats
the purpose of getting married at all. Marriage is a commitment between
two people to remain together until death parts them; this is specifically
stated in the matrimonial vows. Allowing two people to decide how long
their marriage should last would not decrease divorce rates because this
"temporary marriage" should not have been considered as a marriage in
the first place.

VOCABULARY/USING A DICTIONARY
1. What are the origins of the word *patriarchy* (para. 5), and what is the definition of the word?
2. What does the word *nurturer* (para. 5) mean, and what connotations does
   the word carry?
3. Define *matrimonial* (para. 9) and explain where the word originated.

RESPONDING TO WORDS IN CONTEXT
1. In paragraph 4, Rivera states, "Issues within families and staggering
   divorce rates can be the reason why people would be reluctant to take
   the long-term plunge." What does *staggering* mean in this context, and
   what part of speech is it?
2. Rivera quotes Stan Charnofsky as saying, "I had an uncle who did joint
   physical custody for his children growing up . . . ." What does the word
   joint mean here?
3. In paragraph 8, John Rodriguez-Saringo states, "It will make us secure in
   some ways a domestic partnership can't." What does *domestic partnership* mean, and how is it different from marriage?

DISCUSSING MAIN POINT AND MEANING
1. Summarize Rivera's argument in one or two sentences.
2. How does Rivera discredit the claim that marriage might be irrelevant in
   today's "more progressive society" (para. 5)?

3. What does the bill described here plan to do, and how might it lower the divorce rate in Mexico?

EXAMINING SENTENCES, PARAGRAPHS, AND ORGANIZATION

1. Why might Rivera have introduced the idea of marriage as an outdated institution based on patriarchy in paragraph 5?

2. How do the statistics in paragraph 4 support or detract from Rivera's argument? Why do you think the author chose to include them?

3. Where does Rivera reveal her own opinion about temporary marriage? Do you think this was the appropriate place in the essay to make her argument?

THINKING CRITICALLY

1. Why might Rivera have chosen a gay male couple to refute the claim that marriage is a relic of a patriarchal society?

2. Rivera closes her essay by saying, "Allowing two people to decide how long their marriage should last would not decrease divorce rates because this 'temporary marriage' should not have been considered a marriage in the first place." Do you think she has supported this argument in the preceding paragraphs? How?

3. What assumptions might Rivera have made about her readers, and how might these assumptions affect her argument?

WRITING ACTIVITIES

1. In a brief essay, state whether or not you think temporary marriage is a good solution to high divorce rates, and support your opinion with specific examples.

2. Write a short essay on how a law like this might affect (a) the way that couples approach marriage and (b) how society views marriage.

3. Using the last line of Rivera's essay as inspiration, write a short essay in which you explore your own thoughts on the definition of marriage and whether this law would either fit in with that definition or go against it.

Effective Openings: Establishing a Clear Context for an Argument

When writing an essay that advances an opinion about a current issue, one of the best approaches a writer can take is to clearly summarize the general context or situation that gave rise to the issue. This approach is very effectively demonstrated in Natalie Rivera's "Could Temporary Marriages Reduce the Alarming Rate of Divorce?" Note how her opening paragraph sets out in clear and direct sentences the situation that has prompted her essay: a recent legislative proposal that would allow couples to specify exactly how long they wish their marriage to last. Rivera does not begin with her position on the issue but starts with a brief and lucid summary that establishes a context for her subject, which she develops in the body of her essay — the social value of "temporary marriage."

1 *A specific proposal sets the [?]*	In September, Mexico City <u>lawmakers proposed legislation that would allow couples to apply for temporary marriage licenses</u>. (1) Under the law <u>couples would be able to choose the length of their marriage</u> (2), starting at
2 *What the proposal allows*	a minimum of two years, and would be able to renew their licenses if they wished to be married longer. According to
3 *What the proposal hopes to accomplish*	Assemblyman Leonoel Luna, who co-authored the bill, the <u>short contract will slow down increasing divorce rates and free couples from the hassle of divorce</u>. (3)

Are You Ready for Marriage?

A common feature of American magazines almost from their beginning in the mid-nineteenth century has been the article on marital advice. These were — and still are — variations of "How to Keep Your Husband Happy" that usually portrayed middle-class housewives whose main tasks in life were to find ways to satisfy their hard-working husbands. This usually involved cooking, entertaining, cleaning, maintaining a household budget, keeping up one's appearance, and being an agreeable companion, conversationally and romantically.

The following "quiz" from a 1950 comic magazine (see p. 86) was directed to single women whose goal in life was to be married. The text asked women to assume they had found Mr. Right and then to picture how they might behave in different situations that could come up in the early stages of marriage. Pictured here are the first two multiple-choice questions: what to do if your husband complains about your spending habits and how to respond when he acts amorously. Other questions ask how the new bride would respond to the husband inviting a business client to dinner on short notice, wanting to go out with the guys, and telling the same joke over and over.

Do you think such a "thought-provoking quiz" could appear in one of today's magazines? Or has our society become much more sophisticated about marital relationships and gender expectations?

ARE YOU READY FOR MARRIAGE?
A Game of MAKE-BELIEVE

OF COURSE YOU WANT TO MARRY! IT'S YOUR CONSTANT DREAM, YOUR DESIRE FOR THE FUTURE! WELL, LET'S PRETEND THAT THE MAN OF YOUR DREAMS IS REALLY YOURS, THAT THE HONEYMOON IS OVER, AND YOU AND YOUR HUSBAND ARE STARTING OUT ON THE ROAD TO A HAPPY MARRIAGE! NOW THERE'S THE CATCH! ARE YOU, AS A NEW BRIDE, MATURE AND UNDERSTANDING ENOUGH TO MAKE THE KIND OF WIFE YOUR HUSBAND DESIRES? WILL YOU HELP HIM IN HIS CAREER — OR HINDER HIM? WILL YOU BUILD A HAPPY HOME—OR A BROKEN ONE? THAT'S WHAT YOU WANT TO KNOW—AND HERE IS YOUR ANSWER, IN THIS THOUGHT-PROVOKING QUIZ! HERE ARE TEN SITUATIONS THAT YOU WILL ALMOST INEVITABLY FACE AT ONE TIME OR ANOTHER! THERE ARE THREE POSSIBLE SOLUTIONS FOR EACH PROBLEM! CHOOSE THE ONE YOU THINK IS RIGHT, ADD UP YOUR SCORE, THEN TURN THE PAGE UPSIDE-DOWN TO SEE WHETHER YOU ARE READY FOR MARRIAGE!

YOUR HUSBAND COMPLAINS ABOUT THE MONEY YOU ARE SPENDING, SO . . .

A. YOU START TO CRY AND CALL HIM AN OLD SKINFLINT!

B. YOU SAY, "DEAR, WHY DON'T WE START A BUDGET SO WE CAN SEE WHERE OUR MONEY GOES?"

C. YOU TELL HIM YOU'LL SEE WHAT YOU CAN DO—AND THEN GO TO YOUR FATHER SECRETLY FOR EXTRA SPENDING MONEY!

YOUR HUSBAND WHISPERS, "COME CLOSER, DARLING, AND LET ME TELL YOU HOW MUCH I LOVE YOU," AND YOU ANSWER . . .

A. "DON'T, YOU'RE MUSSING MY NEW HAIR-DO!

B. OF COURSE, DEAR! IT'S SO HEAVENLY TO BE TOGETHER!

C. I HAVEN'T GOT TIME FOR THAT SORT OF THING. I'VE GOT TO WASH THE DISHES."

Discussing the Unit

SUGGESTED TOPIC FOR DISCUSSION

Is a lifelong, monogamous commitment to another person—the traditional ideal for a marriage—a goal worth upholding or a fairy-tale notion, both unrealistic and limiting? Do individuals and society pay any price when marriage rates decline? Or do the benefits of marriage alternatives, such as cohabitation or a decision to remain single, potentially outweigh the costs? If so, for whom, and under what circumstances?

PREPARING FOR CLASS DISCUSSION

1. At a time of greater financial and reproductive independence for women, what benefits might women still see in marriage? What about the benefits for men? How might these have changed over the past fifty years? Consider these questions with this chapter's essays in mind.

2. In Aja Gabel's article, sociology professor Brad Wilcox says, "People who get married have an expectation of sexual fidelity, and that fidelity tends to engender a sense of trust and security." However, both Kayt Sukel and the research on which she bases her essay (see the piece by Alexander G. Ophir, *et al.*) suggest that monogamy may go against human — or at least mammalian — nature. How might Wilcox respond to Sukel and Ophir? How might Natalie Rivera respond to them?

FROM DISCUSSION TO WRITING

1. Considering the essays in this chapter, and also the "America Then . . . 1950s" feature on page 85, discuss how the definition of a "good marriage" has changed since the 1950s and how it has remained the same.

2. People who prefer cohabitation to marriage often say that marriage is "only a piece of paper." Drawing on your own experiences and observations and the essays in this chapter, discuss whether you agree or disagree with this statement. Also, consider whether the "piece of paper" itself might have any social or economic value.

TOPICS FOR CROSS-CULTURAL DISCUSSION

1. Gabel points to evidence that "marriage among the higher socio-economic classes is going strong." What about lower-income people? In this group, what factors might be contributing to declining rates of marriage and increasing rates of divorce?

2. In some countries and cultural groups, especially in South Asia, arranged marriages are common. In these marriages, parents choose spouses for their children, considering such factors as a potential mate's religion, socioeconomic background, and reputation. In modern Western cultures, however, most people choose their own spouses, usually placing romantic feelings over other considerations. Taking into account the benefits and limitations of marriage as discussed in this chapter, what might be some advantages of an arranged marriage over a "love marriage"? What are some possible drawbacks? Do you think arranged marriages could ever become popular in the United States? Why or why not?

:e This chapter continues online. Visit the e-Page at
bedfordstmartins.com/americanow/epages for an interactive visual assignment.

3

Communicating through Social Media: What Do We Gain? What Do We Lose?

How have Facebook, Twitter, and e-mail changed the way people communicate with each other? Granted, we can now effortlessly be in touch with people—whether they are in the same room with us or on another continent—in an instant, but has that convenience cost us a level of intimacy and privacy that relationships once depended upon when the speed of communication moved much more slowly? In "Electronic Intimacy," Christine Rosen, a writer and editor who grew up in the world of pen and paper, ponders the human gains and losses resulting from our addiction to social networking. She cites a recent psychological study that surprisingly found that the more "friends" people had on Facebook, the more likely they were to believe that other people had better and happier lives than they did.

"The power of a handwritten letter," says popular actor Ashton Kutcher, "is greater than ever. It's personal and deliberate and means more than an e-mail or text ever will." In "Has Texting Killed Romance?" Kutcher wonders whether in our digital age "we are all becoming so in touch with one another that we are in danger of losing touch?"

In her poignant account of Gmail exchanges with her terminally ill boyfriend, Rebecca Armendariz explores another dimension of instant communication, the way it can provide us with an electronic, verbatim transcript of our closest relationships. In "Chat History," she looks back on some twenty months of messages that chart in specific detail their first meeting, his struggle with cancer, and his untimely death: years later, she writes, "I sometimes type his email address in the search box in my Gmail. Hundreds of results pop up, and I'll pick a few at random to read."

Although he, too, recognizes the power and convenience of social media, Shawn Ghuman, a student at Virginia Tech, also worries about its cost. In "Is Technology Destroying Social Bonds?" Ghuman considers why we are now neglecting face-to-face conversation with others and seem to prefer to "articulate our thoughts and feelings through short messages, often using smiley faces and abbreviations like 'lol' to express emotions."

The e-Page for this chapter takes a close—and very funny—look at that ubiquitous social media phenomenon, the "humble brag."

Christine Rosen

Electronic Intimacy

[*Wilson Quarterly*, Spring 2012]

BEFORE YOU READ

How do you form and maintain friendships and romantic relationships? Do you think today's apps and other forms of modern communication are an adequate substitute for face-to-face interaction? What, if anything, is lost or gained when you find yourself relying on electronic media as a way to connect to others?

WORDS TO LEARN

revelation (para. 3): disclosure (noun)

mediate (para. 3): to settle (verb)

inextricably (para. 6): without the ability to be untangled (adv)

ambient (para. 7): all-encompassing (adj)

disquiet (para. 9): uneasiness (noun)

copious (para. 10): large amounts (adj)

cognitively (para. 10): connected to mental processes (adv)

predetermine (para. 10): decide in advance (verb)

algorithm (para. 10): steps for solving a mathematical problem (noun)

purport (para. 10): to claim (verb)

deluge (para. 11): flood (noun)

peruse (para. 13): to look over carefully (verb)

cheeky (para. 13): disrespectful, often boldly so (adj)

simulacrum (para. 13): superficial likeness (noun)

caveat (para. 13): warning (noun)

cohere (para. 14): to stick together (verb)

serendipity (para. 17): luck or happiness found by chance (noun)

erode (para. 18): to destroy slowly (verb)

deleterious (para. 18): harmful (adj)

glean (para. 18): to gather bit by bit (verb)

languid (para. 19): drooping; sluggish (adj)

antidote (para. 19): remedy (noun)

accrue (para. 19): to increase over time (verb)

sporadic (para. 21): occasional (adj)

Christine Rosen lives in Washington, D.C., where she is the senior editor of The New Atlantis: A Journal of Technology & Society. *Her past books include* Preaching Eugenics: Religious Leaders and the American Eugenics Movement *(2004) and* My Fundamentalist Education *(2005). Her newest book,* The Extinction of Experience, *is set to be published in 2013. Her essays and reviews have appeared in, the* New York Times Magazine, *the* Wall Street Journal, *the* Washington Post, *and the* New Republic, *among others.*

W e met at music school in Vermont in the 1980s. He was the   1
golden boy, popular and cocksure. I wore thick glasses and
played the bassoon. Somehow we formed a friendship, much
to the annoyance of his string of romantic conquests and my friends, who
disliked him. When August came we parted ways, close but not entirely
connected. Two weeks later, I received my first letter from him. It was
still broiling hot in Florida as I stood by the mailbox and tore open the
envelope. My friend had gone to the trouble to find my address, and, by
including his own on the back of the envelope, signaled his expectation
that I should write back.

During the next few years we wrote regularly about all kinds of   2
things — the music we were listening to, our parents' willful misunder-
standing of our monumental teenage torments. A "pen pal" is what everyone called him. But that childish phrase always bothered me. It sounded
too limited and casual, nothing like an expression of the way our letter
writing felt. I went through the day filing away little experiences to replay
later in a letter to him, and eagerly awaited his responses. Once he wrote
"It's here! It's here!" on the back of an envelope containing a letter that
was tardier than usual. He understood perfectly my anticipation of his
letters because he shared it.

Years passed, and our friendship deepened. We spoke on the tele-   3
phone occasionally and reunited during one more summer at camp, but
most of our communication occurred through letters. After hundreds
of small revelations, we made large ones to each other — but only to each
other. Our letters were always handwritten. Private. Mediated only by the
technology of pen and paper and the postal service.

I don't recount this long-ago exchange to lament the lost era of let-   4
ter writing. These days, I rarely put pen to paper. Instead, like most of us, I
rely on e-mails or text messages, which I simultaneously embrace for their
brilliant efficiency and loathe for the conformity they impose.

But I wonder how humans' chosen forms of communication alter our   5
emotional experience of connection. Our
feelings for each other haven't changed. We
continue to seek validation and happiness
and contact with others. We still flush with
pleasure when we spy a particular person's
e-mail in our in-box. But does the way we
communicate with each other alter that experience significantly?

> Our feelings for
> each other haven't
> changed.

In preparing to write to someone, we prime the emotional pump. We   6
think about how we feel; ideally, we reflect for a moment. The medium
of pen and paper encourages this. E-mail and texting and interactions
on Facebook encourage more efficient and instantaneous affirmation or

rejection of our feelings. They also introduce something new — a form of social anxiety caused by the public nature of so many of our communications. A study published earlier this year in the journal *Cyberpsychology, Behavior, and Social Networking* found that the more time and more "friends" people had on Facebook, the more likely they were to agree with the statement that others had better, happier lives than they did, and the less likely they were to believe that life is fair. Researchers have confirmed what many of us already know: Using social networking sites is pleasurable. But the pleasure of publicizing our connections on social networking sites is inextricably linked to the anxiety we experience about the meaning of those connections and what they reveal about the value of our offline lives.

We are living in an age of electronic intimacy. Its hallmark is instantaneous global communication inseparable from an ambient awareness that we are or should be connected to others. Scientists have documented that we experience a dopamine[1] rush when we receive a new e-mail in our in-boxes. The flip side of that rush is the vague social anxiety we feel when we see that we have no new messages. This is new emotional terrain.   7

Smartphones are the Geiger counters of this electronic intimacy. They are supremely efficient at delivering information, allowing us constantly to measure the levels of connection radiating throughout our social network. Such connection is a genuine pleasure. But is more of it better?   8

Surely, some of the disquiet about the revolution we are experiencing stems from the fact that a world that supports the marvel of instantaneous communication is also one in which we must decide who is and is not worthy of our communications — the average Facebook user has 130 "friends," after all. The possibilities are endless — we can talk one on one, broadcast our feelings to a small group of friends, or weigh in as an anonymous Internet commentator and be heard by millions of strangers. Yet most of us have also suffered decision fatigue when faced with this proliferation of choices. Why this particular person, why now? We have always had to answer these questions, but never this often or on this scale.   9

Our new communications technologies have fulfilled their promise to help us find people with whom we might form intimate relationships. But they have done so by giving us an overwhelming amount of choice and a copious amount of false hope. A recent meta-analysis of online dating published in the journal *Psychological Science in the Public Interest* found that people "become cognitively overwhelmed" when they search through hundreds of dating profiles. To cope, they must "objectify" the   10

---

[1] dopamine (para. 7): Chemical found in the brain, linked to human sensation of pleasure.

people they are sizing up for some sort of emotional connection. And despite the many claims online dating sites make about their "scientific" matching systems, the study found that none of the systems devised to predetermine compatibility reliably predicted the long-term success of relationships. Algorithms that purport to match the athletic cat lover with the poetry-reading outdoors-man might lead to a first date, but they are no better than blind luck at ensuring lasting love.

Even when we already have a thriving social network, it can be a chal-   11
lenge to keep up with everyone in it. In social networking's most extreme form, we end up engaging in a kind of intimacy porn as we keep tabs on hundreds of our Facebook "friends," follow the Twitter feeds of others, and respond to a daily deluge of e-mail. All the while, we are expected to keep our own electronic presence up to date. The extent of this transformation is evident in the marketing slogans of telecommunications companies. In the late twentieth century, the Bell System urged customers to "reach out and touch someone." The company's advertisements assumed that we would prefer to see our loved ones face to face. If we couldn't, the ads suggested, a conversation on the telephone was the next-best thing.

Contemporary telecommunications companies emphasize some-   12
thing fundamentally different: individual control over a communications empire premised on speed and efficiency. Sprint calls itself "The NOW Network" and promises that you can do business, talk to friends, and travel the globe, all "without limits"; AT&T urges us to "Rethink Possible." In one recent advertisement, two men sit together in a coffee shop conducting a business meeting by sending e-mails back and forth to each other instead of speaking.

Perhaps the current state of affairs explains our spasms of nostalgia   13
for the days of written correspondance. Peruse the cards and paper for sale on Web sites such as Etsy, an online marketplace of handmade goods, and you could be forgiven for thinking that Brooklyn's economy is built almost entirely on cheeky letterpress stationery produced out of people's basements. The literary magazine *The Rumpus* has launched a service called Letters in the Mail; for $5, subscribers are mailed an honest-to-god letter from a writer such as Dave Eggers, Stephen Elliott, or Elissa Schappel. "Think of it as the letters you used to get from your creative friends, before this whole Internet/e-mail thing," the Web site urges. But since this is a simulacrum of a pen pal relationship, a helpful caveat is included: Return addresses are appended "at the author's discretion."

As much as I rely on modern forms of communication today, I don't   14
think I would have become friends with that boy at summer camp if we had used them. The pace of an e-mail or text exchange would have been too quick, and our weird bond would not have had time to emerge

amid such public and impatient forms of communication as Facebook or Twitter. For both of us, there would have been too much risk involved in publicly acknowledging our affinity for each other. Once our friendship cohered, the last thing I wanted to do was "share" it by displaying it to the rest of the world.

But our new world of electronic intimacy paradoxically demands that   15
we share those intimacies early and often. It turns the private bonds of friendship and connection into a mass spectator sport, a game in which we are all simultaneously players and viewers (and one in which Facebook and other companies profit richly from our participation). I wonder about the nearly eight million American children age 12 and younger who are currently registered on Facebook (having easily evaded restrictions created in response to federal laws prohibiting data collection on children under 13). By the time they are 15, they will have cultivated dozens of online friends. How many of those connections will become what sociologists are starting to call "migratory friendships" — relationships that form online but eventually move to the physical world and face-to-face interaction?

I hope a great many will, even though moving beyond the efficiency   16
and convenience of online friendship to real-world connection isn't always easy. Of course, future generations will have the benefit of new communications technologies offering solutions to our problems connecting with each other. Flirting apps such as IFlirt4U and Axe Auto Romeo promise to outsource the awkwardness of first encounters to your smartphone. (The Axe app even lets you set the flirt level to "warm," "hot," or "steamy.") And a recent patent application filed by Apple hints that the company is developing a program that would function as a form of iDating, scanning the data on your smartphone to locate like-minded people in your immediate area and suggesting ways to initiate conversations with them.

But these technologies seem aimed less at encouraging intimacy than   17
manufacturing serendipity — an oxymoronic notion that has gained surprising traction in Silicon Valley. "You never know when you might come across a little planned serendipity," the mobile geotagging company Foursquare says on its Web site. In an interview he gave in 2010 while he was still CEO of Google, Eric Schmidt claimed that serendipity "can be calculated now. We can actually produce it electronically."

Manufactured serendipity suggests that Google's algorithms and   18
your smartphone's sophisticated data collection systems are better life guides than your own intuition. Certainly they have their uses, but our reliance on them to map our emotional lives poses dangers, too. As psychologist Julia Frankenstein of the University of Freiburg has found, the use of global positioning system devices significantly erodes our capacity to create "mental maps," a skill that brings with it countless cognitive

benefits. Might texting and e-mailing and tweeting eventually have the same deleterious effect on, for instance, our ability to experience longing? In a world of electronic intimacy, we elevate immediacy and availability, from which we glean a great deal of pleasure. But it is a pleasure tinged with pleonexia[2] — we always want more.

Then again, longing is so last century. It doesn't seem to suit an age of enhanced reality, when our devices cater to our need for immediate gratification and we describe ourselves — rather than our appliances — as "plugged in." Nor does it suit a culture in the grips of what sociologists call "time famine." No wonder we turn to time management gurus for advice on how to extract the most out of every minute of the day, and rely on social networking sites to keep our far-flung friends and family informed about our lives. Longing suggests languid hours for contemplation — a luxury for most people today. But perhaps we should see it instead as a necessity, an antidote to the excesses of a hectic, wired world. During the economic downturn, retailers revived their layaway policies; couldn't we practice a kind of emotional layaway program? Like instant credit, instant friendship in the Facebook mold yields immediate rewards. But it also has hidden costs — costs that tend to accrue long after the pleasures of that first connection have faded.

19

We will adapt, as we always have done. But perhaps we should permit ourselves a small lament, after all, for what we are leaving behind. As Charles Swann observes in Marcel Proust's *Remembrance of Things Past,* "Even when one is no longer attached to things, it's still something to have been attached to them."

20

During college, my correspondence with my friend was sporadic. We visited each other a few times, and even made a hilariously doomed attempt at a romantic relationship from which we emerged even more grateful for each other's friendship. We never made the transition to e-mail. Eventually we lost touch altogether.

21

That's life — or at least that is what the life of a friendship used to be. A closed door usually stayed closed forever. No longer. Last year my sister tracked down my summer camp friend on Facebook. From what I could gather from his profile, he is a married schoolteacher who enjoys bass fishing in his spare time. This is the moment when I should recount how we reconnected on Facebook and reminisced about the old days. But we didn't. I never contacted him. His Facebook profile assures me that he has lots of friends. He looks happy, as far as I can tell. I barely recognized him.

22

---

[2] pleonexia (para. 18): Comes from the Greek and refers to an insatiable desire or greediness, similar to what is felt in the throes of addiction.

VOCABULARY/USING A DICTIONARY

1. What does it mean to *lament* (para. 4) something? What does it mean to *loathe* (para. 4) something?
2. What connotations are implicit in the word *conformity* (para. 4)? How would you define the word?
3. From what language is the word *terrain* (para. 7) derived? What is its definition?

RESPONDING TO WORDS IN CONTEXT

1. Rosen uses an idiom in paragraph 6 when she writes, "In preparing to write to someone, we prime the emotional pump." What does it mean to *prime a pump*? How do you understand Rosen's alteration of the expression?
2. What is a *mass spectator sport* (para. 15)? Given your understanding of what one is, how do you understand Rosen's analogy to Facebook?
3. What is a *Geiger counter* (para. 8)? Explain the analogy being made between that device and smartphones.

DISCUSSING MAIN POINT AND MEANING

1. Why would Rosen's relationship with the boy she met at camp not have blossomed if electronic media had been available?
2. When we write to each other now, how does our approach to writing differ from how we approached it in the past? What details does Rosen point out about how we connect now through writing?
3. In the section of the essay that brings up serendipity, how does Rosen compare the use of manufactured serendipity to our use of global positioning devices?

EXAMINING SENTENCES, PARAGRAPHS, AND ORGANIZATION

1. What is the effect of starting an essay with the lines: "We met at music school in Vermont in the 1980s. He was the golden boy, popular and cocksure. I wore thick glasses and played the bassoon." What does it reveal about the "he" and "I"?
2. How does Rosen's return to her music camp friend at the end of the essay underscore her position on friendship and the idea of "electronic intimacy"?
3. What is the effect of including Sprint and AT&T advertising slogans in paragraph 12?

THINKING CRITICALLY

1. In the essay, Rosen and her friend eventually lose touch with each other. She writes, "That's life—or at least that is what the life of a friendship

used to be." Do you think it is a good or bad thing that Facebook and other media allow friendships to continue long past their life outside the computer?

2. Why do you think Rosen never contacted her old friend, even after her sister found him on Facebook? How would such a contact have altered the story?

3. How do texting, e-mailing, and tweeting affect feelings of longing, according to Rosen? Do you think that she's right?

WRITING ACTIVITIES

1. After exploring Facebook or another social networking site, ask yourself how well you know the people you encounter there. Do you feel that you know them? Is it necessary to have met them and spent time with them in person before you answer that question? Why or why not?

2. In a brief essay, compare the quality of your off-line friendships with the quality of social media friendships. What is special or attractive about each kind of friendship?

3. Consider recent interactions you've had on social media over the last twenty-four hours. Look back at some of the texts, tweets, posts, etc., you've sent out into the world. Keeping one or two electronic writings in mind, sit down and write a one-page letter to one person who may have received that information from you. What are the differences between the correspondences? Which do you prefer, and why?

Ashton Kutcher

Has Texting Killed Romance?

[*Harper's Bazaar*, January 2011]

BEFORE YOU READ

How have texting, IM'ing, and other modes of communication via technology changed the way you interact with your friends? Your parents? How do you think your relationships might be different without these innovations?

WORDS TO LEARN

servers (para. 1): centralized data storage (noun)

mitigate (para. 3): to lessen the force of (verb)

quip (para. 4): a clever or witty remark (noun)

I was shooting a scene in my new film, *No Strings Attached,* in which I say to Natalie Portman, "If you miss me . . . you can't text, you can't e-mail, you can't post it on my [Facebook] wall. If you really miss me, you come and see me." I began to think of all of the billions of intimate exchanges sent daily via fingers and screens, bouncing between satellites and servers. With all this texting, e-mailing, and social networking, I started wondering, are we all becoming so in touch with one another that we are in danger of losing touch?   1

It used to be that boy met girl and they exchanged phone numbers. Anticipation built. They imagined the entire relationship before a call ever happened. The phone rang. Hearts pounded. "Hello?" Followed by a conversation that lasted two hours but felt like two minutes and would be examined with friends for two weeks. If all went well, a date was arranged. That was then.   2

Now we exchange numbers but text instead of calling because it mitigates the risks of early failure and eliminates those deafening moments of   3

Ashton Kutcher is an American television and film actor, producer, and co-founder of Katalyst Media. He is most famous for his breakout role in That 70s Show *and his hosting of MTV's* Punk'd. *In 2010, he was named one of* Time *magazine's "Top 100 Most Influential People," and he recently wrote the foreword for* Engage: The Complete Guide for Brands and Businesses to Build, Cultivate, and Measure Success in the New Web *(Wiley, 2011).*

silence. Now anticipation builds. *Bdoop.* "It was NICE meeting u." Both sides overanalyze every word. We talk to a friend, an impromptu Cyrano: "He wrote *nice* in all caps. What does that mean? What do I write back?" Then we write a response and delete it 10 times before sending a message that will appear 2 care, but not 2 much. If all goes well, a date will be arranged.

> Natural selection may be favoring the quick-thumbed quip peddler over the confident, ice-breaking alpha male.

Whether you like it or not, the digital age has produced a new format for modern romance, and natural selection may be favoring the quick-thumbed quip peddler over the confident, ice-breaking alpha male. Or maybe we are hiding behind the cloak of digital text and spell-check to present superior versions of ourselves while using these less intimate forms of communication to accelerate the courting process. So what's it really good for? 4

There is some argument about who actually invented text messaging, but I think it's safe to say it was a man. Multiple studies have shown that the average man uses about half as many words per day as women, thus text messaging. It eliminates hellos and goodbyes and cuts right to the chase. Now, if that's not male behavior, I don't know what is. It's also great for passing notes. There is something fun about sharing secrets with your date while in the company of others. Think of texting as a modern whisper in your lover's ear. 5

Sending sweet nothings on Twitter or Facebook is also fun. In some ways, it's no different than sending flowers to the office: You are declaring your love for everyone to see. Who doesn't like to be publicly adored? Just remember that what you post is out there and there's some stuff you can't unsee. 6

But the reality is that we communicate with every part of our being, and there are times when we must use it all. When someone needs us, he or she needs all of us. There's no text that can replace a loving touch when someone we love is hurting. 7

We haven't lost romance in the digital age, but we may be neglecting it. In doing so, antiquated art forms are taking on new importance. The power of a hand-written letter is greater than ever. It's personal and deliberate and means more than an e-mail or text ever will. It has a unique scent. It requires deciphering. But, most important, it's flawed. There are errors in handwriting, punctuation, grammar, and spelling that show our vulnerability. And vulnerability is the essence of romance. It's the art of being uncalculated, the willingness to look foolish, the courage to say, "This is me, and I'm interested in you enough to show you my flaws with the hope that you may embrace me for all that I am but, more important, all that I am not." 8

VOCABULARY/USING A DICTIONARY

1. What are the origins of the word *quip*? How else can it be used?
2. What does *courting* (para. 4) mean? Where does the word come from?
3. In paragraph 8, Kutcher states that "antiquated art forms are taking on new importance." What is the definition of *antiquated*?

RESPONDING TO WORDS IN CONTEXT

1. Kutcher states, "Sending sweet nothings on Twitter or Facebook is also fun" (para. 6). What are *sweet nothings*? How have they changed over time?
2. In the third paragraph, Kutcher suggests that texting makes a friend into an "impromptu Cyrano." Who is Cyrano, and what does his name imply?
3. Kutcher concludes that romance is a willingness to say, "'This is me, and I'm interested in you enough to show you my flaws with the hope that you may embrace me for all that I am but, more important, all that I am not" (para. 8). What does the word *embrace* mean in this context, and what can it mean in a different context?

DISCUSSING MAIN POINT AND MEANING

1. In one sentence, summarize Kutcher's argument in this piece.
2. How does Kutcher answer the question posed in the title? Has texting killed romance, according to Kutcher?
3. What possibilities does Kutcher suggest might be the reasons for the popularity of text messaging and e-mailing over more traditional modes of communication?

EXAMINING SENTENCES, PARAGRAPHS, AND ORGANIZATION

1. What new idea does Kutcher introduce in paragraph 5? Does it contribute to his argument? Why or why not?
2. In paragraph 3, Kutcher uses quotes and text messages to tell a story and illustrate a point. Is this method effective? What is he trying to prove with these quotes and texts?
3. What is the overall organizing principle for this essay? Does Kutcher provide a thesis and then support it, or does he work toward a conclusion? Is this method effective?

THINKING CRITICALLY

1. Kutcher wrote this essay to make an argument regarding how technology is changing the face of romance, but there is also an alternative reason behind the publication of this piece. What is that reason, and how might it affect the reliability or bias of the writer?
2. Does Kutcher successfully answer the question presented in the title? Why or why not? What would you add to the argument to improve it?

3. Is Kutcher qualified to comment authoritatively on this subject? Why or why not? If not, who might be better qualified and why?

WRITING ACTIVITIES

1. Kutcher argues, "The power of a handwritten letter is greater than ever" (para. 8). Write a short essay in which you explore the difference in tone and meaning between an e-mail and a handwritten letter. When is one appropriate and the other inappropriate? Why do we make these distinctions?

2. Write an essay responding to Kutcher's argument. Do you agree that text messages are, for the most part, unromantic? Why or why not? Do you disagree that we are neglecting romance in the digital age? Explain your opinion.

3. Aside from romance, what are some other aspects of communication that have changed through digitalization? Using Kutcher's essay as a model, write your own argument either defending or decrying an aspect of technology that has changed the way we communicate with each other.

Rebecca Armendariz

Chat History

[*GOOD*, September 2011]

BEFORE YOU READ

Texting, instant messaging, and e-mailing are all quick forms of communication that are replacing face-to-face and phone conversations. What are some of the benefits of these technologies, and what are some of the detriments?

WORDS TO LEARN

dissection (para. 4): the act of cutting something apart for examination or analysis (noun)

tandem (para. 11): having seats arranged one behind the other (adj)

Rebecca Armendariz is a writer based in Washington, D.C. Her work has been published in the Guardian, *the* Onion AV Club, Hairpin, Gridskipper, *the* Big Takeover, *and* GOOD *magazine. Former online editor for the* Washington Blade, *she now works as a Web specialist for* Altarum. *She enjoys tea, reading magazines, and stand-up comedians.*

Clark and I met on the Thursday before Labor Day, August 30, 2007. I don't know exactly when we first said I love you, but the first email exchange containing the phrase, which he casually includes before signing off, is dated October 3 of that year.

Nearly four years later, I sometimes type his email address in the search box in my Gmail. Hundreds of results pop up, and I'll pick a few at random to read. The ease of our everyday interactions is what kills me. The way we spoke to each other about what I'd bring home for dinner or whether it was a PBR or a Grolsch kind of night. In nearly every conversation, there is something that releases the pressure from my chest by forcing a giant laugh.

Clark: did you eat?
Me: yes i had soup and chips but whatever someone else has smells delish
Clark: k just as long as you ate something
how do you spell Bodasifa?
from Point Break?
Me: let me look it up
Bodhisattva
Clark: ?
really?
sattva?
Me: yep
it's a buddhism thing

I can break down Clark's illness into one diagnosis (metastatic melanoma), one prognosis (between 4 and 14 months to live), three surgeries, three clinical trials, seven hospital stays, three doses of chemotherapy, and five weeks of hospice care. The first surgery, a deep lymphnode dissection of the left groin, and its subsequent days-long hospital stay, spanned the first week of April 2008. The second surgery, which removed the cancer's recurrence from underneath the tender flesh of the first, was June 11. He was hospitalized from November 11–19 and again from December 1–6. On February 20, 2009, he had emergency surgery to remove a tumor the size of a baseball from his gut. He started chemotherapy on April 15.

Me: i am sorry i wigged out last night.
Clark: oh baby do not say sorry
Me: i really was just exhausted! that's obvious.
Clark: I totally understand
i know you were so tired and I know that you want
to make sure I'm going to be okay and safe

and really makes me want to cry
Clark: i feel the same way about you
I want to always want to make sure you are safe
and warm and comfortable
Clark: and I didn't mean to yell but you are so stubborn
Me: no i know
haha SO ARE YOU, for the record

Clark died two months later. He was 33. I was 25.   6

I spent a lot of time after his death looking at photographs of us   7
camping, at a friend's wedding, with my family at our first Thanksgiving.
I listened to "The Ocean" by Sunny Day Real Estate, the song he heard
when he imagined me walking down the aisle at our wedding. I cried
when Archers of Loaf, the one band Clark insisted make an appearance
on any playlist, announced its reunion tour. I watched YouTube videos
of his band, Statehood, scanning for hints of what his voice sounded like,
afraid I'd already forgotten.

The memories of my life as Clark's caretaker buzz in the back of my   8
brain at a low hum. Two years ago, I was on autopilot when I changed his
diaper or scrubbed the smell of urine from the armchair he sat and slept
in. I didn't question how I found the strength to support his crumbling
frame as we hobbled to the bathroom. Without even thinking about it,
I'd roll my jeans halfway up my calves and get into the bathtub to pull
him up. I shaved his face and gave him his painkillers at perfectly timed
intervals. I dressed him.

Now my breath quickens when the answer to a clue in my cross-   9
word, "Body fluid buildup," is "edema," the condition in Clark's left leg
that caused it to swell and dwarf his right. My eyes sting as I read a newspaper article describing the latest study to come out of a cancer conference, which involves a drug trial that Clark was too sick to participate in.
I slink off to the bathroom with my head down, ignoring my friends at
the bar, when I catch a glimpse of his obituary, which hangs on the back
of a door at the Black Cat, the bar where we met.

I go looking for evidence of our partnership that's not tied to a mem-   10
ory of me sleeping on two chairs pushed together next to his hospital
bedside. My Gmail is a priceless hoard of
us making plans, telling inside jokes, calling
each other "snoodle" and "bubbies." I type
his name into the search field and enter a
world of the unscripted dialogue that filled
our 9-to-5 existence. I become immersed
in the coziness of our union. In hundreds

> This is a history of
> our relationship
> that we didn't
> intend to write.

of chats automatically saved to my account, we express our love for each other readily and naturally in our own private speech. This is a history of our relationship that we didn't intend to write, one that runs parallel to the one authored by his uncontainable illness.

> Me: i love you :)
> Clark: you do?
> Me: yes more den anythin
> Clark: I see
> well, I'd say we have a problem because I
> love you
> your love might clash with my love, resulting into
> a shitstorm of unicorns, babies, puppy dogs, and
> couples ice skating
> it could get ugly
> Me: hahahahahahahhaha
> and tandem bikes

 11

 I remember the pharmaceutical names of his medications — amitryptyline, Zoloft, methadone. It's only thanks to my archive of our Gchat conversations — me from my work computer, he from our apartment's couch or his hospital bed — that I remember that we called gabapentin his "Guptas." They were brown, like the skin of Dr. Gupta, his kidney specialist. The Dilaudid pills he took for breakthrough pain were "hydros," a nickname for the drug listed on the label, hydromorphone hydrochloride. He'd imitate a surfer when asking for them.

 12

> Clark: man, my left leg is useless
> I really hope this chemo helps
> I can barely use it anymore
> Me: i know
> it will work.
> Clark: figure I'll notice there first
> Me: you never know
> Clark: when are you leaving?
> can I get a nap in?
> Me: yes!
> see you in like 45 minutes snoopy
> Clark: cause i can't seem to think of when I can get a nap in BEFORE
> practice cause when you get home I just want to hang with you
> Me: yes, take a nap!
> Clark: k i love you
> Me: i will get gatorades and ensures. and be right home. love you.
> Clark: LOVE YOU!

 13

It was winter 2008 and Clark was taking part in a trial, his second, at the National Institutes of Health. It involved a drug called high-dose IL-2, which stimulates white blood cells to grow and divide in an attempt to overtake the cancer. The treatment has a slim chance of success but it's one of the only regimens approved specifically for melanoma by the FDA. Patients are typically bedridden with dizzying flu-like symptoms and are uncharacteristically irritable or moody. Clark was no exception. 14

He had a high fever and soiled the bed again and again during his second IL-2 treatment. During this stint at the hospital, the fourth dose of drug sent him mentally over the edge. He screamed at me. I left the hospital in tears. 15

It was the only time during his illness that I elected not to sleep next to him. When I arrived at my friend Alyson's, I had a text message from him that said, "You left me, so I'm leaving you." Two hours later, he called me sobbing, apologizing. He barely remembered specifics the next day, but I still get a lump in my throat when I think about it. We had this conversation three days after we returned home: 16

> Clark: you make me so happy
> everyday is wonderful with you
> Me: really?
> Clark: no
> Me: you promise?
> Clark: not really
> I'm just playing with your emotions
> Me: :(
> Clark: YES REALLY
> stupid pants

17

In December 2008, Clark called my mother to apologize for the fact that I wasn't going to be home to spend Christmas Day with them. I know it's not uncommon for people my age to be away from their families during the holidays, but my mother, brother, sister, and I had never spent a Christmas apart. Clark and I opened presents at his mother's house that year. My mom told him not to worry. "There'll be plenty of other Christmases," she said. 18

"Come on, Mom," he said. 19

She told me this after he was gone, and it haunts me. Did he always know he was going to die, or did he think there was a chance? Did he believe me when I told him stories of the people whose tumors had shrunk to nothing, seemingly by magic? It was easier for me to play cheerleader; I wasn't the one gritting my teeth through the pain. 20

Clark: babies, did they say the next treatment is rough? like IL-2? 21
Me: the one they want to do to you?
Clark: yes
Me: i don't think anything compares to IL2.
but i think it is semi rough. i think it's less puking, pooping, ill feeling and more weak, tired. however, IL2 has a really low success rate, the other treatment has a high one.
i was reading testimonies of people who have been cured by the treatment, this was a few months ago, and the one guy wrote that absolutely nothing compares to IL2.
honey?
Clark: i can't stop crying
its hard to read the computer
i'm so happy
Me: yes baby
Clark: :-D
we are going to do it baby
Me: i'm so happy too
i know we are

Chemotherapy was our last-ditch effort to beat back the cancer. 22
There was the tiniest chance that it would work. If all went according to plan, the chemo would shrink his tumors to manageable levels, and we'd return to the NIH to participate in a different clinical trial, the one with the best success rate.

Clark: I would go to my mothers
chill there 23
u can start having a life again
Me: baby, my life is being with you and fighting this cancer
that's what it is
i do not resent you, and i never will
i love you and we're in this together

After three weeks of chemo, it was clear we were losing. Cancer had 24
eaten away at his hip, attacked his spinal cord, and created a blockage in his large intestine that necessitated a colostomy bag. We then chose to stop trying to wipe out his disease and focus only on treating his pain. He lasted five more weeks.

Clark: dr. kitano called
Me: to say what? 25
Clark: email coming

um, the message said that she understands our concerns and thinks
they are still able to provide us the original treatment and just wanted
to talk to us more about it

Me: WHAT!

Clark: um, she still wants us to keep the appt. on Tuesday

Me: oh my god

I close my eyes and hear him tell me through exhaustion and tears   26
how much he's going to miss me after he dies. How beautiful I look sitting by the window of his hospice room.

                                                                        27

Me: got her email

oh my god

they're going to do it

Clark: whenever Kitano does something totally rad i play that "Are
you ready for the sex girls" song from Revenge of the Nerds in my head

Me: HAHAHAHAHA

tell her that.

Clark: i should make her a mix tape

Now I live with my best friend, Cella. Some days I go to send her a   28
message, searching for her name and the colored dot that accompanies it.
I'll try her even if she appears offline, because I need to tell her I'll pick up
coffee on the way home or ask if I can open the wine she left in the fridge.

And there it is: his name is right under hers. I move the cursor over   29
it, and the thumbnail pops up with all of his information. His address,
clarkstatehood@gmail.com. His icon, a photo of Patrick Swayze from
Road House. A little gray dot, just like the one next to Cella's name. As if
he's just not available to chat at the moment.

Clark is offline.   30

VOCABULARY/USING A DICTIONARY

1. What is the definition of the word *slink* (para. 9)? What are some synonyms?
2. What does *archive* (para. 12) mean, and what are the origins of the word?
3. Name one synonym of the word *regimen* (para. 14) and provide its definition.

RESPONDING TO WORDS IN CONTEXT

1. In paragraph 4, Armendariz writes, "I can break down Clark's illness into
   one diagnosis (metastatic melanoma) [and] one prognosis (between 4
   and 14 months to live) . . ." What is the difference between *diagnosis* and
   prognosis?
2. In one of her chats, Armendariz says, "I am sorry I wigged out last night"
   (para. 5). What does *wigged out* mean, and when would it be an appropriate term to use? When would it be inappropriate?

3. Armendariz says, "My Gmail is a priceless hoard of us making plans, telling inside jokes ..." (para. 10). What does *hoard* mean?

DISCUSSING MAIN POINT AND MEANING

1. What do you think is the main point of this essay?
2. What is the tone of this essay, and how does it reflect the situation?
3. What emotions do you think the author was trying to elicit? As a reader, what did you feel while you were reading the piece?

EXAMINING SENTENCES, PARAGRAPHS, AND ORGANIZATION

1. What does Armendariz mean when she says, "The ease of our everyday interactions is what kills me" (para. 2)? How does this set the tone for the rest of the essay?
2. How do the chat transcripts function in the essay? How do they contribute to the narrative, and why might the author have chosen to include them rather than just describe them?
3. What is the significance of the last line in the essay?

THINKING CRITICALLY

1. The media often criticize using technology as a form of communication: Gchat, texting, and e-mailing are usually portrayed as impersonal and sterile ways of talking. Does this essay reflect that idea? Why or why not?
2. Do the chat transcripts provide the reader with enough detail about the relationship between the writer and Clark? Why or why not?
3. How do chats like this differ from letters or e-mails? How might they affect someone differently than a long-form letter upon reading them after a death, as the author does here?

WRITING ACTIVITIES

1. Write a short essay in which you describe a particularly important or moving conversation you had using Gchat (or another instant messenger). Why was it important, and if you are able to go back and read the conversation, how does rereading it affect you?
2. Write a short essay in which you analyze the structure of "Chat History." Discuss why the chat transcripts appear when they do in the essay, and explore the difference in tone and word choice between the chat transcripts and the formal narrative.
3. Write a short narrative essay in the style of Armendariz's, switching between prose and conversation. If you do not have access to a text or IM conversation, do your best to recreate a meaningful conversation that you have had, and reflect on what that conversation means to you as you look back on it.

Shawn Ghuman (student essay)

Is Technology Destroying Social Bonds?

[*Collegiate Times*, Virginia Tech, February 22, 2012]

BEFORE YOU READ
How often do you use social media like Facebook and Twitter to communicate with friends? Has it replaced other forms of communication in your life?

WORDS TO LEARN
witty (para. 5): characterized by quick, sharp humor (adj)

Over the past decade, social media has developed into a style of communication fit for our generation. People are able to present themselves in unimaginable ways, allowing them to express interests and dislikes. But most importantly, Facebook, Twitter, and other networking sites serve as tools for procrastination.

While chatting with friends, reading statuses, and skimming tweets, I wonder what happened to traditional communication in the current tech-savvy era. Our lives seemingly revolve around receiving digital messages, as we spend countless hours staring at screens and communicating with people online even though they are geographically close.

I understand social media is a beautiful thing, providing us an opportunity to stay instantly in touch with others locally, nationally, and internationally. Still, these advances come with costs. Rather than speaking face-to-face with others, we articulate our thoughts and feelings through short messages, often using smiley faces and abbreviations like "lol" to express emotions.

Reality check. The newfound ease that comes with social media may be causing anxiety among those of us afraid of in-person conversations. Is it a fear that natural discourse is not cool enough anymore? Think about being at a party but having no one to talk to. What is the first thing you do? You look at your phone. Your inbox has become a security blanket to cushion your uneasiness. The addictive use of social media may also stem from a fear of being misunderstood. We can

> We can edit and re-edit digital messages as much as we like.

Shawn Ghuman is a junior at Virginia Tech, with a major in Communications.

edit and re-edit digital messages as much as we like until we decide we've perfectly conveyed our thoughts.

We can make ourselves sound intelligent, meaningful, or witty. Cell phones have become the faces of their users, and messages have become direct reflections of our personalities. People can sound like whomever they choose. However, there are rules regarding messaging. Guys should only text girls three days after they first meet, or else they will come across as desperate. If people respond to a text message within a minute, they will be perceived as overly anxious. But what about participating in real, genuine conversation these days? That seems scarier than anything.

Have you ever been on a date with someone you spent so much time messaging online and then discovered you had nothing to say to him or her in person? Somehow, you felt more comfortable speaking to that person through texts and Facebook messages than in a face-to-face conversation. That experience is more common than people think and can only be described as awkward.

I can't help but wonder what life would be like if it were similar to that of *Friends* or *Seinfeld,* when "social media" meant only telephones and answering machines. People's lives might reflect who they truly are, not what is on your Facebook profile or how many "likes" you received on your latest status update.

Digital communication has taken away from what makes humans thrive — the ability to express thoughts through in-person discussion. The more people use social media, the more self-conscious they become, behaving more like guarded shells of their former selves.

My call to action is not for people to stop texting or deactivate their Facebooks, but rather to measure their lives by the days they lead.

Texting and typing are tools that have only given a bigger role to the thumb; they are not the only way to communicate. A previous generation was referred to as Gen X. The way our generation is socializing, it ought to be known as Generation teXt.

VOCABULARY/USING A DICTIONARY

1. What is the definition of *discourse* (para. 4), and what are the origins of the word?
2. The word *awkward* (para. 6) has many different definitions. How is the word used most often now?
3. What are the origins of the word *anxious* (para. 5)?

RESPONDING TO WORDS IN CONTEXT

1. In the sentence, "The addictive use of social media may also stem from a fear of being misunderstood" (para. 4), how is the word *stem* being used?

2. When Ghuman writes, "But what about participating in real, genuine conversation these days" (para. 5), what does the word *genuine* refer to, and what is he implying?
3. In paragraph 8, Ghuman argues, "Digital communication has taken away from what makes humans thrive." What does *thrive* mean?

DISCUSSING MAIN POINT AND MEANING

1. What do *Friends* and *Seinfeld* represent in this essay? What point is the author making about those shows?
2. What is the author asking readers to do regarding social media? Does he think social media should be abandoned altogether?
3. How does Ghuman believe social media is changing modern communication?

EXAMINING SENTENCES, PARAGRAPHS, AND ORGANIZATION

1. Who is the intended audience for this essay? How did you determine your answer?
2. What is the purpose of the second-to-last paragraph? What does Ghuman want that paragraph to accomplish?
3. What phrase signals that Ghuman is going to stop discussing the benefits of social media and start discussing the negative aspects of it?

THINKING CRITICALLY

1. Do you agree with Ghuman's statement, "Digital communication has taken away from what makes humans thrive—the ability to express thoughts through in-person discussion" (para. 8)? Why or why not?
2. Ghuman concedes that social media makes communication easier and faster. Expand on this point; what other benefits does social media have? How can it improve communication for individuals and businesses?
3. Social media also bombards users with advertisements and marketing campaigns. How do you think this affects your daily life? Has social media changed your buying habits in any way?

WRITING ACTIVITIES

1. Write a short essay describing how your life would be different without social media. Use specific examples of how you use texts, Facebook, or Twitter in your daily life, and how it would change if you were to stop using social media.
2. How else has technology changed human interaction? List three advancements not mentioned by Ghuman and describe whether you believe they are detrimental or helpful.

3. Write a response to Ghuman's essay in which you either defend social media as a useful tool or further support the idea that it is detrimental to in-person communication. Cite examples from your personal experience to support this claim.

Including the Reader

Experienced writers know that readers like to feel included as part of the audience and that their personal experiences are being taken into account. One way to accomplish this is to switch at times to the second person singular — that is, to directly address "you" the reader. This is especially the case when the writer feels that a particular experience is so commonly felt that readers will immediately identify with it. This has the added advantage of persuading the reader that the writer knows what he or she is talking about.

Note how Shawn Ghuman in the fourth paragraph of "Is Technology Destroying Social Bonds?" makes his point about the way social media can at times ease our anxiety. He switches from speaking in the first person plural ("we," "us," "our") about "our" general experiences with social media to someone's ("your") specific experience at a party. That switch to "you" puts the reader directly into the picture and vividly reinforces the writer's general observation about social anxiety.

1 *People in general ("us")*	Reality check. The newfound ease that comes with social media may be causing anxiety <u>among those of us afraid</u> (1) of in-person conversations. Is it a fear that natural discourse is not cool enough anymore? <u>Think about being at a party but having no one to talk to. What is the first thing you do? You look at your phone. Your inbox has become a security blanket to cushion your uneasiness.</u> (2)
2 *Now moves to second person singular ("you")*	
3 *Returns to first person plural ("we")*	The addictive use of social media may also stem from a fear of being misunderstood. <u>We can edit</u> (3) and re-edit digital messages as much as we like until we decide we've perfectly conveyed our thoughts.

STUDENT WRITER AT WORK
Shawn Ghuman

B.A. What inspired you to write this essay? And publish it in your campus paper?

S.G. It's incredible the amount of time we spend staring at devices and procrastinating on social media sites, and when that crosses over into our personal lives, it becomes much more significant. The story was just a way for me to put something I thought was so apparent in perspective for people. I think opinion writing is all about showing people another way to think about something, kind of like what a comedian does, but through prose rather than jokes.

B.A. What response have you received to this piece?

S.G. The comments toward the piece were positive, and they reinforced that people see social media the way I do, as a possible detriment to interpersonal communication.

B.A. Have you written on this topic since? Have you read or seen other work on the topic that has interested you?

S.G. I personally have not written on the subject since, but I have seen several pieces from authors that have contributed to this same realization. There have been recently published studies that claim that our usage of smartphones is actually addictive.

B.A. How long did it take for you to write this piece? Did you revise your work? What were your goals as you revised?

S.G. I'm not sure how long it took, but it often takes me two to three hours to put all my thoughts down. Revision is a necessary step in the writing process because a stream of consciousness is never properly filtered. My goals were to make the story as genuine as possible, consequently making the story tough to counterargue.

B.A. Do you generally show your writing to friends before submitting it? To what extent did discussion with others help you develop your point of view on the topic?

S.G. I'm the kind of person who will ask others just to gain a feel for how they would respond to one of my ideas. Bouncing your ideas off others is crucial to the creative process because conversation only leads to better thoughts. It's better to have a dissident than to have groupthink. For this story, my discussion with others allowed me to justify some of the ideas I had concluded.

B.A. Do you plan to continue writing for publication?

S.G. Yes, definitely.

B.A. What advice do you have for other student writers?

S.G. If your passion is truly writing, the ease of putting words to paper will be clear in your mind. The only way to find that out is if you put yourself out there and start writing. It could be your college newspaper, a blog, or even a diary.

Discussing the Unit

SUGGESTED TOPIC FOR DISCUSSION
Social media and other forms of electronic communication allow us to connect with far more people—more frequently—than was possible in the past. Do texts, e-mails, and social media exchanges offer the potential of strengthening social bonds, or do electronic connections run more wide than deep? What is lost when e-exchanges replace phone or face-to-face conversations? Conversely, does communicating electronically offer any unique advantages?

PREPARING FOR CLASS DISCUSSION
1. Both "Has Texting Killed Romance?" and "Is Technology Destroying Social Bonds?" assert that in certain text-messaging and social-media exchanges, people present edited versions of themselves—versions that while perhaps less flawed than the senders or posters really are also lack complexity and truth. In what situations might such discrepancies between a text or post and reality be especially problematic? Why?

2. Most of the essays in this chapter focus mainly on what is lost through electronic communication compared with face-to-face communication, phone calls, and letters. Rebecca Armendariz's piece, however, suggests there are circumstances under which the power of e-communications may equal or even exceed that of, say, a phone call or letter. What are these circumstances? What gives the writing done in these instances such power?

FROM DISCUSSION TO WRITING
1. The essays in this chapter discuss several of the drawbacks of social media and other forms of electronic communication; however, they do not touch on one of the other major concerns critics have about social

networks: that they can extend the reach of bullies, a development that clearly works against building social bonds. Do you believe that this is a legitimate concern? If so, why? If not, explain why you think that worries about cyberbullying are overblown.

2. Imagine that social media, texting, and e-mail vanish overnight. What would happen? How would it affect your social life? Would you feel hopelessly alone, or would you still find ways to feel connected to others? How might society be affected? Would millions wander the streets aimlessly, or would many people see an improvement in their lives?

TOPICS FOR CROSS-CULTURAL DISCUSSION

1. Today's students came of age with social media as a way of life; students of previous generations did not. Based on the essays from this chapter and on your own experiences and observations, how would you define the Social Media Generation—or "Generation teXt," in Shawn Ghuman's words? How might you distinguish this generation from Americans older than forty, who grew up forming connections through face-to-face interactions, phone calls, and, in some cases, letters?

2. Beginning in 2010, crowd-sourced videos, Twitter feeds, and other social media kept the world up-to-date about the uprisings spreading through the Middle East and North Africa. As this development shows, social media allows people not only to build and maintain social connections but also to get the word out about important news developments, especially when traditional media can't, or won't, do so. Compared with traditional news coverage, what might be the benefits and drawbacks of news reports coming from "citizen journalists" using social media? Do social media have the potential to be a lasting and popular news source, not only overseas but also in the United States? Why or why not?

This chapter continues online. Visit the e-Page at
bedfordstmartins.com/americanow/epages for an interactive visual assignment.

4

How Important Are Racial and Ethnic Identity?

Jean de Crevecoeur, a Frenchman who moved to America in the eighteenth century, wrote that an immigrant to the United States "becomes an American by being received in the broad lap of our great Alma Mater. Here individuals of all nations are melted into a new race of men." The metaphor of a melting pot, in which people of various origins are blended together to become one unified compound, has remained a popular image of our society. Attempts to forge a truly homogeneous American society, however, have met with limited success — and consistent opposition.

One challenge is that racial and ethnic identity are deeply felt and persistent, not only for recent immigrants but also for their children and grandchildren. In a society in which defining oneself is increasingly important, our cultural and geographic roots, even when they are generations old (note the success of ancestry.com), are becoming a significant source of self-understanding as well as personal pride. But they can also be a source of confusion and displacement and, especially since the attacks of 9/11, have led to a constant racial and ethnic tension as people from all sorts of backgrounds have found themselves subjected to constant surveillance at airports and borders. In "The Terminal Check," one of America's finest essayists, Pico Iyer, describes how, as a dark-skinned individual who has possessed a number of different passports, he has learned "over decades to accept such indignities or injustices." What Iyer finds interesting today is the way average, and even affluent, white Americans, because of 9/11, are now experiencing what people from the poorer nations of the world had long grown accustomed to.

In "My Homeland Security Journey," a Pakistani American student supports Iyer's point by detailing her encounters with airport security. Meher Ahmad, a junior at the University of Wisconsin–Madison, noticed that after the 9/11 attacks, when she was in the fourth grade, she suddenly became "acutely aware of the fact that [she] was Pakistani and not American." At airports today, more than a decade after 9/11, she understands that she can't escape her own identity. But can identity be escapable? With more mixed marriages today than ever before in history, will racial identity be something of our own choosing? If we can check both black and white in census boxes or application forms, will the concept of race become insignificant? In a highly provocative essay, "As Black as We Wish to Be," Thomas Chatterton Williams, a prominent author, believes that—given the options today—"Mixed race blacks have an ethical obligation to identify as black." Why? Williams explains that a growing "new multiracial community could flourish and evolve at black America's expense." He points out that many fear African Americans will be "at risk of being undercounted as blacks compete more than ever with other minorities and immigrants for limited resources and influence."

Identity, of course, isn't an issue only confronting immigrants and African Americans. It affects the lives of those who were the first Americans. A recent ad for the American Indian College Fund depicts the importance of studying at Native American schools as a way to preserve a precious but vanishing heritage.

"Project Implicit," the e-Page for this chapter, gets you to examine your conscious and unconscious preferences about a range of topics. At the same time, you will have the opportunity to advance research in an ongoing survey.

Pico Iyer

The Terminal Check

[*Granta*, #116, Summer 2011]

BEFORE YOU READ

Have you ever been treated with suspicion in a foreign country because of your appearance or nationality? Some might be annoyed or surprised by such treatment, while others might find it routine. How would you react if you were minding your own business in a different country and someone questioned your presence there?

WORDS TO LEARN

displaced (para. 1): out of sorts, not quite right (adj)

impunity (para. 16): freedom from punishment (noun)

dubious (para. 16): uncertain (adj)

interrogation (para. 16): inquiry, questioning (noun)

passable (para. 17): acceptable (adj)

grousing (para. 19): complaints (noun)

ruddy (para. 19): having a fresh, healthy red color (adj)

quixotically (para. 19): foolishly; oddly (adv)

alight (para. 20): to land; to settle (verb)

aggrieved (para. 21): distressed (adj)

I'm sitting in the expansive spaces of Renzo Piano's four-storey airport outside Osaka, sipping an Awake tea from Starbucks and waiting for my bus home. I've chosen to live in Japan for the past twenty years, and I know its rites as I know the way I need tea when feeling displaced, or to head for a right-hand window seat as soon as I enter a bus. A small, round-faced Japanese man in his early thirties, accompanied by a tall and somewhat cadaverous man of the same age, approaches me. 1

"Excuse me," says the small, friendly-seeming one; they look like newborn salarymen in their not-quite-perfect suits. "May I see your passport?" 2

Pico Iyer is a British-born writer and author of over ten books, most recently, The Man within My Head *(2012). A regular essayist for* Time *since 1986, his work has also appeared in* Harper's *magazine, the* New York Times, *the* New York Review of Books, *and* National Geographic.

When I look up, surprised, he flashes me a badge showing that he's a   3
plain-clothes policeman. Dazed after crossing sixteen time zones (from
California), I hand him my British passport.

"What are you doing in Japan?"   4

"I'm writing about it." I pull out my business card with the red   5
embossed logo of *Time* magazine.

"*Time* magazine?" says the smiling cop, strangely impressed. "He   6
works for *Time* magazine," he explains to his lanky and impassive partner.
"Very famous magazine," he assures me. "High prestige!"

Then he asks for my address and phone number and where I plan to   7
be for the next eighty-nine days. "If there is some unfortunate incident,"
he explains, "some terrorist attack," (he's sotto voce now) "then we will
know you did it."

Six months later, I fly back to the country I love once more. This time I   8
need to withdraw some yen[1] from an ATM as I stumble out of my trans-
Pacific plane, in order to pay for my bus home.

"You're getting some money?" says an attractive young Japanese   9
woman, suddenly appearing beside me with a smile.

"I am. To go back to my apartment."   10

"You live here?" Few Japanese women have ever come up to me in   11
public, let alone without an introduction, and shown such interest.

"I do."   12

"May I see your passport?" she asks sweetly, flashing a badge at me,   13
much as the pair of questioners had done two seasons before.

"Just security," she says, anxious not to put me out, as my Japanese   14
neighbors stream, unconcerned, towards the Gakuenmae bus that's about
to pull out of its bay.

I tell my friends back in California about these small disruptions and   15
they look much too knowing. It's 9/11, they assure me. Over the past
decade, security has tightened around the world, which means that
insecurity has increased proportionally. Indeed, in recent years Japan
has introduced fingerprinting for all foreign visitors arriving at its airports, and takes photographs of every outsider coming across its borders; a large banner on the wall behind the immigration officers in
Osaka — as angry-looking with its red-and-black hand-lettering as a student banner — explains the need for heightened measures in the wake of
threats to national order.

---

[1] yen (para. 8): Monetary unit used in Japan.

But the truth of the matter is that, for those of us with darker skins, and from nations not materially privileged, it was ever thus. When I was eighteen, I was held in custody in Panama's airport (because of the Indian passport I then carried) and denied formal entry to the nation, while the roguish English friend from high school with whom I was travelling was free to enter with impunity and savor all the dubious pleasures of the Canal Zone. On my way into Hong Kong — a transit lounge of a city if ever there was one, a duty-free zone whose only laws seem to be those of the marketplace — I was hauled into a special cabin for a lengthy inter-rogation because my face was deemed not to match my (by then British) passport. In Japan I was strip-searched every time I returned to the coun-try, three or four times a year — my lifelong tan moving the authorities to assume that I must be either Saddam Hussein's cousin or an illegal Iranian (or, worst of all, what I really am, a wandering soul with Indian forebears). Once I was sent to a small room in Tokyo reserved for anyone of South Asian ancestry (where bejewelled women in saris loudly com-plained in exaggerated Oxbridge accents about being taken for common criminals).

16

Another time, long before my Japanese neighbors had heard of Osama bin Laden, I was even detained on my way *out* of Osaka — and the British Embassy hastily faxed on a Sunday night — as if any male with brown skin, passable English, and a look of shabby quasi-respectability must be doing something wrong if he's crossing a border.

17

But now, having learned over decades to accept such indignities or injus-tices, I walk into a chorus of complaints every time I return to California, from my pale-skinned, affluent neighbors. They're patting us down now, my friends object, and they're confiscating our contact-lens fluid. They're forcing us to travel with tiny tubes of toothpaste and moving us to wear loafers when usually we'd prefer lace-ups. They're taking away every bottle of water — but only after bottles of water have been shown to be weapons of mass destruction; they're feeling us up with blue gloves, even here in Santa Barbara, now that they know that underwear can be a lethal weapon.

18

I listen to their grousing and think that the one thing the 9/11 attacks have achieved, for those of us who spend too much time in airports, is to make suspicion universal; fear and discomfort are equal-opportunity employers now. The world is flat in ways the high-flying global theore-ticians don't always acknowledge; these days, even someone from the materially

19

> Fear and discom-fort are equal-opportunity employers now.

fortunate parts of the world — a man with a ruddy complexion, a woman in a Prada suit — is pulled aside for what is quixotically known as "random screening."

It used to be that the rich corners of the world seemed relatively safe, 20 protected, and the poor ones too dangerous to enter. Now, the logic of the terrorist attacks on New York and Washington has reversed all that. If anything, it's the rich places that feel unsettled. It used to be that officials would alight on people who look like me — from nations of need, in worn jeans, bearing the passports of more prosperous countries — as likely troublemakers; now they realize that even the well-born and well-dressed may not always be well-intentioned.

I understand why my friends feel aggrieved to be treated as if they 21 came from Nigeria or Mexico or India. But I can't really mourn too much that airports, since 9/11, have become places where everyone may be taken to be guilty until proven innocent. The world is all mixed up these days, and America can no longer claim immunity. On 12 September 2001, *Le Monde* ran its now famous headline: WE ARE ALL AMERICANS. On 12 September 2011, it might more usefully announce: WE ARE ALL INDIANS.

VOCABULARY/USING A DICTIONARY

1. What is the root of the word *cadaverous* (para. 1)? What does it mean?
2. In paragraph 16, Iyer describes his traveling companion as *roguish*. Describe the behavior of a *rogue*.
3. *Sotto voce* (para. 7) is borrowed from what language? Give its translation.

RESPONDING TO WORDS IN CONTEXT

1. What sort of *rites* (para. 1) are you familiar with? What's the difference between a *rite* and a *ritual*?
2. Define *prestige* (para. 6). How might you guess at the definition based on context if you aren't sure of the definition?
3. Iyer says he has learned to accept the "indignities and injustices" (para. 18) of the reactions he encounters while traveling. What is an *indignity*? What is an *injustice*? How do their meanings differ?

DISCUSSING MAIN POINT AND MEANING

1. How do Iyer's friends explain his treatment abroad? What is Iyer's response to their explanation?
2. Iyer comments on his own nationality and appearance throughout the essay. What references does he make, and why?
3. When Iyer says in paragraph 21, "the world is all mixed up these days," what sort of mix up is he referring to?

EXAMINING SENTENCES, PARAGRAPHS, AND ORGANIZATION

1. What details does Iyer include in the first sentence of his essay? Why are they important?
2. Iyer begins the essay with his personal story, and he ends it by bringing in the reactions of his friends to similar treatment. Why do you think he organizes his information in this way?
3. Why do you think Iyer includes so many different stories of his personal travels in the essay?

THINKING CRITICALLY

1. Are you surprised at how security officials speak to and act with Iyer? Why or why not?
2. Consider the moments when Iyer's tone becomes humorous. Point out any examples and explain how they affected you.
3. Do you think, as Iyer does, that in terms of heightened measures of security, "for those of us with darker skins, and from nations not materially privileged, it was ever thus" (para. 16)? Why or why not?

WRITING ACTIVITIES

1. As you write an essay on a topic that interests you (or using a draft of an essay you have already begun), try to work in some lines of dialogue as Iyer has done in his essay. See if you can move naturally in your writing from the dialogue to the greater points you are making. In small groups, make suggestions to help each other connect the dialogue effectively with the rest of the writing.
2. Do you think security screening is important? Is it fair? Explain in a brief essay.
3. Does Iyer's piece make you want to speak out against the sort of treatment he encounters? Does it make you think we should stop complaining about the security measures being enforced? Write a detailed letter to an official that argues against the sort of racial profiling Iyer has experienced, or write one that expresses gratitude for and defends the securities in place.

Meher Ahmad (student essay)

My Homeland Security Journey

[*The Progressive*, May 2012]

BEFORE YOU READ

Have you ever been stopped in an airport because of the way you look or where you were born? Do you think it's appropriate for the Department of Homeland Security to stop travelers from certain countries or of certain ethnicities for security reasons? Why or why not?

WORDS TO LEARN

clamor (para. 2): to shout loudly for attention (verb)

flustered (para. 6): confused or agitated (adj)

Urdu (para. 6): a form of Hindustani that is an official language of Pakistan (noun)

I grew up in a suburb of Indianapolis called Carmel and never found myself to be any different from my predominantly white friends, except for the odd unibrow joke and clarifying the pronunciation of my name during roll call.

On 9/11, hours after our teacher choked back tears to tell our fourth grade class the Twin Towers had been attacked, we all sat watching the news on the television. Some of us were crying, but we didn't quite comprehend why. A clip came on of people cheering around the world. First there was a reel of young Palestinians clamoring for the camera's attention. Someone in class pointed to the TV and said, "They did it!" I thought, "Why would they be celebrating when all these people are covered in ash and my teacher is crying?"

Then the newscast cut to a similar crowd of Pakistani boys jumping on cars in the street. Whoever pointed at the Palestinians was still pointing at the TV, this time suggesting that Pakistanis had done it. I could not even begin to grasp why Pakistanis would be happy about the attack, let alone what they had to do with all of the people running from a collapsing

Meher Ahmad is a senior at the University of Wisconsin–Madison, with a major in international studies and Middle East studies. She wrote "My Homeland Security Journey" while an intern at The Progressive *magazine, where the piece was published.*

building in New York. Even if no one turned to me after the clip ended, I was acutely aware of the fact that I was Pakistani and not American.

Nearly eleven years after 9/11, virtually every Pakistani family in the area has a Homeland Security tale to tell.   4

My Homeland Security journey began in the summer of 2002, the first time I flew since 9/11 for a family vacation to Hawaii. I was eleven years old. At the airport waiting to check in, I was playing Game Boy with my kid brother on the floor, ignoring the exchange the airline official was having with my parents.   5

But when I looked up, the attendant was flustered and scared, I could tell. A feeling of panic reached my stomach, which only worsened when a police officer showed up. My brother and I wondered, "Why are we under arrest?" "What's happening?" "What's wrong?" We tugged at our parents' pant legs, and they told us sweetly in Urdu that we weren't under arrest and to please stop bothering them, be quiet, and sit over there, for God's sake.   6

My parents tell me now that the FBI was crosschecking our names, and while we waited for hours at the check-in desk, an agent in the Washington, D.C., office verified our identifies. After a while, a friendly looking man in a white shirt and blue jeans escorted us to our newly booked flight, as our original one had taken off long ago. He told us it was most likely my name that had set off the security flag.   7

The man we sat next to on the flight wasn't an ordinary passenger. My mom murmured to me as we squeezed past him that it figures she would be the one person next to such a big man on the long flight. He answered in perfect Urdu, our secret language for making fun of strangers in public. With a visage not unlike Brad Pitt's, he was the last person I would think to speak Urdu fluently, but after describing to us his time in Islamabad as a former CIA agent, I could see why he did. Strange as it was, we arrived in Hawaii, and I shelved the journey in the back of my mind.   8

Suspicion greeted us every time we traveled, and in my teenage years I responded with sarcasm. I'd ask the TSA agent why I was being stopped, just so I could roll my eyes when they repeated it was a random search.   9

A few years of that bratty attitude didn't bring me any satisfaction, and now as an experienced navigator of airport security, I remain as polite and cooperative as possible. After all, it isn't the fault of the TSA agent, who probably just wants to go home, that I'm being stopped. Instead of a smirk, I sport a smile. I know the drill, so let's get this over with.   10

As I approached the row of agents in Chicago O'Hare this winter, I made bets with my father and brother about my chances of getting stopped.   11

> It's like slowing down when you see a cop car in the rearview mirror even if you're driving five below.

We reached the desk and slipped our passports through the glass. A few minutes after looking through my family's passports, the immigration officer finally picked mine up. He glanced up at me; I was staring intently back at him so as to signal complete confidence, a cover for the self-consciousness seasoned with a hint of doubt that creeps into my head every time I hand my passport over to American immigration. It's like slowing down when you see a cop car in the rearview mirror even if you're driving five below.

I ran a reel of situations through my head that the agent might mis-construe. What if my interviews with women in the Islamic Action Front in Jordan could be used against me? What if the fact that I was in Cairo after the Coptic riots was misconstrued? I went to the West Bank; could that be it? **12**

The immigration officer made a brief phone call to a shadowy figure that I liken to the Wizard of Oz. I won the bet. We were escorted to the cubicle-like office of O'Hare's Homeland Security. **13**

I tried to make myself comfortable on the impossibly narrow benches in the waiting room and glanced at a few posters with waving American flags that reminded me of my rights within that space. I was a suspect yet again. **14**

A month before I landed in O'Hare, I found myself in a similarly tiny cordoned-off area where unsightly travelers like myself were corralled at the Allenby Bridge into Israel from Jordan. Surrounded by Arabs, mostly Palestinians who had likely been waiting for more than an hour before I joined them, I noticed the crowd wasn't frustrated or defeated. They were playing games on their cell phones, reading the newspaper, conversing with their neighbors. It didn't seem to bother them that they had been waiting for so long; it was the norm. **15**

I had known that I was going to join them in their wait when the Israeli immigration officer opened my passport. I'm used to the disappointed look on security personnel's faces when I hand them my passport because before 2004, I carried a Pakistani one. Pakistani passports are notoriously easy to forge. On my old passport, my name was misspelled (written in ballpoint pen), crossed out, and rewritten with an arrow pointing to the correct spelling. I could understand why its validity was always in question. **16**

But now, with a fresh American passport and citizenship, I expected to be presumed innocent. This thing has holograms and chips in it: What more could you want? But my passport isn't the kind an immigration officer likes to see: **17**

Name: Ahmad, Noor Meher   18
Birthplace: Islamabad, Pakistan
Places Traveled: Pakistan, Jordan, Egypt, Turkey, Lebanon, Israel,
    United Kingdom

In Israel, they didn't pretend that the thorough and condescend-   19
ing questioning of my identity was random, as I'm always assured in
the United States. It was blatantly discriminatory, and as I waved to
my Caucasian American friends, who told me before they would wait
in solidarity outside of the terminal, I was strangely comforted by the
openly racist security policy of the IDF.

Back in O'Hare, the scene was tenser. My flight had come from   20
Istanbul and it was full of people that ended up in the same waiting room
as us. Though nobody told us not to talk, everyone kept quiet and spoke
only in hushed tones. After an hour of anxiously watching the clock get
closer to the time our connecting flight departed, I saw the Homeland
Security agent come toward me to give me my passport back. He was
smiling as if he just handed me a steaming apple pie.

After sprinting through the terminal, we ended up missing our flight,   21
and that's when the helplessness of our situation hit me. There was nothing I could have done to get out of that gray waiting room faster. I couldn't
prove to the agent that I was an all-American girl, that I drink Coca-Cola
and frequently indulge in *The Real Housewives* series. I couldn't avoid my
own identity.

Eleven years after my classmate pointed his finger at Pakistanis cele-   22
brating 9/11, I've now encountered a growing mass of finger-pointers. It
used to be the only place I felt uncomfortably different was at an Arby's
in rural Indiana. Now, I can sense the glares on my back as agents search
my bags in plain view of my fellow passengers. It doesn't feel like they'll
stop pointing any time soon.

VOCABULARY/USING A DICTIONARY

1. What does the word *visage* mean (para. 8)? What are its origins?

2. Explain the origins of the word *cordoned* (para. 15) and how it is used
today versus its original meaning.

3. What synonyms can you find for the word *misconstrued* (para. 12)?

RESPONDING TO WORDS IN CONTEXT

1. In paragraph 15, Ahmad states that she was in a "tiny cordoned-off
area where unsightly travelers like myself were corralled at the Allenby
Bridge. . . ." What does *corralled* mean in this sentence, and what connotations does the word carry?

2. When Ahmad recounts the story of her security experience in O'Hare, she describes the security agent who returns her passport as "smiling as if he just handed me a steaming apple pie." Why might the author have chosen this metaphor, and what might be the significance of the "apple pie" reference here?

3. In paragraph 10, Ahmad writes, "Instead of a smirk, I sport a smile." What does the word *sport* mean in this context?

DISCUSSING MAIN POINT AND MEANING

1. How did Ahmad's behavior towards security and immigration officers change over time?

2. How does Ahmad feel about American search policies compared to the IDF policies?

3. What do you think Ahmad's purpose was for writing this essay, and what statements does she make?

EXAMINING SENTENCES, PARAGRAPHS, AND ORGANIZATION

1. How is Ahmad's essay organized? Is the organization effective? Why or why not?

2. In paragraph 15, Ahmad interrupts her narrative of her experience at Chicago O'Hare to talk about her last trip to Israel. Why do you think the essay is structured this way rather than chronologically, and what was the purpose of including the Israel incident?

3. How does Ahmad follow her statement, "But now, with a fresh American passport and citizenship, I expected to be presumed innocent"? Why might she have presented the information in this way?

THINKING CRITICALLY

1. Do you agree with Ahmad's statement that the openly racist IDF immigration policies are favorable to the U.S. policies? Why or why not?

2. In light of Ahmad's essay, do you believe that U.S. security policies should be changed? If so, what changes should be made and why? If not, why do you think the current policies are effective?

3. Ahmad illustrates the racial divide that is present at U.S. airport security, but how else might her Pakistani heritage affect her life and experiences in the United States?

WRITING ACTIVITIES

1. Write a short essay in which you respond to the message in Ahmad's essay. Has the essay changed your perception of how Pakistani Americans are treated? Why or why not?

2. Write a short narrative of a time you felt discriminated against or treated unfairly. Have your thoughts about the incident evolved over time? Describe how you felt at the time of the incident versus how you feel about it now.

3. Do you believe that the U.S. security policies should be upheld? Write a short argument essay that either supports current U.S. policy or calls for a change. If you believe they should remain, explain why; if you believe they should be changed, cite your reasons for thinking so and provide examples of alternative policies that you think would be superior.

LOOKING CLOSELY

Varying Sentences

When you read essays that sound choppy or monotonous or both, it is usually because the writer has constructed the same type of sentences over and over. Here's an example: "This summer I went on a trip to Spain. Our group visited three cities, Madrid, Barcelona, and Seville. Madrid was very hot and crowded. We saw a bullfight there at Las Ventas bullring. I was disgusted by the way the bulls are treated. Bullfighting is inhumane and should be outlawed." Note that the sentences all sound alike. The writer makes no effort to combine thoughts or information, and the overall effect is a dull and repetitive "da-dum, da-dum, da-dum." That's why good writers make a conscious attempt to vary their sentence structures. Observe how Meher Ahmad, a student at the University of Wisconsin–Madison, uses different structures, lengths, and sentence openings in "My Homeland Security Journey." Note especially how Ahmad opens each sentence in a different way to avoid monotony and to create a sense of movement.

<u>Back in O'Hare</u>, the scene was tenser. <u>My flight had come</u> from Istanbul and it was full of people that ended up in the same waiting room as us. <u>Though nobody told us</u> not to talk, everyone kept quiet and spoke only in hushed tones. <u>After an hour</u> of anxiously watching the clock get closer to the time our connecting flight departed, I saw the Homeland Security agent come toward me to give me my passport back. <u>He was smiling</u> as if he had just handed me a steaming apple pie.

STUDENT WRITER AT WORK
Meher Ahmad

R.A. What inspired you to write this essay?

M.A. I have wanted to write about my experiences with security in airports for many years now, but I hadn't found the right place to publish my story. I had mentioned my experiences to an editor at *The Progressive*, where I was an intern at the time, who encouraged me to write for the magazine's "First Person Singular" section.

R.A. What was your main purpose in writing this piece?

M.A. Aside from relaying accounts of various times I have been stopped in airports and borders, I felt that as a young adult reflecting on the decade that has passed since September 11 I had a little more perspective than I had when I was younger. I have read multiple "ten years later" pieces about the situation in the United States, and the world, really, since 9/11 and this was one aspect of what I've grown up with in that decade.

R.A. Are your opinions unusual or fairly mainstream given the general climate of discourse on campus?

M.A. My opinion on specific policies is less transparent in this article, but on several issues, I would say that my opinion strays from the mainstream opinions on campus. There's a sense that Madison, Wisconsin, is a very liberal city, and while this is true, I get the sense that there's a growing conservative student population that would oppose my largely liberal opinions.

R.A. Have you written on this topic since?

M.A. I have not written about this topic specifically. I wrote an OpEd for the school newspaper that I work for, the *Badger Herald,* which touched on growing racism against Muslim Americans, however.

R.A. How long did it take for you to write this piece? Did you revise your work?

M.A. I wrote two drafts before submitting it to the editors at *The Progressive,* and it was edited about three times after that. I revised it several times and reorganized several portions of it multiple times. The revisions allowed for a more continuous and direct narrative.

R.A. Do you generally show your writing to friends before submitting it?

M.A. I usually only show my writing to a good friend before submitting it, but I usually discuss the topics I like to write about with my friends and classmates. A lot of my thoughts are formed from class discussions or the material that I read for school.

R.A. Was this piece edited?

M.A. Matthew Rothschild, the Editor-in-Chief of *The Progressive,* edited this piece.

R.A. What topics most interest you as a writer?

M.A. My interest in the Middle East generally directs my interests in writing. Specifically, I find the rise of populist Islamic political movements in burgeoning Arab democracies to be an issue I keep returning to. However, I'm also interested in income inequality and its link to capitalism and corporations, as well as the odd music review.

R.A. Are you pursuing a career in which writing will be a component?

M.A. I'm hoping to begin a career in journalism as a foreign correspondent in the Middle East, but I'm unsure as to what I'll be doing when I graduate just yet.

R.A. What advice do you have for other student writers?

M.A. As a student, I didn't publish a lot of articles because I was self-conscious of my writing. With practice, I've learned to be more confident, but I think the key to that is getting my articles published wherever I can. Campus publications are a great place to get your articles in print, and they're a great way to gain experience in writing. So my advice is to submit, even if you're hesitant you'll be turned down.

Thomas Chatterton Williams

As Black as We Wish to Be

[*New York Times*, March 18, 2012]

BEFORE YOU READ
Do you agree with the U.S. Census's decision to allow people to identify as more than one race? Why or why not? How do you think this decision might affect racial politics?

WORDS TO LEARN

stigmatization (para. 17): to affiliate with disgrace (noun)

miscegenation (para. 18): marriage between different races (noun)

exhortations (para. 19): statements of urgent advice (noun)

My first encounter with my own blackness occurred in the checkout line at the grocery store. I was horsing around with my older brother, as bored children sometimes do. My blond-haired, blue-eyed mother, exasperated and trying hard to count out her cash and coupons in peace, wheeled around furiously and commanded us both to be still. When she finished scolding us, an older white woman standing nearby leaned over and whispered sympathetically: "It must be so tough adopting those kids from the ghetto." 1

The thought that two tawny-skinned bundles of stress with Afros could have emerged from my mother's womb never crossed the lady's mind. That was in the early 1980s, when the sight of interracial families like mine was still an oddity, even in a New Jersey suburb within commuting distance from Manhattan. What strikes me most today is that despite how insulting the woman's remark was, we could nonetheless all agree on one thing: my brother and I were black. 2

Now we inhabit a vastly different landscape in which mixing is increasingly on display. In just three decades, as a new Pew Research 3

Thomas Chatterton Williams lives in New York and holds a BA from Georgetown University in philosophy and a master's degree from New York University in Cultural Reporting and Criticism. His writing has been published in the New York Times, n+1, *and the* Washington Post, *where his controversial piece "Yes, Blame Hip-Hop" first appeared. He is the author of* Losing My Cool: How a Father's Love and 15,000 Books Beat Hip-Hop Culture *(2010).*

Center study shows, the percentage of interracial marriages has more than doubled (from 6.7 percent in 1980 to approximately 15 percent in 2010), and some 35 percent of Americans say that a member of their immediate family or a close relative is currently married to someone of a different race. Thanks to these unions and the offspring they've produced, we take for granted contradictions that would have raised eyebrows in the past.

As a society, we are re-evaluating what such contradictions mean. The idea that a person can be both black and white — and at the same time neither — is novel in America.   4

Until the year 2000, the census didn't even recognize citizens as belonging to more than one racial group. And yet, so rapid has the change been that just 10 years later, when Barack Obama marked the "Black, African Am., or Negro," box on his 2010 census form, many people wondered why he left it at that.   5

If today we've become freer to concoct our own identities, to check the "white" box or write in "multiracial" on the form, the question then forces itself upon us: Are there better or worse choices to be made?   6

I believe there are. Mixed-race blacks have an ethical obligation to identify as black — and interracial couples share a similar moral imperative to inculcate certain ideas of black heritage and racial identity in their mixed-race children, regardless of how they look.   7

The reason is simple. Despite the tremendous societal progress these recent changes in attitude reveal in a country that enslaved its black inhabitants until 1865, and kept them formally segregated and denied them basic civil rights until 1964, we do not yet live in an America that fully embodies its founding ideals of social and political justice.   8

As the example of President Obama demonstrates par excellence, the black community can and does benefit directly from the contributions and continued allegiance of its mixed-race members, and it benefits in ways that far outweigh the private joys of freer self-expression.   9

> The black community can and does benefit directly from the contributions and continued allegiance of its mixed-race members.

We tend to paint the past only in extremes, as having been either categorically better than the present or irredeemably bad. Maybe that's why we live now in a culture in which many of us would prefer to break clean from what we perceive as the   10

racist logic of previous eras — specifically the idea that the purity and value of whiteness can be tainted by even "one drop" of black blood. And yet, however offensive those one-drop policies may appear today, that offensiveness alone doesn't strip the reasoning behind them of all descriptive truth.

In fleeing from this familiar way of thinking about race, we sidestep 11
the reality that a new multiracial community could flourish and evolve at
black America's expense. Indeed, the cost of mixed-race blacks deciding
to turn away could be huge.

With the number of Americans identifying as both black and white 12
having more than doubled in the first decade of this century—from
785,000 to 1.8 million—such demographic shifts are bound to shape
social policy decisions, playing a role in the setting and reassessing of
national priorities at a time when Washington is overwhelmed with debt
obligations and forced to weigh special interests and entitlement programs
against each other.

Consider the impact that a broad re-definition of blackness might 13
have on the nation's public school system. In the past few years, the federal government has implemented new guidelines for counting race and
ethnicity, which for the first time allow students to indicate if they are
"two or more races."

That shift is expected to change the way test scores are categorized, 14
altering racial disparities and affecting funding for education programs.
For this reason and others, the N.A.A.C.P. and some black members of
Congress have expressed concern that African-Americans are at risk of
being undercounted as blacks compete more than ever with other minorities and immigrants for limited resources and influence.

Scholars have long maintained that race is merely a social construct, 15
not something fixed into our nature, yet this insight hasn't made it any
less of a factor in our lives. If we no longer participate in a society in which
the presence of black blood renders a person black, then racial self-identification becomes a matter of individual will.

And where the will is involved, the question of ethics arises. At a 16
moment when prominent, upwardly mobile African-Americans are
experimenting with terms like "post-black," and outwardly mobile ones
peel off at the margins and disappear into the multiracial ether, what
happens to that core of black people who cannot or do not want to do
either?

Could this new racial gerrymandering result in that historically stig- 17
matized group's further stigmatization? Do a million innocuous personal
decisions end up having one destructive cumulative effect?

LAST year, I married a white woman from France; the only thing that 18
shocked people was that she is French. This stands in stark contrast to my
parents' fraught experience less than 10 years after the landmark 1967

case *Loving v. Virginia* overturned anti-miscegenation laws. It is no longer radical for people like my wife and me to come together.

According to the Pew report, while 9 percent of white newlyweds in 2010 took nonwhite spouses, some 17 percent of black newlyweds, and nearly one-quarter of black males in particular, married outside the race. Numbers like these have made multiracial Americans the fastest-growing demographic in the country. Exhortations to stick with one's own, however well intentioned, won't be able to change that.   19

When I think about what my parents endured — the stares, the comments, the little things that really do take a toll — I am grateful for a society in which I may marry whomever I please and that decision is treated as mundane. Still, as I envision rearing my own kids with my blond-haired, blue-eyed wife, I'm afraid that when my future children — who may very well look white — contemplate themselves in the mirror, this same society, for the first time in its history, will encourage them not to recognize their grandfather's face.   20

For this fear and many others, science and sociology are powerless to console me — nor can they delineate a clear line in the sand beyond which identifying as black becomes absurd.   21

Whenever I ask myself what blackness means to me, I am struck by the parallels that exist between my predicament and that of many Western Jews, who struggle with questions of assimilation at a time when marrying outside the faith is common. In an essay on being Jewish, Tony Judt observed that "We acknowledge readily enough our duties to our contemporaries; but what of our obligations to those who came before us?" For Judt, it was his debt to the past alone that established his identity.   22

Or as Ralph Ellison explained — and I hope my children will read him carefully because they will have to make up their own minds: "Being a Negro American involves a *willed* (who wills to be a Negro? I do!) affirmation of self as against all outside pressures." And even "those white Negroes," as he called them, "are Negroes too — if they wish to be."   23

And so I will teach my children that they, too, are black — regardless of what anyone else may say — so long as they remember and wish to be.   24

VOCABULARY/USING A DICTIONARY

1. Williams asks, "Could this new racial gerrymandering result in that historically stigmatized group's further stigmatization" (para. 17)? What does *gerrymandering* mean, and what are the origins of the word?
2. What does the word *inculcate* mean (para. 7), and what part of speech is it?
3. What are two definitions of the word *margin* (para. 16)?

RESPONDING TO WORDS IN CONTEXT

1. Williams writes, "The idea that such a person can be both black and white—and at the same time neither—is novel in America" (para. 4). What does the word *novel* mean in this context?
2. In the phrase, "Scholars have long maintained that race is merely a social construct, not something fixed into our nature . . . " (para. 15), what does *construct* mean, and what part of speech is it?
3. What is the definition of the word *tawny* (para. 2), and what does it refer to in this article?

DISCUSSING MAIN POINT AND MEANING

1. What is Williams's main argument, and where does he state it in this article?
2. What are some of the reasons Williams provides as support for his argument that multiracial people should identify as black?
3. What does Williams mean when he says that science and sociology cannot "delineate a clear line in the sand beyond which identifying as black becomes absurd" (para. 21)? How does this apply to Williams's own children and grandchildren?

EXAMINING SENTENCES, PARAGRAPHS, AND ORGANIZATION

1. What technique does Williams use to open the article? Is this an effective opening? Why or why not?
2. Williams states that "a new multiracial community could flourish and evolve at black America's expense" (para. 11). What examples does he provide to support this statement?
3. Why does Williams quote Tony Judt in paragraph 22? What does this quote lend to Williams's argument?

THINKING CRITICALLY

1. In paragraph 15, Williams states, "Scholars have long maintained that race is merely a social construct, not something fixed into our nature." Do you agree with this statement? Is race merely a social construct? Why or why not?
2. Williams concedes that his children may look white, but he still expects them to identify as black. Do you think this is plausible? What types of problems or conflict might result from this self-identification? What types of problems might result if they identified as white?
3. Williams makes a parallel of his own predicament of identification to that of Jewish self-identification. What other groups or races might have a similar predicament, and how might it differ from that of Williams?

WRITING ACTIVITIES

1. In a short essay, respond to Williams's claim that multiracial people should identify as black. Do you agree with his claim? What aspects of Williams's argument convinced you, or if you disagree, why did Williams's argument not sway your opinion?

2. Write a brief essay in which you explore race and self-identification. How do you think the idea of race is changing in an increasingly multiracial society?

3. In a short essay, discuss the importance (or non-importance) of categorization on a larger scale. We all identify with a certain group, be it a country, a political party, a specific race, or even a generation. Discuss the benefits and limitations of categorization, and use at least two quotes from Williams's essay to support your claims.

American Indian College Fund

Think Indian

[*Collegefund.org*, 2008–present]

BEFORE YOU VIEW

What does the expression "Think Indian" mean to you? Why do you think the designers of the ad (see p. 138) chose those two words? Why doesn't the ad's headline read instead "Think Native American"?

The American Indian College Fund, founded in 1989, is a Denver-based non-profit organization that distributes scholarships to Native American students and supports tribal colleges across the country. According to its president, Dr. Cheryl Crazy Bull, "Students at tribal colleges are among the most resilient, talented individuals in higher education today. They eagerly study, research, serve, and learn together. They overcome tremendous economic and personal obstacles in order to achieve their dreams of a higher education that provides them with both employment and the security of their rich tribal identity. Today this is even more important because economic policies and political approaches to social change are having a challenging impact on already impoverished tribal communities. Tribal college students with their talents and education can change the future of tribal nations."

Advertisement for the American Indian College Fund.

DISCUSSING MAIN POINT AND MEANING

1. The top headline of the ad suggests a way to "Think Indian." What connection do you find between thinking Indian and saving a plant? Furthermore, how would saving a plant "save a people"?

2. Because they attempt to persuade so many people, ads tend to rely on the simplest language and avoid difficult vocabulary. How many people do you expect know what "Echinacea" refers to? Did you know it's the technical name of a flower that's commonly known as a "purple coneflower" and a member of the Daisy family? What do you think was the purpose in using an unfamiliar botanical term in the advertising copy?

3. A "poster child" is a person who is seen as representative of a particular group. The AICF ad is meant to appeal to a particular group of people—American Indians—without alienating them or being derogatory. How is Allyson Two Bears, the Indian shown in the ad, a poster child for American Indian college students? Could she be a poster child for all college students? Explain why or why not.

EXAMINING DETAILS, IMAGERY, AND DESIGN

1. What is the focal point or the first thing you notice in the advertisement? Before reading any of the text, what did you initially think it was trying to sell or argue?

2. The ad uses several different typefaces. In what ways are they different? What different kinds of information do they convey?

3. What is the significance of the flowery sketch surrounding the photo of Allyson Two Bears? Why do you think the designer favored a drawing of the flowers instead of a photograph?

THINKING CRITICALLY

1. As a student, what do you think is the most important factor when looking for a college? Do you belong to any cultural groups? Do you think maintaining your cultural identity and heritage is an important part of your college education?

2. Historically, education has been used to assimilate American Indians into white industrialized society. From 1879 to 1918, the Carlisle Indian Industrial School in Carlisle, Pennsylvania, took American Indian children from their reservations and taught them industrial skills while also working to assimilate them by cutting their hair, which was taboo to many tribes, teaching them in English, forbidding their native language, and changing their names. In what way is the "Think Indian" advertising campaign having a conversation with this particular type of history? How can education be used to change or preserve culture?

3. What do you think are the benefits of maintaining a cultural identity? Are there any drawbacks? If one group or culture decides to separate itself from other groups or cultures to preserve its heritage, is that considered simply a strategy for cultural survival? Or is it discrimination?

IN-CLASS WRITING ASSIGNMENTS

1. This advertisement is meant to persuade students to choose a particular college based on their unique identity. In a short essay, explain why, beyond the academic programs available, you chose the college you now attend. What about the community attracted you? How does your particular school support your identity? Has it caused you to change your identity in any way to fit in or conform?

2. How would you "sell" your school to prospective students? Sketch out or describe an advertisement you would create to convince students to come to your school. Picture your audience—who are its members? What will appeal most to them? What would you emphasize in the advertising copy? What visuals would you include, and why?

3. Read over carefully the section on Opinion Ads in the Introduction (pp. 41–45) paying special attention to the analysis of the sample ACLU advertisement. Then, in a short critical essay, apply that type of analysis to "Think Indian." Remember to consider both the specific wording of the text and the details of visual design in your analysis.

Discussing the Unit

SUGGESTED TOPIC FOR DISCUSSION

Although the first African American president took leadership of the United States in 2008, race and ethnicity remain prominent and controversial issues in America. Is color blindness a goal worth achieving, especially given reports that racial discrimination continues and that people who appear to be Muslim may be singled out for security screenings in airports and other locations? Or is color blindness actually problematic? Specifically, could downplaying one's membership in a non-white racial or ethnic group have negative consequences, both for individuals and society?

PREPARING FOR CLASS DISCUSSION

1. Compare Pico Iyer's experiences with security officials with those of Meher Ahmad. How are their views of their experiences similar or different? What do both of their stories say about what it means to look like, or actually be, a Muslim while traveling in the United States or overseas?

2. Considering Iyer's, Ahmad's, and Williams's essays, list some circumstances in which identifying with a specific ethnic or racial group might be beneficial to an individual or to society. Conversely, list circumstances when such identification might be problematic. What do these distinctions say about the importance of race and ethnicity in modern society?

FROM DISCUSSION TO WRITING

1. After the election of Barack Obama, some social observers commented that America was entering, or had already entered, a "post-racial" phase. In the words of Touré, a critic of this term, post-racialism means that "race no longer matters and anyone can accomplish anything because racism is behind us." Considering the essays by Iyer, Ahmad, and Williams, do you think there will ever be a post-racial America? Why or why not? Although a world where race no longer matters would, ideally, be free of discrimination, what problems might commentators like Williams see in it?

2. At the end of his essay Williams writes, "And so I will teach my children that they, too, are black—regardless of what anyone else may say—so long as they remember and wish to be." Imagine that you are the parent of children who are members of more than one racial or ethnic group. The children do not have to be both black and white, as in Williams's case. (And if you already are the parent of children of mixed races or ethnicities, consider them in particular.) Then describe how you would prefer them to identify themselves, racially or ethnically, both privately and in the larger culture. Like Williams, be sure to explain the reasons for your decision. If you think it would be better that your children not focus too much on their racial or ethnic identity, explain why.

TOPICS FOR CROSS-CULTURAL DISCUSSION

1. Ahmad points out that while security agents in the United States politely suggested that their scrutiny of her was random, Israeli agents' questioning of her was "blatantly discriminatory" and "openly racist." What explains this cultural difference? What would happen if U.S. security agents took up practices that were obviously discriminatory?

2. In his essay, Williams refers to scholars' assertion that race is a social construct, something created by social or cultural practices, "not something fixed into our nature." Could any other aspects of who we are or what is important to us, such as gender or religious belief, also be considered social constructs? Why or why not?

 This chapter continues online. Visit the e-Page at bedfordstmartins.com/americanow/epages for an interactive research project.

5

The American Consumer: Is Everything for Sale?

The United States became a predominately consumer society towards the end of the nineteenth century when, as a result of the Industrial Revolution and cheap labor, the nation found itself overproducing goods and looked for ways to stimulate consumption among a rapidly growing population. This economic and cultural process resulted in the creation of modern advertising, as companies turned more and more to experts to help them move their products. One can see these changes reflected in old advertisements: Ads created prior to the Civil War depict mainly the *production* of goods, showing pictures of factories and manufacturing, but ads a decade or so after the Civil War began to depict the *consumption* of goods, showing images of Americans buying or using products. Though now much more colorful and dynamic, advertising is still essentially consumer-oriented; very few ads or commercials any longer depict how products are made.

In "What Isn't for Sale?" Michael J. Sandel, a noted Harvard political philosopher, examines what he considers the latest development of our consumer society. He worries that the marketing of products, once primarily an economic matter, has become a social and cultural issue. He sees the country being quickly transformed into a "market society." "A market society," he argues, "is a way of life in which market values seep into every aspect of human endeavor . . . a place where social relations are made over in the image of the market." Sandel regards this social transformation as one of the most urgent moral issues of our time and calls for a national debate on the subject that will help us decide "where markets serve the public good and where they do not belong."

Do you think that our "consumer culture is bad for the environment, bad for the economy, and bad for your souls"? Writing for the hi-tech magazine *Wired*, James Livingston, a Rutgers University historian, advises readers as they prepare for the December holidays that if they do think that way, "Well, you're wrong." Our consumer society has had exactly the opposite impact, Livingston argues. In fact, he titled his recent book, *Against Thrift: Why Consumer Culture Is Good for the Economy, the Environment, and Your Soul.*

Also reacting to our overwhelming holiday consumption habits are two Moraine Valley Community College students. One, Amel Saleh, wonders, as the title of her essay states, "Is the Holiday Season Too Materialistic?," while the other student, Lauren Smith, defends holiday spending in her response, "No, the Holiday Season Just Brings Out the Giver in All of Us." The final print selection profiles one of our nation's greatest economists, Thorstein Veblen, who was among the first to study America's peculiar notions of what he termed "conspicuous consumption." He explained the significance of status as far back as 1899.

And the e-Page for this chapter presents presidential campaign commercials, showing how we truly do market everything, including the candidates themselves.

Michael J. Sandel

What Isn't for Sale?

[*The Atlantic*, April 2012]

BEFORE YOU READ

Do you think there is a limit to what can be bought and sold? Where would you draw the line between an ethical sale and purchase, and something that should never be assigned monetary value?

WORDS TO LEARN

prestige (para. 16): widespread respect or admiration (noun)

heady (para. 17): having a strong effect (adj)

inveigh (para. 20): to speak or write about with anger or hostility (verb)

corrosive (para. 27): causing corrosion or damage (adj)

vitriol (para. 35): bitter or cruel criticism (noun)

sectarian (para. 36): denoting groups or sects (adj)

technocratic (para. 38): of a government controlled by industry (adj)

There are some things money can't buy—but these days, not many. Almost everything is up for sale. For example: 1

• *A prison-cell upgrade: $90 a night.* In Santa Ana, California, and some other cities, nonviolent offenders can pay for a clean, quiet jail cell, without any non-paying prisoners to disturb them. 2

• *Access to the carpool lane while driving solo: $8.* Minneapolis, San Diego, Houston, Seattle, and other cities have sought to ease traffic 3

Michael J. Sandel has taught political philosophy at Harvard University since 1980; his popular undergraduate course, "Justice," was the first Harvard course to be made freely available online and on public television. His books include What Money Can't Buy: The Moral Limits of Markets *(2012),* Justice: What's the Right Thing to Do? *(2009),* The Case against Perfection: Ethics in the Age of Genetic Engineering *(2007), and* Public Philosophy: Essays on Morality in Politics *(2005), among others. A former Rhodes Scholar, Sandel has been recognized by both Harvard-Radcliffe Phi Beta Kappa and the American Political Science Association for excellence in teaching. His work has been translated into nineteen languages.*

congestion by letting solo drivers pay to drive in carpool lanes, at rates that vary according to traffic.

• *The services of an Indian surrogate mother: $8,000.* Western couples seeking surrogates increasingly outsource the job to India, and the price is less than one-third the going rate in the United States.   4

> The right to shoot an endangered black rhino: $250,000.

• *The right to shoot an endangered black rhino: $250,000.* South Africa has begun letting some ranchers sell hunters the right to kill a limited number of rhinos, to give the ranchers an incentive to raise and protect the endangered species.   5

• *Your doctor's cellphone number: $1,500 and up per year.* A growing number of "concierge" doctors offer cell-phone access and same-day appointments for patients willing to pay annual fees ranging from $1,500 to $25,000.   6

• *The right to emit a metric ton of carbon dioxide into the atmosphere: $10.50.* The European Union runs a carbon-dioxide-emissions market that enables companies to buy and sell the right to pollute.   7

• *The right to immigrate to the United States: $500,000.* Foreigners who invest $500,000 and create at least 10 full-time jobs in an area of high unemployment are eligible for a green card that entitles them to permanent residency.   8

Not everyone can afford to buy these things. But today there are lots of new ways to make money. If you need to earn some extra cash, here are some novel possibilites: 9

• *Sell space on your forehead to display commercial advertising: $10,000.* A single mother in Utah who needed money for her son's education was paid $10,000 by an online casino to install a permanent tattoo of the casino's Web address on her forehead. Temporary tattoo ads earn less.   10

• *Serve as a human guinea pig in a drug-safety trial for a pharmaceutical company: $7,500.* The pay can be higher or lower, depending on the invasiveness of the procedure used to test the drug's effect and the discomfort involved.   11

• *Fight in Somalia or Afghanistan for a private military contractor: up to $1,000 a day.* The pay varies according to qualifications, experience, and nationality.   12

• *Stand in line overnight on Capitol Hill to hold a place for a lobbyist who wants to attend a congressional hearing: $15–$20 an hour.* Lobbyists pay line-standing companies, who hire homeless people and others to queue up.   13

• *If you are a second-grader in an underachieving Dallas school,* 14
read a book: $2. To encourage reading, schools pay kids for each book
they read.

We live in a time when almost everything can be bought and sold. Over 15
the past three decades, markets — and market values — have come
to govern our lives as never before. We did not arrive at this condition
through any deliberate choice. It is almost as if it came upon us.

As the Cold War ended, markets and market thinking enjoyed unri- 16
valed prestige, and understandably so. No other mechanism for organizing the production and distribution of goods had proved as successful at
generating affluence and prosperity. And yet even as growing numbers of
countries around the world embraced market mechanisms in the operation
of their economies, something else was happening. Market values were
coming to play a greater and greater role in social life. Economics was becoming an imperial domain. Today, the logic of buying and selling no longer
applies to material goods alone. It increasingly governs the whole of life.

The years leading up to the financial crisis of 2008 were a heady time 17
of market faith and deregulation — an era of market triumphalism. The
era began in the early 1980s, when Ronald Reagan and Margaret That-
cher proclaimed their conviction that markets, not government, held the
key to prosperity and freedom. And it continued into the 1990s with the
market-friendly liberalism of Bill Clinton and Tony Blair, who modera-
ted but consolidated the faith that markets are the primary means for
achieving the public good.

Today, that faith is in question. The financial crisis did more than 18
cast doubt on the ability of markets to allocate risk efficiently. It also
prompted a widespread sense that markets have become detached from
morals, and that we need to somehow reconnect the two. But it's not
obvious what this would mean, or how we should go about it.

Some say the moral failing at the heart of market triumphalism was 19
greed, which led to irresponsible risk-taking. The solution, according to
this view, is to rein in greed, insist on greater integrity and responsibility
among bankers and Wall Street executives, and enact sensible regulations to prevent a similar crisis from happening again.

This is, at best, a partial diagnosis. While it is certainly true that greed 20
played a role in the financial crisis, something bigger was and is at stake.
The most fateful change that unfolded during the past three decades
was not an increase in greed. It was the reach of markets, and of market
values, into spheres of life traditionally governed by nonmarket norms.
To contend with this condition, we need to do more than inveigh against
greed; we need to have a public debate about where markets belong — and
where they don't.

Consider, for example, the proliferation of for-profit schools, hos- 21
pitals, and prisons, and the outsourcing of war to private military
contractors. (In Iraq and Afghanistan, private contractors have actually
outnumbered U.S. military troops.) Consider the eclipse of public police
forces by private security firms — especially in the U.S. and the U.K.,
where the number of private guards is almost twice the number of public
police officers.

Or consider the pharmaceutical companies' aggressive marketing 22
of prescription drugs directly to consumers, a practice now prevalent
in the U.S. but prohibited in most other countries. (If you've ever seen
the television commercials on the evening news, you could be forgiven for thinking that the greatest health crisis in the world is not mala-
ria or river blindness or sleeping sickness but an epidemic of erectile
dysfunction.)

Consider too the reach of commercial advertising into public 23
schools, from buses to corridors to cafeterias; the sale of "naming
rights" to parks and civic spaces; the blurred boundaries, within journalism, between news and advertising, likely to blur further as newspapers and magazines struggle to survive; the marketing of "designer"
eggs and sperm for assisted reproduction; the buying and selling, by
companies and countries, of the right to pollute; a system of campaign
finance in the U.S. that comes close to permitting the buying and selling
of elections.

These uses of markets to allocate health, education, public safety, 24
national security, criminal justice, environmental protection, recreation,
procreation, and other social goods were for the most part unheard-of
30 years ago. Today, we take them largely for granted.

Why worry that we are moving toward a society in which everything 25
is up for sale?

For two reasons. One is about inequality, the other about corrup- 26
tion. First, consider inequality. In a society where everything is for sale,
life is harder for those of modest means. The more money can buy, the
more affluence — or the lack of it — matters. If the only advantage of
affluence were the ability to afford yachts, sports cars, and fancy vaca-
tions, inequalities of income and wealth would matter less than they do
today. But as money comes to buy more and more, the distribution of
income and wealth looms larger.

The second reason we should hesitate to put everything up for sale 27
is more difficult to describe. It is not about inequality and fairness but
about the corrosive tendency of markets. Putting a price on the good
things in life can corrupt them. That's because markets don't only allocate goods; they express and promote certain attitudes toward the goods

being exchanged. Paying kids to read books might get them to read more, but might also teach them to regard reading as a chore rather than a source of intrinsic satisfaction. Hiring foreign mercenaries to fight our wars might spare the lives of our citizens, but might also corrupt the meaning of citizenship.

Economists often assume that markets are inert, that they do not affect   28 the goods being exchanged. But this is untrue. Markets leave their mark. Sometimes, market values crowd out nonmarket values worth caring about.

When we decide that certain goods may be bought and sold, we   29 decide, at least implicitly, that it is appropriate to treat them as commodities, as instruments of profit and use. But not all goods are properly valued in this way. The most obvious example is human beings. Slavery was appalling because it treated human beings as a commodity, to be bought and sold at auction. Such treatment fails to value human beings as persons, worthy of dignity and respect; it sees them as instruments of gain and objects of use.

Something similar can be said of other cherished goods and practices.   30 We don't allow children to be bought and sold, no matter how difficult the process of adoption can be or how willing impatient prospective parents might be. Even if the prospective buyers would treat the child responsibly, we worry that a market in children would express and promote the wrong way of valuing them. Children are properly regarded not as consumer goods but as beings worthy of love and care. Or consider the rights and obligations of citizenship. If you are called to jury duty, you can't hire a substitute to take your place. Nor do we allow citizens to sell their votes, even though others might be eager to buy them. Why not? Because we believe that civic duties are not private property but public responsibilities. To outsource them is to demean them, to value them in the wrong way.

These examples illustrate a broader point: some of the good things   31 in life are degraded if turned into commodities. So to decide where the market belongs, and where it should be kept at a distance, we have to decide how to value the goods in question — health, education, family life, nature, art, civic duties, and so on. These are moral and political questions, not merely economic ones. To resolve them, we have to debate, case by case, the moral meaning of these goods, and the proper way of valuing them.

This is a debate we didn't have during the era of market triumpha-   32 lism. As a result, without quite realizing it — without ever deciding to do so — we drifted from having a market economy to being a market society.

The difference is this: A market economy is a tool — a valuable and   33 effective tool — for organizing productive activity. A market society is a way of life in which market values seep into every aspect of human endeavor. It's a place where social relations are made over in the image of the market.

The great missing debate in contemporary politics is about the role and reach of markets. Do we want a market economy, or a market society? What role should markets play in public life and personal relations? How can we decide which goods should be bought and sold, and which should be governed by nonmarket values? Where should money's writ not run? 34

Even if you agree that we need to grapple with big questions about the morality of markets, you might doubt that our public discourse is up to the task. It's a legitimate worry. At a time when political argument consists mainly of shouting matches on cable television, partisan vitriol on talk radio, and ideological food fights on the floor of Congress, it's hard to imagine a reasoned public debate about such controversial moral questions as the right way to value procreation, children, education, health, the environment, citizenship, and other goods. I believe such a debate is possible, but only if we are willing to broaden the terms of our public discourse and grapple more explicitly with competing notions of the good life. 35

In hopes of avoiding sectarian strife, we often insist that citizens leave their moral and spiritual convictions behind when they enter the public square. But the reluctance to admit arguments about the good life into politics has had an unanticipated consequence. It has helped prepare the way for market triumphalism, and for the continuing hold of market reasoning. 36

In its own way, market reasoning also empties public life of moral argument. Part of the appeal of markets is that they don't pass judgment on the preferences they satisfy. They don't ask whether some ways of valuing goods are higher, or worthier, than others. If someone is willing to pay for sex, or a kidney, and a consenting adult is willing to sell, the only question the economist asks is "How much?" Markets don't wag fingers. They don't discriminate between worthy preferences and unworthy ones. Each party to a deal decides for him- or herself what value to place on the things being exchanged. 37

This nonjudgmental stance toward values lies at the heart of market reasoning, and explains much of its appeal. But our reluctance to engage in moral and spiritual argument, together with our embrace of markets, has exacted a heavy price: it has drained public discourse of moral and civic energy, and contributed to the technocratic, managerial politics afflicting many societies today. 38

A debate about the moral limits of markets would enable us to decide, as a society, where markets serve the public good and where they do not belong. Thinking through the appropriate place of markets requires that we reason together, in public, about the right way to 39 value the social goods we prize. It would be folly to expect that a more morally robust public discourse, even at its best, would lead to agreement on every contested question. But it would make for a healthier public life. And it would make us more aware of the price we pay for living in a society where everything is up for sale.

VOCABULARY/USING A DICTIONARY

1. Sandel uses the word *triumphalism* (para. 17) numerous times to describe the economy in the early 2000s. What does *triumphalism* mean?
2. What does *proliferation* (para. 21) mean? In what other contexts might you see that word?
3. What is the definition of *intrinsic* (para. 27), and what are the origins of the word?

RESPONDING TO WORDS IN CONTEXT

1. Sandel states that after the Cold War, economics was becoming an *imperial domain* (para. 16). What does the author mean by those words?
2. In the sentence, "Hiring foreign mercenaries to fight our wars might spare the lives of our citizens, but might also corrupt the meaning of citizenship" (para. 27), what does the word *mercenary* mean? What might the word mean in a different context?
3. Why do you think Sandel chose to call the debates that take place on the floor of Congress "ideological food fights" (para. 35)? What does he mean by that phrase?

DISCUSSING MAIN POINT AND MEANING

1. Briefly describe the difference between a market economy and a market society.
2. What does Sandel suggest needs to happen before the market can return to "serving the public good"?
3. What main reasons does Sandel give for the market economy becoming a market society? Why did that evolution occur?

EXAMINING SENTENCES, PARAGRAPHS, AND ORGANIZATION

1. What purpose does the list of sellable items and services at the beginning of the essay serve?
2. What point is Sandel trying to make when he introduces the idea of selling slaves and children (para. 30)?
3. How does Sandel present the answer to his question, "Why worry that we are moving toward a society in which everything is up for sale?" Why might this question—and its answer—be posed in the middle of the essay rather than at the beginning?

THINKING CRITICALLY
1. Where would you draw the line between sellable items and moral limits? Do you think some of the items listed for sale here cross that line? Why or why not?
2. Do you agree with Sandel's argument that the practice of encouraging citizens to "leave their moral and spiritual conviction behind when they enter the public square" be abandoned? Why or why not?
3. What might be some of the social implications of making institutions like prisons, schools, and hospitals for-profit rather than public?

WRITING ACTIVITIES
1. In a brief essay, respond to Sandel's claim that "even if you agree that we need to grapple with big questions about the morality of markets, you might doubt that our public discourse is up to the task." Do you agree that public discourse has become ineffective? Address one of the three areas that Sandel mentions—television, talk radio, and the floor of Congress—to support your argument.
2. Do you agree with Sandel's claim that more than greed was at fault for the financial crisis, or do you think that greed was the major contributing factor? Support your argument in a short written response.
3. Does your high school, college, or favorite professional sports team venue have a corporate sponsor? Do you think it is ethical to allow corporations into schools? How might a school's corporate sponsorship differ from that of a professional sports team?

James Livingston

Americans, Thou Shalt Shop and Spend for the Planet

[*Wired*, December 2011]

BEFORE YOU READ

Do you spend a significant amount of money around the holidays on gifts? If so, how does buying gifts make you feel? If not, why don't you buy gifts? Is it an economic concern, or more personal?

WORDS TO LEARN

equity (para. 2): value or worth (noun)
chasten (para. 4): to restrain (verb)
curtail (para. 4): to reduce or restrict (verb)

aggregate (para. 5): formed by the combination of many units (adj)

You're the most affluent people on the planet, you Americans. The choices available to you, in food, clothing, gadgets, travel, education, and entertainment, are almost without limit, and you love to shop, especially at this time of year. But all the while, you hate yourself for it. Even if you've got money to burn on gifts, you're probably spending less. 1

You've been conditioned to feel ashamed of excess. You know that you consume too many global resources, that you save too little. You know that when equipped with credit cards or home equity, you can't delay the immediate gratification of your desires — you just can't seem to save for a rainy day. You know that while consumer spending may be good for recovery in the short run, it's a drain on long-term economic growth and a threat to the environmental integrity of the planet. You want to tighten 2

James Livingston is the author of five books, among them, Against Thrift: Why Consumer Culture Is Good for the Economy, the Environment, and Your Soul *(2011) and* Origins of the Federal Reserve System *(1986). His published essays include studies of Shakespeare, banking reform, cartoon politics, pragmatism, diplomatic history, Marxism, slavery and modernity, feminism, corporations and cultural studies, psychoanalysis, capitalism, and socialism. He has been teaching history at Rutgers since 1988.*

your belt, control your impulses, defer your desires — and you want your fellow citizens to do the same, because you believe it would promote the common good. You're convinced that consumer culture is bad for the environment, bad for the economy, and bad for your souls.

Well, you're wrong.   3

Many economists, journalists, and politicians would have you   4
believe that your desire to buy things is turning the earth into a landfill.

> Consumers have been the leaders in demanding alternatives to the most pressing environmental threats of our time.

But in fact, consumers have been the leaders in demanding alternatives to the most pressing environmental threats of our time: fossil fuels and industrialized food. About 40 years ago, you switched allegiances and started buying Japanese-made cars, because they cost less, lasted longer, and got better mileage than American-made vehicles. You'll make a similar move to American hybrids when the auto industry — chastened by bankruptcy and socialized by government mandates — gets its act together. Your purchasing decisions also helped fuel the food revolution that has changed everything about what, how, and where we eat. Now you can (and do) select healthier food options, checking the nutrition labels imposed on corporate agribusiness by your demands for better buying information. Progress in both areas has been curtailed for 30 years by a distribution of national income that rewards corporate profits at the expense of wages, thus depriving consumers of the ability to vote with their pocketbooks for better products. But when presented with real choices backed by discretionary income, you consumers typically do the right thing, whether it's springing for a hybrid or shopping at the farmer's market.

Many economists, journalists, and politicians would also have you   5
believe that consumer culture is wrecking the economy. They say consumers have to spend more in the short term to strengthen the economic recovery, but they also say that we need to increase private investment and reduce consumer spending in the long run if we want balanced growth. But in fact, historical evidence shows that since 1910, private investment as a percentage of GDP has been declining steadily, with no effect on aggregate demand and thus none on growth. Consumer spending, not private investment, has made up the difference. Cutting taxes on business in the name of job creation just leads to ever-larger surpluses idling in corporate coffers, or eager speculation in the next bubble, or both — as we saw in the 1920s and as you've seen in spades since the Reagan tax cuts of 1981. If balanced growth is the goal, what we really

need to do is redistribute income, shifting away from higher corporate profits and toward better wages for shoppers like you.

Many economists, journalists, and politicians will have you believe that consumer culture will lead to a vapid, empty life. In fact, consumer culture is what you do when you're off the clock, at your leisure. It's the time when you can treat people — your friends, your family — as ends in themselves, not means to the advancement of your career. You can't be businesslike when you're buying gifts and spending money for fun, because then your goal in interacting with others is the acquisition of an emotional surplus, not money in the bank. This spending is far better for your soul than what happens when you're using the expense account to entertain clients, in hopes of getting new business and fattening the bottom line. 6

So ignore what the economists, journalists, and politicians would have you believe. Happy holidays. Get to the mall and knock yourself out. 7

VOCABULARY/USING A DICTIONARY

1. What does the word *agribusiness* (para. 4) mean? Where does it come from?
2. What part of speech is the word *vapid* (para. 6), and what does it mean?
3. Provide the origin and the definition of the word *surplus* (para. 6).

RESPONDING TO WORDS IN CONTEXT

1. In paragraph 4, Livingston says, "consumers typically do the right thing, whether it's springing for a hybrid or shopping at the farmer's market." What does the word *springing* (para. 4) mean in this context?
2. What does the word *bubble* mean in paragraph 5?
3. What is Livingston trying to convey with the phrase "emotional surplus" (para. 6)?

DISCUSSING MAIN POINT AND MEANING

1. In one sentence, summarize Livingston's argument.
2. Why does Livingston think consumerism is healthy?
3. What two examples of advancement does Livingston offer as proof that consumers can make effective change?

EXAMINING SENTENCES, PARAGRAPHS, AND ORGANIZATION

1. Paragraph 3 in this essay consists of one sentence: "Well, you're wrong." Why is this sentence given its own paragraph, and how does it add or detract from Livingston's argument?
2. What is the purpose of the repetition of the phrase "many economists, journalists, and politicians" (paras. 4–6)? Do you think the repetition is effective in supporting Livingston's argument? Why or why not?

3. How would you describe the tone of this essay? How do you think it affects the message of the piece?

THINKING CRITICALLY

1. Livingston mentions two instances of consumers demanding alternatives. What additional examples can you think of that consumers have demanded and received? Do you agree with Livingston that consumption is the best way to incite change?

2. In paragraph 5, Livington states, "If balanced growth is the goal, what we really need to do is redistribute income, shifting away from higher corporate profits and toward better wages for shoppers like you." What is Livingston proposing here? Do you agree with his opinion? Why or why not?

3. Livingston states, "Consumer culture is what you do when you're off the clock, at your leisure" (para. 6). Is your leisure time primarily consumed by consumer culture? Do you view this as positive or negative?

WRITING ACTIVITIES

1. In a short essay, respond to Livingston's closing remarks that Americans should "get to the mall and knock [themselves] out." Address whether or not you agree with Livingston's pro-consumer arguments and give specific examples for support.

2. Because this essay is so short, Livingston has to gloss over many ideas. Choose one of Livingston's main ideas—consumers drive change, the redistribution of wealth will help the economy rebound, etc.—and expand on it. Your task here is to find an idea that can be discussed more fully and to provide the support.

3. Using Livingston's essay as an example, write an essay that refutes a commonly held claim. Do your best to emulate Livingston's brief, somewhat humorous tone, while still bringing your own voice into the essay.

Amel Saleh (student essay)

Is the Holiday Season Too Materialistic? Yes

[*The Glacier*, Moraine Valley Community College, December 2011]

BEFORE YOU READ

Do you think the holidays are too materialistic? How would the holidays change if gift giving became less important or common?

T he holiday season is driven entirely by materialism. We spend more money in the month of December than any other. People are conditioned to "expect" gifts and this ultimately ruins the true meaning of the holidays. 1

As a capitalistic society, America loves to spend money. This gluttonous act encourages holiday-season shoppers and recipients to become more materialistic as a whole. As soon as the summer season comes to a close, the next big break on everyone's mind is usually the winter break. Along with that comes a long holiday season completely centered on materialism. 2

Despite the fact that the United States holds 4.5 percent of the world's population, we consume 40 percent of its toys. According to psychcentral.com, a first-grader is able to recognize 200 brands and obtains 70 new toys a year. Are we raising our kids with ethical values or outright greed? By the time children reach adolescence, they will demand pricey clothes and brands to describe who they are and define their social status. Can you afford top-of-the-line clothes while paying for so many other things? When those teenagers become adults they will expect to do little work for a lot in return. They are more likely to suffer personality disorders like narcissism, separation anxiety, paranoia, and attention deficit disorder. The effect of the holiday season does a lot more personal harm than you might think. 3

Amel Saleh and Lauren Smith are students at Moraine Valley Community College, where they contribute to The Glacier, *the school's newspaper.*

Now, I'm not saying to refrain from buying gifts for your loved ones. 4
By all means, buy them gifts! Just don't overindulge and do try to make
them meaningful. Lavishing our loved ones with gifts robs them of something far more precious: shared time and experiences. Bake cookies with
them, watch holiday movies, congregate with family and friends, and
have that spontaneous snowball fight that'll result in a hot cocoa chat
session. Give them something to remember
while enjoying the spirit of it all.

> Give them some-
> thing to remember
> while enjoying the
> spirit of it all.

Holiday presents play a big part in this 5
season, yet they seem to place a veil over
the true meaning of this month. This season
isn't just for Christmas — it's for Hanukkah
and Kwanzaa as well. This month is when
we reflect on the year entirely. It's the year's
closing chapter. We should smile to have
made it through another year with the ones we love. This time of year
is when we realize life is beautiful, and that is something one cannot
gift-wrap.

DEBATE

Lauren Smith (student essay)

Is the Holiday Season Too Materialistic? No

[*The Glacier*, Moraine Valley Community College, December 2011]

A s the holiday season comes closer and closer, the easiest thing for 1
anyone to do is to follow old traditions.
   Shopping for loved ones is just one of those unavoidable tra- 2
ditions, and this tradition is in no way too materialistic. Yes, sometimes
it can be a little overwhelming to be in the midst of all the shopping and
planning for upcoming events, and at times people can exhaust themselves, but essentially that is not what the holiday season is about. This
season is about spending time with family, and improving yourself by
giving.
   In our society, many people measure success by the material things 3
they are able to own and to give their families. During the holiday season,

people feel this way more than ever. As rude and overbearing as these people can sometimes be, they should not be the stereotype of every holiday shopper. Even those families that can't afford everything they want this season are still able to appreciate the time they are given with each other.

As long as there are charities and organizations that can provide for less fortunate people, this season cannot be selfish or materialistic. In most cases, during this period people are able to receive the things that they really need. For instance, every year my mother would purchase a gift for a foster child that her employer decided to sponsor. Sometimes the things that these children would ask for would be as simple as a winter coat or an action figure. For some people, the holiday season provides the right circumstances to really help others who find themselves in bad times. Most gifts bought and given to family members or friends are special, because any other time of the year they would not receive those items. **4**

I have never considered the holidays as being too materialistic, because each gift that is given or received is done so with love and selflessness. Even those who do not receive anything during this time should appreciate that they are most likely with people who love them. No, this season is not about material things alone; for some, giving material things is the easiest way to show others that they are **5**

> Each gift that is given or received is done so with love and selflessness.

being thought of and loved. So, if someone wants to spend money on you just to prove that they mean it when they say "Happy Holidays," let them. You never know what they might have gotten you.

VOCABULARY/USING A DICTIONARY

1. What is a synonym for the word *gluttonous* (Saleh, para. 2)?
2. What part of life does the word *adolescence* (Saleh, para. 3) refer to?
3. What does the verb *exhaust* (Smith, para. 2) mean, and what are the origins of the word?

RESPONDING TO WORDS IN CONTEXT

1. In Saleh's first sentence, "The holiday season is driven entirely by materialism," what does the word *driven* mean?
2. Saleh states, "Holiday presents play a big part in this season, yet they seem to place a veil over the true meaning of this month" (para. 5). What does she mean by the phrase "place a veil over"?

3. Smith states of materialistic people, "As rude and overbearing as these people can sometimes be, they should not be the stereotype of every holiday shopper" (para. 3). What does the word *stereotype* mean here, and who does it refer to?

DISCUSSING MAIN POINT AND MEANING

1. What examples does Saleh give to support her claim that the holidays are too materialistic? What support does Smith provide to prove her argument that they are not?
2. Does Saleh believe gift-giving should be eliminated from the holiday season? What solution does she propose to make the holidays less materialistic?
3. What point does Smith's anecdote about her mother make?

EXAMINING SENTENCES, PARAGRAPHS, AND ORGANIZATION

1. What is the purpose of the statistics Saleh introduces in the third paragraph of her essay?
2. Based on their thesis statements and support, who wrote a more effective persuasive argument? Why?
3. Reread the conclusion paragraphs of both essays. Which conclusion is most effective? Use specific examples from the text to support your answer.

THINKING CRITICALLY

1. What assumptions does Saleh make about her readers? What assumptions does Smith make about hers? How do these assumptions affect the authors' arguments?
2. Do you agree with Saleh or Smith? If you agree with Saleh, what do you think can be done to solve the problem of materialism during the holidays? If you agree with Smith, why do you think gift-giving should remain as important as it is?
3. While the two authors disagree on the basic argument presented here, they agree on many aspects of the holidays. What do they agree on, and how does each author treat the same facts to support their opposing viewpoints?

WRITING ACTIVITIES

1. Choose either Saleh's or Smith's essay and write a brief response as though you were grading the piece. Do not state whether you agree or disagree with the argument, but state whether the argument was well stated and supported. Suggest specific areas to improve on for revision.

2. Write a short essay in which you compare and contrast the arguments of Saleh and Smith, and come to a conclusion on whether the holidays are too materialistic based on the arguments presented here.

3. The word *materialism* usually carries negative connotations. As Smith points out in her essay, "Many people measure success by the material things they are able to own and buy for their families." Write briefly on whether materialism in general is a good or bad thing, in your opinion, and support your claim with specific examples.

Supplying Evidence

When we construct an opinion essay, we need to offer evidence that supports our position. Without evidence, our opinions will seem personal and impressionistic and will not carry any weight with readers who may be inclined to disagree with us. Evidence is very often a matter of objective facts that will be difficult to refute or statistical information. Note how Amel Saleh in "Is the Holiday Season Too Materialistic?" introduces statistical information to support her main point that our society overconsumes, especially during the holiday period. Saleh cites a popular Web site that provides her with some interesting data that allow her to support her claim about America's materialism.

1

The writer backs up her claims about U.S. materialism with statistical information.

Despite the fact that the United States holds 4.5 percent of the world's population, we consume 40 percent of its toys. According to psychcentral.com, a first-grader is able to recognize 200 brands and obtains 70 new toys a year. (1)

The Powerful Theory of Conspicuous Consumption

If any one principle of consumption holds true for today's America, it is this: People no longer buy something merely because they need it; they buy it because it's available. How this principle of consumption became a major factor in American life and economy is a fascinating story that begins sometime in the 1880s, with the rise of advertising, the birth of large department stores, the success of the Industrial Revolution, and the rapid expansion of mass media. It is, in effect, a story about the invention of the modern "consumer," a largely irrational creature hardly imagined in classic economics. This new phenomenon was brilliantly

The Granger Collection.

Thorstein Veblen (1857–1929), creator of the theory of conspicuous consumption.

identified by a maverick economist named Thorstein Veblen in a 1899 book called *The Theory of the Leisure Class.*

Veblen (1857–1929), the American-born son of Norwegian immigrant parents, was one of the first to point out — long before radio, television, mega shopping malls, and the Internet — the enormous power of what he memorably called "conspicuous consumption" — the desire to demonstrate one's prestige and status based on one's material acquisitions. And long before Madison Avenue discovered the power of envy (the modern consumer may be defined as someone who desperately wants whatever others possess), Veblen argued that after self-preservation, "emulation is probably the strongest of economic motives." Veblen saw emulation as wasteful and irrational; he once said that "man is not a logical animal, particularly in his economic activity."

His economic theory still retains a remarkable explanatory power and is the precursor to such best-selling books as *Freakonomics* (2005), which attempt to explain the "hidden side of everything." Although Veblen would never have imagined such an item of apparel, he would nevertheless be able to explain through his theory why someone would

Many social leaders in New York and other large cities—people who demand and have the best of everything—are users of **Columbia** Electric Broughams, Landaus, Landaulets, Hansoms, Coupés, Victoria-Phaëtons and Opera Busses. These vehicles are built from exclusive designs, and are sold for private service only. Let us send you a handsomely printed list of prominent purchasers and our special Town Carriage Catalogue.

ELECTRIC VEHICLE CO., Hartford, Conn.

NEW YORK
134-138 West 39th St.

CHICAGO
1413 Michigan Ave.

BOSTON
74 Stanhope St.

Member Association of Licensed Automobile Manufacturers

A 1904 advertisement promoting a luxury car.

pay hundreds of dollars for designer-ripped blue jeans. He had a keen eye for detecting "conspicuous waste." He saw that people tended to place enormous value on useless objects and skills, often because these were evidence of one's capacity for "wasteful expenditure." Too many things that we spend time and money on lavishly he considered simply "decorative" and as having no useful function; for example, he satirizes the affluent American male's preoccupation with his "lawn," which is merely a cow pasture that must be kept closely cropped but without benefit of a cow. At one point he amusingly contrasts Americans' preference for dogs over cats. Why? Dogs are more useless and expensive to keep and therefore are afforded a higher stature as domestic pets.

Veblen received an undergraduate degree in economics from Carleton College and then took a PhD in philosophy at Yale. But his disposition and his unorthodox economic theories kept him moving from one academic position to another. In 1919 he helped develop the now famous New School for Social Research in New York City. Besides *The Theory of the Leisure Class*, he published over ten books and many articles.

Discussing the Unit

SUGGESTED TOPIC FOR DISCUSSION

The term "consumerist" often carries negative connotations. How do the authors in this chapter uphold or refute negative connotations? Do you think of consumerism as being something inherently bad, or do essays like James Livingston's (p. 153) and Lauren Smith's (p. 158) more reflect your idea of consumerism?

PREPARING FOR CLASS DISCUSSION

1. Do you believe that consumerism is an absolute? That is, can a person only be either consumerist or not? If so, explain why. And if not, discuss your idea of moderation or finding a middle ground. Either way, relate your ideas to at least two of the essays in this unit.

2. Is it acceptable to alter your spending habits and level of consumerism around the holidays? Think about the contrast between Black Friday, the day after Thanksgiving when stores have massive sales, and Buy Nothing Day, which falls on the same day but encourages people to stay at home and purchase nothing. How would you characterize these two extremes? For example, do they encourage responsible behavior? Why or why not?

FROM DISCUSSION TO WRITING

1. Michael Sandel and James Livingston appear to have very different ideas about consumerism and responsible spending, but their essays are not exact opposites or examples of the pros and cons of the same point. Write an essay in which you explore the differences in Sandel's and Livingston's arguments, and explain how a reader might agree or disagree with both essays.

2. All of the authors in this section have chosen to examine a specific argument in favor of or against the current state of consumerism in the United States. Which argument did you find most compelling, and why? Compare the argument to at least one other essay in this chapter that you did not find as convincing, and explain why that essay was not as effective.

TOPICS FOR CROSS-CULTURAL DISCUSSION

1. Is the debate about consumerism strictly an American one? Do other countries struggle with the same ideas that are presented here? Amel Saleh and Lauren Smith specifically discuss the holiday season—is the United States unique in its commercialization of the holidays?

2. How do you think the rest of the world perceives American consumer culture? Where do you believe these perceptions come from? Why do you believe these perceptions exist?

This chapter continues online. Visit the e-Page at bedfordstmartins.com/americanow/epages for a video assignment.

6

College Sports: Is It Time to Change the Game?

College sports have long been a focal point of criticism and calls for reform. As far back as 1905, President Theodore Roosevelt urged changes to improve the safety of college football at a time when game plans—in the words of *Atlanta Journal-Constitution* columnist Steve Hummer—seemed "lifted from Attila the Hun's playbook." In recent years, college sports have seemed especially fraught with scandals, financial and otherwise, adding to longstanding criticisms of college athletics. How much do they really benefit players, who aren't paid anything for their contributions to their schools? And is it fair for universities to spend large sums of money on sports programs while raising tuition and fees? We've gotten to a point where something really needs to change, critics say. But what? And how?

One celebrated sports writer, Buzz Bissinger, author of *Friday Night Lights*, calls for drastic measures. In "Why College Football Should Be Banned," Bissinger argues that such a ban could allow more money to be spent on academics, noting that a large proportion of football programs post financial losses rather than gains.

For her part, writer Megan Greenwell asserts that banning college sports, especially football, would be a "paternalistic and short sighted" solution to the problems facing college athletics. In "Do College Sports Affect Students' Grades? A Defense of the NCAA," she argues for more thoughtful, measured reforms, including paying athletes or allowing them to receive compensation for endorsements. Additionally, Greenwell dismisses criticisms that students' grades suffer when their schools' teams are defeated. Instead, she says, students gain far more than they lose from college sports.

In the chapter's final essay, "Compensation for College Athletes?," Pensacola State College student Tim Ajmani also makes the case for paying these athletes. Furthermore, in cases where athletes have been penalized for receiving compensation from boosters and other sources, Ajmani believes that the NCAA and the athletes' colleges have acted unfairly: "They reap the benefits of the athletes competing in their sports. But they also punish them to protect their institutions' integrity and character."

The e-Page at the end of the chapter offers a glimpse into a filmed online debate on the question of whether college football should be banned. Buzz Bissinger, as well as *New Yorker* staff writer Malcolm Gladwell, participated in this lively debate. Go online to watch, and decide for yourself.

Buzz Bissinger

Why College Football Should Be Banned

[*Wall Street Journal*, May 8, 2012]

BEFORE YOU READ

Should colleges and universities continue to spend so much money on their football programs despite the fact that their tuitions are going up? What is the role of football in college life, and what is the benefit or harm to students enrolled in schools with costly football programs?

WORDS TO LEARN

sacrosanct (para.1): sacred (adj)

abate (para. 5): to lessen, to decrease (verb)

precarious (para. 6): uncertain (adj)

detriment (para. 6): loss or disadvantage (noun)

tier (para. 6): rank (noun)

deficit (para. 8): amount by which money falls short of an expected amount (noun)

superfluous (para. 9): unnecessary (adj)

largess (para. 10): generous giving (noun)

toniest (para. 10): most expensive and stylish (adj)

beneficiaries (para. 12): the ones who benefit from something (noun)

The average student gets nothing from football programs that remain sacrosanct despite tuition increases. 1

In more than 20 years I've spent studying the issue, I have 2 yet to hear a convincing argument that college football has anything to do with what is presumably the primary purpose of higher education: academics.

A New York City native, H. G. "Buzz" Bissinger is a Pulitzer Prize-winning author of four works of nonfiction, including New York Times *bestseller* Friday Night Lights *(1990) and his most recent,* Father's Day *(2012). Over the course of his career, Bissinger has been a reporter and magazine writer with published work in* Vanity Fair, *the* New York Times Magazine, *and* Sports Illustrated, *and a co-producer and writer for the ABC television drama* NYPD Blue. *Two of his works,* Friday Night Lights *and* Shattered Glass, *have been adapted for film;* Friday Night Lights *also inspired the television series of the same title.*

That's because college football has no academic purpose. Which   3
is why it needs to be banned. A radical solution, yes. But necessary in
today's times.

Football only provides the thickest layer of distraction in an atmo-   4
sphere in which colleges and universities these days are all about distraction, nursing an obsession with the social well-being of students as
opposed to the obsession that they are there for the vital and single purpose of learning as much as they can to compete in the brutal realities of
the global economy.

Who truly benefits from college football? Alumni who absurdly   5
judge the quality of their alma mater based on the quality of the football team. Coaches such as Nick Saban of
the University of Alabama and Bob Stoops
of the University of Oklahoma who make
obscene millions. The players themselves
don't benefit, exploited by a system in
which they don't receive a dime of compen-
sation. The average student doesn't benefit, particularly when football
programs remain sacrosanct while tuition costs show no signs of abating
as many governors are slashing budgets to the bone.

> Who truly benefits from college football?

If the vast majority of major college football programs made money,   6
the argument to ban football might be a more precarious one. But too
many of them don't — to the detriment of academic budgets at all too
many schools. According to the NCAA, 43% of the 120 schools in the
Football Bowl Subdivision lost money on their programs. This is the
tier of schools that includes such examples as that great titan of football excellence, the University of Alabama at Birmingham Blazers, who
went 3-and-9 last season. The athletic department in 2008–2009 took
in over $13 million in university funds and student fees, largely because
the football program cost so much. The *Wall Street Journal* reported
New Mexico State University's athletic department needed a 70% subsidy in 2009–2010, largely because Aggie football hasn't gotten to a
bowl game in 51 years. Outside of Las Cruces, where New Mexico State
is located, how many people even know that the school has a football
program? None, except maybe for some savvy contestants on *Jeopardy*.
What purpose does it serve on a university campus? None.

The most recent example is the University of Maryland. The presi-   7
dent there, Wallace D. Loh, late last year announced that eight varsity
programs would be cut in order to produce a leaner athletic budget, a
kindly way of saying that the school would rather save struggling football and basketball programs than keep varsity sports such as track and
swimming, in which the vast majority of participants graduate. Part of

the Maryland football problem: a $50.8 million modernization of its stadium in which too many luxury suites remain unsold. Another problem: The school reportedly paid $2 million to buy out head coach Ralph Friedgen at the end of the 2010 season, even though he led his team to a 9-and-4 season and was named Atlantic Coast Conference Coach of the Year. Then, the school reportedly spent another $2 million to hire Randy Edsall from the University of Connecticut, who promptly produced a record of 2-and-10 last season.

8 In an interview with the *Baltimore Sun* in March, Mr. Loh said that the athletic department was covering deficits, in large part caused by attendance drops in football and basketball, by drawing upon reserves that eventually dwindled to zero. Hence cutting the eight sports.

9 This is just the tip of the iceberg. There are the medical dangers of football in general caused by head trauma over repetitive hits. There is the false concept of the football student-athlete that the NCAA endlessly tries to sell, when any major college player will tell you that the demands of the game, a year-round commitment, make the student half of the equation secondary and superfluous. There are the scandals that have beset programs in the desperate pursuit of winning — the University of Southern California, Ohio State University, University of Miami, and Penn State University, among others.

10 I can't help but wonder how a student at the University of Oregon will cope when in-state tuition has recently gone up by 9% and the state legislature passed an 11% decrease in funding to the Oregon system overall for 2011 and 2012. Yet thanks to the largess of Nike founder Phil Knight, an academic center costing $41.7 million, twice as expensive in square footage as the toniest condos in Portland, has been built for the University of Oregon football team.

11 Always important to feed those Ducks.[1]

12 I actually like football a great deal. I am not some anti-sports prude. It has a place in our society, but not on college campuses. If you want to establish a minor league system that the National Football League pays for — which they should, given that they are the greatest beneficiaries of college football — that is fine.

13 Call me the Grinch. But I would much prefer students going to college to learn and be prepared for the rigors of the new economic order, rather than dumping fees on them to subsidize football programs that, far from enhancing the academic mission instead make a mockery of it.

---

[1] Ducks (para. 11): The name of the football team connected with the University of Oregon.

VOCABULARY/USING A DICTIONARY
1. How are *academics* (para. 2) different from *sports*?
2. What does the phrase *alma mater* (para. 5) mean?
3. What is a *titan* (para. 6)?

RESPONDING TO WORDS IN CONTEXT
1. Bissinger makes reference to "the brutal realities of the global economy" (para. 4). What do you think he is referring to?
2. How are football players "exploited" (para. 5) by college football?
3. *Jeopardy* contestants are remarked upon as "savvy" (para. 6). What is the opposite of *savvy*?

DISCUSSING MAIN POINT AND MEANING
1. Does Bissinger think football is a terrible sport that should be banned outright? Under what circumstances does he wish to ban the sport, and what are his feelings about it overall?
2. How does Bissinger establish himself as an authority on the issue he is writing about?
3. How might football programs harm the students who take part in them rather than help them?

EXAMINING SENTENCES, PARAGRAPHS, AND ORGANIZATION
1. How much time does Bissinger give to clarifying what colleges and universities are for, if not for college sports? Do you think he could have spent more time clarifying that position? What does he focus on instead?
2. Explain what Bissinger means by the sentence, which is in fact a paragraph: "Always important to feed those Ducks." What is the effect of that sentence/paragraph?
3. What sections of the essay validate the conclusion that "the average student doesn't benefit" (para. 5) from college football programs?

THINKING CRITICALLY
1. Do you believe that the maintenance of college football programs benefits a university overall? Why or why not?
2. Do you agree with Bissinger's statement that colleges and universities today are more preoccupied with "the social well-being of students as opposed to the obsession that they are there for the vital and single purpose of learning as much as they can to compete" (para. 4)? What do you think priorities for colleges and universities should be?
3. What about Bissinger's essay is "Grinch"-like (para. 13)? What do you think that means? Is his tone appropriate? Why or why not?

WRITING ACTIVITIES

1. If your college or university has a football team, research some of the same facts that Bissinger includes in his essay. How much is your tuition? How much money goes to football? Is football a distraction for the student body, as Bissinger says, or does it provide an important contribution to their experience? Does it "enhance the school's academic mission" (para. 13) in any way? Research this information and write a brief paper using your own school as an example.

2. In a brief essay, compare and contrast the importance of academics and sports in your life. Without taking a side, debate the pros and cons that come with stressing both areas in a college education.

3. Write a list of qualities you admire about your school. What makes it outstanding, in your opinion? Even if sports are not on your list, write a list of qualities you admire about a particular sport. Then write a list of things that describe college football. How do these lists compare with one another? Are there areas of overlap and divergence? In small groups, discuss your answers.

Megan Greenwell

Do College Sports Affect Students' Grades? A Defense of the NCAA

[*GOOD*, January 3, 2012]

BEFORE YOU READ

What expectations do you have of college sports? Do you think that college sports are an important aspect of a university, or of the college experience? Why or why not?

WORDS TO LEARN

alarmist (para. 3): a person who publicly exaggerates a danger (noun)
salient (para. 4): most noticeable or important (adj)

coalesce (para. 8): to come together and form a whole from parts (verb)

Megan Greenwell, a graduate of Barnard College at Columbia University, is a former editor-in-chief of the Columbia Daily Spectator *and former managing editor of* GOOD *magazine. Greenwell is an active blogger and columnist, and her articles have appeared in* GOOD, The Classical, *and the* Washington Post.

L ast year is likely to go down as the worst in the history of college football. When a Yahoo Sports investigation in August revealed that a University of Miami booster had provided illegal benefits to players for years, it seemed inconceivable that the scandal would only be the second-worst to hit the NCAA in 2011.

Then, just before Christmas, a trio of economists declared that "big-time sports are a threat to American higher education." The National Bureau for Economic Research published the study, which examined the relationship between a university's success on the football field and its students' grades — not those of the players, but their classmates and fans. Using data from the University of Oregon, where they are based, the three researchers concluded that students — especially male students — earn lower grades when the Ducks are winning games. "Our estimates suggest that three fewer wins in a season would be expected to increase male GPAs by approximately 0.02, or to reduce the gender gap by seven to nine percent," the authors write.

Although there is plenty of blame to go around for college sports' failings, the alarmist discussions about whether colleges would be better off without athletics — particularly football — are paternalistic and shortsighted.

That students are inclined to go out drinking instead of studying after a huge win shouldn't surprise anyone, but it's ridiculous to assume they'd be studying otherwise. As an alumna of the college with the longest losing streak in college football history, I can assure the researchers that we found other excuses to imbibe. This is especially salient once you consider the report's expanded findings, which show that students who enter college underprepared are the most likely to see their grades drop after the football team wins. In other words, students who are pre-disposed to struggle in college are more likely to struggle when major distractions are present. Shocking, right? The researchers proceed to take their point further, asserting that a Rose Bowl-winning team (go Ducks!) threatens not just men's grades on their Econ 101 final, but the entire American higher-education system.

> It's all part of a pattern of ludicrous claims about how college sports are ruining America.

It's all part of a pattern of ludicrous claims about how college sports are ruining America. After Penn State assistant football coach Jerry Sandusky was arrested for raping dozens of boys, some in the team locker room, plenty of commentators used Sandusky's crimes as evidence that sports should not exist — a case that never would have been made about a businessman raping children in the board room, or a priest in the sacristy.

The calls to eliminate or "deprofessionalize" college sports existed long before anyone but the most diehard Penn State fans knew Sandusky's name. Last April, notorious hater-of-everything Ralph Nader launched a crusade to eliminate athletic scholarships on the grounds that college players are no different from professional ones. That would come as news to the 100 percent of NCAA athletes who earn no salary, and Nader's proposed solution would make many players unable to afford college at all. 6

There are plenty of problems with the current system of big-time college athletics, from the devaluing of academics to the plantation mentality that allows universities to make huge profits on the backs of unpaid athletes. But fixing those problems requires thinking creatively about real solutions, not throwing the baby out with the bathwater. Paying college athletes, or allowing them to accept endorsement revenue, makes much more sense than eliminating their ability to play in college. Getting serious about their academic performance, even at the expense of practice time, is a better response than forcing "student-athletes" to choose between the two. Requiring university athletics officials to report crimes to the police and getting serious about enforcing punishments for sexual abuse is a more appropriate solution to the Jerry Sandusky case than shutting locker rooms for good. 7

College sports provide a way for students to pursue their athletic passions even if they have no hope of going pro. Sports give students something to coalesce around, creating a campus community. And yes, college sports teams sometimes make huge profits, and that's not inherently a bad thing (so does Warren Buffett, and few people think he's evil). These upsides seem almost too obvious to merit saying. Let's hope in 2012 we won't need to. 8

VOCABULARY/USING A DICTIONARY

1. What is the definition of the word *paternalistic* (para. 3)?
2. State the definition and the origins of the word *imbibe* (para. 4).
3. Define *sacristy* (para. 5) and discuss the word's origins.

RESPONDING TO WORDS IN CONTEXT

1. In paragraph 5, Greenwell states, "It's all part of a pattern of ludicrous claims about how college sports are ruining America." What does the author mean by the word *ludicrous,* and what connotations does that word carry?

2. Greenwell refers to some university sports programs as having a "plantation mentality" (para. 7). What does that phrase mean, and what point is Greenwell making?
3. How is the word *merit* used in the sentence "These upsides seem almost too obvious to merit saying" (para. 7)? What part of speech is *merit* in this context?

DISCUSSING MAIN POINT AND MEANING

1. What is Greenwell arguing in this piece? Is the argument clear and focused? Why or why not?
2. What examples does Greenwell provide to support her statement that 2011 will be remembered as "the worst in the history of college football"?
3. What possible solution does Greenwell propose to improve college athletics?

EXAMINING SENTENCES, PARAGRAPHS, AND ORGANIZATION

1. Why does Greenwell introduce the study performed in Oregon, and how does she use that study to either support or refute her main argument?
2. In paragraph 6, Greenwell introduces Ralph Nader. What does she think of Nader's plan for college athletics, and how does she convey that opinion?
3. What purpose does the last paragraph serve in this essay? How does it support or forward the author's argument?

THINKING CRITICALLY

1. Do you agree or disagree with the idea that some athletic programs have, as Greenwell states, a "plantation mentality"? Why or why not?
2. Do you believe the current athletic programs in colleges are detrimental or beneficial? Use the examples in Greenwell's essay to support your stance.
3. Describe Greenwell's tone in this essay. How does her tone affect her argument?

WRITING ACTIVITIES

1. Write a short essay in which you explore how you would improve the current state of college athletics. Cite Greenwell's essay as a source, and use it as support for your argument, or as a claim you can refute.
2. Greenwell concludes that college athletics build a necessary community at universities and provide students "something to coalesce around." Has this been true in your personal experience? Write a short essay in which you draw from your own experience to respond to Greenwell's statement.

Tim Ajmani (student essay)

Compensation for College Athletes?

[*The Corsair*, Pensacola State College, April 25, 2012]

BEFORE YOU READ
Do you believe that college athletes should be compensated for their time in addition to receiving scholarships? Why or why not?

O ne of the biggest issues involving the NCAA today is whether or not student athletes should be compensated for their services to their school's athletic programs. A highly debated subject, the topic has perhaps gained more and more controversy due to recent support by high-profile coaches. The NCAA has also been negatively perceived for its strict and sometimes questionable enforcement of its policies involving extra benefits for student athletes.

1

Scandals like the ones at Miami and Ohio State haven't helped its case. A big part of why student athletes are involved in receiving improper benefits is the nature of college athletics. If you compare the NFL or the NBA to college football or basketball, what is the difference between them? Both are high-revenue-producing businesses. Both make their players famous. Both tempt their players to participate in questionable activities. In some ways, college sports are just as, if not more, popular and successful than their professional counterparts.

2

Consider the situation that the University of Kentucky basketball program is in. It just won a national championship. Its entire starting lineup, including three true freshman players,[1] declared for the NBA draft afterwards. Critics of Kentucky and Head Coach John Calipari harp on the fact that his so-named "one-and-dones" have ruined the landscape of college basketball. But they are missing the point.

3

Calipari isn't doing anything illegal. He is abiding by the current system set in place by the NCAA and succeeding at an extremely high

4

---

[1] true freshman players (para. 3): College athletes who compete the first year they enter college. Many college freshmen choose to "red shirt," which means they sit out competition, but are able to practice with the team in order to develop their skills.

Tim Ajmani attended Pensacola State College, where he was a writer and a section editor for The Corsair. *He is currently a computer engineering major at the University of Florida.*

level (it also helps that he is a superb coach with a knack for producing NBA-ready talent). The NBA's policy for players entering the draft centers on the fact that they have to be at least one year out of high school. And remember, many of these basketball players, as well as many college athletes, come from places where they have experienced financial hardship.

It shouldn't be a surprise to anyone that these athletes want to 5 make a good income as soon as they can. However, would they be as eager to leave school if they were being compensated for competing on their college teams? I understand that college athletes already (for the most part) are on scholarship and receive many benefits because of their campus celebrity. But if they were to be given a little income for themselves, which they could use for their individual purposes, it could provide a little more incentive to stay in school and get their degrees.

And this brings me back to NCAA violations involving supposed 6 illegal benefits. These same players and programs that the NCAA is punishing for violations are being taken advantage of, far worse than they would like to admit. You have street agents[2] providing favors for these athletes and expecting the athletes to give favors in return (which is how most violations come out in the news).

Then you have the colleges themselves. Think of the Reggie Bush 7 saga years ago at the University of Southern California. The school distanced themselves from Bush because of the sanctions that the NCAA put on their athletic programs because of violations that Bush committed while at USC. But do you hear them apologizing for all of the money that Bush made them during his time there?

In today's world, college athletes are 8 pawns in a huge chess game. These are young men and women that are still finding their way in the world. And as much as the NCAA, colleges, and universities want to deny, they do take advantage of them. They reap the benefits of the athletes competing in their sports. But they also punish them to protect their institutions' integrity and character. They are just as at fault as their athletes at times, particularly in some of their strange rulings of cases that arise.

> College athletes are pawns in a huge chess game.

The reality is that the notion of compensating student athletes isn't 9 as cut-and-dry as people believe it is.

---

[2] street agents (para. 6): Middlemen who sell signatures and camp visits of high school athletes to interested parties.

VOCABULARY/USING A DICTIONARY

1. What does the word *controversy* mean (para. 1) and what are the word's origins?
2. What is the definition of the word *revenue* (para. 2), and from what language does the word come?
3. The word *sanction* has two very different meanings (para. 7). Provide both definitions and indicate which definition is applicable to this essay.

RESPONDING TO WORDS IN CONTEXT

1. What does Ajmani mean by the phrase "In today's world, college athletes are pawns in a huge chess game"? How is the word *pawn* being used?
2. What does the term *starting lineup* mean (para. 3), and why would Ajmani emphasize that the starting lineup left?
3. In the sentence "Critics of Kentucky and Head Coach John Calipari harp on the fact that his so-named 'one-and-dones' have ruined the landscape of college basketball" (para. 3), how is the word *harp* being used? What do you think the coach means by the phrase "one-and-dones"?

DISCUSSING MAIN POINT AND MEANING

1. Does Ajmani have a clear argument in this essay? If so, what is it?
2. What does Ajmani believe about NCAA violations and illegal benefits?
3. How does Ajmani portray Kentucky head coach John Calipari?

EXAMINING SENTENCES, PARAGRAPHS, AND ORGANIZATION

1. What is the purpose of the Reggie Bush example in paragraph 7?
2. What point does Ajmani illustrate in paragraph 3, when he discusses the University of Kentucky?
3. Ajmani uses several rhetorical questions throughout his essay. Cite at least two and explain their meaning within the context of the argument.

THINKING CRITICALLY

1. What assumptions does Ajmani make about his readers, and where are these assumptions made apparent? Cite specific examples from the text.
2. In paragraph 2, Ajmani states, "In some ways, college sports are just as, if not more, popular and successful than their professional counterparts." Do you agree with this statement? Why or why not?
3. Can you think of any other activities or jobs that create massive revenue that the workers or players do not see the benefits of? Be as specific as possible.

WRITING ACTIVITIES

1. College athletes undoubtedly help earn money for the universities they play for. Keeping in mind both sides of the argument and the essays you've read on the topic, write a short essay in which you argue that it is or is not ethical to not pay college athletes.

2. Whether you agree with Ajmani or not, write a short essay in which you argue against paying college athletes. Cite specific reasons as to why college athletes should *not* be paid, and reference at least one claim made in Ajmani's essay.

3. The final line of Ajmani's essay is: "The reality is that the notion of compensating student athletes isn't as cut-and-dry as people believe it is." Maintaining Ajmani's argument, write three alternate final lines and provide a brief explanation of why each closing line would function well within Ajmani's argument.

LOOKING CLOSELY

The Art of Argument: Anticipating Opposition

When you take a position you think will be unpopular or controversial, an effective strategy is to anticipate the objections you may receive. In this way, you indicate that you have thought carefully about your position, and you make it more difficult for those who resist your argument to reject your claims outright. In nearly all effective argument and debate, the writer or speaker will attempt to anticipate arguments likely to be made by the other side. This doesn't mean that you have answered the opposing arguments satisfactorily, but it does mean that the opposing side will need to take into account your awareness of its position.

In "Compensation for College Athletes?" Tim Ajmani, a student at Pensacola State College, realizes that one objection readers may have to his opinion that college athletes should be paid for their services is that most of these athletes are already being compensated in the form of scholarships and other benefits. By mentioning this, Ajmani shows his readers that he is aware that those who might disagree with him would object to his position: they would argue that college athletes are already obtaining payment in other forms. Note that he makes his awareness clear by stating "I understand that college athletes. . . ." After showing his understanding of this key fact, Ajmani then goes on to say why "a little income for themselves" could "provide a little more incentive to stay in school and get their degrees."

1 *Recognizes the financial motive to leave school*	It shouldn't be a surprise to anyone that these athletes want to make a good income as soon as they can. However, would they be as eager to leave school if they were being compensated for competing on their college teams? (1) I understand that college athletes already (for the most part) are on scholarship and receive many benefits because of their campus celebrity.(2) But if they were to be given a little income for themselves, which they could use for their individual purposes, it could provide a little more incentive to stay in school and get their degrees. (3)
2 *Acknowledges that many already receive scholarships*	
3 *Counters that position by claiming that some income would offer incentive to stay in school*	

STUDENT WRITER AT WORK
Tim Ajmani

R.A. What inspired you to write this essay? And publish it in your campus paper?

T.A. As a Community Conversations Editor, most of my inspiration for columns and blogs came from discussions and debates on campus between students.

R.A. What response have you received to this piece? Has the feedback you have received affected your views on the subject?

T.A. We actually put out a poll for feedback on the topic, and based on the results, most readers generally disagreed with the argument that athletes should be compensated in some way. I was a little surprised because of recent events that have transpired, but it really didn't change my views on the subject.

R.A. Have you written on this topic since? Have you read or seen other work on the topic that has interested you?

T.A. I have not written on the topic since I published the column. But I'm seeing more and more debate regarding the stance that athletes should be financially compensated for their participation in their school's athletics, particularly from sports networks like ESPN.

R.A. How long did it take for you to write this piece? Did you revise your work? What were your goals as you revised?

T.A. It probably took me about two to three hours in terms of a draft, with another one to two revising. I usually write a column in one sitting when I have a clear head with clear focus. Writing a piece in spurts doesn't work for me. I made three complete revisions checking over the work, looking for content and grammatical errors.

R.A. What topics most interest you as a writer?

T.A. As a writer, I'd definitely have to say any debate regarding sports. I love expressing my views and ideas on anything regarding issues in the collegiate and professional sports world.

R.A. Are you pursuing a career in which writing will be a component?

T.A. Yes, writing is a very important component in the engineering field.

R.A. What advice do you have for other student writers?

T.A. When writing, don't rush things. Take the time and effort to proofread your work again after your final revision. You wouldn't believe how many times I've spotted things that needed to be corrected after I thought I was finished.

Discussing the Unit

SUGGESTED TOPIC FOR DISCUSSION

This unit explores the effect of advertising money on college sports programs and the way in which college sports programs can distract everyone from academics. Are institutions of higher learning selling out by focusing on their sports programs? Are they harming their student body by doing so? Where do you draw the line between enthusiasm for football games and the commercialization of college football?

PREPARING FOR CLASS DISCUSSION

1. Is it "time to change the game," as the subheading of this chapter suggests? How have the arguments found in this chapter influenced your answer?

2. What is the role of sports in higher education? Why has such importance been placed on how sports teams represent a particular school? Do you feel that importance is misplaced? Why or why not?

FROM DISCUSSION TO WRITING

1. What is the least appealing aspect of college sports today? Using the essays in this chapter, write a brief essay that outlines what is most disappointing or contemptible about how college sports operate in the current climate.

2. In "Why College Football Should Be Banned," Buzz Bissinger asks, "Who truly benefits from college football?" How would you answer that question? Looking at all the answers provided in this chapter, write an essay that compares their responses to your own.

TOPICS FOR CROSS-CULTURAL DISCUSSION

1. American colleges are the only ones in the world that include athletic programs, the most successful and influential of which are hyped to the point of being broadcast across the nation by major sponsors. What does that suggest about cultural differences between the United States and other countries? Does that mean other countries don't value sports the way Americans do, or does it indicate they value sports differently? Explain.

2. Schools in several states are mentioned in the essays in this chapter. Do the states mentioned reflect a particular region of the country? Which regions are more affected by the money poured into sports programs based on the schools pointed out in these essays? Do you imagine the culture of sports is different in these regions?

e This chapter continues online. Visit the e-Page at **bedfordstmartins.com/americanow/epages** for a video assignment.

7

Is Society Becoming Less Violent?

The prominent Harvard cognitive scientist Steven Pinker made cultural headlines recently with a study that claimed acts of violence were declining throughout the world. Pinker examined this trend both historically and statistically and concluded that—despite daily examples to the contrary—"Violence has been in decline for thousands of years, and today we may be living in the most peaceful era in the existence of our species." Pinker's study and main points are summarized in an essay adapted from his book *Violence Vanquished*. It's this essay Ashland University student Jacob Ewing responds to in "Steven Pinker and the Question of Violence." Ewing doesn't question Pinker's statistics, which he concedes are probably correct, but he does challenge Pinker's restricted definition of violence and his various explanations for its apparent decline.

What might people living in the inner cities of Chicago, Detroit, New Orleans, St. Louis, or Baltimore make of Pinker's argument? In those urban areas—and many others—violence and crime affect the everyday lives of many people. In "Defusing Violence," Alex Kotlowitz, the noted American author and activist, points out that a Chicago "police superintendent conceded that his officers can't respond to every call of a gun fired because there are so many gunshots," and he goes on to say that "For the past ten years homicide has been the leading cause of death for African American men between the ages of fifteen and twenty-four." While working on a film about violence in Chicago, Kotlowitz followed a "violence interrupter," someone formerly of the streets who proved to him the effectiveness of intervening in disputes before they escalate.

If there is one aspect of American society in which violence predominates—and is in no way vanishing—it is surely in our movies, music, and video games. Especially video games, argues Annette John-Hall, a Philadelphia newspaper columnist who claims that, despite their amazing violence, the games may actually be therapeutic : "Yes, young people are playing violent video games," she writes in "Using Video Games to Reduce Violence," "but as a way to decrease their aggressive thoughts, not increase them." Yet, some recent research suggests a contrary view, notably studies in neuroscience that show that young adult males who play violent video games undergo brain changes that are "similar to those seen in teens with destructive sociopathic disorders. . . ." For more on this research, look up Alice Park's reporting for *Time* magazine, "How Playing Violent Video Games May Change the Brain," online. The e-Page at the end of the chapter invites you to "test your gun law IQ" with an interactive quiz.

Steven Pinker

Violence Vanquished

[*Wall Street Journal*, September 24, 2011]

BEFORE YOU READ

Are we living in a world that is more peaceful or more violent than the world of the past? If violence is on the decline, what measurement do we use to prove that to be true?

WORDS TO LEARN

insurrection (para. 1): a revolt, rebellion, or resistance that occurs against a civil authority or government (noun)

millennia (para. 4): plural form of *millennium*, a period of 1,000 years (noun)

incredulity (para. 5): disbelief (noun)

carnage (para. 5): slaughter (noun)

genocide (para. 6): deliberate and systematic extermination of a group of people based on race, politics, or culture (noun)

anarchy (para. 8): lawlessness (noun)

horticultural (para. 8): having to do with gardening and plants (adj)

subside (para. 10): to become quiet; to abate (verb)

benevolent (para. 11): characterized by goodwill (adj)

welfare (para. 11): well-being (noun)

homicide (para. 12): murder (noun)

consolidation (para. 14): unification (noun)

commerce (para. 14): an exchange of commodities (noun)

despotism (para. 16): tyranny; rule by someone with unlimited power (noun)

initiate (para. 18): to begin (verb)

inept (para. 20): without skill; incompetent (adj)

insurgency (para. 20): rebellion (noun)

proxy (para. 23): one who acts in place of another (noun)

cascade (para. 24): an object resembling a waterfall (noun)

obliterate (para. 24): to destroy completely (verb)

pogrom (para. 24): an organized massacre, usually pertaining to the massacre of Jews (noun)

repeal (para. 25): to revoke (verb)

snipe (para. 27): to attack (verb)

Steven Pinker is a professor of psychology at Harvard University, where he conducts highly acclaimed research on visual cognition. He writes frequently for the New Republic, *the* New York Times, Time, *and other publications, and is the author of eight books. He has been named Humanist of the Year (2006) and is listed in* Foreign Policy *and* Prospect *magazines' "The World's Top 100 Public Intellectuals" and in* Time *magazine's "The 100 Most Influential People in the World Today."*

judiciary (para. 29): court system (noun)

circumvent (para. 29): to go around; to avoid (verb)

altruism (para. 31): the practice of showing concern for others, unselfishly motivated (noun)

parochial (para. 33): limited; provincial (adj)

complacency (para. 36): feeling of security or self-satisfaction without awareness of actual dangers (noun)

thwart (para. 36): to oppose or foil (verb)

irredeemable (para. 36): not redeemable; hopeless (adj)

tribulation (para. 38): distress or suffering (noun)

impetus (para. 38): a driving force (noun)

On the day this article appears, you will read about a shocking act of violence. Somewhere in the world there will be a terrorist bombing, a senseless murder, a bloody insurrection. It's impossible to learn about these catastrophes without thinking, "What is the world coming to?" 1

But a better question may be, "How bad was the world in the past?" 2

Believe it or not, the world of the past was *much* worse. Violence has been in decline for thousands of years, and today we may be living in the most peaceable era in the existence of our species. 3

The decline, to be sure, has not been smooth. It has not brought violence down to zero, and it is not guaranteed to continue. But it is a persistent historical development, visible on scales from millennia to years, from the waging of wars to the spanking of children. 4

This claim, I know, invites skepticism, incredulity, and sometimes anger. We tend to estimate the probability of an event from the ease with which we can recall examples, and scenes of carnage are more likely to be beamed into our homes and burned into our memories than footage of people dying of old age. There will always be enough violent deaths to fill the evening news, so people's impressions of violence will be disconnected from its actual likelihood. 5

Evidence of our bloody history is not hard to find. Consider the genocides in the Old Testament and the crucifixions in the New, the gory mutilations in Shakespeare's tragedies and Grimm's fairy tales, the British monarchs who beheaded their relatives, and the American founders who dueled with their rivals. 6

Today the decline in these brutal practices can be quantified. A look at the numbers shows that over the course of our history, humankind has been blessed with six major declines of violence. 7

The first was a process of pacification: the transition from the anarchy   8
of the hunting, gathering, and horticultural societies in which our species spent most of its evolutionary history to the first agricultural civiliza-
tions, with cities and governments, starting about 5,000 years ago.

For centuries, social theorists like Hobbes[1] and Rousseau[2] specu-   9
lated from their armchairs about what life was like in a "state of nature."
Nowadays we can do better. Forensic archeology — a kind of "CSI:
Paleolithic"[3] — can estimate rates of violence from the proportion of
skeletons in ancient sites with bashed-in skulls, decapitations, or arrow-
heads embedded in bones. And ethnographers can tally the causes of
death in tribal peoples that have recently lived outside of state control.

These investigations show that, on average, about 15% of people in   10
prestate eras died violently, compared to about 3% of the citizens of the
earliest states. Tribal violence commonly subsides when a state or empire
imposes control over a territory, leading to the various "paxes" (Romana,
Islamica, Brittanica, and so on) that are familiar to readers of history.

It's not that the first kings had a benevolent interest in the welfare of   11
their citizens. Just as a farmer tries to prevent his livestock from killing
one another, so a ruler will try to keep his subjects from cycles of raiding
and feuding. From his point of view, such squabbling is a dead loss —
forgone opportunities to extract taxes, tributes, soldiers, and slaves.

The second decline of violence was a civilizing process that is best   12
documented in Europe. Historical records show that between the late
Middle Ages and the 20th century, European countries saw a 10- to
50-fold decline in their rates of homicide.

The numbers are consistent with narrative histories of the brutality   13
of life in the Middle Ages, when highwaymen made travel a risk to life and
limb and dinners were commonly enlivened by dagger attacks. So many
people had their noses cut off that medieval medical textbooks specu-
lated about techniques for growing them back.

Historians attribute this decline to the consolidation of a patchwork   14
of feudal territories into large kingdoms with centralized authority and

---

[1] Hobbes (para. 9): Thomas Hobbes. English philosopher who wrote the book
Leviathan, about the structure of society and government. In that book, he
wrote that people live lives that are "nasty, brutish, and short."

[2] Rousseau (para. 9): Jean-Jacques Rousseau. French philosopher who wrote
about an idealized state of nature, in stark contrast to Hobbes's, in *Discourse on
Inequality* and *On the Social Contract*.

[3] Paleolithic (para. 9): Refers to the early stage of the Stone Age.

an infrastructure of commerce. Criminal justice was nationalized, and zero-sum plunder gave way to positive-sum trade. People increasingly controlled their impulses and sought to cooperate with their neighbors.

The third transition, sometimes called the Humanitarian Revolution, took off with the Enlightenment.[4] Governments and churches had long maintained order by punishing nonconformists with mutilation, torture, and gruesome forms of execution, such as burning, breaking, disembowelment, impalement, and sawing in half. The 18th century saw the widespread abolition of judicial torture, including the famous prohibition of "cruel and unusual punishment" in the eighth amendment of the U.S. Constitution. 15

At the same time, many nations began to whittle down their list of capital crimes from the hundreds (including poaching, sodomy, witchcraft, and counterfeiting) to just murder and treason. And a growing wave of countries abolished blood sports, dueling, witchhunts, religious persecution, absolute despotism, and slavery. 16

The fourth major transition is the respite from major interstate war that we have seen since the end of World War II. Historians sometimes refer to it as the Long Peace. 17

Today we take it for granted that Italy and Austria will not come to blows, nor will Britain and Russia. But centuries ago, the great powers were almost always at war, and until quite recently, Western European countries tended to initiate two or three new wars every year. The cliché that the 20th century was "the most violent in history" ignores the second half of the century (and may not even be true of the first half, if one calculates violent deaths as a proportion of the world's population). 18

Though it's tempting to attribute the Long Peace to nuclear deterrence,[5] non-nuclear developed states have stopped fighting each other as well. Political scientists point instead to the growth of democracy, trade, and international organizations — all of which, the statistical evidence shows, reduce the likelihood of conflict. They also credit the rising valuation of human life over national grandeur — a hard-won lesson of two world wars. 19

The fifth trend, which I call the New Peace, involves war in the world as a whole, including developing nations. Since 1946, several organizations have tracked the number of armed conflicts and their human toll world-wide. The bad news is that for several decades, the decline of interstate wars was accompanied by a bulge of civil wars, as newly 20

---

[4] Enlightenment (para. 15): Important philosophical movement of the eighteenth century (also known as the Age of Reason).

[5] nuclear deterrence (para. 19): The theory that the buildup of nuclear weapons and accompanying threat of mutual annihilation would prevent the use of such weapons.

independent countries were led by inept governments, challenged by insurgencies, and armed by the cold war superpowers.

The less bad news is that civil wars tend to kill far fewer people than wars between states. And the best news is that, since the peak of the cold war in the 1970s and '80s, organized conflicts of all kinds — civil wars, genocides, repression by autocratic governments, terrorist attacks — have declined throughout the world, and their death tolls have declined even more precipitously.   21

The rate of documented direct deaths from political violence (war, terrorism, genocide, and warlord militias) in the past decade is an unprecedented few hundredths of a percentage point. Even if we multiplied that rate to account for unrecorded deaths and the victims of war-caused disease and famine, it would not exceed 1%.   22

The most immediate cause of this New Peace was the demise of communism, which ended the proxy wars in the developing world stoked by the superpowers and also discredited genocidal ideologies that had justified the sacrifice of vast numbers of eggs to make a utopian omelet. Another contributor was the expansion of international peacekeeping forces, which really do keep the peace — not always, but far more often than when adversaries are left to fight to the bitter end.   23

Finally, the postwar era has seen a cascade of "rights revolutions" — a growing revulsion against aggression on smaller scales. In the developed world, the civil rights movement obliterated lynchings and lethal pogroms, and the women's-rights movement has helped to shrink the incidence of rape and the beating and killing of wives and girlfriends.   24

In recent decades, the movement for children's rights has significantly reduced rates of spanking, bullying, paddling in schools, and physical and sexual abuse. And the campaign for gay rights has forced governments in the developed world to repeal laws criminalizing homosexuality and has had some success in reducing hate crimes against gay people.   25

Why has violence declined so dramatically for so long? Is it because violence has literally been bred out of us, leaving us more peaceful by nature?   26

This seems unlikely. Evolution has a speed limit measured in generations, and many of these declines have unfolded over   27

> ## Why has violence declined so dramatically for so long?

decades or even years. Toddlers continue to kick, bite, and hit; little boys continue to play-fight; people of all ages continue to snipe and bicker, and most of them continue to harbor violent fantasies and to enjoy violent entertainment.

It's more likely that human nature has always comprised inclina- 28
tions toward violence and inclinations that counteract them — such as
self-control, empathy, fairness, and reason — what Abraham Lincoln
called "the better angels of our nature." Violence has declined because
historical circumstances have increasingly favored our better angels.

The most obvious of these pacifying forces has been the state, with 29
its monopoly on the legitimate use of force. A disinterested judiciary
and police can defuse the temptation of exploitative attack, inhibit the
impulse for revenge, and circumvent the self-serving biases that make all
parties to a dispute believe that they are on the side of the angels.

We see evidence of the pacifying effects of government in the way 30
that rates of killing declined following the expansion and consolidation
of states in tribal societies and in medieval Europe. And we can watch
the movie in reverse when violence erupts in zones of anarchy, such as
the Wild West, failed states, and neighborhoods controlled by mafias and
street gangs, who can't call 911 or file a lawsuit to resolve their disputes
but have to administer their own rough justice.

Another pacifying force has been commerce, a game in which every- 31
body can win. As technological progress allows the exchange of goods and
ideas over longer distances and among larger groups of trading partners,
other people become more valuable alive than dead. They switch from
being targets of demonization and dehumanization to potential partners
in reciprocal altruism.

For example, though the relationship today between America and 32
China is far from warm, we are unlikely to declare war on them or vice
versa. Morality aside, they make too much of our stuff, and we owe them
too much money.

A third peacemaker has been cosmopolitanism — the expansion of 33
people's parochial little worlds through literacy, mobility, education, science, history, journalism, and mass media. These forms of virtual reality
can prompt people to take the perspective of people unlike themselves
and to expand their circle of sympathy to embrace them.

These technologies have also powered an expansion of rationality 34
and objectivity in human affairs. People are now less likely to privilege
their own interests over those of others. They reflect more on the way
they live and consider how they could be better off. Violence is often
reframed as a problem to be solved rather than as a contest to be won.
We devote ever more of our brainpower to guiding our better angels. It
is probably no coincidence that the Humanitarian Revolution came on
the heels of the Age of Reason and the Enlightenment, that the Long
Peace and rights revolutions coincided with the electronic global village.

Whatever its causes, the implications of the historical decline of vio- 35
lence are profound. So much depends on whether we see our era as a

nightmare of crime, terrorism, genocide, and war or as a period that, in the light of the historical and statistical facts, is blessed by unprecedented levels of peaceful coexistence.

Bearers of good news are often advised to keep their mouths shut, lest they lull people into complacency. But this prescription may be backward. The discovery that fewer people are victims of violence can thwart cynicism among compassion-fatigued news readers who might otherwise think that the dangerous parts of the world are irredeemable hell holes. And a better understanding of what drove the numbers down can steer us toward doing things that make people better off rather than congratulating ourselves on how moral we are. 36

As one becomes aware of the historical decline of violence, the world begins to look different. The past seems less innocent, the present less sinister. One starts to appreciate the small gifts of coexistence that would have seemed utopian to our ancestors: the interracial family playing in the park, the comedian who lands a zinger on the commander in chief, the countries that quietly back away from a crisis instead of escalating to war. 37

For all the tribulations in our lives, for all the troubles that remain in the world, the decline of violence is an accomplishment that we can savor — and an impetus to cherish the forces of civilization and enlightenment that made it possible. 38

VOCABULARY/USING A DICTIONARY

1. Do you know what a *skeptic* is? What is the definition of *skepticism* (para. 5)?
2. Define *infrastructure* (para. 14). How might you guess its definition by examining parts of the word separately?
3. What does *pacification* (para. 8) mean? From what language does it derive?
4. *Decline* is often used as a verb, meaning "to refuse." In this essay, it is used as another part of speech. What part of speech is *decline* (para. 3), and what does it mean?

RESPONDING TO WORDS IN CONTEXT

1. Pinker refers to the *footage* of some visual media (para. 5). How do you define *footage* in this context? What is its literal meaning?
2. Twice, Pinker uses the word *utopian* in this essay. In one instance, he says that genocides "sacrifice[d] a vast number of eggs to make a utopian omelet" (para. 23), and in the other, he speaks of our current way of living as one that might appear "utopian to our ancestors" (para. 37). Considering the context of his examples, what do you think *utopian* means?
3. Pinker makes a distinction between a *state* and an *empire* in paragraph 10. What is the difference between those terms?

DISCUSSING MAIN POINT AND MEANING

1. Does Pinker think we are evolving into more peaceful beings? Explain his argument.
2. Over this history of humankind, what was one of the earliest lifestyle changes that led to a more peaceful coexistence?
3. What types of past violence does Pinker mention, and how are they used to support his position that things have improved?

EXAMINING SENTENCES, PARAGRAPHS, AND ORGANIZATION

1. Examine the two questions that Pinker begins with and how they differ. Are the questions an effective introduction to the essay? Why or why not?
2. Both *behead* and *decapitate* mean "to cut the head off of." Pinker uses *beheaded* in paragraph 6 and *decapitated* in paragraph 9. Would it make a difference if they were switched? Examine how the particular word choice fits its paragraph.
3. Pinker's essay is one of the longer ones in this textbook. How does he organize his material? Why is this mode of organization effective in a longer essay?

THINKING CRITICALLY

1. Has Pinker left any important areas of "declines of violence" (para. 7) out of his essay? Identify anything that you think has been overlooked.
2. The title of this essay is "Violence Vanquished." Do you think, in light of the violence that still exists, that this is a misleading title? Why or why not?
3. How do you understand "the better angels of our nature" (para. 28)? How do you view humankind's struggle between violent impulses and the desire to counteract them?

WRITING ACTIVITIES

1. What do you think of Pinker's examples? Do you believe that we live in a more violent time or one less violent than times past? In a short essay, explain why you think what Pinker is saying is true or not true.
2. Describe, in writing, a historical event that illustrates the violence of its period or is an example of nonviolent behavior in an otherwise violent time. Research your work after you have described the particular event and see if your research stands in agreement with or in opposition to what you've written.
3. Write an essay that considers the effect of one of the "six major declines of violence" (para. 7) on your own life. Quote examples used in Pinker's essay as you explore their effect of your personal experience. How would your life be different if a particular "decline" had not occurred?

Jacob Ewing (student essay)

Steven Pinker and the Question of Violence

[Ashland University, April 27, 2012]

BEFORE YOU READ

After reading Steven Pinker's "Violence Vanquished" (p. 187), what do you believe about Pinker's claims? Do you find them convincing, or do you think that his interpretation of the data provided left something to be desired?

WORDS TO LEARN

pacifying (para. 5): bringing peace to or quelling anger (adj)

Note: Jacob Ewing's essay was written in response to the following assignment:

Steven Pinker's recent book The Better Angels of Our Nature: Why Violence Has Declined *has provoked a great deal of conversation. After reading carefully the essay, "Violence Vanquished," adapted from his book by the* Wall Street Journal, *join the controversy by writing a short response to Pinker in which you confirm and/or challenge some of his findings and conclusions. Be sure to select several specific claims that Pinker makes and systematically point out their merits or weaknesses. You may bring in additional readings to support your points.*

I n his essay "Violence Vanquished," which appeared in the *Wall Street Journal* (September 24, 2011), the Harvard Professor of Psychology, Steven Pinker, claims that the modern era is the most peaceful time in the history of the human species. He says that now more than ever before, we are less likely to die a violent death at the hands of another human being. He cites statistics that show how violence of all kinds — murder, war, genocide, and so on — have decreased across the board.

Pinker is aware that this fact seems not only unlikely but blatantly wrong, especially in light of the seemingly endless acts of violence that characterize so much of today's news. Yet, despite the horrors in Darfur, Syria, and Iraq and in virtually every major American city, Pinker is likely right in his general claim that violence is diminishing across the globe. It would be hard to argue with his statistics that prove that violence among human beings is at its lowest point in history.

1

2

Jacob Ewing is a student at Ashland University, majoring in English and Spanish.

But there are still some major issues to consider when evaluating Pinker's position. For instance, what exactly constitutes violence in this argument? It would first be helpful to analyze the author's definition. Throughout the piece, he discusses violence in terms of how likely one is to die at the hands of another human being. This is a convenient statistic, especially for an argument as numbers-driven as Pinker's, but violence extends well beyond just murder or warfare. Rape, assault, bullying — these are all ways in which human beings act violent toward one another, yet none of these phenomena are mentioned in his article.

There are still other types of violence that permeate society. Most young boys have, at a certain point in their childhood, gotten into a wrestling match or a fist fight, often with someone very close to them — a brother, a cousin, a best friend. Now, this type of violence is not on par with murder, but it is certainly an aspect of our society that goes unmentioned by Pinker's analysis. Violence manifests itself in modern society in a variety of ways, many of which Pinker ignores and some of which are not extreme enough to even be on his radar.

> Violence manifests itself in modern society in a variety of ways.

In the latter half of the article, Pinker attempts to determine what exactly has caused the decline in violence he has described. He appeals first to modern governments, saying, "The most obvious of these pacifying forces has been the state, with its monopoly on the legitimate use of force." Here again, Pinker's point is not as simple as it appears. The state's ability to monopolize the use of force has absolutely helped quell vigilante justice and personal vendettas, but it has also created a potential for violence that is absolutely unprecedented.

Indeed, one could assume that at this moment, several of the world's major powers have the ability to launch a nuclear attack with weapons far more powerful than those used on Japan at the end of the Second World War, when a single plane dropping one atomic bomb over Hiroshima left over 100,000 human beings dead. The number of deaths that could result in a nuclear attack today is unthinkable. With modern weapons that absolutely dwarf the original atomic bomb, and with so many states having access to such weapons, Pinker's assertion that the state has brought about an alleviation of violence becomes less evident. He would be quick to point out that such an attack has not happened; it might be better to say that such an attack has not happened yet. As Robert Jervis says in his article "Pinker the Prophet," "If we think we're playing Russian roulette, then the fact that we were lucky does not count quite so strongly for our living in a less violent time."[1]

---

[1] *The National Interest*, Issue 116, Nov./Dec. 2011, p. 57.

Pinker also cites the global market as a source for this newfound 7
peace. He points out how unlikely it is for a war to break out between
the United States and China because "they make too much of our stuff,
and we owe them too much money." But the fallacy of this point comes
a paragraph earlier, when Pinker describes commerce as "a game in
which everybody can win." This sentiment holds true when considering two nations like the United States and China — strong centralized
governments, stable economies, freedom from internal conflict. This
allows trade to occur between these two nations in a peaceful, mutually-
beneficial manner.

But what about countries that aren't fortunate enough to be a world 8
power? What about countries where the extraction of precious natural
resources has resulted in some of the most gruesome violence of the
twentieth century? One only need analyze the history of the diamond
trade in Africa to realize the type of violence that can come as a direct
result of commerce. Diamonds are a precious commodity, and any
opportunity to make money in a place like Sierra Leone is likely to end
in violence. Even more recently, the mining of coltan — a mineral used in
most cell phones and laptops — has been the source for violence in the
Democratic Republic of Congo. In these cases, commerce and trade have
actually created violence — not alleviated it.

Pinker is constantly alluding to the Enlightenment as another 9
source for what he calls "the most peaceable era in the existence of our
species." It would be hard to argue that the Enlightenment didn't at least
help people realize that killing one another may not be the best thing to
do. That seems obvious now. But what about people who are raised in
our enlightened society, taught about playing nice and the sanctity of
life and the golden rule, yet still kill people? The list of school-shootings
over the past twenty years is already terrifying and growing by the year.
These acts are carried out by people who are presumably enlightened,
products of our education system, who have had the opportunity to
learn how important and beautiful and sacred life is; yet the shootings
still happen.

Pinker is quick to mention how "about 15% of people in prestate eras 10
died violently," but fails to mention that the populations of these societies were savages by contemporary standards. Death happened at a much
higher rate, but these people were wholly unable to comprehend the
philosophical implications of the deaths they were causing. It was their
way of life, and they didn't have the advanced knowledge to consider that
life might be lived some other way. The same cannot be said about modern day murderers. If our society is truly as enlightened as Pinker likes
to think it is — as we all like to think it is — then the fact that so many
people still function outside of the collective societal reasoning, the fact

that murders happen every day, should be far more shocking than the fact unenlightened savages killed one another at a higher rate than we do today.

Pinker's assertion that violence is in consistent decline is both   11 intriguing and inspiring, but is not as solid as it appears on the surface. To his credit, Pinker readily concedes that violence still has an enormous presence in human society. But the way in which he measures violence — human death caused by another human being — is not necessarily the full story on the matter. Furthermore, his desire to appeal to state power, global commerce, and the modern enlightened mind all have some important implications, as noted above, to which his article does not do justice.

The final claim that Pinker never addresses is an omission for which   12 no one could blame him. One of the most frequent instances of violence over the past decade has been natural disasters — earthquakes, tsunamis, hurricanes, and so on. The amount of human life lost as a result is enormous, yes, but it wouldn't have anything to do with an assessment like Pinker's. Or would it? If one day, the world of science comes to discover that these patterns in extreme weather were caused by human beings, by the way modern society functions, is Pinker's argument changed at all? Are we considerably more violent if that is the case, even if it is unintentional? This is undoubtedly speculative, but if Pinker's project is to consider how violence works on the macro-level, it might not be a bad idea to at least consider the possibility that human beings kill one another in more ways than we realize.

VOCABULARY/USING A DICTIONARY

1. What is the definition of the word *permeate* (para. 4)?
2. What are the origins of the word *quell* (para. 5)?
3. What is the definition of the word *commodity* (para. 8), and what part of speech is it?

RESPONDING TO WORDS IN CONTEXT

1. In paragraph 3, Ewing states, "Rape, assault, bullying—these are all ways in which human beings act violent toward one another, yet none of these phenomena are mentioned in his article." How is the word *phenomena* used here? Is it appropriate for the context? Why or why not?
2. In the sentence, "With modern weapons that absolutely dwarf the original atomic bomb, and with so many states having access to such weapons, Pinker's assertion that the state has brought about an alleviation of violence becomes less evident" (para. 6), what does the word *dwarf* mean, and what part of speech is it?

3. The title of Pinker's essay is "Violence Vanquished." What is the meaning of the word *vanquished,* and based on Ewing's assessment of Pinker's claims, do you believe this word to be appropriate in the title? Why or why not?

DISCUSSING MAIN POINT AND MEANING

1. How does Ewing's definition of violence differ from Pinker's?
2. How does Ewing refute Pinker's claim that the global market is a source of non-violence? Is Ewing's argument effective? Why or why not?
3. According to Ewing, what is the major cognitive difference between modern-day murderers and "savages" who killed each other on a more regular basis?

EXAMINING SENTENCES, PARAGRAPHS, AND ORGANIZATION

1. How does Ewing choose to organize his essay? Is this an effective way to respond to an article? Why or why not?
2. In paragraph 2, Ewing states, "It would be hard to argue with [Pinker's] statistics that prove that violence among human beings is at its lowest point in history." Why do you think Ewing makes this concession, and how does it affect his argument?
3. What is the purpose of the concluding paragraph? How does it support the rest of the essay?

THINKING CRITICALLY

1. Examine the difference between Pinker's definition of violence for the purposes of his argument, and Ewing's definition of violence. Why might Pinker have chosen that measurement of violence for his study?
2. When discussing school shootings, Ewing implies that modern violence is actually more violent simply because humans are enlightened. Do you agree with this assessment? If so, how might you measure violence? If not, do you support Pinker's method of measuring violence?
3. Which of Ewing's arguments do you find the most convincing? Which are the least convincing? Explain your reasoning.

WRITING ACTIVITIES

1. In a short essay, respond to both Ewing's and Pinker's essays. Try to put the texts in conversation with each other, choosing which points to highlight from each, and discussing the strengths and weaknesses of both arguments.
2. If you were going to write a response to Pinker's essay, how would you respond? In a brief essay, explain how you would structure an argument either supporting or refuting Pinker's claims, and then explore how your essay might be different from Ewing's. Look at different aspects such as structure, tone, and overall argument.

Effective Endings

Writers often end their opinion essays by summarizing their main points and position. But there are other — and sometimes more interesting — ways to conclude an essay and engage the reader. Note how Jacob Ewing in "Steven Pinker and the Question of Violence" ends not by summarizing what he'd said earlier but instead by introducing an entirely new point into discussion. He does this in a questioning style that opens up a new perspective on the Pinker article he is critically examining: How would Pinker explain the incredible violence that has affected millions on the planet who have suffered through tsunamis, major hurricanes, and massive earthquakes? These events are certainly violent. Although Pinker is looking at violence primarily as death at the hands of other human beings, Ewing wonders how we might view weather-related violence if it could be attributed to predominately human causes. If so, that would necessitate redefining violence in ways Pinker may not have anticipated.

1
Final paragraph raises a new point about violence

2
Ends by enlarging the potential definition of violence

The final claim that Pinker never addresses is an omission for which no one could blame him. One of the most frequent instances of violence over the past decade has been natural disasters — earthquakes, tsunamis, hurricanes, and so on. The amount of human life lost as a result is enormous, yes, but it wouldn't have anything to do with an assessment like Pinker's. Or would it? If one day, the world of science comes to discover that these patterns in extreme weather were caused by human beings, by the way modern society functions, is Pinker's argument changed at all? (1) Are we considerably more violent if that is the case, even if it is unintentional? This is undoubtedly speculative, but if Pinker's project is to consider how violence works on the macro-level, it might not be a bad idea to at least consider the possibility that human beings kill one another in more ways than we realize. (2)

STUDENT WRITER AT WORK
Jacob Ewing

R.A. What was your main purpose in writing this piece?

J.E. I wanted to question some of the specific claims that Pinker makes about why we as a society are less violent. His tone in the piece has an air of finality, as though no arguments could be made to the contrary. I wanted to ask a few more questions before we closed the discussion. To be sure, Pinker's tone can be attributed to the nature of persuasive writing. I'm willing to bet that Pinker would be glad to have a conversation on the subject.

R.A. How long did it take for you to write this piece? Did you revise your work? What were your goals as you revised?

J.E. The piece didn't take long at all, maybe a week. I revise as I write, so I didn't end up with too many drafts. The goal of my revisions was, as always, clarity and fluidity.

R.A. Do you generally show your writing to friends before submitting it? Do you collaborate or bounce your ideas off others?

J.E. I discussed the topic a few times before I wrote the essay. I'm always in favor of discussing ideas before writing, especially in a piece like this — one that is inherently argumentative or contrarian.

R.A. What do you like to read?

J.E. I read mostly nonfiction, usually essays. I read books more than anything else, but I also enjoy the *New Yorker* and *McSweeney's*. Grantland.com is also a great Web site for sports writing; I read that quite a bit.

R.A. What topics most interest you as a writer?

J.E. The self, I'd say. Most of my essays come back to those sorts of questions in the end: Who am I really, and how do I even go about answering that question?

R.A. Do you plan to continue writing for publication?

J.E. That's the goal.

R.A. Are you pursuing a career in which writing will be a component?

J.E. Not just a component, but pretty much the whole basis. I want to be a writer.

Alex Kotlowitz

Defusing Violence

[*The Rotarian*, February 2012]

BEFORE YOU READ
What's the best way to help communities beset by violence cope with the escalating violence they face every day? How can effectively working toward defusing violence become an effort made by a community?

WORDS TO LEARN

impoverished (para. 1): poor (adj)

shrine (para. 1): places or objects that are considered sacred (noun)

tally (para. 1): a count (noun)

rigorous (para. 2): strict; tough (adj)

deterrent (para. 2): something that discourages or inhibits (noun)

shortcoming (para. 4): an imperfection; a flaw (noun)

emulate (para. 4): to imitate (verb)

epiphany (para. 4): an insight (noun)

glib (para. 4): offhand (adj)

credibility (para. 5): quality of being trustworthy (noun)

empathize (para. 5): to experience empathy (sensitivity to another's experience) (verb)

rant (para. 7): wild talk (noun)

agitated (para. 8): excited or excitedly troubled (adj)

lure (para. 8): to attract or entice (verb)

defuse (para. 8): to make less dangerous (verb)

cajole (para. 9): to persuade or coax (verb)

grievance (para. 9): complaint (noun)

instinctively (para. 9): innately (adv)

potentially (para. 10): possibly (adv)

mediation (para. 11): an attempt to reconcile (noun)

profound (para. 12): deep; wide-reaching (adj)

intercept (para. 13): to seize or halt (verb)

persist (para. 14): to carry on; to persevere (verb)

Alex Kotlowitz is best known for the best-selling novel There Are No Children Here: The Story of Two Boys Growing Up in the Other America *(1991), which was selected by the New York Public Library as one of the 150 most important books of the century. He is also the author of* The Other Side of the River: A Story of Two Towns, a Death and America's Dilemma, *and most recently,* Never a City So Real. *Kotlowitz has contributed to public radio, as well as many magazines and newspapers. He is a writer-in-residence at Northwestern University, and a visiting professor at the University of Notre Dame.*

In the impoverished neighborhoods on Chicago's South and West sides, violence has come to define the landscape. At the end of the last school year, a marquee at Manley High School read: *Have a Peaceful Summer.* Signs for neighborhood block clubs, ordinarily a mark of celebration, detail all that's prohibited. One warns: *No Drug Selling.* Another cautions: *No Gambling.* A city sign declares: *Safe School Zone—increased penalties for gang activities and the use, sale or possession of drugs or weapons in this area.* On street corners and on stoops, in front of stores and in gangways, makeshift shrines appear—candles, empty liquor bottles, stuffed animals, poster board with scrawled remembrances—monuments to the fallen, victims of the epidemic of shootings in our central cities. Politicians have called for the National Guard. Chicago's police superintendent conceded that his officers can't respond to every call of a gun fired because there are so many gunshots. So many children have been murdered that a few years back, the *Chicago Tribune* began to keep a tally of public school students killed. 1

Chicago is not alone. Thirteen cities have higher murder rates, including four—New Orleans, Baltimore, St. Louis, and Detroit—where the rate is more than twice that of Chicago. For the past 10 years, homicide has been the leading cause of death for African American men between the ages of 15 and 24. The response traditionally has been more rigorous policing and longer prison sentences, the notion being that the threat of getting locked up for a long stretch would be a deterrent to anyone even thinking about picking up a gun. But with over 1.5 million people in America's prisons, that feels like a lost argument. Moreover, lock people up, and most come back to their communities one day. (In Chicago alone, an estimated 20,000 to 27,000 men return from prison each year, and most of them to seven neighborhoods.) It's enough to make even the most committed and persistent among us throw up our hands. 2

Yet time and again I have met people in these communities who haven't given up, who see promise where others see despair. 3

Consider Cobe Williams. Now 37, Cobe grew up on Chicago's South Side, in a neighborhood marked by abandoned homes and struggling families. His father was in prison for much of Cobe's youth and, shortly after getting released, when Cobe was 12, was beaten to death by a group of men. Despite his dad's shortcomings, Cobe looked up to him, so he spent many of his teen years trying to emulate his father's life: running with a gang, selling drugs, shooting at others and 4

> Time and again
> I have met people
> in these communi-
> ties who haven't
> given up, who see
> promise where
> others see despair.

getting shot at. Cobe served three stints in prison for a total of 12 years. In his last appearance in court, he had an epiphany of sorts. His four-year-old son ran up to him in tears, and at that moment, Cobe realized he wanted to do better than his dad. He wanted to be a real father to his son. It would perhaps be too glib to suggest that he's changed. Rather, he's figured out who he always was — and who he wants to be.

Cobe is trying to return what he has taken from his community. He   5
works for CeaseFire, a violence prevention program that views shootings through a public health lens. Organizers believe the spread of violence mimics the spread of an infectious disease, so they have hired individuals like Cobe, men and women formerly of the street, to intervene in disputes before they escalate — to interrupt the next shooting. Hence the job title: violence interrupter. Given their pasts, these people have credibility on the streets. And because they've been there themselves, they can empathize with someone intent on revenge. For a year, the film director Steve James and I followed Cobe and two of his colleagues, recording them as they went about their work for our documentary, *The Interrupters.*

One day, Cobe received a call from a young man, Flamo, whom he'd   6
met in the county jail some years earlier and who has a reputation on the streets for, as Cobe says, "taking care of business." Someone had called the police on Flamo, reporting that he had guns in his house. When the police came, Flamo wasn't home, but they found some guns and arrested his brother, who was in a wheelchair as a result of having been shot, and handcuffed his mother. By the time Cobe got to Flamo's house — with us in tow — Flamo had been downing vodka, was packing a pistol, and was waiting for a friend to bring him a stolen car so he could "take care of business." He knew who had called the police and was looking for payback. Boiling with rage, at one point he violently kicked a wall in his house: "You ain't just crossed me, you crossed my mama. For my mama . . . I come in your crib and kill every . . . body."

Cobe told us later he had thought this was a lost cause, a failed inter-   7
ruption. But about 10 minutes into his rant, Flamo turned to Cobe and asked, "How can you help me? Right now. How can you help me?"

It was a plea, really. If Cobe were the police, he might have arrested   8
Flamo at that point, but instead, Cobe did something so simple it seems almost laughable: He asked Flamo to lunch. They headed to a nearby chicken shack, where Flamo, still agitated, called a friend to get some bullets. But Cobe asked Flamo who would take care of his kids if he got locked up. He reminded Flamo that his mother needed him. He bought some time. Cobe then lured Flamo down to CeaseFire's office and invited him to attend the weekly meeting of the Interrupters — men and women with résumés similar to Cobe's whose job, like his, is to suss out simmering disputes in their neighborhoods and try to defuse them.

By the time the meeting was over, Flamo had calmed down enough that he no longer was intent — at least at the moment — on exacting revenge.

I suppose the story could end here, but what's so striking is how Cobe 9 stayed with Flamo, calling him, taking him out for meals, cajoling him to get a job. In the end, I came to realize that all Flamo had needed was someone to listen, someone to acknowledge his grievance, someone to believe in him. Cobe knew this instinctively. In his own life, Cobe had a grandmother who refused to give up on him. Despite all the trouble he had gotten into, Cobe told me, "She never turned her back on me."

Over the course of the 14 months of filming, it became apparent 10 that the one constant for those like Cobe and Flamo, for those who were able to emerge from the wreckage of their lives and their neighborhoods, for those who were able to walk away from a potentially violent encounter, was to have someone in their lives with high expectations for them, someone who treated them with a sense of dignity and decency, someone who wasn't afraid to slap them across the head when they did something wrong (when Cobe was a teenager, his grandmother had refused to bond him out of jail) but who never viewed them as inherently bad. Someone who saw something in them that others didn't.

Cobe and the others around the CeaseFire Interrupters table practice 11 old-fashioned conflict mediation, which is used by a handful of community organizations across the United States, including some that have directly replicated CeaseFire's public health approach. But what Cobe and his colleagues have come to realize is that keeping someone from shooting someone one day is no guarantee that person won't shoot someone the next week — so they stay with that person. They don't let go.

This is not to discount all the forces working against those who are 12 growing up in the profound poverty of our cities. If we are serious about addressing violence, people — especially young people — must believe in their own futures. And believe they have a future. These are neighborhoods where the schools are still lousy, where blocks are littered with foreclosed homes,[1] where jobs are hard to come by. These are neighborhoods physically and spiritually isolated from the rest of us. These are neighborhoods where young people can look at the city's glittering skyline and realize their place in the world. These are neighborhoods where the American dream is a fiction.

Cobe and his colleagues know that, but they plow ahead, trying to 13 intercept the next potential shooting, trying to pull people off the ledge. But mediating conflicts is more than just persuading people to go their

---

[1] foreclosed (para. 12): The proceeding by which a bank attempts to regain property in the event that a borrower defaults on payments.

separate ways. The Interrupters look to give people a way to walk away while maintaining their self-respect. At one point while we were filming, Ameena Matthews, another of the Interrupters, persuaded a young man who'd just been hit in the mouth with a rock not to retaliate. "I saw that you was walking away, to defend you and your family," Ameena told him. "Man, I thank you. I mean for real. For real, that's what gangster is about right there." She was telling him that it was really "gangster" of him to walk away, that that was the best way he could defend his family. Now that's turning things on their head.

It may seem self-evident, but it's worth contemplating nonetheless: Once people stop believing in you, you stop believing in yourself. The Interrupters recognize that. It's not enough simply to step between two people and push them apart. You need to persist, to listen, and to give them something to hold on to, something that gives them a sense of possibility, whether it's a job, a decent place to live, an education, or just a helping hand. 14

At one point, Flamo told Cobe: "I was really plottin' on how to get them. But you was just in my ear . . . You constantly in my ear. You buggin' — me for a minute. . . . You know how that be — like I'm sleepin', the fly keep landin' on you, you know what I'm sayin'? You's buggin' me till eventually I had to get up and attend to that fly." 15

At a screening of the film in Chicago, a teenage girl from the South Side got up to ask a question. She was near tears. She talked about how hard her life was, how she was getting into fights, how she was doing all she could not to give up. She turned to Flamo, who was in attendance, and asked him: "What do I do? What do I do, *now*?" Flamo pointed to Cobe and told her: "Take my fly." 16

VOCABULARY/USING A DICTIONARY

1. What does *prohibit* mean? What sorts of items are *prohibited* (para. 1)?
2. What does the word *stint* (para. 4) mean in this essay, and what part of speech is it?
3. What's the definition of *intervene* (para. 5)? From what language does it come?

RESPONDING TO WORDS IN CONTEXT

1. What kind of phrase is *suss out* (para. 8)? Where does it come from?
2. Cobe gets to Flamo's house with Kotlowitz's film team "in tow" (para. 6). What does *in tow* mean?
3. Kotlowitz says that Ameena's use of the word *gangster* (para. 13) really "turn[s] things on their head." What does *gangster* mean? What does *gangster* mean when Ameena says it?

DISCUSSING MAIN POINT AND MEANING

1. What is Kotlowitz's documentary about?
2. How did Cobe help Flamo back away from a violent reaction when he was on the cusp of behaving violently?
3. Why is Kotlowitz and James's film called *The Interrupters*? Is it an apt title?

EXAMINING SENTENCES, PARAGRAPHS, AND ORGANIZATION

1. How is the connection between violence and illness made in the essay? Where and how is that connection stressed?
2. Kotlowitz organizes the essay around certain characters and images, just as he organizes his documentary around them. Where does the essay feel most cinematic? Explain.
3. "Defusing Violence" begins with a description of Chicago's South and West sides, stressing the hopelessness and violence found there. Is this an effective way for Kotlowitz to begin his essay? Why or why not?

THINKING CRITICALLY

1. Kotlowitz writes, "Organizers [of CeaseFire] believe the spread of violence mimics the spread of an infectious disease, so they have hired individuals like Cobe, men and women formerly of the street, to intervene in disputes before they escalate—to interrupt the next shooting" (para. 5). How is violence like an infectious disease, and how is it different?
2. Why is CeaseFire effective? Do you think there are other actions that can be taken to help?
3. Prisons are meant to deter people from violence and punish them once they have committed violence; however, Kotlowitz argues that they are ineffective. Do you think he has a point? Is there a way to make the prison system more effective?

WRITING ACTIVITIES

1. Recommend, in writing, that someone watch Kotlowitz's documentary. As you plug the film, try to give your reader a flavor of what he or she will see and convince someone of the importance of the work, based on what you've read in this essay.
2. Do you have a "fly" (para. 15) in your life who is there for you in the way Cobe is there for Flamo? Write a brief character sketch describing that person and his or her influence on you. (If you don't have a "fly," imagine what attributes such a person would have and how he or she might help you.)
3. Imagine living in a neighborhood similar to the one Kotlowitz describes in his first paragraph. With that neighborhood in mind, write a persuasive essay about why CeaseFire should be brought in. What are the worst issues plaguing the community and how do you think CeaseFire might help?

Annette John-Hall

Using Video Games to Reduce Violence

[*Philadelphia Inquirer*, February 3, 2012]

BEFORE YOU READ
How do you feel about violent video games? Were you allowed to play them as a child? If so, how do you think they affected you later in life?

WORDS TO LEARN
credo (para. 13): a statement of beliefs or aims (noun)

aficionado (para. 14): a person who is very knowledgeable and enthusiastic about a subject (noun)

We've heard it for years — a violent culture begets violence. 1

Conventional wisdom says, if you want to understand the 2 not-so-subliminal reasons for incivility, you don't have to look any further than the movies, the music, and the video games — the elements of pop culture we so readily identify with and glorify.

Those blasted video games are the worst. Violent video games, more 3 than violent television shows or movies, can increase aggressive thoughts and behaviors because they're interactive. At least that's what the American Psychological Association says.

Always sounded a little simplistic to me. I can't imagine a video game 4 having more of an influence on a kid than a parent. But when Philadelphia has suffered 34 homicides in 33 days, you can't help but wonder about everything.

> Parents are using video games as effective tools for raising their children.

What I do know is, I didn't expect to 5 come to this conclusion.

How about this: Yes, young people are 6 playing violent video games, but as a way to decrease their aggressive thoughts, not increase them.

And parents are using video games as 7 effective tools for raising their children.

Annette John-Hall is a columnist for the Philadelphia Inquirer. *A native of Berkeley, California, she is a former sports writer for the* San Jose Mercury News, *the* Rocky Mountain News, *and the* Oakland Tribune.

That "aha" moment presented itself at the University Family Fun Center in University City, where Eric Small reigns as the gaming king supreme with a joystick as scepter. 8

It wasn't always this way a decade or so ago when many of the city's arcades, including Family Fun, were considered hot spots for crime. 9

But that was before Small, 39, better known as "Big E," took his childhood passion for gaming and parlayed it into international tournaments held right here in Philly. Next up is Winter Brawl 6, Feb. 18 and 19 at the Sheraton Suites Philadelphia Airport, where Small expects more than 1,000 gamers to take it out on each other — but only on the video screens. 10

"Never had a problem," says Small, who is as affable as he is a physical contradiction to his name. "I have security at the door to make sure nobody walks out with a PlayStation, but [the competition] is all friendly arguing and bickering." 11

Small's gamers battle in games like *Street Fighter* and *Soul Calibur V*, master assassins and superheroes fighting to the death. 12

You would think any game that takes Leonardo da Vinci's quote "Our life is made by the death of others" as its credo was just the kind of violent indoctrination that easily impressed minds don't need. 13

But actually, says Kenneth Scott, a *Street Fighter* aficionado, its effect is the opposite. 14

"If I was mad at school, I would go home and play *Street Fighter*," says Scott, a student at Community College of Philadelphia. "It was therapeutic." 15

(I can just see Scott taking cleansing breaths as he blows his on-screen enemies to smithereens.) 16

I'll admit I don't see the appeal. Watching Scott playing *Street Fighter* has all the nuance of typists working in those back-in-the-day steno pools[1] — frantically banging on buttons seemingly with no rhyme or reason. But gamers say there is a method to the kill — the deft combination of hand-eye coordination with a chess player's anticipation. 17

"I used to teach my sons through video games. It's about pattern recognition and being adaptive," says Victor Melbourne, 38, a childhood pal of Small's and a longtime gamer. "You can get some good bonding time in, too. I'd lose to them on purpose and sneak the knowledge in later. . . . It's like putting medicine in ice cream." 18

Small credits gaming with expanding his own horizons. He has traveled as far away as Japan to promote his tournaments. 19

Tournament competition allows kids to meet and interact with new people, says Vada Golphin, 19. The homies he sees hanging on the corner don't get that. 20

---

[1] steno pool (para. 17): A group of office workers known as stenographers who were assigned the task of typing letters and documents written in shorthand.

They just become targets for real violence.   21

"Here," Golphin says, "the violence ends once the game is over. Any   22
beef you have stays on the screen."

VOCABULARY/USING A DICTIONARY

1. What does the word *subliminal* mean (para. 2), and how was it originally used?
2. What is a *scepter* (para. 8), and what are the origins of the word?
3. What does the word *affable* (para. 11) mean? List two similes as well as the definition.

RESPONDING TO WORDS IN CONTEXT

1. In paragraph 2, John-Hall uses the phrase *conventional wisdom*. What does this phrase mean?
2. What does John-Hall mean when she says that Small is "as affable as he is a physical contradiction to his name" (para. 11)?
3. In paragraph 17, John-Hall writes, "Watching Scott playing *Street Fighter* has all the nuance of typists working in those back-in-the-day steno pools." What does *nuance* mean in this context, and what statement is she making about watching Scott play *Street Fighter*?

DISCUSSING MAIN POINT AND MEANING

1. Does John-Hall's argument follow or refute conventional wisdom?
2. List three positive outcomes of video games that John-Hall mentions in her essay.
3. How would you categorize John-Hall's essay? Is it an argument? A journalistic article? A personal essay? What specifically in the piece supports your categorization?

EXAMINING SENTENCES, PARAGRAPHS, AND ORGANIZATION

1. What type of support does John-Hall use as evidence for her argument?
2. How does John-Hall organize her essay? Do you find this organization effective? Why or why not?
3. How do the quotes John-Hall chooses to use support her argument? Choose one quote that you think is particularly effective and examine why that quotation works well within the context of the essay.

THINKING CRITICALLY

1. Do you agree or disagree with John-Hall's argument about video games and violence? Why?
2. John-Hall's essay focuses on the violence in video games, but she also mentions several other aspects of pop culture that are often blamed for

inciting violence. Do you think video games differ from these other types of media? Why or why not?

3. Think of another piece of conventional wisdom that you find to be untrue and explain why you don't think it should be a commonly held belief.

WRITING ACTIVITIES

1. Write a short essay in which you explore how video games have affected your life. Do you play them regularly? Does that affect your daily interaction with people? If you don't play, have you seen video games affect the people around you, in either a positive or a negative way?

2. Even if you agree with John-Hall's argument, evaluate her essay point by point, and for every support for her argument, think of a way to counter that support. Essentially, you want to build an argument against her by refuting her reasons for support.

3. In a short essay, evaluate why John-Hall might have chosen the three people she did to interview. What do they all have in common, and why might John-Hall have thought they were representative of the violent video game-playing community?

Spotlight on Law and Society

Robert Atwan

Can the State Prohibit the Sale of Violent Video Games to Minors?

[*U.S. Supreme Court, Brown v. Entertainment Merchants Association*, June 27, 2011]

The United States Supreme Court in June 2011 struck down a California law   1
that prohibited the sale or rental of violent video games to children under the age of eighteen. The California law, enacted in 2005, was based primarily on psychological research that showed "a connection between exposure to violent video games and harmful effects on children." But the Court refused to buy into these studies, countering that the "studies have been rejected by every court to consider them . . . and with good reason: They do not prove that violent video games cause minors to act aggressively (which would at least be a beginning)." The Court did not find compelling one study which "found that children who had just finished playing violent video games were more likely to fill in the blank letter in 'explo_e' with a 'd' (so that it reads 'explode') than with an 'r' ('explore')."

At first, the California law might appear to be a morally conservative   2
step to help curtail violence. Yet, it was opposed by one of the Supreme

continued

Court's most notable conservatives, Antonin Scalia, who wrote the majority decision. Scalia basically maintained that the law violated the First Amendment of the Constitution; video games, he argued, were a form of protected speech. He thought, too, that if the law's purpose was to prevent the exposure of minors to violence, then why not prohibit depictions of violence in other forms, such as Saturday morning TV cartoons? Why single out video games? He thought this focus on just the games raised "serious doubts about whether the State is pursuing the interest it invokes or is instead disfavoring a particular speaker or viewpoint." In addition, he argued, that the law violated the rights of young people whose parents or guardians approved of the games.

Scalia thought that "California's argument would fare better if there were   3 a longstanding tradition in this country of specially restricting children's access to depictions of violence, but there is none." "Certainly," he wrote, "the books we give children to read — or read to them when they are younger — contain no shortage of gore. Grimm's Fairy Tales, for example, are grim indeed. As her just deserts for trying to poison Snow White, the wicked queen is made to dance in red hot slippers till she fell dead on the floor, a sad example of envy and jealousy'. . . . Cinderella's evil stepsisters have their eyes pecked out by doves. And Hansel and Gretel (children!) kill their captor by baking her in an oven." A cursory glance at a typical high school reading list shows that violence isn't confined to video games alone: "Golding's *Lord of the Flies* recounts how a schoolboy called Piggy is savagely murdered by other children while marooned on an island."

Although six of the other justices sided with Scalia, two of them had   4 some reservations about the Court's decision. Justices Samuel Alito and Chief Justice John Roberts were skeptical that video games could be easily lumped with books, movies, and other kinds of protected speech. In his concurring opinion, Samuel Alito warned that new technologies could be grounds for new judicial thinking about free expression. Both Alito and Roberts sympathized with the goals of the California legislators:

"The California statute that is before us in this case represents a pio-   5 neering effort to address what the state legislature and others regard as a potentially serious social problem: the effect of exceptionally violent video games on impressionable minors, who often spend countless hours immersed in the alternative worlds that these games create. Although the California statute is well intentioned, its terms are not framed with the precision that the Constitution demands, and I therefore agree with the Court that this particular law cannot be sustained.

I disagree, however, with the approach taken in the Court's opinion.   6 In considering the application of unchanging constitutional principles to new and rapidly evolving technology, this Court should proceed with caution. We should make every effort to understand the new technology. We should take into account the possibility that developing technology may have important societal implications that will become apparent only with time. We should not jump to the conclusion that new technology is fundamentally the same as some older thing with which we are familiar. And we should not hastily dismiss the judgment of legislators, who may be in a better position than we are to assess the implications of new technology. The opinion of the Court exhibits none of this caution. . . .

When all of the characteristics of video games are taken into account,   7
there is certainly a reasonable basis for thinking that the experience of playing a video game may be quite different from the experience of reading a book, listening to a radio broadcast, or viewing a movie. And if this is so, then for at least some minors, the effects of playing violent video games may also be quite different. The Court acts prematurely in dismissing this possibility out of hand."

In the two dissenting opinions, Justices Stephen Breyer and Clar-   8
ence Thomas agreed with the California legislators, arguing that the Court viewed the First Amendment too broadly and that there is a long-standing history of American courts protecting minors since colonial times. In a pages-long appendix to the dissent, they attached an enormous number of research studies showing that "there is substantial (though controverted) evidence supporting the expert associations of public health professionals that have concluded that violent video games can cause children psychological harm."

Although the California law was struck down, the differences of opinion   9
expressed by the Supreme Court regarding the protection of minors, free speech, the value of research studies, and new technologies, indicate that the video-game violence issue may be far from settled.

DRAWING CONCLUSIONS

1. Do you think that the violence depicted in video games is similar to that depicted in literature or film? What do you make of that comparison? In what ways does the violence in video games differ? How important are those differences in deciding whether video games constitute an entirely different medium of expression?

2. Read over carefully the statement by Justice Alito. Though he agreed to overturn the California law, in what way do his comments undercut the authority of the majority decision? What legal possibilities is he opening up?

3. Do you think that psychological research conducted by professionals could sway a court's decision one way or the other? Why or why not? In your opinion, what sort of study could have a decisive impact on legal thinking in this matter?

Discussing the Unit

SUGGESTED TOPIC FOR DISCUSSION

The essays in this unit debate whether our current time period is more or less violent than other times in history. Do you think violence is being vanquished? Is it possible to diffuse areas of violence in the United States, such as the violence found in the South and West sides of Chicago? What does it take to get a society, or a species, to be less violent?

PREPARING FOR CLASS DISCUSSION

1. Have we moved away from the violence found in past times? What information do you find in the essays that supports this idea?
2. How have people helped each other overcome violence? What are some examples these essays offer of existing violence today?

FROM DISCUSSION TO WRITING

1. Are the CeaseFire Interrupters in Kotlowitz's essay at all comparable to Pinker's "better angels"? In writing, compare the two ideas and discuss any parallels you see between them.
2. Each essay describes violence in its own way. How do their definitions of violence match your own? Can you add anything to the list of what constitutes violence?
3. In what ways can Annette John-Hall's column be used to support Pinker's claim that the world is growing less violent?

TOPICS FOR CROSS-CULTURAL DISCUSSION

1. What do you think of the discrepancies in Pinker's argument, pointed out by Ewing? Does Pinker's essay take a particular view of Western culture when he says violence is diminishing? What differences has Ewing noted about other cultures?
2. What about the culture of Chicago's South and West sides is changed by the CeaseFire Interrupters? Where is that apparent in the essay?

This chapter continues online. Visit the e-Page at bedfordstmartins.com/americanow/epages for an interactive quiz.

8

The American Language Today: How Is It Changing?

Can educators blame the new media technology for encouraging sloppy writing and careless expression, or are the new styles of writing and spelling an inevitable result of texting, tweeting, and other types of new messaging? What about spelling? Do we need to reinforce old rules, create new ones, or abandon rules entirely? In "Spelling Matters," Mikita Brottman, writing for a specialized magazine of higher education, believes that poor spelling indicates an inattention to detail and defends standards of English: "Is it really fussy to suggest that someone with a PhD should be able to spell the name of her own specialty?" But taking a different view, another educator, Anne Trubek, reminds us that spelling rules are historically recent and aren't set in stone. In "Use Your Own Words," she argues that "with new technologies, the way we write and read (and search and data-mine) is changing, and so must spelling."

Anyone who sends and receives messages knows that the once rarely used exclamation point has now become one of the most common forms of punctuation. In "We Get the Point!" journalist Christopher Muther complains about the overuse of false emphasis—using an exclamation point just to say "Thanks!"—but at the same time realizes their usefulness in electronic communication, in which it is too easy to sound abrupt and unfriendly. As Muther puts it, "In the digital era, a sentence without an exclamation doesn't pack the same wallop it once did."

In "Words Are What We Make of Them," University of Hawai'i student Shayna Diamond takes a broader look at our language today. She believes that an oppressive, narrow-minded "politically-correct" attitude has grown into a "socially expected norm" that stifles free expression: "The absurdly closed-minded and over-analytical atmosphere," she writes, "that has been adopted under the guise of protecting others does nothing but smother self-expression and limit the possibility of becoming a more tolerant and understanding people."

How did people text message before the days of the Internet and the smart phone? "America Then . . . 1844" features the cutting-edge communication technology of its time: the telegram, an item most young people have only seen, if at all, in old movies.

The e-Page at the end of the chapter is a thought-provoking video that argues that grammar and spelling aren't taken into account when ranking Web page reliability, but they tend to line up with how reliable the site actually is.

Does Spelling Count?

BEFORE YOU READ

What does another's ability (or inability) to spell tell you about him or her? Do you think standardized spellings of words are important? If changes in communication (like text messaging, for example) move us away from rules that have been in place for hundreds of years, will anyone care? More importantly, will we still be able to understand each other?

Mikita Brottman

Spelling Matters

[*The Chronicle of Higher Education*, January 15, 2012]

WORDS TO LEARN

diversity (para. 1): variety (noun)

protocol (para. 2): etiquette; code of behavior (noun)

egregious (para. 2): glaringly bad (adj)

paramount (para. 4): of utmost importance (adj)

pedant (para. 4): someone who makes a great show of his or her learning (noun)

assumption (para. 4): something taken for granted or assumed (noun)

proficiency (para. 5): skill (noun)

arcane (para. 9): mysterious; obscure (adj)

A couple of years ago, I was on a hiring committee for a position in counseling psychology that had proved difficult to fill. During one of our meetings, we were handed the résumé of an applicant the chair was eager to hire, not only because her experience and qualifications seemed tailor-made for the post, but also because she was

1

Mikita Brottman is a psychoanalyst, author, and cultural critic. She currently teaches in the Department of Humanistic Studies at the Maryland Institute College of Art. Her articles have appeared in The Chronicle of Higher Education, *the* Fortean Times, Baltimore Style, Film Quarterly, *and the* American Journal of Psychoanalysis, *among others.*

a diversity candidate (which, I gathered, meant a candidate who was not Caucasian). Looking over the document, however, I noticed three spelling errors on the first page, one of which was in the candidate's field of expertise, which she had described as "complimentary medicine." I glanced at my colleagues. Would anyone else mention it? If not, should I?

I hesitated for two reasons: First, I was the only humanist on a com- 2 mittee of psychologists, and I didn't want to seem like a nit-picker; and second, I was a newcomer to the institution and unfamiliar with pro- tocol. Still, when everyone else expressed approval of the candidate, I couldn't stop myself. In my experience, I said, egregious misspellings in a résumé are grounds for instant rejection. When asked for examples, I pointed to the phrase "complimentary medicine." Two members of the committee still did not see a problem, compelling me to explain the dif- ference between "complimentary" and "complementary."

Even then, the error was not taken seriously. One person described it as a 3 "typo." "I always get mixed up between 'insure' and 'ensure,'" said another. The dean suggested that this candidate, while obviously a strong clinician, might not be especially polished when it came to "the academic side of things."

I left the meeting feeling both indignant — what is a university, after 4 all, but a place where "the academic side of things" is paramount? — but also afraid I'd come across as a pedant or, worse, a racist. Beyond this, while I've never thought of myself as a grammar Nazi, I was baffled, not so much by my colleagues' disregard for standards of acceptable Eng- lish as by their assumption that such errors shouldn't stand in the way of hiring a person who, in all other respects, was just what they were looking for. The assumption of my colleagues was that to be an effective therapist and a successful teacher of clinical skills, polished writing isn't necessary.

That may very well be true, but still, a certain level of proficiency 5 should surely be taken for granted. Is it really fussy to suggest that someone with a PhD should be able to spell the name of her own specialty? To me, as to most of my colleagues in the humanities, grammar and style are inseparable from "meaning," whereas to the other members of the hiring committee, spelling mistakes were minor issues that had little bearing on the underlying information. The same problem arose when I gave low grades, in a clinical-psychology course, to papers full of grammar, syntax, and punctuation mistakes. The students were indignant and offended, and complained to the program chair. ("This isn't an English class!")

It wasn't an English class, true, but in most universities in the United 6 States, English is the medium of instruction, and regardless of subject, I expect my students to abide by the rules of ordinary English prose. That, at least, was what I said at the time.

But the more I think about it now, the trickier the question becomes. 7 After all, I realize, there are always limits to the errors I correct. I don't correct em dashes that should be en dashes, for example; I don't correct misplaced hyphens, I don't fuss about spaces after periods, extra dots in an ellipsis, or margin widths. My corrections are always limited to more-obvious errors (at least, obvious to me), such as misplaced apostrophes, subject-object agreement, illogical fragments, and run-on sentences. But if I'm going to pay attention to errors, shouldn't I try to be consistent?

Another question: If a student is permitted to reach the PhD level without being able to spell the name of her specialty, should she be solely to blame? Did her supervisor never notice or draw attention to the error? What if the candidate were not a native speaker? Should she have been given leeway? Researchers in the field of language-order dyslexia[1] have suggested that difficulties with spelling could be rooted in our genes, and in the way that our brains are wired. Biology, it seems, influences not only those with dyslexia but also people without the syndrome, so those with spelling problems can, to a certain extent, blame their genetic makeup. If that is true, should "bad" spellers be given the same rights as everyone else, despite their problematic prose? 8

Finally, if there are plenty of professors who do not recognize what (to me, at least) are blindingly obvious errors, perhaps the problem is not theirs, but mine. Perhaps I am, in fact, an old-fashioned pedant, pre-judiced against the modern age with its relaxed spelling rules. Perhaps I'm naïve to expect job candidates not to make spelling mistakes on their résumés. In the end, my pointing out the candidate's bad spelling did not make her look stupid or foolish or incompetent or careless — it just made me look picky and arcane. Perhaps it's me, not the job candidate, who needs re-educating. 9

But I'm glad I stood my ground by at least speaking out. In an age of spell-check and grammar-check, it's not very difficult to avoid large and obvious errors of this kind. After all, when I type "complimentary medicine" into a search engine, I'm immediately asked, "Do you mean complementary medicine?" Indeed, at a time when most job searches are yielding hundreds of résumés, bad spelling can be a godsend — a way of weeding out those who are thoughtless and 10

> Bad spelling can be a godsend — a way of weeding out those who are thoughtless and inattentive to detail.

inattentive to detail, or who simply don't think that spelling matters. To my mind, while accurate spelling may be only one aspect of attention to detail, dismissing it is symptomatic of a potentially more significant lack of care.

---

[1] dyslexia (para. 8): A reading disorder that makes it hard for the sufferer to read and spell.

Anne Trubek

Use Your Own Words

[*Wired*, February 2012]

WORDS TO LEARN

innocuous (para. 1): harmless (adj)

collate (para. 1): to arrange; to order (verb)

cite (para. 2): to quote; to mention (verb)

arbitrary (para. 3): unsupported or whimsical (adj)

determinate (para. 5): definite; conclusively determined (adj)

concise (para. 6): brief; succinct (adj)

inertia (para. 6): the state of rest or inactivity (noun)

ensure (para. 7): to guarantee (verb)

A misspelled tweet describing a crush as adorable is changed to say she is "affordable." The text message "I like himm" is changed to "I like Himmler.[1]" Damn you, autocorrect! By now most of us have had unfortunate experiences with autocorrection software — innocuous messages turned anatomical or lunch plans morphed into love notes. (Pro tip: Don't ever abbreviate Wednesday.) Damn You Autocorrect! is even the name of a popular website that collates hilariously obtuse examples of texts perverted by software assistants.

Our supposedly helpful correction software isn't doing us any favors, and not just because it routinely turns easily decipherable errors into bizarre non sequiturs. And definitely not for any of the reasons your third-grade English teacher might cite: that it makes us lazy or robs us of our ability to spell. No, autocorrect and spellcheckers are wrongheaded because they reinforce a traditional spelling standard. Consistent spelling was a great way to ensure clarity in the print era. But with new technologies, the way that we write and read (and search and data-mine) is changing, and so must spelling.

---

[1] Himmler (para. 1): Refers to Heinrich Himmler, a leader of the Nazi party.

Anne Trubek is a writer, editor, and associate professor of Rhetoric and Composition & English at Oberlin College. She has published articles in the New York Times, The Atlantic, Wired, *the* Washington Post, *and* The Chronicle of Higher Education, *among others, and is the author of* A Skeptic's Guide to Writers' Houses *(2010).*

English spelling is a terrible mess anyway, full of arbitrary contriv-   3
ances and exceptions that outnumber rules. Why *receipt* but *deceit*? *Water*
but *daughter*? *Daughter* but *laughter*? What is the logic behind the *ough* in
through, dough, and *cough*? Instead of trying to get the letters right with
imperfect tools, it would be far better to loosen our idea of correct spelling.

The notion that words can and should be spelled only one way is a   4
fairly recent invention. "The phrase 'bad speller' rarely appears in English-
language books before the 1770s," Jack Lynch notes in his book *The
Lexicographer's Dilemma.* Until William Caxton used a printing press
in 1475, English words were reproduced by scribes in scriptoria. There
were no dictionaries (or Google) to check for "proper" spelling. Most
words were spelled several different ways — there were at least 114 vari-
ants of *through*. (Even the spelling of something as personal as a name was
inconsistent; there are six surviving instances of Shakespeare's signature,
and they're all spelled differently.) Even after the advent of print, variant
spellings were the rule. Typesetters would alter spellings to help them
justify type (perhaps this is how *deceit* lost its *p*?).

And it's not like things are set in stone — in fact, advocating for a   5
more sensible English spelling system is a noble American tradition. In
1768, Benjamin Franklin published "A Scheme for a New Alphabet and
Reformed Mode of Spelling," a treatise that laid out a detailed plan for
making spelling sensible. He invented three new vowels and removed *c,
j, q, w, x,* and *y* from our alphabet. Noah Webster (of *Webster's Dictionary*) agreed with many of Franklin's suggestions and came up with more
of his own, some of which were accepted: Webster is why the American spelling of *color* has no *u*. Mark Twain placed the blame for spelling
errors on "this present silly alphabet, which I fancy was invented by a
drunken thief," and proposed a "sane, determinate" alternative with "a
system of accents, giving to each vowel its own soul and value."

So who shud tell us how to spel? Our-   6
selves. Language is not static — or constantly degenerating, as many claim. It is
ever evolving, and spelling evolves, too, as
we create new words, styles, and guidelines
(rules governing use of the semicolon date

> So who shud tell
> us how to spel?
> Ourselves.

to the 18th century, meaning they're a more recent innovation than the
steam engine). The most widely used American word in the world, *OK,*
was invented during the age of the telegraph because it was concise. No
one considers it, or abbreviations like ASAP and IOU, a sign of corrup-
tion. More recent textisms signal a similarly creative, bottom-up play
with language: "won" becomes "1," "later" becomes "l8r." After all, new
technology creates new inertia for change: The apostrophe requires an

additional step on an iPhone, so we send text messages using "your" (or "UR") instead of "you're." And it doesn't matter — the messagee will still understand our message.

Standardized spelling enables readers to understand writing, to aid communication and ensure clarity. Period. There is no additional reason, other than snobbery, for spelling rules. Computers, smartphones, and tablets are speeding the adoption of more casual forms of communication — texting is closer to speech than letter writing. But the distinction between the oral and the written is only going to become more blurry, and the future isn't auto-correct, it's Siri.[2] We need a new set of tools that recognize more variations instead of rigidly enforcing outdated dogma. Let's make our own rules. It's not like the English language has many good ones anyway.

7

VOCABULARY/USING A DICTIONARY

1. In paragraph 5, Trubek incorporates stories of those who made *advocating* for sensible English spelling rules their mission. What is an *advocate*? And what does it mean to *advocate*?
2. In Brottman's essay she refers to a job candidate's *résumé* (para. 1). What is a *résumé*? Why are the accent marks important? From what language is it borrowed?
3. The word *justify* (Trubek, para. 4) has more than one meaning. What does the word *justify* mean, and what do you think it means in the context of Trubek's essay?
4. *Symptomatic* (Brottman, para. 9) is what part of speech? What is a *symptom*?

RESPONDING TO WORDS IN CONTEXT

1. The word *message* (Trubek, paras. 1 and 6) and the word *messagee* (para. 6) differ by only one letter. Define each term.
2. Trubek states that until the invention of the printing press, "English words were reproduced by scribes in scriptoria" (para. 4). Even if you don't know the definition of the word *scriptoria*, how might you guess its definition from its root or from the words in the quoted clause?
3. Brottman takes issue with the job candidate's use of the word *complimentary*, when she meant *complementary*. Even if you don't exactly know what "complementary medicine" is, how might you guess what it means from the definition of the word *complementary*? How might you guess at the definition of *complimentary*?
4. What does Brottman mean when she talks about "the way our brains are *wired*" (para. 8)?

---

[2] Siri (para. 7): A voice-activated "personal assistant" software available on the iPhone.

DISCUSSING MAIN POINT AND MEANING

1. Why does Brottman believe the résumé errors might be grounds for immediately disqualifying such a promising candidate?
2. How do changes in technology influence changing spelling rules? How do you understand the history of the current rules given Trubek's explanation?
3. In paragraph 3 of "Use Your Own Words," several English spelling inconsistencies are mentioned. In "Spelling Matters," Brottman points out two confusingly close word pairs in the English language (*compliment/ complement, insure/ensure*). How do these inconsistencies and confusions illustrate the contradictory points the authors are making?

EXAMINING SENTENCES, PARAGRAPHS, AND ORGANIZATION

1. Brottman focuses on only one of the "three spelling errors on the first page" of the candidate's résumé. Does it matter that you don't know what the others are? Why do you think she chose not to discuss them all?
2. What is the effect of Trubek including the misspelled sentence "So who shud tell us how to spel"?
3. Trubek uses several historical figures and examples to illustrate her point about the evolution of language and changes in spelling. What is it about these particular figures and examples that lends weight to her argument?
4. Consider the repetition of the word *perhaps* in Brottman's penultimate paragraph. What effect does Brottman achieve by structuring that paragraph that way before her conclusion?

THINKING CRITICALLY

1. Explain how you see language being shaped by the technologies we use.
2. Do you believe we are evolving back into an oral tradition rather than a written one, given what Trubek is saying? Why or why not?
3. Do you think Brottman is being overly sensitive to misspellings, or does she have a point? How would you have responded if you had been on that hiring committee? Choose a side and explain.
4. Does the response of Brottman's colleagues to the résumé error surprise you? Does Trubek's call for individualized rules of spelling surprise you? Do Brottman's own misgivings about the topic reflect your own?

WRITING ACTIVITIES

1. Discuss the language being used in texts, tweets, and e-mails. What kind of changes are taking place to the English language based on what you see there? See if the changes follow any discernible "rules."
2. In a brief essay, consider your own feelings about standardized spellings. What sort of difficulties have you encountered as you learned the rules of English? How does standardized English help or hinder your communication? In your final paragraph, disregard the rules of spelling and spell as you think

you should in a world without fixed rules. Then ask a classmate to read your last paragraph and see whether or not your ideas make sense.

3. Brottman reminds us that she is in the Humanities and the others on the university hiring committee with her are in the Sciences. Trubek is a professor at Oberlin, although we do not necessarily know by her essay in what field. Is it important to know the rules of English in any particular field? Why? Write a brief essay exploring the importance or unimportance of spelling and grammar rules in your area of expertise. If possible, try to write from the middle ground and consider what effect such knowledge or lack thereof has on you and your associates.

Christopher Muther

We Get the Point!

[*Boston Globe*, April 26, 2012]

BEFORE YOU READ

When do you include exclamation points in your daily correspondences? Do you think you overuse them? Why or why not?

WORDS TO LEARN

pact (para. 1): agreement (noun)
chide (para. 3): to scold (verb)
serial (para. 3): occurring in a series; consecutive (adj)
curmudgeonly (para. 4): grouchy (adj)
faux (para. 4): fake (adj)
slang (para. 5): informal use of language; jargon (noun)
abrupt (para. 6): curt, rude (adj)
wallop (para. 10): a heavy blow (noun)
diatribe (para. 11): invective; verbal attack (noun)

emasculated (para. 11): weakened; undermined (adj)
condone (para. 13): to approve; to accept (verb)
mitigate (para. 16): to make less severe (verb)
dowager (para. 17): elderly woman of high social rank (noun)
kindred (para. 18): similar (adj)
ambassador (para. 23): an official representative (noun)
soothe (para. 25): to calm or relieve (verb)

I can still remember the pact I made with a co-worker five years ago. We began to notice an alarming increase in the number of exclamation points crammed into e-mails and text messages. False enthusiasm was giving us

---

Christopher Muther is a columnist and style writer for the Boston Globe.

a headache. The English language had taken enough of a beating, and there was no need for this kind of sucker punch. We would have no part of it.

The problem was that nearly every e-mail I received ended with an overzealous "Thanks!" E-mails and texts cheerfully chimed "Can't wait to see you!," and I recall more than a few "How are you!" e-mails. Since when did an exclamation point wrestle a helpless question mark into submission? 2

The co-worker and I agreed that we would not fall prey to the trend. But I'm now ashamed to admit that I'm just as guilty as those I once chided. I've become a serial exclamation pointer. 3

Before you judge me, Judy, hear me out. Without an omnipresent exclamation point, my electronic communication sounded as if it was written by a certain curmudgeonly and crusty green muppet who resides in a trash can. I could feel the shame creeping into my fingertips the first few times I started adding this faux emphasis to pleasantries. Now there is no turning back. 4

This exclamation epidemic has become so dire that there's now a name for it — the very unpleasant slang bangorrhea. Urban Dictionary goes a step further by calling bangorrhea a "grammedical" condition. Even grammar snobs are fighting figurative infection. 5

"Even though I know better than to use stunt punctuation instead of thoughtful language, I often find my hand hesitating over the exclamation point," confesses Martha Brockenbrough, author of *Things That Make Us [Sic]* and the founder of the blog the Society for the Promotion of Good Grammar. "Should I use one? Does it seem amateurish? Without it, does my e-mail sound bossy and abrupt?" 6

When is an exclamation point appropriate? Merriam-Webster defines it as "A mark ! used especially after an interjection or exclamation to indicate forceful utterance or strong feeling" or "a distinctive indication of major significance." 7

Does "Thanks!" or "See you later!" fall under either of those definitions? Those of us who learned our grammar from the Saturday morning *Schoolhouse Rock* animated shorts may disagree. Allow me to quote from the 1974 song "Interjections!" 8

"Interjections (Hey!) show excitement (Yow!) or emotion (Ouch!). / They're generally set apart from a sentence by an exclamation point, /Or by comma when the feeling's not as strong." 9

In the digital era, a sentence without an exclamation doesn't pack the same wallop it once did. 10

These lessons were drilled into my brain between episodes of *Scooby-Doo*. By high school, I saw enough red ink on my research papers to know an exclamation point was for excitement only. But in the digital era, a sentence without an exclamation doesn't pack the same wallop it once did.

At one time, the exclamation point indicated shouting ("Watch out   11
Nancy Drew! That crook has a gun!"). Now shouting means a Kanye West-style caps lock Twitter diatribe. Exclamation points are no longer tough; they've been emasculated into sweet little blue birds delivering happy thoughts.

I'm not the first, and certainly not the last, to speak up about excla-   12
mation point abuse. Author Terry Pratchett famously said, "Five exclamation marks, the sure sign of an insane mind." F. Scott Fitzgerald offered, "An exclamation point is like laughing at your own joke." Everyone from Mark Twain to Craig Ferguson has spoken out against this inhumane treatment of punctuation.

It would be easy to blame text-happy tweens for the exclamation   13
point avalanche. I'm not one to point fingers, but I'm going to make an exception and point in the direction of David Shipley and Will Schwalbe. In 2008, they wrote a book called *Send: The Essential Guide to Email for Office and Home*. It created a minor sensation, partially because the authors condoned the use of exclamation points.

" 'I'll see you at the conference,' is a simple statement of fact," they   14
wrote. " 'I'll see you at the conference!' lets your fellow conferee know that you're excited and pleased about the event."

A round of talk shows and cheeky feature stories followed. The   15
exclamation point door was ajar, and now there may be no shutting it.

"In e-mail, I think that exclamation points serve some useful func-   16
tions, because they can convey extra meaning in brief messages," says Jean Berko Gleason, a Boston University psycholinguist. "They can mitigate the brusqueness of a brief reply by indicating the writer's enthusiasm, sincerity, surprise — it all depends on the situation."

Given that even academics are warming up to e-mails peppered with   17
exclamation points, I feel like the dowager countess from *Downton Abbey*. I'm rolling my eyes at change and bemoaning crazy new things, such as electricity, weekends — and the overuse of exclamation points in e-mails.

Fortunately, I found a cranky kindred spirit in Jeff Rubin, the   18
founder of National Punctuation Day. Mark your calendar, that holiday takes place on Sept. 24.

"That particular punctuation mark conveys a very special message."   19
Rubin says, "More so than most punctuation marks. It's overused in text messaging and e-mails. That's mostly where you see it. If you go back 20 or 30 years before we had this stuff. I saw the same thing in handwritten letters. I have friends who used to write to me longhand and use 10 exclamation points."

Author and former social media coach Judy Dunn ponders the same 20
question that troubles me about the exclamation epidemic: "When
you overuse it, it takes the power out of it. So what am I supposed to be
excited about if it's everywhere? If everything is exciting then nothing is
exciting, because it's all the same."

Turns out, a lot of us are really excited about nothing. 21

Brockenbrough said a recent survey of her e-mail inbox found that 22
2,599 of the 3,756 e-mails included exclamation points. (In my inbox,
I found I had more than 2,000 e-mails containing exclamation points.)

"That's what the exclamation point has become," she says. "The 23
ambassador of good intentions."

Because I realize there is no winning this fight, I've started to think 24
of a compromise: A new punctuation mark. It should fall somewhere
between a period and an exclamation point, and be reserved exclusively
for e-mail. I'm not the only one who's had this thought.

Also suggesting a new punctuation mark is Lera Boroditsky, an 25
assistant professor of psychology at Stanford University who studies
language and cognition. But in the meantime, she tries to soothe my
exclamation-battered nerves by looking on the bright side.

"Let me give you an answer, and hopefully you'll feel less offended 26
by the exclamation point. People are using the written word in a much
more conversational manner," Boroditsky says, "What people do with
written language is that they adapt it to meet their needs."

Boroditsky tells me I should welcome this evolution, because the 27
more communicative we are in e-mail and text messages, the better our
emotions will be understood.

Following her advice, I'm going to embrace the exclamation point 28
for just a sentence to make sure my feelings on the subject are not misunderstood.

I'm sick of exclamation point abuse! 29

Thanks, I feel much better now. 30

VOCABULARY/USING A DICTIONARY

1. In paragraph 2, Muther refers to an *overzealous* ending to an e-mail. What
does it mean to be *overzealous*, and how does that differ from being *zealous*?
2. What part of speech is *dire* (para. 5)? What does it mean?
3. How is [sic] (para. 6) different from *sick*?

RESPONDING TO WORDS IN CONTEXT

1. What does it mean literally to *fall prey* to something? How is this different from how Muther and his co-worker could "fall prey to the trend"
(para. 3) of using exclamation points in e-mails?

2. Muther talks about an "omnipresent exclamation point" in paragraph 4. What do you think *omnipresent* means? How might you guess at its meaning?

3. How do you understand what is meant by the *sucker punch* (para. 1) the English language receives from the increase of exclamation points used in e-mails?

DISCUSSING MAIN POINT AND MEANING

1. What, according to Muther, does the "exclamation point epidemic" (para. 5) consist of?

2. What does Muther think our writing has lost due to overuse of the exclamation point? What sort of evidence does he bring into the argument to back up his thesis?

3. Muther offers only one suggestion about how to fix the exclamation point problem. What is his answer about what can be done?

EXAMINING SENTENCES, PARAGRAPHS, AND ORGANIZATION

1. Where does Muther use language that likens exclamation point overuse to an illness (or epidemic)?

2. Describe the tone of this essay. Is it formal or informal? How can you tell?

3. Muther uses references to several television shows throughout the essay. Can you identify them? Are they effective as a rhetorical tool? Why or why not?

THINKING CRITICALLY

1. Do you think that "Thanks!" and "See you later!"—common words and phrases found in e-mails—qualify as interjections (as defined by *Schoolhouse Rock*)? Why or why not?

2. Why is "exclamation point abuse" (para. 29) rampant in electronic communication? Do you think it may seep into other modes of writing as well?

3. Do you agree with Brockenbrough's quotation in Muther's essay that defines the exclamation point as "the ambassador of good intentions" (para. 23)? What do you think that means?

WRITING ACTIVITIES

1. Muther says he found more than 2,000 e-mails in his inbox that included exclamation points. Take a guess at the number in your own archive. Do you think it's similar? Try to find a few examples. What can you gather from them about when and why exclamation points are being used? Do you use them the same way in your replies?

2. How well do you know the rules governing punctuation marks? In small groups, write down the most commonly used marks (period, comma, question mark, exclamation point, quotation marks, colon, and semi-colon, for example) and beside each one write a rule that indicates when the mark should or should not be used. Then have each group member look up rules for a particular mark in a grammar book or a Web site about grammar/punctuation. See if any of the answers generated by the group matches a formal rule. Are any answers off base? Were any important rules overlooked?

3. Find an example of your own writing from this or another class. In any paragraph, change the punctuation so that you use exclamation points a majority of the time. How does the inclusion of so many exclamation points affect the tone of your writing? Do you think it adds or detracts from the meaning you are trying to convey? How? Would your experience of so many exclamation points be different in an e-mail?

Shayna Diamond (student essay)

Words Are What We Make of Them

[*Ka Leo*, University of Hawai'i at Manoa, February 5, 2012]

BEFORE YOU READ

Is political correctness a form of intolerance and censorship, or does it serve the public good by protecting people from offensive language? Do words in themselves have the power to wound, or do offensive words lose their force without a malicious intent behind them?

WORDS TO LEARN

potent (para. 1): powerful (adj)

misconstrue (para. 1): to misinterpret (verb)

inflection (para. 1): a change in the voice (noun)

callous (para. 1): hardened; unfeeling (adj)

rapt (para. 3): completely absorbed (adj)

amoral (para. 3): without morals (adj)

pariah (para. 3): an outcast of society (noun)

boorish (para. 4): uncouth (adj)

malicious (para. 5): intentionally mean (adj)

Shayna Diamond is a student at the University of Hawai'i at Manoa, where she majors in English and serves as desk editor for the opinions section of the student newspaper.

Words are the most potent source of influence in the world. Yet they are so ambiguous that they can be easily misconstrued. Regardless of what you're trying to say, even the slightest change of inflection can change the entire meaning. Even things out of your control, like your words being taken out of context, can completely alter the message that you were trying to get across. The result is often someone stomping off in explanation of just how offensive and callous you are — without taking the time to make sure that's really what you meant.

In order to avoid stepping on anyone's sensitive toes and instead of trying to understand one another, our society has developed an unspoken code regarding what we can and cannot say. In order to put this incredibly bigoted and narrow-minded attitude in a positive light, it's usually referred to as being "politically correct" and it has somehow mutated into a socially expected norm.

> Our society has developed an unspoken code regarding what we can and cannot say.

Musicians, comedians, and politicians alike are expected to possess a "better" vocabulary than that of the commoners watching their shenanigans with rapt attention. However if one of them drops an "f-bomb" and our oh-so-virginal ears hear it, he or she is thrust into the spotlight as an amoral pariah and must live out the rest of his or her shame-filled days as a politically-incorrect and insensitive individual.

Yet we've all seen exceptions to politically correct behavior, such as comedians and poets who use such "offensive" words to express themselves. Comedian Louis C. K. actually addresses this very topic in *Chewed-Up*, his standup show from 2008. Are people like him regarded as boorish or less intelligent because they freely use colorful language? When was it decided that words with constantly changing meanings were offensive in all situations? Was there a vote? I must have missed the email.

The bottom line is that the level of offense we take to any given word or phrase is dictated not by society or its rules, but by each and every one of us as individuals. If we don't want to be offended, we need only to stop seeing words as malicious. And if we don't want what we say to be taken as offensive, we need only to watch the way in which we express ourselves. After all, we define words, and our inconsistency — along with the ever-changing nature of the events around us — will alter those definitions on a rapid and regular basis. If we can take the time to be offended, can't we take the time to reflect on why we're offended in the first place, and perhaps what the speaker's intentions were?

The absurdly closed-minded and over-analytical atmosphere that has been adopted under the guise of protecting others does nothing but smother self-expression and limit the possibility of becoming a more tolerant and understanding people. 6

The words that we use don't define who we are; the way we use them and our intentions in using them do. It's our actions and emotions that create the force and influence behind our words, and that trigger the responding emotions and actions of others. Words are nothing but complex combinations of symbols and patterns of pronunciation. It's our thoughts and our reactions that give words power. 7

VOCABULARY/USING A DICTIONARY

1. What does *ambiguous* (para. 1) mean? What's the opposite of *ambiguous*?
2. What is a *guise* (para. 6)?
3. What part of speech is the word *trigger* in paragraph 7? How would you define it?

RESPONDING TO WORDS IN CONTEXT

1. Why is the use of the word *bigot* (para. 2) an interesting choice on Diamond's part, given her discussion about the code of political correctness? Would a counterargument perhaps find occasion to use the word *bigoted* as well?
2. Diamond writes, "Musicians, comedians, and politicians alike are expected to possess a 'better' vocabulary than that of the commoners watching their shenanigans with rapt attention" (para. 3). In the context of this essay, what does Diamond mean by the *shenanigans* of musicians, comedians, and politicians?
3. How do you understand what is meant by "our inconsistency" in paragraph 5? To what does this refer?

DISCUSSING MAIN POINT AND MEANING

1. What two things does Diamond suggest we change so that political correctness isn't necessary?
2. What gives words their power, according to Diamond?
3. In this essay, what example does Diamond incorporate to illustrate her point that political correctness "does nothing but smother self-expression and limit the possibility of becoming a more tolerant and understanding people" (para. 6)?

EXAMINING SENTENCES, PARAGRAPHS, AND ORGANIZATION

1. What effect do Diamond's rhetorical questions have? What do they add to the essay?

2. Diamond uses various adjectives in order to make her feelings on this topic clear. What are some of the most effective adjectives used to emphasize her point?
3. What is the benefit of switching into second person in the fourth paragraph after the third-person perspective in paragraphs 2 and 3? What would be the effect of not switching to second person?

THINKING CRITICALLY

1. Diamond says "words are . . . so ambiguous that they can be easily misconstrued" (para. 1). Do you agree or disagree with this statement? Why?
2. Can language be harmful? What function does politically correct language serve if you view it as something other than censorship?
3. Do you believe Diamond is right when she says, "The words that we use don't define who we are; the way we use them and our intentions in using them do" (para. 7)? Why or why not?

WRITING ACTIVITIES

1. Take a look at a famous musician's, comedian's, or politician's Web site. Do you find the language he or she uses particularly edgy, even offensive? If so, where is it offensive? If not, do you think he or she is intentionally using politically correct language to express himself or herself? Write a brief essay giving an overview of the Web site and discussing the way the person uses language. Refer to Diamond's essay as you construct your argument.
2. Have you ever felt offended by a word? In a freewriting exercise, think of the word that offended you and write down as many of the reasons *why* it offended you as you can. Consider whether or not limiting the use of that word by others feels like a valid or too-extreme response. Then, in a short essay, reflect on your reaction to that particular word and the reasons for your decision about limiting or not limiting its use.
3. Research "political correctness" on the Web. What examples of offensive words and politically correct replacements do you find? After you've gathered a page or two of research, share your findings in small groups. Together try to come up with a list of three words you believe are truly offensive, three words you agree may not need to be "corrected," and three words about which the group disagrees. Discuss as a class.

Establishing Your Main Point

As you learn to express opinions clearly and effectively, you need to ask yourself a relatively simple question: Will my readers understand my main point? In composition, a main point is sometimes called a thesis or a thesis statement. It is often a sentence or two that summarizes your central idea or position. It need not include any factual proof or supporting evidence — that can be supplied in the body of your essay — but it should represent a general statement that clearly shows where you stand on an issue, what you are attacking or defending, and what exactly your essay is about. Although main points are often found in opening paragraphs, they can also appear later on in an essay, especially when the writer wants to set the stage for his or her opinion by opening with a relevant quotation, a topical reference, an emotional appeal, or a general observation.

This is how Shayna Diamond, a student at the University of Hawai'i, proceeds in "Words Are What We Make of Them." She begins with a point about the way people are too quick to take offense or misconstrue what is being said. She then goes on in the next paragraph to express the main point of her essay — that we now live in a society that is suppressing free expression.

1

Diamond states the main point of the essay

In order to avoid stepping on anyone's sensitive toes and instead of trying to understand one another, <u>our society has developed an unspoken code regarding what we can and cannot say.</u> (1) In order to put this incredibly bigoted and narrow-minded attitude in a positive light, it's usually referred to as being "politically correct" and it has somehow mutated into a socially expected norm.

STUDENT WRITER AT WORK
Shayna Diamond

R.A. What inspired you to write this essay? And publish it in your campus paper?

S.D. I wrote this piece because I felt it was the best way to communicate with my peers and professors on campus. I feel that people are too easily offended by language and are unaware that words are powerless without your consent. It's your interpretation and personal upset over words that give them power. Don't let words upset you, and debating or making your point clear is suddenly a much easier task. I published this essay with *Ka Leo* as my very first piece with them because I wanted them to know how I thought and felt before I became more involved.

R.A. How long did it take for you to write this piece? Did you revise your work? What were your goals as you revised?

S.D. I wrote this piece fairly quickly. I would say that from the time I sat down to write it, it took an hour. However, since it was my first submission I found myself nervously revising it again and again, trying to make sure that every point was made clearly and that my voice was truly my own. I finally decided to just send it in and see what they thought, and the next thing I knew, it was already in print.

R.A. Do you generally show your writing to friends before submitting it? Do you collaborate or bounce your ideas off others?

S.D. I generally discuss an idea with peers before writing it, but I tend to avoid showing my writing to friends before submitting it, because I would prefer that they see the finished article once it has gone through the proper editing procedures. I also try not to discuss it in detail until after it has been published so that I don't influence their opinion. I prefer when someone else formulates their own opinion based on the facts and argument that I have presented. It makes for better discussions and debates later.

R.A. What do you like to read?

S.D. I love reading and writing all kinds of literature, but am generally drawn to horror, humor, screenwriting, and plays. Admittedly, I love watching *The Daily Show* and often daydream about getting to meet and work with the writers there.

R.A. What topics most interest you as a writer?

S.D. International, humanitarian, and philosophical topics interest me the most because they can relate to everyone, and many people are often directly affected by such issues and don't even know it.

R.A. Do you plan to continue writing for publication?

S.D. If I should be so privileged, I would love to continue writing for publication.

R.A. What advice do you have for other student writers?

S.D. Verify everything and don't be afraid of your own voice.

The Telegram

Radio relay towers, about 50 miles apart, will gradually replace thousands of miles of telegraph poles and wires.

Now, telegrams "leapfrog" storms
through RCA Radio Relay

With the radio relay system, developed by RCA, Western Union will be able to send telegraph messages without poles and wires between principal cities.

"Wires down due to storm" will no longer disrupt communications. For this new system can transmit telegrams and radiophotos by invisible electric microwaves. These beams span distances up to fifty miles between towers and are completely unaffected by even the angriest storms. Moreover, the radio relay system is less costly to build and maintain.

This revolutionary stride in communications was made possible by research in RCA Laboratories—the same "make it better" research that goes into *all* RCA products.

And when you buy an RCA Victor radio or television set or Victrola* radio-phonograph, or even a radio tube replacement, you enjoy a unique pride of ownership. For you know, if it's an RCA it is one of the finest instruments of its kind that science has achieved.

Radio Corporation of America, RCA Building, Radio City, New York 20, N.Y.... Listen to The RCA Victor Show, Sundays, 4:30 P.M., Eastern Time, over NBC Network.

Research in microwaves and electron tubes at RCA Laboratories led to the development by the RCA Victor Division of this automatic radio relay system. Here you see a close-up view of a microwave reflector. This system also holds great promise of linking television stations into networks.

RADIO CORPORATION of AMERICA

*Victrola, T. M. Reg. U. S. Pat. Off.

An ad (c. 1940) promoting the technology of the telegram.

An undated telegram, probably sent in the early 1940s, from the legendary jazz musician Louis Armstrong (1901–1971) to his manager.

Long before text-messaging and e-mail, and earlier than fax machines and long-distance telephone calls, there was the telegram. Through much of the nineteenth and the first half of the twentieth centuries, sending a telegram was the easiest and fastest way of communicating with someone at a distance. European inventors and scientists experimented with various machines to send written messages as early as the 1790s. In the United States, working independently, a Yale graduate and well-known portrait painter Samuel F. B. Morse (1791–1872) received a patent for an electrical telegraph in 1837. Because so many others had worked up telegraphic systems with codes, it is difficult to credit Morse as *the* inventor of the telegraph. What he did essentially was, with the assistance of other scientists and instrument designers, to develop the first "user-friendly" machine with a convenient code of dots and dashes representing the alphabet and numeric system. Though there were other codes, the Morse code quickly became the worldwide standard.

Despite some successful early demonstrations, Morse encountered difficulties for years in persuading Congress to grant him the money to lay a telegraph line between Washington, D.C., and Baltimore so he could prove once and for all the value of his idea. The central idea, of course, was that messages could be sent by means of electrical current. He and his small group of associates kept fine-tuning the system, extending the power of batteries and transmission capacity, and simplifying the machine's "finger-key" and the code so that more words could be tapped out per minute. In 1844, Congress finally approved funds. After a few errors — Morse first tried laying the wires underground and then found it worked better to string them on poles — Washington, D.C., was electrically connected with Baltimore. On May 24, 1844, Morse sent from the U.S. Supreme Court a one-sentence message, the first electrical telegram. The message, apparently chosen by the daughter of a patent official, was "What hath God wrought!" She borrowed the exclamation from the King James Bible: "Surely there is no enchantment against Jacob, neither is there any divination against Israel: according to this time it shall be said of Jacob and of Israel, What hath God wrought!" (Num. 23:23).

Over the next decade, Morse's telegram system grew tremendously, as America became "wired" for the first time. In 1857, the Western Union Company, which became synonymous with *telegram*, was born. In January 2006, Western Union, unable to compete with the ease of e-mail, sent its last telegram. An entire verbal culture, one that often prided itself on brief, economical messages (since senders paid for telegraphs by the word) came to an end, as one technology inevitably replaced another.

Discussing the Unit

SUGGESTED TOPIC FOR DISCUSSION

As we move forward in the twenty-first century, many changes to language, grammar, and punctuation have begun to take hold. Sometimes the rules of grammar and punctuation feel not quite set in stone. The language of political correctness may or may not be important. Are the rules that govern our spelling and punctuation of value? Is the language of political correctness beneficial, or does it in fact keep us from understanding one another?

PREPARING FOR CLASS DISCUSSION

1. How familiar are you with the rules of spelling, grammar, and punctuation? Did any information you came across in these essays surprise you or teach you anything about your own language?
2. How do technologies affect our ability to use and correct our language? What are some of the past technologies mentioned in these essays, and which ones are revolutionizing our approaches now?

FROM DISCUSSION TO WRITING

1. Compare two of the essays in this unit and point out where the essayists are in agreement or disagreement with each other. Write a brief essay that points out their similarities or differences.

2. Are you easygoing about the words you use? Are you relaxed about rules of grammar? In a short essay, describe how your approach toward language and the rules that govern it matches the approach of one of the other essayists.

TOPICS FOR CROSS-CULTURAL DISCUSSION

1. Consider how the twenty-first century might be termed a culture of technology, and the ways in which we communicate with each other. What has changed in recent history? Describe our culture of technology.

2. In "Words Are What We Make of Them," Shayna Diamond argues that the meanings of words often change, and the use of politically correct language is detrimental to us as a society. Imagine that we abandon politically correct language for that reason. For this to work, what are the responsibilities of the race, gender, or ethnic culture who is the subject of non-politically correct language? What are the responsibilities of the speaker?

This chapter continues online. Visit the e-Page at
bedfordstmartins.com/americanow/epages for a video assignment.

9

Education: Does College Still Matter?

For years, a college education has been seen as a path to personal, intellectual, and financial success. However, at a time of economic instability, the financial benefits of a college degree have received the most attention. According to a report from the Georgetown University Center on Education and the Workforce, full-time workers holding a bachelor's degree make, on average, 74 percent more over the course of their careers than workers who've obtained only a high school diploma. But with tuition costs and student-loan debts soaring, more and more people are questioning the value of a college education. Given its high cost, is it really the best choice for everyone? And do students, parents, and educational institutions need to focus more on majors that will provide the most financial bang for the tuition buck? Or is emphasizing the economic benefits of college selling short the other, less quantifiable advantages it offers students—for example, the potential to be better, and happier, citizens and thinkers?

In "Three Reasons College Still Matters," professor and writer Andrew Delbanco acknowledges the economic importance of a college education. But he adds, "The best reason to care about college . . . is not what it does for society in economic terms but what it can do for individuals, in both calculable and incalculable ways." Among the incalculable benefits of college, Delbanco says, are the ways in which it can provide students with the cultural and historical background they need to be informed, thoughtful participants in a democracy. Delbanco also praises the intellectual and spiritual satisfactions of college, where students of all classes "have the capacity to embrace the precious chance to think and reflect before life engulfs them."

In contrast, professor and researcher Alex Tabarrok argues that "[t]he obsessive focus on a college degree has served neither taxpayers nor students well." In "Tuning In to Dropping Out," he says the college dropout rate in the United States, the highest in the industrialized world, is just one sign that college—and even the traditional high school education—isn't for everyone. Instead, Tabarrok contends, we need to do a better job of creating alternatives to both paths, such as vocational and apprenticeship programs like those in Europe. Additionally, Tabarrok makes the case that taxpayers should subsidize only those students pursuing degrees that provide "spillover" benefits to the larger economy—degrees in fields such as microbiology, chemical engineering, and computer science. He adds that "there is little justification for subsidizing sociology, dance, and English majors."

In "Not All College Majors Are Created Equal," financial-advice columnist Michelle Singletary agrees that students need to consider how much their majors will be worth in the job market. She concludes, "I wouldn't want to discourage people from pursuing a career they love, even if the pay isn't very high. However, that choice should be made with the understanding of which job opportunities might be available and weighing what you can expect to earn annually against the cost of taking on debt to finance your education."

But in the final essay of the chapter, "A College Degree Is a Worthy Achievement," Maria Dimera, a student at Santa Monica College, urges potential college attendees not to let concerns about loan debt, tuition, and job prospects discourage them from pursuing a degree, which, she says, is "more than just a piece of paper. It is an experience and an accomplishment that no one can take away, no matter what comes after college." According to Dimera, obtaining scholarships and applying to more affordable institutions are just a couple of ways to put college within reach.

The e-Page at the end of the chapter offers a look into a virtual classroom of the Khan Academy, whose goal is to provide a "free world-class education to anyone anywhere." What does the existence of the Khan Academy suggest about the education of the future?

Andrew Delbanco

Three Reasons College Still Matters

[*Boston Globe Magazine*, March 4, 2012]

BEFORE YOU READ

Do you think college and higher education should be available to everyone? Why or why not? Do you think higher education should be focused on specific careers or tasks, or do you think it should encompass multiple areas of study, from arts and humanities to science and engineering?

WORDS TO LEARN

supplant (para. 3): to replace (verb)

dissenters (para. 7): people whose opinion differs from the majority (noun)

punditry (para. 12): opinions of experts or authorities (noun)

trepidation (para. 15): fear (noun)

utilitarian (para. 16): regarding usefulness over beauty (adj)

For a relatively few students, college remains the sort of place that Anthony Kronman, former dean of Yale Law School, recalls from his days at Williams, where his favorite class took place at the home of a philosophy professor whose two golden retrievers slept on either side of the fireplace "like bookends beside the hearth" while the sunset lit the Berkshire Hills "in scarlet and gold." For many more students, college means the anxious pursuit of marketable skills in overcrowded, under-resourced institutions. For still others, it means traveling by night to a fluorescent office building or to a "virtual classroom" that only exists in cyberspace. 1

It is a pipe dream to imagine that every student can have the sort of experience that our richest colleges, at their best, provide. But it is a nightmare society that affords the chance to learn and grow only to the wealthy, brilliant, or lucky few. Many remarkable teachers in America's community 2

Andrew Delbanco is the director of American Studies at Columbia University, where he also serves as the Julian Clarence Levi Professor Chair in the Humanities. He is the author of several books, and his essays regularly appear in the New York Review of Books. *In 2001, he was both elected Fellow of the American Academy of Arts and Sciences and named "America's Best Social Critic" by* Time *magazine.*

colleges, unsung private colleges, and underfunded public colleges live this truth every day, working to keep the ideal of democratic education alive. And so it is my unabashed aim to articulate in my forthcoming book, *College: What It Was, Is, and Should Be*, what a college — any college — should seek to do for its students.

What, then, are today's prevailing answers to the question, what is college for? The most common answer is an economic one. It's clear that a college degree long ago supplanted the high school diploma as the minimum qualification for entry into the skilled labor market, and there is abundant evidence that people with a college degree earn more money over the course of their lives than people without one. Some estimates put the worth of a bachelor of arts degree at about a million dollars in incremental lifetime earnings.

> It is alarming that for the first time in history, we face the prospect that the coming generation of Americans will be less educated than its elders.

For such economic reasons alone, it is alarming that for the first time in history, we face the prospect that the coming generation of Americans will be less educated than its elders.

Within this gloomy general picture are some especially disturbing particulars. For one thing, flat or declining college attainment rates (relative to other nations) apply disproportionately to minorities, who are a growing portion of the American population. And financial means have a shockingly large bearing on educational opportunity, which, according to one authority, looks like this in today's America: If you are the child of a family making more than $90,000 per year, your odds of getting a BA by age 24 are roughly 1 in 2; if your parents make less than $35,000, your odds are 1 in 17.

Moreover, among those who do get to college, high-achieving students from affluent families are four times more likely to attend a selective college than students from poor families with comparable grades and test scores. Since prestigious colleges serve as funnels into leadership positions in business, law, and government, this means that our "best" colleges are doing more to foster than to retard the growth of inequality in our society. Yet colleges are still looked to as engines of social mobility in American life, and it would be shameful if they became, even more than they already are, a system for replicating inherited wealth.

Not surprisingly, as in any discussion of economic matters, one finds dissenters from the predominant view. Some on the right say that pouring more public investment into higher education, in the form of enhanced subsidies for individuals or institutions, is a bad idea. They argue against the goal of universal college education as a fond fantasy and, instead, for a sorting system such as one finds in European countries: vocational training for the low scorers, who will be the semiskilled laborers and functionaries; advanced education for the high scorers, who will be the diplomats and doctors.

Other thinkers, on the left, question whether the aspiration to go   8
to college really makes sense for "low-income students who can least afford to spend money and years" on such a risky venture, given their low graduation rates and high debt. From this point of view, the "education gospel" seems a cruel distraction from "what really provides security to families and children: good jobs at fair wages, robust unions, affordable access to health care and transportation."

One can be on either side of these questions or somewhere in the   9
middle, and still believe in the goal of achieving universal college education. Consider an analogy from another sphere of public debate: health care. One sometimes hears that eliminating smoking would save untold billions because of the immense cost of caring for patients who develop lung cancer, emphysema, heart disease, or diabetes. It turns out, however, that reducing the incidence of disease by curtailing smoking may actually end up costing us more, since people who don't smoke live longer and eventually require expensive therapies for chronic diseases and the inevitable infirmities of old age.

In other words, measuring the benefit as a social cost or gain does   10
not quite get the point — or at least not the whole point. The best reason to end smoking is that people who don't smoke have a better chance to lead better lives. The best reason to care about college — who goes, and what happens to them when they get there — is not what it does for society in economic terms but what it can do for individuals, in both calculable and incalculable ways.

The second argument for the importance of college is a political   11
one, though one rarely hears it from politicians. This is the argument on behalf of democracy. "The basis of our government," as Thomas Jefferson put the matter near the end of the 18th century, is "the opinion of the people." If the new republic was to flourish and endure, it required, above all, an educated citizenry.

This is more true than ever. All of us are bombarded every day with   12
pleadings and persuasions — advertisements, political appeals, punditry of all sorts — designed to capture our loyalty, money, or, more narrowly, our vote. Some say health care reform will bankrupt the country, others that it is an overdue act of justice; some believe that abortion is the work of Satan, others think that to deny a woman the right to terminate

an unwanted pregnancy is a form of abuse. The best chance we have to maintain a functioning democracy is a citizenry that can tell the difference between demagoguery and responsible arguments.

Education for democracy also implies something about what kind of 13 education democratic citizens need. A very good case for college in this sense has been made recently by Kronman, the former Yale dean who now teaches in a Great Books program for Yale undergraduates. In his book *Education's End,* Kronman argues for a course of study that introduces students to the constitutive ideas of Western culture, including, among many others, "the ideals of individual freedom and toleration," "a reliance on markets as a mechanism for the organization of economic life," and "an acceptance of the truths of modern science."

Anyone who earns a BA from a reputable college ought to understand 14 something about the genealogy of these ideas and practices, about the historical processes from which they have emerged, the tragic cost when societies fail to defend them, and about alternative ideas both within the Western tradition and outside it. That's a tall order for anyone to satisfy on his or her own — and one of the marks of an educated person is the recognition that it can never be adequately done and is therefore all the more worth doing.

There is a third case for college, seldom heard, perhaps because it 15 is harder to articulate without sounding platitudinous and vague. I first heard it stated in a plain and passionate way after I had spoken to an alumni group from Columbia, where I teach. The emphasis in my talk was on the Jeffersonian argument — education for citizenship. When I had finished, an elderly alumnus stood up and said more or less the following: "That's all very nice, professor, but you've missed the main point." With some trepidation, I asked him what that point might be. "Columbia," he said, "taught me how to enjoy life."

What he meant was that college had opened his senses as well as his 16 mind to experiences that would otherwise be foreclosed to him. Not only had it enriched his capacity to read demanding works of literature and to grasp fundamental political ideas, it had also heightened and deepened his alertness to color and form, melody and harmony. And now, in the late years of his life, he was grateful. Such an education is a hedge against utilitarian values. It slakes the human craving for contact with works of art that somehow register one's own longings and yet exceed what one has been able to articulate by and for oneself.

If all that seems too pious, I think of a comparably personal comment I 17 once heard my colleague Judith Shapiro, former provost of Bryn Mawr and then president of Barnard, make to a group of young people about what they should expect from college: "You want the inside of your head to be an interesting place to spend the rest of your life."

What both Shapiro and the Columbia alum were talking about is 18
sometimes called "liberal education"—a hazardous term today, since it
has nothing necessarily to do with liberal politics in the modern sense of
the word. The phrase "liberal education" derives from the classical tradition of *artes liberales,* which was reserved in Greece and Rome—where
women were considered inferior and slavery was an accepted feature of
civilized society—for "those free men or gentlemen possessed of the
requisite leisure for study." The tradition of liberal learning survived and
thrived throughout European history but remained largely the possession of ruling elites. The distinctive American contribution has been the
attempt to democratize it, to deploy it on behalf of the cardinal American
principle that all persons, regardless of origin, have the right to pursue
happiness—and that "getting to know," in poet and critic Matthew
Arnold's much-quoted phrase, "the best which has been thought and said
in the world" is helpful to that pursuit.

This view of what it means to be educated is often caricatured as snob- 19
bish and narrow, beholden to the old and wary of the new; but in fact it is
neither, as Arnold makes clear by the (seldom quoted) phrase with which
he completes his point: "and through this knowledge, turning a stream of
fresh and free thought upon our stock notions and habits."

In today's America, at every kind of institution — from underfunded 20
community colleges to the wealthiest Ivies — this kind of education is at
risk. Students are pressured and programmed, trained to live from task to
task, relentlessly rehearsed and tested until winners are culled from the
rest. Too many colleges do too little to save them from the debilitating
frenzy that makes liberal education marginal — if it is offered at all.

In this respect, notwithstanding the bigotries and prejudices of ear- 21
lier generations, we might not be so quick to say that today's colleges mark
an advance over those of the past.

Consider a once-popular college novel written a hundred years ago, 22
Stover at Yale, in which a young Yalie declares, "I'm going to do the best thing
a fellow can do at our age, I'm going to loaf." The character speaks from
the immemorial past, and what he says is likely to sound to us today like
a sneering boast from the idle rich. But there is a more dignified sense in
which "loaf" is the colloquial equivalent of contemplation and has always
been part of the promise of American life. "I loaf and invite my soul," says
Walt Whitman in that great democratic poem "Song of Myself."

Surely, every American college ought to defend this waning possibil- 23
ity, whatever we call it. And an American college is only true to itself when
it opens its doors to all—the rich, the middle, and the poor—who have
the capacity to embrace the precious chance to think and reflect before life
engulfs them. If we are serious about democracy, that means everyone.

VOCABULARY/USING A DICTIONARY

1. What does *demagoguery* mean (para. 12)? Why is an argument or pundit that uses demagoguery irresponsible?
2. What is the origin of the word *platitude*? What does it mean for something to be *platitudinous* (para. 15)?
3. What does the word *culled* mean (para. 20)? What part of speech is it?

RESPONDING TO WORDS IN CONTEXT

1. In paragraph 16, how does Delbanco use the word *utilitarian*? Is it a positive or negative term?
2. Delbanco uses a quote from *Stover at Yale* that states, "I'm going to do the best thing a fellow can do at our age, I'm going to loaf" (para. 22). What does *loaf* mean in this context? What part of speech is it?
3. Delbanco writes, "This view of what it means to be educated is often caricatured as snobbish and narrow . . ." (para. 19). What does *caricatured* mean in this sentence? How does it differ from being *characterized*?

DISCUSSING MAIN POINT AND MEANING

1. What are the three reasons Delbanco argues that college still matters?
2. What type of education does Delbanco argue is the most important, and how does he support that argument?
3. What is Delbanco's conclusion about American education?

EXAMINING SENTENCES, PARAGRAPHS, AND ORGANIZATION

1. What is the effect of dividing the essay into three clear supporting points?
2. What is the purpose of the health care analogy in paragraphs 9 and 10?
3. How would you describe the tone of this essay, and how does it affect the argument being presented?

THINKING CRITICALLY

1. Do you think a liberal education is more beneficial than a more focused education? Why or why not?
2. Is the title of this article representative of the content? Why or why not? How might the title be improved?
3. Do you agree with Delbanco's statement that "every American college ought to defend this waning possibility [to loaf], whatever we call it"? Why or why not?

WRITING ACTIVITIES

1. In a short essay, explore the benefits of a vocational or narrowly focused education. After examining Delbanco's argument and thinking about the

converse, decide which side of the argument you side with and explain your decision.

2. Although Delbanco was able to narrow down the reasons college still matters to three, come up with another reason of support for Delbanco's argument. Write a few paragraphs that expand and support your point.

3. Many students feel pressured to choose a major or path of study in college that will prove lucrative when they graduate. In a brief essay, write about what you would study if practicality or marketability were no object after graduation. If this is already what you are studying, what made you make that decision? If it is not what you are studying, why have you chosen your current path?

Alex Tabarrok

Tuning In to Dropping Out

[*The Chronicle Review*, March 9, 2012]

BEFORE YOU READ

How essential do you think college is to success? Are you planning on following a traditional education plan, or are you going to take the vocational education route? Why does your choice make sense to you?

WORD TO LEARN

subsidize (para. 8): to help pay for by a grant or other sum of money, usually by the government (verb)

Rick Scott, Florida's governor, created a firestorm recently when he suggested that Florida ought to focus more of its education spending on science, technology, engineering, and mathematics (STEM) and less on liberal arts. Scott got this one right: We should focus higher-education dollars on the fields most likely to benefit everyone, not just the students who earn the degrees. Scott, however, missed another part of the equation: We need to focus more attention on the

Alex Tabarrok is Associate Professor of Economics at George Mason University. He is also the co-author of both FDAReview.org and the Modern Principles *introductory economics textbook series. He directs research at the Independent Institute, is a research fellow at Mercatus Center, and regularly blogs with* Modern Principles *co-author Tyler Cowen at MarginalRevolution.com.*

students who are being left behind, the millions of college and high-school dropouts.

Over the past 25 years, the total number of students in college has increased by about 50 percent. But the number of students graduating with degrees in STEM subjects has remained more or less constant. 2

Consider computer technology. In 2009 the United States graduated 37,994 students with bachelor's degrees in computer and information science. That's not bad, but we graduated more students with computer-science degrees 25 years ago! 3

The story is the same in other technology fields such as chemical engineering, math, and statistics. Few disciplines have changed as much in recent years as microbiology, but in 2009 we graduated just 2,480 students with bachelor's degrees in microbiology — about the same number as 25 years ago. Who will solve the problem of antibiotic resistance? 4

If students aren't studying science, technology, engineering, and math, what are they studying? 5

In 2009 the United States graduated 89,140 students in the visual and performing arts, more than in computer science, math, and chemical engineering combined and more than double the number of visual-and-performing-arts graduates in 1985. 6

There is nothing wrong with the arts, psychology, and journalism, but graduates in these fields have lower wages and are less likely to find work in their fields than graduates in science and math. Moreover, more than half of all humanities graduates end up in jobs that don't require college degrees, and those graduates don't get a big income boost from having gone to college. 7

Most important, graduates in the arts, psychology, and journalism are less likely to create the kinds of innovations that drive economic growth. Economic growth is not the only goal of higher education, but it is one of the main reasons taxpayers subsidize higher education through direct government college support, as well as loans, scholarships, and grants. The potential wage gains for college graduates is reason enough for students to pursue a college education. We add subsidies to the mix, however, because we believe that education has positive spillover benefits for society. One of the biggest of those benefits is the increase in innovation that highly educated workers theoretically bring to the economy. 8

> The potential wage gains for college graduates is reason enough for students to pursue a college education.

Thus, an argument can be made for subsidizing students in fields 9
with potentially large spillovers, such as microbiology, chemical engineering, and computer science. But there is little justification for subsidizing sociology, dance, and English majors.

The obsessive focus on a college degree has served neither taxpay- 10
ers nor students well. Only 35 percent of students starting a four-year
degree program will graduate within four years, and less than 60 percent
will graduate within six years. Students who haven't graduated within six
years probably never will. The U.S. college dropout rate is about 40 percent, the highest college dropout rate in the industrialized world. That's
a lot of wasted resources. Students with two years of college education
may get something for those two years, but it's less than half of the wage
gains from completing a four-year degree. No degree, few skills, and a lot
of debt is not an ideal way to begin a career.

College dropouts are telling us that college is not for everyone. 11
Neither is high school. In the 21st century, an astounding 25 percent of
American men do not graduate from high school. A big part of the problem is that the United States has paved a single road to knowledge, the
road through the classroom. "Sit down, stay quiet, and absorb. Do this
for 12 to 16 years," we tell the students, "and all will be well." Lots of
students, however, crash before they reach the end of the road. Who can
blame them? Sit-down learning is not for everyone, perhaps not even for
most people. There are many roads to an education.

Consider those offered in Europe. In Germany, 97 percent of stu- 12
dents graduate from high school, but only a third of these students go
on to college. In the United States, we graduate fewer students from high
school, but nearly two-thirds of those we graduate go to college. So are
German students poorly educated? Not at all.

Instead of college, German students enter training and apprentice- 13
ship programs — many of which begin during high school. By the time
they finish, they have had a far better practical education than most American students — equivalent to an American technical degree — and, as
a result, they have an easier time entering the work force. Similarly, in
Austria, Denmark, Finland, the Netherlands, Norway, and Switzerland,
between 40 to 70 percent of students opt for an educational program
that combines classroom and workplace learning.

In the United States, "vocational" programs are often thought of as 14
programs for at-risk students, but that's because they are taught in high
schools with little connection to real workplaces. European programs
are typically rigorous because the training is paid for by employers who
consider apprentices an important part of their current and future work
force. Apprentices are therefore given high-skill technical training that

combines theory with practice — and the students are paid! Moreover, instead of isolating teenagers in their own counterculture, apprentice programs introduce teenagers to the adult world and the skills, attitudes, and practices that make for a successful career.

Elites frown upon apprenticeship programs because they think college is the way to create a "well-rounded citizenry." So take a look at the students in Finland, Sweden, or Germany. Are they not "well rounded"? The argument that college creates a well-rounded citizen can be sustained only by defining well rounded in a narrow way. Is someone who can quote from the school of Zen well rounded? Only if they can also maintain a motorcycle. Well-roundedness comes not from sitting in a classroom but from experiencing the larger world. 15

The focus on college education has distracted government and students from apprenticeship opportunities. Why should a major in English literature be subsidized with room and board on a beautiful campus with Olympic-size swimming pools and state-of-the-art athletic facilities when apprentices in nursing, electrical work, and new high-tech fields like mechatronics are typically unsubsidized (or less subsidized)? College students even get discounts at the movie theater; when was the last time you saw a discount for an electrical apprentice? 16

Our obsessive focus on college schooling has blinded us to basic truths. College is a place, not a magic formula. It matters what subjects students study, and subsidies should focus on the subjects that matter the most — not to the students but to everyone else. The high-school and college dropouts are also telling us something important: We need to provide opportunities for all types of learners, not just classroom learners. Going to college is neither necessary nor sufficient to be well educated. Apprentices in Europe are well educated but not college schooled. We need to open more roads to education so that more students can reach their desired destination. 17

VOCABULARY/USING A DICTIONARY

1. What is the definition of *apprenticeship* (para. 13)? How has it evolved over time?
2. *Mechatronics* (para. 16) is an example given of a new high-tech field. What is *mechatronics*?
3. What does the word *vocational* mean, and how does a *vocational* (para. 14) education differ from an *apprenticeship*, if at all?

RESPONDING TO WORDS IN CONTEXT

1. In paragraph 9, Tabarrok states that "an argument can be made for subsidizing students in fields with potentially large spillovers, such as

microbiology, chemical engineering, and computer science." What does the word *spillover* mean in this context, and what does it relate to?

2. "Sit down, stay quiet, and absorb," (para. 11) is what Tabarrok claims students are told in modern American education. What does *absorb* mean in this context?

3. One of the arguments Tabarrok uses to support the effectiveness of apprenticeships is that they are not "isolating teenagers in their own counterculture" (para. 14). What is the definition of *counterculture*, and what does it mean here?

DISCUSSING MAIN POINT AND MEANING

1. Why does Tabarrok think a liberal arts degree is less valuable than a science or engineering degree?

2. What support does Tabarrok provide to show that apprenticeships are practical and successful?

3. What is Tabarrok's overall argument regarding education? Does he propose a solution to what he views is America's education dilemma?

EXAMINING SENTENCES, PARAGRAPHS, AND ORGANIZATION

1. Tabarrok introduces a number of statistics in the second paragraph. Why do you think these statistics are introduced, and do you find their inclusion successful? Why or why not?

2. In the conclusion, Tabarrok states, "Our obsessive focus on college schooling has blinded us to basic truths. College is a place, not a magic formula." Analyze the tone of these sentences — what do you think Tabarrok is trying to accomplish in the conclusion?

3. Throughout the article, Tabarrok puts quotation marks around numerous words: "vocational" (para. 14); "well-rounded citizenry" (para. 15); "well rounded" (para. 15). What do you think the purpose of these quotation marks is?

THINKING CRITICALLY

1. What is your reaction to Tabarrok's claim that liberal arts education has diminishing returns for American society? Do you agree? Why or why not?

2. Is Tabarrok's argument clear and well supported? Where do you think he could have improved his support, and what do you think was his most effective method of supporting his argument?

3. In paragraph 11, Tabarrok writes, "College dropouts are telling us that college is not for everyone. Neither is high school." Do you agree with Tabarrok's conclusions that he draws from the presented drop-out statistics?

WRITING ACTIVITIES

1. Write a short essay in which you explore the debate of traditional American university education vs. vocational education. You may want to look back at Andrew Delbanco's essay, "3 Reasons College Still Matters" (p. 243) to help form an argument.

2. What do you think are the benefits of a vocational education? Building on the support that Tabarrok presents, further the argument that vocational education should be de-stigmatized in American education.

3. Are you a "sit-down learner," or do you learn better through doing tasks and learning as you go? Write a short essay that explores the differences between these two learning styles and how education could adapt to be effective for all kinds of learners.

Michelle Singletary

Not All College Majors Are Created Equal

[*Washington Post*, January 14, 2012]

BEFORE YOU READ

What obstacles to employment do college graduates face when they enter the workforce these days? Are you worried that your major won't help you find a job? What practical considerations should you make when choosing a path to pursue in college?

WORDS TO LEARN

relevant (para. 7): having something to do with the matter at hand (adj)

attain (para. 10): to reach or accomplish (verb)

substantially (para. 14): amply or much (adv)

marginally (para. 15): slightly (adv)

caveat (para. 16): warning (noun)

align (para. 17): to adjust into a line (verb)

Michelle Singletary is an author and nationally syndicated columnist ("The Color of Money") for the Washington Post. *She has appeared on personal finance segments for programs on NBC, MSNBC, ABC, CBS, PBS, and NPR, and she has served as keynote speaker at the NFL Rookie Symposium in addition to countless universities and churches across the nation.*

I have this game I play when I meet college students. 1

"What's your major?" I ask. 2

The student might say, "English," "psychology," "political science" 3
or "engineering."

And then, in my mind, after factoring 4
in some other information, I say to myself
"job" or "no job," depending on the major.

> I say to myself
> "job" or "no job,"
> depending on the
> major.

An English major with no internships 5
or any plan of what she might do with the
major to earn a living? No job.

A political science major with no 6
internships that could lead to a specific job opportunity? No job, I think.

Engineering major with three relevant internships in the engineer- 7
ing field? Ding. Ding. We have a winner. Job.

Certainly a college degree is the ticket to many jobs. The unem- 8
ployment rate for people with only a recent high school diploma is 22.9
percent, and it's an astonishing 31.5 percent among recent high school
dropouts. Nonetheless, the lack of career planning before a school is
chosen, a major is selected, and debt is borrowed is shocking to me. Not
enough students — and their families who are also taking on student
loans — are asking what their college major is worth in the workforce.

For years, long before the Great Recession[1] and today's almost 9 per- 9
cent unemployment rate among new college graduates, I've been beg-
ging students and their parents to consider the fallout from their choice
to borrow heavily to attend a school when the student has no clue about
the expected career opportunities of a chosen major.

Too many students aren't sure what job they could get after four, five, 10
or even six years of studying a certain major and racking up education
loans. Many aren't getting on-the-job training while they are in school
or during their semester or summer breaks. As a result, questions about
employment opportunities or what type of job they have the skills to
attain are met with blank stares or the typical, "I don't know."

And don't get me started on people who borrow heavily to get an 11
advanced degree without really knowing whether it will lead to a fatter
paycheck that can easily service the debt. In some cases it will, but for
some academic disciplines, the salary bump isn't as much as people expect.

Maybe a new report from the Georgetown Center on Education and 12
the Workforce will help encourage students to make better choices about

---

[1] Great Recession (para. 9): Also known as the Global Recession, a financial
crisis felt throughout the world economy that began in 2008, the effects of
which were still felt in 2012.

which college and degrees they pursue. *Hard Times: College Majors, Unemployment and Earnings: Not All College Degrees Are Created Equal* answers the question that many people are asking in the aftermath of the recession. Is college still worth it?

For most it is. But it all depends on your major, the report concludes.   13

"It was true in the 1970s that the purpose of going to college was to   14
get a degree because you could move through a lot of occupations," said Anthony P. Carnevale, director of the Georgetown Center. "But since then, the difference among degrees has grown substantially."

Median annual earnings among recent college graduates vary from   15
$55,000 among engineering majors to $30,000 in the arts. Education, psychology, and social work majors have relatively low unemployment, but their earnings are also low and only improve marginally with experience and graduate education.

"Today's best advice, then, is that high school students who can go   16
on to college should do so — with one caveat," the report's authors write. "They should do their homework before picking a major because, when it comes to employment prospects and compensation, not all college degrees are created equal."

A series of reports released by the Georgetown Center has focused   17
on matching jobs with majors. In 2010, the center warned about the growing disconnect between the types of jobs that employers need to fill and the number of people who have the education and training to fill them. The report, *Help Wanted: Projections of Jobs and Education Requirements Through 2018*, argues that students should align their postsecondary educational choices with available careers.

In the *Hard Times* report, the center found that the unemployment   18
rate for recent graduates is highest in architecture (13.9 percent) because of the collapse of the construction and home-building industry. Not surprisingly, unemployment rates are generally higher in non-technical majors, such as the arts (11.1 percent), humanities and liberal arts (9.4 percent), social science (8.9 percent), and law and public policy (8.1 percent).

A college education is not an investment in your future if you are   19
taking out loans just for the college experience. It's not an investment if you're not coupling your education with training. It's not an investment if you aren't researching which fields are creating good-paying jobs now and 30 years from now.

I wouldn't want to discourage people from pursuing a career they   20
love, even if the pay isn't very high. However, that choice should be made with the understanding of which job opportunities might be available and weighing what you can expect to earn annually against the cost of taking on debt to finance your education.

VOCABULARY/USING A DICTIONARY

1. What part of speech is *median* (para. 15)? How might your familiarity with the etymology of the word lead you to its definition? What other words are related to *median*?

2. What is an *internship* (para. 5)? What is an *investment* (para. 19)?

3. What is the literal definition of *aftermath* (para. 12)? What has the word come to mean?

RESPONDING TO WORDS IN CONTEXT

1. What is *fallout* (para. 9)? What does it mean in the context of this essay?

2. What is an example of a *non-technical* (para. 18) major? What might a technical major be?

3. The Georgetown Center on Education and the Workforce issued a report that discusses *employment prospects and compensation* (para. 16) for recent college graduates. What do those terms refer to?

DISCUSSING MAIN POINT AND MEANING

1. What, for Singletary, determines whether or not a recent college graduate is likely to get a job?

2. What economic developments have an effect on how Singletary believes parents and students should think about the so-called "college experience"?

3. In her essay, Singletary cites several reports. What is the purpose of these reports? What do they tell students about how to prepare for college?

EXAMINING SENTENCES, PARAGRAPHS, AND ORGANIZATION

1. The phrase "not all college majors are created equal" (title) is an allusion. What does it allude to? How does knowing the allusion enhance the effect of the phrase?

2. When Singletary refers to the *worth* (para. 8) of a college major, what is she referring to? How do you know?

3. Which do you find more compelling: the short sentences and dialogue that begin this essay or the longer evidence-driven paragraphs of the middle and conclusion? Why?

THINKING CRITICALLY

1. What is the main reason for going to college? Is it to find a job? Explain.

2. What problems do students face when they take out large loans for their college education? Why would someone take out such hefty loans?

3. If going to college doesn't guarantee you a high-paying job, *is* it still worth it, as Singletary asks? Why or why not?

WRITING ACTIVITIES

1. Create a list of majors you are familiar with and try to come up with five possible jobs for each that one might apply for after earning a college degree. Are some majors more difficult to pair with jobs? Is Singletary too quick to judge which college students will get jobs based on their majors, or do you think she is correct in her assumptions?

2. In a brief essay, discuss how college can be viewed as an investment. Does your idea of what kind of investment college is match Singletary's view? Explain.

3. What sort of fears do you have about finding employment once you finish college? Does Singletary's essay do anything to quell those fears? Does her essay add to those fears? Write a personal essay that discusses your future plans and makes use of Singletary's argument to help explain your feelings about your future.

Maria Dimera (student essay)

A College Degree Is a Worthy Achievement

[*The Corsair*, Santa Monica College, October 8, 2011]

BEFORE YOU READ

Do you believe the value of a college education should be measured in terms of money? If so, why? If not, why not?

WORDS TO LEARN

enroll (para. 1): to register (verb)
allegedly (para. 2): according to what is asserted without proof (adv)
ponder (para. 5): to consider (verb)
eternity (para. 9): endless time (noun)

incur (para. 10): to acquire or bring upon oneself (verb)
discontinue (para. 11): to put an end to (verb)
expiration (para. 14): the point at which something ends (noun)

Maria Dimera is a journalism student at Santa Monica College, where she has served as a staff writer for the campus newspaper.

The decision of whether or not to enroll in college often comes down to the financial aspect. With the nation's current economic difficulties, college students have already suffered many fee hikes and can only hope for a break. How many increases do students need to endure until it becomes too burdensome to attend a community college?

In fall 2011, Santa Monica College's tuition fee increased from $26 to $36, and will allegedly increase another $10 in the summer of 2012. Although a 10-dollar increase isn't the end of the world, California community colleges should only be considering $46-per-unit fees as the last resort.

For international student Anna Jonsson, paying $36 per unit would be ideal. "As an international student," said Jonsson, "I pay approximately $250 per unit. It's like seven times more than an average American student, so they should be glad they don't have to pay what I pay." Despite the high tuition fee, Jonsson embraces the opportunity to get a college degree abroad. "It's worth every penny."

As an international student, I completely agree with Jonsson. Although most students can make ends meet and pay for college, the recent increase is not joyful news for anyone. The increase, however, will not affect students who qualify for a fee waiver, which is great for them, since they can still apply and get one.

In today's world, many ponder the importance and benefits of a college degree. Bobby Simmons, a communications professor at SMC, believes that "a college education is more important than ever before, both in terms of economic opportunity, and in terms of developing oneself as an engaged member of a community."

> In today's world, many ponder the importance and benefits of a college degree.

Of course, learning is available in many different forms. College may not be for everyone, and some students will give up on earning a degree. These students either blame debt, lack of a guaranteed job, or they may simply consider it a waste of time. College students shouldn't let these issues pull them back from earning a degree, but rather push them ahead to succeed.

Plenty of colleges and other institutions offer grants and scholarships for students who could use the extra cash. Many SMC students have won thousands of dollars in scholarships. More students should take advantage of these awards and find other possible ways to pay for college, especially when facing financial strain.

"Not every institution is a smart investment, and students have to make good decisions about how to spend scarce resources. Part of the process is recognizing that what you are seeking is not a degree as much as an education," said Simmons, who has earned two bachelor's degrees, two master's degrees, and is closing in on a doctorate. 8

A college degree can leave behind a burden of discouragingly juicy debt that will take an eternity to repay, but a degree has a lot more to offer. It is entirely different from a high school diploma, since it's the ticket to one's desired field and higher pay. 9

SMC journalism professor Lyndon Stambler said, "In today's economy, students are finding that college degrees pay off, providing that they don't incur excessive debt." 10

Choices made while in college and afterwards play an important role in decision-making. While some may discontinue educational pursuits past an associate degree, others will go on to pursue a bachelor's or master's, which can help them to a better job. Still, other jobs may only require a basic education, and an associate degree will be enough to launch or advance a career. 11

"Even with the fee increases, which place additional financial stress on students, SMC is still affordable compared to most four-year universities. Students can spend a couple of years at SMC trying to figure out if they want to make the much bigger investment of attending a four-year university," said Stambler. 12

Many think that a college degree has less value today than it did a few decades ago, but a college degree is more than just a piece of paper. It is an experience and an accomplishment that no one can take away, no matter what happens after college. 13

The phrase, "It's not what you know, but who you know," is familiar among many, but it seems that "who you know" reflects a temporary situation, while "what you know" has no expiration date. 14

VOCABULARY/USING A DICTIONARY

1. What does the prefix *inter* mean? Based on that definition, how do you define the word *international* (para. 3)? What other words do you know that share that same prefix?

2. How do you define the word *increase* (para. 1)? How is it different from the word *decrease*?

3. From what language does the word *doctorate* (para. 8) come?

RESPONDING TO WORDS IN CONTEXT

1. What is a *waiver* (para. 4)? In Dimera's essay, what might possibly be *waived* for a qualified student?

2. How does one *embrace* (para. 3) an opportunity? How is the meaning in this context similar to the literal meaning?
3. What does a *communications* (para. 5) professor teach?

DISCUSSING MAIN POINT AND MEANING

1. How, according to Dimera, might students relieve some of the financial strain they may be under as they pay for their education?
2. What reasons are given in this essay as to why enrolled students drop out of college?
3. What are the benefits to a college education, as outlined by Dimera?

EXAMINING SENTENCES, PARAGRAPHS, AND ORGANIZATION

1. Dimera's position on the cost of college isn't revealed until paragraph 4. How does the delay of her thesis affect your experience of her argument?
2. How does Dimera put a different spin on the familiar adage, "It's not what you know, but who you know" (para. 14)?

THINKING CRITICALLY

1. Do you agree with the highly motivated fellow student Dimera quotes, who states that her college education is "worth every penny" (para. 3)?
2. Is a college degree "the ticket to one's desired field and higher pay"? Why or why not?
3. Research the tuition and estimated costs of the institution you currently attend and compare them to another college or university in the United States. Where do the prices seem similar (if at all)? How do they differ? In a brief essay, compare and contrast the school you attend with another random school, and explain why you have made a smart investment or what your current school might be lacking.

WRITING ACTIVITIES

1. Write a personal essay that discusses your struggles and stories as you deal with the financial burden of higher education. In it, argue whether or not the struggles or victories of your college experience are worth it. Be sure to include a concluding paragraph.
2. What are the benefits of a two-year college over a four-year college or university? What are the benefits of a four-year college over a two-year one?
3. Do you think "what you know" or "who you know" is more important? Write an essay that explores this question.

Moving from General to Specific

A common and effective way to begin an essay is to move from a general point to a specific instance. A writer may open an essay by claiming that ever since its beginnings the English language has undergone incessant change: The original Old English of the Anglo Saxons is unreadable today. That could prepare the way for the following paragraph to show specifically how the new social media, through texting, tweets, etc., are also changing the English language we know and that such changes are natural and inevitable.

Note how Santa Monica Community College student Maria Dimera starts with a general observation and then moves immediately to a specific instance. In "A College Degree Is a Worthy Achievement," Dimera opens her essay with a general statement about the growing costs of a college education in today's distressed economy. She then turns in her next paragraph to the situation at her particular school, providing very specific numbers to show the increasing costs. The first paragraph offers readers a general view of the cost of college in today's economy, while the second paragraph supports her generalization and brings us closer to what these costs actually are. In structuring her opening this way, Dimera follows a time-tested rhetorical pattern that has been used by writers and speakers for centuries.

1
Opens with general statement about costs of college today

The decision of whether or not to enroll in college often comes down to the financial aspect. (1) With the nation's current economic difficulties, college students have already suffered many fee hikes and can only hope for a break. How many increases do students need to endure until it becomes too burdensome to attend a community college?

2
Moves to specific increased costs at a specific college

In fall 2011, Santa Monica College's tuition fee increased from $26 to $36, and will allegedly increase another $10 in the summer of 2012. (2) Although a 10-dollar increase isn't the end of the world, California community colleges should only be considering $46-per-unit fees as the last resort.

STUDENT WRITER AT WORK
Maria Dimera

R.A. What inspired you to write this essay? And publish it in your campus paper?

M.D. I thought it was an important topic that affects all students. Most of us are debating whether or not to get a degree. Is it worth it these days?

R.A. What was your main purpose in writing this piece?

M.D. My purpose was for students to feel motivated to get a degree. It's one thing when you hear it from professors, parents, and family, but it's different when you hear the encouragement from a fellow student.

R.A. How long did it take for you to write this piece? Did you revise your work? What were your goals as you revised?

M.D. We have five days from the day we get the assignment to finish the piece, so five days would have been the maximum. I had to go over my work a few times before sending it in to the editor. My goal was to present fewer facts and more opinions, including my own and those of the professors and students I interviewed.

R.A. Do you generally show your writing to friends before submitting it? Do you collaborate or bounce your ideas off others?

M.D. Other than the people I interviewed, no one else saw my work while I was writing. I like to keep opinion pieces to myself so that I don't get influenced by others and come off my original opinion. Sometimes it's good to hear different opinions, but a school topic like this is quite personal to me. The professors I interviewed shared the same opinion as me, so there was no hesitation or change of heart when I wrote the piece.

R.A. What topics most interest you as a writer?

M.D. I'm most interested in opinion, fashion, music, travel, relationships, film and TV, and entrepreneurship.

R.A. Are you pursuing a career in which writing will be a component?

M.D. I am currently working on my first novel, a romance piece that I hope will be on the bookshelves soon.

R.A. What advice do you have for other student writers?

M.D. If writing is your passion, then stick with it. Write something every day even if it's only two hundred words, a diary entry, or a blog post. The field is competitive, but with the availability of the Internet, being a guest blogger or writer is something anyone can do. But you must have drive and passion.

Discussing the Unit

SUGGESTED TOPIC FOR DISCUSSION

The questions in many of the essays in this unit ask not only, "Does college matter?" but also, "What is the purpose of college?" Is the purpose of college to find a job after graduation, or is it something less practical? As college is becoming increasingly more expensive and nonetheless expected in the workforce, what should the primary focus of a college career be?

PREPARING FOR CLASS DISCUSSION

1. Compare and contrast Andrew Delbanco's and Michelle Singletary's arguments. On what points do they agree? On what points do they differ? How do your beliefs about the importance of college align (or not) with the authors'?

2. One reality many students are going to face is the rising cost of higher education and the increasing reliance on student loans. How do you think students should measure the costs vs. benefits of a college education? What factors did you take into consideration when deciding where to go to college?

FROM DISCUSSION TO WRITING

1. Think of your own college experience. What prompted you to go? Write a short essay in which you describe the various factors that have affected how you view higher education and why you decided to attend college.

2. Both Tabarrok and Singletary argue that majors in the sciences are more valuable and practical than those in the arts. Tabarrok goes so far as to say that students who earn a degree in one of the STEM programs should be subsidized monetarily, while those who are studying the arts should be free to do so, but without financial subsidy. In an essay, argue for or against this idea, using essays from the chapter as sources to support your argument.

TOPICS FOR CROSS-CULTURAL DISCUSSION

1. As college degrees have become increasingly necessary for entry-level employment, how might the gap between lower-, middle-, and upper-class citizens evolve? How can colleges and educational systems help to bridge the gap (if they need to)?

2. Andrew Tabarrok introduces his readers to the German apprenticeship program and compares it to the American "vocational" program. How might the United States be able to follow Germany's lead and encourage students who decide against college to pursue vocational training?

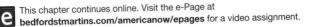 This chapter continues online. Visit the e-Page at
bedfordstmartins.com/americanow/epages for a video assignment.

The Economy: Are We Making Progress?

One pillar of the American dream has been the belief that everyone, even the poorest among us, has the potential to get ahead—and even make it big—with enough hard work and persistence. But for many Americans, the 2008 economic collapse and the long recession that followed it have made this belief feel more like a fairy tale than a real possibility. Accompanying declining faith in the American dream is what seems to be an ever-widening gap between the 1 percent of Americans who hold the greatest share of the nation's wealth and everyone else—that is, the "99 percent" characterized by the Occupy protesters, whose demonstrations started in New York City and spread throughout the country in late 2011. Have disparities in opportunities and wealth across income groups brought us to the point of "class warfare," as some commentators have suggested? Or are lower- and middle-class Americans actually making more progress than we've been led to believe? And what about the Occupy movement? Has it sparked any lasting and meaningful changes?

In "We Are Not All Created Equal," author and journalist Stephen Marche says the notion that all Americans have an equal opportunity to succeed is "the most dangerous lie the country tells itself. More than anything else, class now determines Americans' fates." This development does not bode well, Marche argues, for the already ailing middle class.

Professors Bruce D. Meyer and James X. Sullivan take a less pessimistic view in "American Mobility." The authors write, "Over the past three decades, growth in the U.S. economy has produced considerable, and demonstrable, improvement in material well-being for both the middle class and the poor." According to Meyer and Sullivan, statistics and methods traditionally used to calculate Americans' economic health overstate inflation and ignore certain factors—such as home size and car ownership—that contribute to individuals' quality of life.

Yet Meyer and Sullivan do not disagree that class divisions exist, and as writers Barbara and John Ehrenreich note in "The Making of the 99%," before the economic crash of 2008, these divisions made it hard for those outside the 1 percent to find common ground. However, the authors contend that the crash and the resulting Occupy movement brought together people from a variety of social and economic backgrounds, and "[w]hat started as a diffuse protest against economic injustice became a vast experiment in class building. The 99 percent, which might have seemed to be a purely aspirational category just a few months ago, began to will itself into existence." The authors add that if the 99 percent is to become "a force to change the world, eventually we will undoubtedly have to confront some of the class and racial divisions that lie within it."

The final essay in the chapter, by Clark University student Breanna Lembitz, offers a look inside the Occupy Wall Street movement, in which Lembitz served as a medical staffer, a public-discussion facilitator, and a member of the group's finance team, before she and the other demonstrators were arrested and the protest site dismantled. Despite some difficult experiences with it, Lembitz believes the movement was worthwhile: "We held the attention of the world for months, and we will continue to educate and mobilize people, and the people themselves will continue to build communities. We have a power that refuses to quit."

The e-Page feature for this chapter is an interactive infographic created by *The New York Times*, which asks its readers, "What's Your Economic Outlook?"

Stephen Marche

We Are Not All Created Equal

[*Esquire*, January 2012]

BEFORE YOU READ

What have you been taught about the American dream? Do you believe in complete social mobility and the idea that if you work hard, you will be successful?

WORD TO LEARN

clandestine (para. 3): purposefully secretive or deceptive (adj)

There are some truths so hard to face, so ugly and so at odds with how we imagine the world should be, that nobody can accept them. Here's one: It is obvious that a class system has arrived in America — a recent study of the thirty-four countries in the Organization for Economic Cooperation and Development found that only Italy and Great Britain have less social mobility. But nobody wants to admit: If your daddy was rich, you're gonna stay rich, and if your daddy was poor, you're gonna stay poor. Every instinct in the American gut, every institution, every national symbol, runs on the idea that anybody can make it; the only limits are your own limits. Which is an amazing idea, a gift to the world — just no longer true. Culturally, and in their daily lives, Americans continue to glide through a ghostly land of opportunity they can't bear to tell themselves isn't real. It's the most dangerous lie the country tells itself.

> Every instinct in the American gut, every institution, every national symbol, runs on the idea that anybody can make it.

More than anything else, class now determines Americans' fates. The old inequalities — racism, sexism, homophobia — are

---

Stephen Marche is a book author and frequently writes opinion pieces for the New York Times, *the* Wall Street Journal, *the* New Republic, Salon.com, *and the* Toronto Star *as well as "A Thousand Words about Our Culture," a monthly column for* Esquire *magazine.*

increasingly antiquated. Women are threatening to overwhelm men in the workplace, and the utter collapse of the black lower middle class in the age of Obama — a catastrophe for the African-American community — has little to do with prejudice and everything to do with brute economics. Who wins and who loses has become simplified, purified: those who own and those who don't. Meanwhile Great Britain, the source of the class system, has returned, plain and simple, to its old aristocratic masters. Reverting to type, the overlords and the underclass seem little removed from their eighteenth-century predecessors. The overlords preach shared sacrifice from their palaces and the underclass riots and the middle classes quietly judge. Everybody knows where he stands.

Not in America. In the United States, the emerging aristocracy   3
remains staunchly convinced that it is not an aristocracy, that it's the result of hard work and talent. The permanent working poor refuse to accept that their poverty is permanent. The class system is clandestine.

And yet the most cherished dreams are the hardest to awaken   4
from. The best-made shows on television now — some of the most beautifully shot, most beautifully articulated television shows ever made — capture in achingly precise detail the era that economists call the Great Compression, that shimmering, virtuous period before the 1970s when the middle class swelled so much that it came to believe it could never stop swelling — the original dangerous illusion. *Pan Am* is an unlikely parable of American fluidity. Being stuck in a tube in the air, serving coffee, and having your ass grabbed achieves glamour by virtue of the characters' ease of movement. Don Draper is a new Gatsby — he transforms himself from penniless vet to salesclerk to partner in an ad firm. Meanwhile, in Sitcomland, *Modern Family* has replaced working-class heroes like Homer Simpson and Ralph Kramden with the top 1 percent, and yet everyone, including the audience, seems to accept them as representative.

Meaningful, substantive approaches to class are going to have to   5
come from elsewhere. This month, the second season of *Downton Abbey* returns to PBS, and we may as well all have a look, because if we are going to have a European-style class system, we better begin to import their values. The scenery is extremely lovely. The arrangements are very cozy. British aristocrats always look like they're daring the world to line them all up against a wall and erase the entire parasitical group of them, but at Downton, at least, the ruling class is somewhat aware of the arbitrary nature of its status. The American ruling class could learn from their humility. At Downton Abbey, where everyone has a place, at least

the boy who cleans the boots and knives isn't a bad person because of his job.

Herman Cain's comment in a recent interview on the Occupy Wall Street movement, which is by no means an uncommon opinion, was this: "If you're not rich, blame yourself." The old Calvinist strain that connects prosperity to divine election runs deep. Work hard and stay late and you get to be a banker or doctor; drop out of high school or start using drugs and you'll end up at McDonald's. Even among liberals, the new trend toward behavioral economics demonstrates how poor people fare worse on tests requiring self-control, how their personal weaknesses create cycles of poverty. You don't have to be on talk radio to believe that the poor must be doing something wrong.

The Great Outcry that has filled the country with inchoate rage is the bloody mess of this fundamental belief in the justice of American outcomes crashing headfirst into the new reality. The majority of new college grads in the United States today are either unemployed or working jobs that don't require a degree. Roughly 85 percent of them moved back home in 2011, where they sit on an average debt of $27,200. The youth unemployment rate in general is 18.1 percent. Are these all bad people? None of us — not Generation Y, not Generation X, and certainly not the Boomers — have ever faced anything like it. The Tea Partiers blame the government. The Occupiers blame the financial industry. Both are really mourning the arrival of a new social order, one not defined by opportunity but by preexisting structures of wealth. At least the ranters are mourning. Those who are not screaming or in drum circles mostly pretend that the change isn't happening.

Post-hope, it is hard to imagine even any temporary regression back to the days of the swelling American middle class. The forces of inequality are simply too powerful and the forces against inequality too weak. But at least we can end the hypocrisy. In ten years, the next generation will no longer have the faintest illusion that the United States is a country with equality of opportunity. The least they're entitled to is some honesty about why.

VOCABULARY/USING A DICTIONARY

1. What does the word *parasitical* mean (para. 5), and what are the origins of the word?

2. The word *aristocracy* (para. 3) has multiple meanings. Which one pertains most to this essay?

3. What is the definition of *inchoate* (para. 7)?

RESPONDING TO WORDS IN CONTEXT

1. In paragraph 2, Marche states that the collapse of the black lower-middle class "has less to do with prejudice and everything to do with brute economics." What does the word *brute* mean in this context?
2. Marche claims, "The old Calvinist strain that connects prosperity to divine election runs deep" (para. 6). What does the word *Calvinist* refer to?
3. In the sentence, "Meaningful, substantive approaches to class are going to have to come from elsewhere" (para. 5), what is the meaning of *substantive*?

DISCUSSING MAIN POINT AND MEANING

1. What does Marche believe about the American dream?
2. How has social mobility changed over the last fifty years, and how does Marche believe it will continue to change?
3. What does Marche suggest society thinks being poor is indicative of?

EXAMINING SENTENCES, PARAGRAPHS, AND ORGANIZATION

1. Marche's opening sentence makes a bold claim about the ability to face truths. How does this sentence prepare the reader for the essay that follows?
2. In paragraph 4, Marche introduces pop culture references as support for the changing landscape of wealth and social mobility. What are these references, and what do they lend to—or detract from—the argument?
3. Many of Marche's sentences depend upon contrasting two opposing entities or ideas (e.g., rich vs. poor). Go through the essay and identify several examples of such sentences. How do they reinforce Marche's overall argument? What is their effect on you as a reader?

THINKING CRITICALLY

1. How has social mobility changed in your lifetime? Do you see as much opportunity for young people as there used to be?
2. Marche argues that perceived worth and goodness are attached to monetary success—that is, wealthy equals good and poor equals bad. Following this logic, how do you think the middle class is perceived?
3. Why do you think shows like *Modern Family* and *Mad Men* are popular today? What do you think their popularity says about the current outlook on economic mobility in America?

WRITING ACTIVITIES

1. Write an essay that responds to Herman Cain's statement, "If you're not rich, blame yourself." Discuss not only whether you agree or disagree with this statement, but why you think this is a common opinion.

2. One of the assumptions that Marche makes to support his argument is that Americans do not acknowledge a class system, and are therefore unable to change it. Do you consider yourself or your family part of a class? Why or why not? Write a short essay in response to the idea of the American class system and whether you think it exists or not.

3. What do you think the solution to the problem of this class system is? Do you agree with Marche, that we should acknowledge it so it doesn't get worse? Or do you think that social mobility is still an option, and conceding a class system would be detrimental to American society?

Bruce D. Meyer and James X. Sullivan

American Mobility

[Commentary Magazine, March 2012]

BEFORE YOU READ

What have you heard from your family or friends, seen on television, or read online recently about the middle and lower classes? Do you believe that the quality of life in recent years has increased or decreased?

WORDS TO LEARN

eminent (para. 11): famous or respected in their field (adj)

O ver the past three decades, the American economy has grown considerably. Accounting for population growth and price changes, GDP has increased by more than 60 percent. There is a prevailing sentiment, however, that the middle class and the poor have

1

Bruce D. Meyer is a professor in the Harris School of Public Policy Studies at the University of Chicago. His recent work includes research on unemployment insurance, immigration and self-employment, and the effects of welfare on single mothers. Meyer has advised the U.S. Department of Labor, U.S. Bureau of Labor Statistics, and the New York State Office of Temporary and Disability Assistance, among others.

James X. Sullivan is an associate professor of economics at the University of Notre Dame. He has published many articles with Bruce D. Meyer on income inequality and poverty in the United States, which have appeared in the Journal of Human Resources, *the* Journal of Public Economics, *the* American Economic Review, *and on both CNN and Fox News networks.*

not enjoyed any of the benefits of this sustained growth. A 2007 CBS News poll found that 60 percent of Americans believed that things had gotten worse for the middle class during the past decade. With the financial collapse of 2008 and the recession that followed it, that percentage is surely much higher today. Conventional wisdom holds that things have also gotten worse for those at the bottom, despite efforts to alleviate the living conditions of the poor. As Robert Siegel, of National Public Radio, recently stated, "It is commonplace to say that we have lost the war on poverty."

2   Much of this sentiment stems from official measures that paint a bleak picture of the middle class and the poor. Official median household income fell between 1999 and 2004, using the conventional adjustment for inflation. Since then, median income has risen but remains below its 1999 level. Official statistics are even gloomier for the poor: The official poverty rate in 2009 was higher than in 1980.

3   But this grim portrait of an America in which life has improved for the wealthy and no one else is inaccurate. Over the past three decades, growth in the U.S. economy has produced considerable, and demonstrable, improvement in material well-being for both the middle class and the poor. They, too, have come along for the ride. One just needs to know where — and how — to look.

> This grim portrait of an America in which life has improved for the wealthy and no one else is inaccurate.

4   With analytical measures that are great advancements on the official methods of the past, we have found in our research significant evidence of such improvement among the middle class and poor. Between 1980 and 2009, income and consumption rose by more than 50 percent in real terms for both groups. Living units became markedly larger and much more likely to feature air-conditioning and other amenities. The quality of the cars these families own also improved considerably.

5   First, we've found strong evidence of improvement in the material well-being of poor families. For Americans in the 10th percentile of wealth, income rose by 44 percent between 1980 and 2009. Even this, however, understates improvements at the bottom. Consumption among the poorest (what goods they actually obtained or used) grew even more during this same period. For those in the bottom 20 percent, or the lowest quintile, the size of living units increased by 200 to 250 square feet, and the fraction of these low-income people who enjoy either central or

window air-conditioning doubled. The share with other amenities also rose noticeably.

There were similar improvements for the middle class. Their houses have become bigger, rising by more than one-quarter of a room without adjusting for household size, and by seven-tenths of a room when accounting for family size. Since 1989, square footage has risen between 300 and 350 square feet. About half of this increase has taken place since 1999, a period during which official median household income fell.

6

The share of middle-quintile individuals with air-conditioning rose from 58 percent to 88 percent between 1981 and 2009. Central air-conditioning rose from 27 percent to 67 percent. Since 1989, the share of people in the middle quintile with a dishwasher has risen from 53 percent to 70 percent; and with a clothes dryer from 79 percent to 88 percent. Again, a large share of this increase has occurred since 1999. Since 1989, the incidence of leaks from plumbing and roofs has fallen sharply, as has the likelihood of living amid peeling paint or with a broken toilet.

7

What accounts for the striking differences between official analyses and our research? First, most analyses of economic well-being rely on narrow income measures that do not reflect the full range of resources, monetary and otherwise, available to the households for consumption of goods and services.

8

They ignore food stamps and do not take into account resources from important antipoverty programs such as the Earned Income Tax Credit (EITC) and housing or school-lunch subsidies. These excluded benefits are generous and have increased significantly over the past few decades. Official analyses also often rely on underreported measures of income. For these reasons, our analyses include comparisons between official pretax income numbers and figures that incorporate taxes and benefits.

9

Second, official statistics exaggerate inflation. Obviously, the higher prices seem, the lower the perceived purchasing power of the poor. But in determining the poverty threshold — the statistical point that separates the poor from the rest of the population — the official statistics rely on an index called the Consumer Price Index for All Urban Consumers, also known as CPI-U. There is broad consensus that the CPI-U overstates inflation and therefore significantly understates improvements in economic well-being. When median incomes are calculated, a similarly biased index is used: the Consumer Price Index Research Series, or CPI-U-RS. Over time, bias in both these indices has

10

significantly muted the rise in household income for both the middle class and the poor.[1]

Hypothetically, an annual misstating of inflation by just 1 percent would lead to a 33 percent difference in determining median incomes between 1980 and 2009. Our best evidence indicates that the annual bias over much of this period has been even greater. In 1996, the Boskin Commission, a group of eminent economists appointed by the Senate Finance Committee, concluded that the annual bias in the CPI-U was 1.1 percentage points that year, but 1.3 percentage points in preceding years. In our results, we make changes to correct for such bias by using an adjustment that subtracts 0.8 percentage points from the growth as figured in the CPI-U-RS index each year. 11

Finally, we believe that consumption provides a more appropriate measure of well-being than does income. It reflects resources that may have been accumulated over time, whereas income may vary in the short term. Consider, for example, a retired couple who own their home outright and who live off of savings. Clearly, their *income* will not reflect the totality of their actual *material well-being*.[2] 12

Income measures also fail to capture disparities in consumption that result from differences in the amount of credit available and credit used. Even if income remains the same, government safety-net programs affect the ability of households to consume because they diminish the need for households to save for a rainy day. (If you know you're going to 13

---

[1] Four types of biases have been identified. Outlet bias refers to the inadequate accounting of the movement of purchases toward low-price discount or big-box stores like Walmart. Substitution bias refers to bias in the use of a fixed list of purchasable items when people substitute away from high-relative-price items so the old market basket becomes less relevant. Quality bias refers to inadequate adjustments for the quality improvements in products over time, while new-product bias refers to the omission of or long delay in the incorporation of new products into the CPI.

[2] Our analyses of material well-being draw upon data from several large, nationally representative surveys covering the period from 1980 through 2009. Our consumption measures and information on automobiles were derived from the Consumer Expenditure survey (CE), which provides quarterly information on family spending. We used the surveys from the first quarter of 1980 through the first quarter of 2010. Measures of income came from the Annual Social and Economic Supplement to the Current Population Survey (CPS), which provides data for approximately 100,000 households annually in recent years. We used data from the 1981 through 2010 surveys, which provide family income information for the previous calendar year. The results that follow were drawn from known and respected data sets.

receive free health care from the time you're 65, you do not have to restrict your spending in the prior two decades to save for health-care expenses, for example.) Consumption is more likely to capture income from self-employment and to reflect private and government transfers. Much of the effort to improve income measures involves making them more like consumption measures, but it is much easier to begin with consumption data. That's what we did.

Our preferred measures of income and consumption as well as data on housing and cars all tell the same story: The material circumstances of the middle class have improved dramatically since 1980. It is crucial to note the pattern of differences between the results from official reports and those from our improved measures. 14

First, official pretax median household income grew by 20 percent in real terms between 1980 and 2000, but then fell by 5 percent during the 2000s. The second measure of pretax money income differs from the first in several ways: Resources are measured at the *family*, rather than household, level and adjusted for differences in family size and composition following National Academy of Sciences recommendations. The median for this second measure follows a pattern very similar to that of the official measure, although the level of the median is about 15 percent higher. 15

The third measure, unlike the first two, accounts for inflation using our adjusted inflation index rather than the biased CPI-U-RS. When the adjusted index is used, median income is seen to have risen by 46 percent between 1980 and 2009, compared with 17 percent when the biased measure is used. 16

It's not the rich 1 percent who have been working to stall the well-being of the middle class; it's bad statistics. 17

In terms of car ownership — the largest and most expensive consumer product — those in the middle-income quintile, or the middle 20 percent, have fared well. Car ownership rates for this quintile are high — close to 95 percent — and have not changed noticeably during the past three decades. But the fraction of families with more than one car rose by more than 4.4 percentage points between 1999 and 2009. Furthermore, these cars were much more likely to have features such as power brakes, power steering, and a sunroof. The number of cars with air-conditioning rose from 47 percent to more than 83 percent between 1981 and 2004. These changes in vehicle characteristics understate the full pattern of quality improvement. There have been widespread improvements in braking and acceleration, as well as in the adoption of air bags, antilock brakes, sophisticated sound systems, and other features. Any discussion of material well-being must take into account these advances in amenities. If 18 the material comforts of high earners can be cited as the excesses of a carefree elite, then honesty demands consideration of the dramatically improved products that are increasingly available to Americans across the economic spectrum.

All our results indicate a notable rise in the material well-being of the   19
poor during the past three decades. Using our preferred measures of income and consumption (and addressing bias in previous methods of calculating inflation), we've shown a sharp decline in poverty. We've also shown that there have been noticeable improvements in the quality of living units and cars for poor families.

The official measure of pretax money income for America's poorest   20
10 percent indicates only modest gains over the past three decades. We see virtually no change between 1980 and 1993. The 10th percentile for the official measure then rose by 19 percent between 1993 and 1999, but it fell in real terms in the most recent decade. But, after making the same adjustments made to the middle-class results, we can see that the income of the 10th percentile has actually risen by 40 percent.

The consumption numbers indicate significantly improved well-   21
being for those near the bottom over most of our time period. Between 1980 and 2009, consumption among the 10th percentile rose by 54 percent in real terms, while after-tax income plus noncash benefits grew by 44 percent. The changes in consumption have often differed from the changes in income, particularly in recent years. During the 2000s, consumption at the 10th percentile grew by 18 percent, while after-tax income plus non-cash benefits grew by less than 4 percent.

Taxes and transfer payments (such as the Earned Income Tax   22
Credit) have had an important impact on the resources of those near the bottom. The 10th percentile of after-tax income plus noncash benefits rose noticeably more than did the 10th percentile of pretax income, and the results showing after-tax income and noncash benefits show a consistently higher level of material well-being for those at the bottom. Elsewhere, we show that this difference is accounted for by taxes rather than noncash benefits (for more details, visit nd.edu/~jsulliv4/Five Decades4.01.pdf).

When we looked at poverty rates, we found striking results. According   23
to the official measures, the poverty rate in the United States between 1980 and 2009 increased by more than 1 percentage point. By our calculations using our adjusted inflation measure, poverty levels fell by more than 3 percentage points. And, even more striking, over the past three decades, a measure of what we might call "consumption poverty" — or the fraction of individuals whose consumption falls below an inflation-adjusted

poverty threshold — fell by nearly 10 percentage points, a decline of 76 percent.

Like their middle-class counterparts, those in the bottom income quintile are living — and driving — much better than they were 30 years ago. Their houses have become bigger, rising by 0.16 rooms on average without adjusting for household size, and by half a room when accounting for family size. Housing-unit size rose after 1999, but by a smaller amount than over the previous decade.   24

The share of bottom-quintile individuals with any air-conditioning rose from 41 percent to 83 percent between 1981 and 2009. Central air-conditioning rose by 39 percentage points from 15 percent to 54 percent. Since 1989, the share of people in the bottom quintile with a dishwasher rose from 22 percent to 42 percent, and the prevalence of clothes dryers for the bottom quintile rose from 48 percent to 68 percent. Most of this increase occurred after 1999, a period during which official poverty *rose*. Over the period since 1989, the incidence of plumbing and roofing leaks fell sharply, as did the likelihood of living amid peeling paint or with a broken-down toilet.   25

Over the past three decades, car-ownership rates grew more noticeably among the poor than among the middle class. In 1981, 69 percent of all households in the bottom quintile owned at least one car. By 2009, 76 percent did. There is also evidence that the quality of cars owned has improved. Among the poorest households, the fraction of cars with power brakes, power steering, or other features rose sharply between 1981 and 2004. The fraction of cars with air-conditioning rose from 47 percent to 77 percent between 1980 and 2004. The share of cars with power brakes, power steering, and air-conditioning was about the same for the bottom and middle quintiles by 2004.   26

These patterns stand in sharp contrast to the noticeable decline in living standards over the past few years, which have hurt both the poor and middle class. Since 2007, median consumption has fallen by 5 percent, and consumption poverty has increased by 21 percent. Many of the calls for radical policy reform have been based on these short-term patterns. But the national crisis as it is currently framed — as one of declining well-being for the middle class and the poor — is not supported by rigorous analysis.   27

If discussion of wealth inequality is to bear fruit and lead to effective policy, it must begin with this honest assessment and not the politicized impressions that have made genuine debate impossible. The recent declines in the material circumstances of the middle class and the poor are due to a severe recession and a sluggish recovery. These short-term setbacks, while very real, do not offset the long-run picture of American progress that is broad and dramatic.   28

VOCABULARY/USING A DICTIONARY
1. What does *consumption* (para. 4) mean, and what are the origins of the word?
2. Define the word *median* (para. 2).
3. What are the origins of *subsidies* (para. 9), and what is the word's definition?

RESPONDING TO WORDS IN CONTEXT
1. In their study, Meyer and Sullivan often refer to "material well-being." What does the word *material* mean in this context, and what part of speech is it?
2. How do Meyer and Sullivan define *poverty threshold* (para. 10)?
3. In paragraph 18, Meyer and Sullivan state, " ... honesty demands consideration of the dramatically improved products that are increasingly available to Americans across the economic spectrum." How is the word *spectrum* being used in this sentence, and how would you define the word?

DISCUSSING MAIN POINT AND MEANING
1. Summarize Meyer and Sullivan's argument in one or two sentences.
2. What is the major flaw Meyer and Sullivan say has falsely skewed the reporting and perception of the decline of the middle and lower classes?
3. List the areas and items that Meyer and Sullivan analyzed to determine the level of "material well-being."

EXAMINING SENTENCES, PARAGRAPHS, AND ORGANIZATION
1. At what point in the essay do the authors introduce the idea of a flawed analysis and exaggerated inflation rates? Why do you think these ideas are presented where they are in the essay?
2. In paragraph 10, Meyer and Sullivan state, "There is a broad consensus that the CPI-U overstates inflation and therefore significantly understates improvements in economic well-being." How does this statement differ from many of the statistic and fact-based statements in the rest of the essay?
3. In the last two paragraphs, Meyer and Sullivan concede that the living standards of the last few years have decreased. What reason do they give for ignoring that decline, and why do you think they left that information until the conclusion of the essay?

THINKING CRITICALLY
1. Do you believe the units of measurement for material well-being used in this essay are indicative of actual well-being? Why or why not?
2. If you were to establish your own criteria for measuring growth, what would that consist of? Explain your choices.

3. If Meyer and Sullivan's claims were widely accepted, what do you think would be the political and social implications? How would the national conversation change if the public began to believe that the middle and lower classes were still improving?

WRITING ACTIVITIES

1. Write a short essay in which you analyze the conclusions Meyer and Sullivan make from their data. Discuss not only whether you agree or disagree with their conclusions, but basing your own analysis on the data presented, discuss why you believe their analysis to be flawed or sound.

2. Look back at question 2 from Thinking Critically. In a short essay, present your criteria for measuring material well-being, and then compare and contrast it to how Meyer and Sullivan measure material well-being.

3. While consumption has increased over the past twenty years, so has personal debt. Write a short essay on how the inclusion of debt statistics would change Meyer and Sullivan's analysis, if you believe it would. If you don't believe it changes their analysis, explain why not.

Barbara Ehrenreich and John Ehrenreich

The Making of the 99%

[*The Nation*, December 14, 2011]

BEFORE YOU READ

How did a movement like Occupy Wall Street come into being? What economic factors led up to the Occupy movement and to the designation of the 99%?

Barbara Ehrenreich is a journalist, activist, and author of fourteen books, including New York Times *bestseller* Nickel and Dimed: On (Not) Getting by in America *(2001),* Bright-Sided: How Positive Thinking Is Undermining America *(2010), and* Bait and Switch: The (Futile) Pursuit of the American Dream *(2006).*

John Ehrenreich is a professor of psychology and director of the Center for Psychology and Society at SUNY College at Old Westbury. He is the author of The Altruistic Imagination: A History of Social Work and Social Policy in the United States (1985) *and* The Humanitarian Companion: A Guide for International Aid, Development and Human Rights Workers (2005), *as well as several articles with Barbara Ehrenreich.*

WORDS TO LEARN

churlish (para. 2): rude (adj)

pension (para. 2): an amount of money paid to someone regularly, usually after retirement (noun)

stridently (para. 4): shrilly or gratingly (adv)

spurious (para. 5): inauthentic (adj)

populism (para. 5): representation of the common people (noun)

innovation (para. 5): something new (noun)

nefarious (para. 6): very wicked (adj)

traction (para. 7): adhesive friction (noun)

hierarchy (para. 8): a system of rank (noun)

depredations (para. 9): ravages (noun)

summarily (para. 9): immediately (adv)

piker (para. 9): someone who gambles or performs tasks on a small scale (noun)

decimate (para. 10): to destroy in great numbers (verb)

venture (para. 10): a risky undertaking (noun)

iconic (para. 10): emblematic (adj)

plausibility (para. 11): the appearance of truth (noun)

pundit (para. 11): an expert (noun)

awry (para. 11): off course (adv)

dictum (para. 12): a saying (noun)

prohibitively (para. 14): discouragingly (adv)

concatenation (para. 14): chain (noun)

destitution (para. 14): poverty (noun)

amenities (para. 16): courtesies (noun)

engender (para. 17): to produce (verb)

meme (para. 18): a widespread cultural reference (noun)

Class happens when some men, as a result of common experiences (inherited or shared), feel and articulate the identity of their interests as between themselves, and as against other men whose interests are different from (and usually opposed to) theirs.

— E. P. Thompson
The Making of the English Working Class

The "other men" (and of course women) in the current American class alignment are those in the top 1 percent of the wealth distribution — the bankers, hedge-fund managers, and CEOs targeted by the Occupy Wall Street movement. They have been around for a long time in one form or another, but they began to emerge as a distinct and visible group, informally called the "superrich," only in recent years. 1

Extravagant levels of consumption helped draw attention to them: private jets, multiple 50,000-square-foot mansions, $25,000 frozen hot 2 chocolate embellished with gold dust. But as long as the middle class could still muster the credit for college tuition and occasional home improvements, it seemed churlish to complain. Then came the financial crash of 2007–08, followed by the Great Recession, and the 1 percent — to whom we had entrusted our pensions, our economy, and our political system — stood revealed as a band of feckless, greedy narcissists, and possibly sociopaths.

Still, until a few months ago, the 99 percent was hardly a group capable of (as Thompson says) "articulat[ing] the identity of their interests." It contained, and still contains, most "ordinary" rich people, along with middle-class professionals; factory workers, truck drivers, and miners; and the much poorer people who clean the houses, manicure the fingernails, and maintain the lawns of the affluent. It was divided not only by these class differences but most visibly by race and ethnicity — a division that has deepened since 2008. African-Americans and Latinos of all income levels disproportionately lost their homes to foreclosures in 2007 and '08, and then disproportionately lost their jobs in the wave of layoffs that followed. On the eve of the Occupy movement, the black middle class had been devastated. In fact, the only movements to have come out of the 99 percent before Occupy emerged were the Tea Party movement and, on the other side of the political spectrum, the resistance to restrictions on collective bargaining in Wisconsin.

But Occupy could not have happened if large swaths of the 99 percent had not begun to discover some common interests, or at least to put aside some of the divisions among themselves. For decades, the most stridently promoted division within the 99 percent was the one between what the right calls the "liberal elite" — composed of academics, journalists, media figures, etc. — and pretty much everyone else.

As *Harper's* columnist Tom Frank has brilliantly explained, the right earned its spurious claim to populism by targeting that "liberal elite," which supposedly favors reckless government spending that requires oppressive levels of taxes, supports "redistributive" social policies and programs that reduce opportunity for the white middle class, creates ever more regulations (to, for instance, protect the environment) that reduce jobs for the working class, and promotes kinky countercultural innovations like gay marriage. The liberal elite, insisted conservative intellectuals, looked down on "ordinary" middle- and working-class Americans, finding them tasteless and politically incorrect. The "elite" was the enemy, while the superrich were just like everyone else, only more "focused" and perhaps a bit better connected.

Of course, the "liberal elite" never made any sociological sense. Not all academics or media figures are liberal (Newt Gingrich, George Will,

Rupert Murdoch). Many well-educated middle managers and highly trained engineers may favor latte over Red Bull, but they were never targets of the right. And how could trial lawyers be members of the nefarious elite, while their spouses in corporate law firms were not?

"Liberal elite" was always a political category masquerading as a sociological one. What gave the idea of a liberal elite some traction, though, at least for a while, was that the great majority of us have never knowingly encountered a member of the actual elite, the 1 percent, who are for the most part sealed off in their own bubble of private planes, gated communities, and walled estates.   7

The authority figures most people are likely to encounter in their daily lives are teachers, doctors, social workers, professors. These groups (along with middle managers and other white-collar corporate employees) occupy a much lower position in the class hierarchy. They make up what we described in a 1976 essay as the "professional managerial class." As we wrote at the time, on the basis of our experience of the radical movements of the 1960s and '70s, there have been real, longstanding resentments between the working-class and middle-class professionals. These resentments, which the populist right cleverly deflected toward "liberals," contributed significantly to the failure of that previous era of rebellion to build a lasting progressive movement.   8

As it happened, the idea of the "liberal elite" could not survive the depredations of the 1 percent in the late 2000s. For one thing, it was summarily eclipsed by the discovery of the actual, Wall Street-based elite and their crimes. Compared with them, professionals and managers, no matter how annoying, were pikers. The doctor or school principal might be overbearing, the professor and the social worker might be condescending, but only the 1 percent took your house away.   9

There was, as well, another inescapable problem embedded in the right-wing populist strategy: even by 2000, and certainly by 2010, the class of people who might qualify as part of the "liberal elite" was in increasingly bad repair. Public sector budget cuts and corporate-inspired reorganizations were decimating the ranks of decently paid academics, who were replaced by adjunct professors working on bare subsistence incomes. Media firms were shrinking their newsrooms and editorial budgets. Law firms had started outsourcing their more routine tasks to India. Hospitals beamed X-rays to cheap foreign radiologists. Funding had dried up for nonprofit ventures in the arts and public service. Hence the iconic figure of the Occupy movement: the college graduate with tens of thousands of dollars in student loan debts and a job paying about $10 a hour, or no job at all.   10

These trends were in place even before the financial crash hit, but it 11
took the crash and its grim economic aftermath, all the "collateral damage," to awaken the 99 percent to a widespread awareness of shared danger. In 2008 the intention of "Joe the Plumber" to earn a quarter-million dollars a year still had some faint sense of plausibility. But a couple of years into the recession, sudden downward mobility had become the mainstream American experience, and even some of the most reliably neoliberal media pundits were beginning to announce that something had gone awry with the American dream.

Once-affluent people lost their nest eggs as housing prices dropped 12
off cliffs. Laid-off middle-aged managers and professionals were staggered to find that their age made them repulsive to potential employers. Medical debts plunged middle-class households into bankruptcy. The old conservative dictum — that it was unwise to criticize (or tax) the rich because you might be one of them someday — gave way to a new realization that the class you were most likely to migrate into wasn't the rich but the poor.

And here was another thing many in the middle class were discover- 13
ing: the downward plunge into poverty could occur with dizzying speed. One reason the concept of an economic 99 percent first took root in America rather than, say, Ireland or Spain is that Americans are particularly vulnerable to economic dislocation. We have little in the way of a welfare state to stop a family or an individual in free fall. Unemployment benefits do not last more than six months or a year, though in a recession they are sometimes extended by Congress. At present, even with such an extension, they reach only about half the jobless. Welfare was all but abolished fifteen years ago, and health insurance has traditionally been linked to employment.

In fact, once an American starts to slip downward, a variety of forces 14
kick in to help accelerate the slide. An estimated 60 percent of American firms now check applicants' credit ratings, and discrimination against the unemployed is widespread enough to have begun to warrant Congressional concern. Even bankruptcy is a prohibitively expensive, often crushingly difficult status to achieve. Failure to pay government-imposed fines or fees can lead, through a concatenation of unlucky breaks, to an arrest warrant or a criminal record. Where other once-wealthy nations have a safety net, America offers a greased chute, leading down to destitution with alarming speed.

> Once an American starts to slip downward, a variety of forces kick in to help accelerate the slide.

The Occupation encampments that enlivened approximately 1,400 cit- 15
ies this fall provided a vivid template for the 99 percent's growing sense
of unity. Here were thousands of people — we may never know the exact
numbers — from all walks of life, living outdoors in the streets and parks,
very much as the poorest of the poor have always lived: without electricity, heat, water, or toilets. In the process, they managed to create self-
governing communities. General assembly meetings brought together
an unprecedented mix of recent college graduates, young professionals,
elderly people, laid-off blue-collar workers, and plenty of the chronically homeless for what were, for the most part, constructive and civil
exchanges. What started as a diffuse protest against economic injustice
became a vast experiment in class building. The 99 percent, which might
have seemed to be a purely aspirational category just a few months ago,
began to will itself into existence.

Can the unity cultivated in the encampments survive as the Occupy 16
movement evolves into a more decentralized phase? All sorts of class,
racial, and cultural divisions persist within that 99 percent, including distrust between members of the former "liberal elite" and those less privileged. It would be surprising if they didn't. The life experience of a young
lawyer or of a social worker is very different from that of a blue-collar
worker whose work life may rarely allow even for the basic amenities of
meal or bathroom breaks. Drum circles, consensus decision-making, and
masks remain exotic to at least the 90 percent. "Middle class" prejudice
against the homeless, fanned by decades of right-wing demonization of
the poor, retains much of its grip.

Sometimes these differences led to conflict in Occupy encamp- 17
ments — for example, over the role of the chronically homeless in Portland
or the use of marijuana in Los Angeles — but amazingly, despite all the
official warnings about health and safety threats, there was no "Altamon[1]
moment": no major fires, and hardly any violence. In fact, the encampments engendered almost unthinkable convergences: people from comfortable backgrounds learning about street survival from the homeless, a
distinguished professor of political science discussing horizontal versus
vertical decision-making with a postal worker, military men in dress uniforms showing up to defend Occupiers from the police.

Class happens, as Thompson said, but it happens most decisively 18
when people are prepared to nourish and build it. If the "99 percent" is
to become more than a stylish meme, if it's to become a force to change

---

[1] Altamont (para. 17): A music festival held in 1969 at the Altamont Speedway in
California, which became a symbol of the death of the 1960s counterculture.

the world, eventually we will undoubtedly have to confront some of the class and racial divisions that lie within it. But we need to do so patiently, respectfully, and always with an eye to the next big action — the next march, or building occupation, or foreclosure fight, as the situation demands.

VOCABULARY/USING A DICTIONARY

1. If someone is *condescending* (para. 9), what is he or she like?
2. What does it mean if something is *decentralized* (para. 16) vs. *centralized*? What does the prefix *de-* indicate?
3. What's the difference between *feckless* (para. 2) and *reckless* (para. 5)? What do these words mean? How are they similar?

RESPONDING TO WORDS IN CONTEXT

1. The Ehrenreichs talk about a *political spectrum* in paragraph 3. What is a *spectrum*?
2. What is common to the words *sociopath* (para. 2) and *sociological* (para. 6)? What do those words mean?
3. The Ehrenreichs use the phrase "economic dislocation" (para. 13). What does it mean to be dislocated? How do you apply that definition to economics?

DISCUSSING MAIN POINT AND MEANING

1. How did the failed housing market and the accompanying recession lead to exposure and demonization of the 1%?
2. What distinction do the Ehrenreichs make between the "liberal elite" and the actual elite?
3. What happened to the economy that led to the creation of a majority of people (the 99%) who identify overwhelmingly with each other's economic plight despite their differences in background?

EXAMINING SENTENCES, PARAGRAPHS, AND ORGANIZATION

1. In paragraph 3, the Ehrenreichs begin to talk about economic divisions by race and ethnicity. They write, "African-Americans and Latinos of all income levels *disproportionately lost* their homes to foreclosures in 2007 and '08, and then *disproportionately lost* their jobs in the wave of layoffs that followed." What is the effect of repeating the words *lost* and *disproportionately* in this sentence?
2. What is the effect of repeating the word *elite* throughout the essay? How does your understanding of the word change as the Ehrenreichs use it? What distinctions do they make as they use it?

3. A section break occurs about three-quarters of the way through the essay. Why do you think the essay is broken into two parts? How do the ideas differ between section 1 and section 2?

THINKING CRITICALLY

1. Do people around you form a "liberal elite" or are you surrounded by "ordinary" Americans? Do you think there is a difference between people as these labels suggest?
2. Do you believe that the Occupy movement could become "a force to change the world" (para. 18)? Do you think it has that kind of power? Should it? Why or why not?
3. Does Ehrenreich's description of America's lack of a safety net make you more or less interested in changing our system? Should American people have a safety net, and is the American system in fact a "greased chute" (para. 14) as Ehrenreich claims?

WRITING ACTIVITIES

1. Take a look at the e-Page for this chapter, "What's Your Economic Outlook" at bedfordstmartins.com/americanow/epages. What can you gather about many Americans' outlooks from what you see there? Ehrenreich states, "The life experience of a young lawyer or of a social worker is very different from that of a blue-collar worker whose work life may rarely allow even for the basic amenities of meal or bathroom breaks" (para. 16). Using two stories from that site as evidence, argue whether or not Ehrenreich's statement is true.
2. Take a look at the e-Page for this chapter, "What's Your Economic Outlook" at bedfordstmartins.com/americanow/epages. In a brief essay, examine your own outlook. Consider several aspects of your life, such as your education, whether or not you have health insurance, and what your expectations are for the future. Describe the good fortune or hardships of your life and determine which "camp" you're in. Do you consider yourself part of the 99%? The 1%? Or do you reject those labels? Does your description match Ehrenreich's?
3. Research and write an essay that explores various factors that led to the economic downturn discussed in this essay. (Pay particular attention to the years Ehrenreich singles out: 2007–2008.) What events took place? What effect did those events have on different people in America? Consider the very poor, the working and middle class, and the affluent, and discuss what ways each particular group was affected.

Breanna Lembitz (student essay)

A Taste of Freedom: What I Got at Occupy Wall Street

[*The Progressive*, February 2012]

BEFORE YOU READ
What do you know about Occupy Wall Street? What do you believe their mission is? Do you agree or disagree with their message? Why or why not?

O n the night of September 24, 2011, I was sitting at my kitchen 1
table at college checking my Facebook. Everyone was talking
about a viral YouTube video of three women who had gotten
pepper-sprayed earlier that day at Occupy Wall Street. I quickly found
the live stream and began intently watching. I wanted to be there. I left
the next morning.

I remember getting out of the subway that first Sunday. My smart- 2
phone told me I was two blocks away but I heard and saw nothing: Had
I missed my opportunity to participate in economic change? I remember
almost turning around, but deciding to go until I had at least seen Zuc-
cotti Park itself.

It was smaller than I expected; the live stream had made it seem as if 3
thousands of people were there. What I saw was fifty or so people milling
around. I walked up to one and said, "Hi, I just got here."

"Cool," he said, and just smiled. 4

I walked a little bit farther and asked someone else what I could do. 5

"Well, you can put your stuff wherever you want; no one has been 6
stealing anything," he said. "In fact, when there is money on the ground,
people will hold it up and ask who it belongs to. You should try checking
in with the info desk. They know what's going on."

I walked over to the info desk, which was one man sitting at a table 7
with a sign that said Info. He told me the medics needed help and the
kitchen always needed people.

I followed his pointing and found the medical team, which was 8
about to have a meeting.

I had brought a comforter, a yoga mat, and a pillow. That night, I laid 9
down my bedding and put a tarp over myself and slept on the ground. It

---

*Breanna Lembitz graduated from Clark University in 2012 with a degree in
economics.*

was cold and hard. It took a couple nights to get used to, but this way of sleeping became the norm for the first few weeks. Where I slept would get soaked each time it rained. I would wake up freezing, in puddles of standing water, with no way to dry myself. I started taking the medical night shifts when it rained. Those nights all I saw were mental health issues and hypothermia.

I watched the numbers in the tiny park increase dramatically; people came from everywhere and squeezed themselves in. It got to a point where there was no longer space to sleep on the ground. Some people simply sat in their spot all day to ensure they would have a place to sleep at night.

I regularly attended the nightly general assemblies at the park, and I gave medical report-backs. They were usually things like, "Hey/ I'm Bre/ I'm on medical/ We help you stay healthy/ We have vitamins/ and earplugs/ come get some!" (The breaks between words and phrases represent the pauses I made in order to effectively use the human mic — the relay system for communicating at Occupy Wall Street, where members of the audience repeat the speaker's words and pass them on.)

I realized that anyone who was not attending the general assembly had no idea what was going on. I wanted people, like the medics who were often on shift during the general assembly, to be able to read a report of what had happened there the night before. I found a dry erase board and a marker, and took notes of all the announcements and report-backs that were made. I continued to take notes and post them on the erase board for about a week. One day, the facilitation group asked me to facilitate.

I was terrified; I have always been a little afraid of public speaking, and this meant standing in front of 200 people and structuring their conversation. I started by explaining what our process was, and anytime anyone strayed from that process I would try to bring them back on track. The more the process worked, the more confident I became. The group then recruited me to facilitate again until I ended up facilitating a meeting of a couple thousand people.

I started hearing rumors about the finance team within the camp. I decided to offer my services so that I could find out what was going on with them. I followed them around and did the grunt work until they trusted me enough to come to the meetings. The meetings were brutal: hours of a bunch of big angry men screaming at each other while counting money.

The first couple weeks of being on the finance team meant counting, by hand, thousands of dollars in cash in sketchy locations and carrying it around in trash bags. It meant being screamed at by everyone on the finance team because I apparently did not understand. It meant being screamed at by the people in the park because they did not understand what was happening with the money. I would also sleep in the park with thousands of dollars in cash in my coat so that I could give the kitchen its money for the day early in the morning. Luckily, I lived next to the medical team and thus had what became the equivalent of twenty-four-hour security guards.

The finance job was terrible, my facilitation job began to be criti- 16
cized, and soon the only noncontroversial thing I could do was help out with the medical team. There was a point in time when I was working from 8 a.m. to 1 a.m. every day. But I could see the real impact we were beginning to make, and I was falling in love.

I met my current boyfriend in the occupation. Being one of the 17
few young single girls staying in the park in the early days, I got a lot of attention. Had it not been for my medical brothers, I don't think I would have felt safe enough to stay in the park long term. I had decided that it was a bad idea to date anyone in the occupation, and made this very clear.

But my boyfriend was sneaky. He figured out that I was a vegetarian 18
and started bringing me food that had non-meat forms of protein. He was constantly checking in on me. He heard me complaining about how water had soaked through my boots, so he found me a waterproof pair that fit.

On November 15, we lay in the tent laughing, trying to figure out if we 19
were going to go get food. I commented on how strange it was that we had been living in a park for seven weeks. It all seemed so surreal. The air was calm and still except for muffled conversations.

Suddenly, there were screams. "Oh, my God! Get out of your tents! 20
Emergency! Emergency! Get out of your tents now!" The feeling of peace and calm disappeared instantly as people all moved to ready themselves.

We bolted upright. I grabbed my backpack. Inside were two bottles 21
of liquid antacid solution to wash pepper spray out of people's eyes, a gas mask I had borrowed from a friend, a bag of cosmetics, and a change of clothes. I ripped the bag of cosmetics out and replaced it with a purse that had books, notepads, and my cell phone charger in it. I slung the bag over my shoulders, pulled on my sneakers, and had the gas mask ready. I was wearing jeans, a T-shirt, a sweatshirt, and the same faux leather jacket with duct-taped red crosses on it that I had been wearing practically the whole time there.

Stepping out of the tent, I saw chaos everywhere. People were scared 22
and running around with sticks. Some built blockades to prevent the police from entering the park; others started chanting and waving their

sticks around in the air. Some occupiers stood motionless, unsure of what to do. The park was completely lit up and surrounded by police. A loudspeaker was blaring unintelligible announcements, and an officer was shouting through a bullhorn trying to serve eviction notices to anyone who would take them.

One of the members of the direct action team told me they had a   23
plan; we needed to move everyone toward the center of the park and hold the kitchen. The cops were systematically moving through the park, tearing open tents and shaking their contents onto the ground, including the occasional terrified and bleary-eyed person. Their procession ended in a line about fifty feet in front of the kitchen.

A white-shirted cop reached for his megaphone. He warned mem-   24
bers of the press that if they did not leave immediately, they would be subject to arrest. They looked confused. Why should they leave? What were the police planning on doing that could not be filmed? Some of the press left; a couple individuals started shouting at the police, and some huddled low, hiding behind a line of protesters.

> We were singing songs, including the national anthem. We were chanting. We were making speeches.

We were singing songs, including the   25
national anthem. We were chanting. We were making speeches. We were terrified and resolved at the same time. Eventually, the cops pushed us into a little circle around the kitchen and waited. Soon a group of men in green suits showed up and started tearing apart the park, picking up anything and everything they found and moving it quickly into dumpsters.

I watched as a huge truck pulled into the park. A crazy circular thing   26
appeared on the top of it, and it began emitting weird, alien-like noises—noises that sounded like a mix of an announcement, a skipping record, and a swarm of insects.

Someone screamed about it being a sound cannon, and we all cow-   27
ered and covered our ears. Someone else had found a bag of garlic and started handing it out, explaining that if we got tear-gassed, we should bite down on it and it would make us feel better. I was skeptical but took a clove for good measure anyway.

On my right arm was a terrified woman. She had placed a plastic   28
crate over her head for "protection against pepper spray or tear gas." She offered to share but I chose my gas mask. She had tears in her eyes as she explained that she did not have a home, this was her home, they were taking it from her, and she had nowhere else to be. She frantically locked down with my arms and said, "Don't let go."

Then the police officers were upon us. They began ripping us apart, dragging first one then another protester. I watched as one man refused to lie with his face on the ground. The officer pushed him down, took his arm, and twisted it over three hundred and sixty degrees. The man laid there, motionless, his broken arm limp behind him.

Off on my right someone was screaming as an officer dealt him blows. My arrest was relatively painless in comparison. A couple officers rolled me over and cuffed me with plastic zip-ties, then stood me up. I tried to move forward to grab my bag, but the officer held the ends of my zip-ties so that when I moved away, my cuffs tightened. He then handed me off to another officer who escorted me out, and finally I was left to stand on the curb. The police-woman behind me told me to get down, and I asked her why. She shoved me and said, "It's been a long time since I've drawn blood, if you want to keep playing cute."

My cuffs were so tight I could not feel my fingers, so I asked to be recuffed. The officers heard my request and looked away. Eventually they brought over a woman cop who informed me that she would be my arresting officer. She was in charge of three young women and took us on to a bus.

In the bus, I asked again to be recuffed and was told that the officers did not have the tool to cut cuffs off. I could not sit down because of the pain, so I leaned with my feet on the ground and the back of my neck against the chair. Eventually, they got the clippers and did recuff all the white people who asked, but they had to be encouraged to recuff anyone else, specifically one woman whose hands were turning blue.

We were told we would be in the bus for five to ten minutes. We ended up being in there for more than two hours, and we spent that time singing freedom songs: "We Shall Overcome," "Lay Down My Sword and Shield," "This Little Light of Mine," and "Three Little Birds," among them.

When we were finally let out of the buses, we were taken to a concrete yard at 1 Police Plaza. There were two lines, one for females, one for males. Each line of people would stop at a desk where we were asked for our names, addresses, and dates of birth.

From there we were moved into our cells. On the walk down the hallway, one of the white shirts turned to another officer and said, "Oh look, you brought me breakfast. So who's doing the searches on these ladies, huh?" They all laughed.

The cell I was put in had a plank, a stainless toilet, and a ceramic sink. It was around the corner from the rest of the protesters and was freezing. I was there with two other girls, and we all curled up and slept. Two of us took the fetal position and fit end to end on the plank, and the third slept on the ground. She woke up shivering so we all huddled around her on the plank to warm her up.

29

30

31

32

33

34

35

36

I awoke to a cough that would not quit. I tried to suppress it, but it would 37
not listen. I was doubled over and could not breathe. I reached in my
pocket, vainly hoping for something, and found the clove of garlic. I
chewed it up raw and immediately felt better, warmer, and more alive.

Upon waking, I also discovered that the guards had brought bags of 38
cheese sandwiches and paper cups for water. The bread was dry and flaky,
and the American cheese left much to be desired, but I was cold, bored,
and hungry, and ate them quickly, washing them down with water. When
I later found out that other girls in the cell had not been given food, I
felt guilty that I had eaten so quickly. I learned to eat only as much as I
needed and save the rest in case others didn't get enough.

We all began mic checking to figure out what time it was, what news 39
we had from the outside world, who all was in cells with us, and anything
else we could think to mic check about. The beauty of the mic check
is that it is impossible to shut up the idea once it has been spoken. It
automatically involves everyone and is extremely successful at sending
concise bits of information.

We sang, we drummed on the walls, we did yoga, but it got old. The 40
cells were small and the toilets were completely exposed to the outside
world. Male officers would walk in and could see into the females' stalls.
They acted as if they thought it was funny.

After a number of songs and hours, they brought us out to be pro- 41
cessed. Walking out meant that we went by the male occupiers' cell. The
guys were all held in one large room that had windows on all sides and
benches inside. It even looked like it might have had carpet.

It seemed so much more fun than where we were. I found out 42
later that they had held a general assembly and had crafted a statement
about why they were there. This statement was the source of a new
chant, one that we would use a lot throughout the next days: "We are
unstoppable, another world is possible." Each and every time a com-
rade walked by, everyone would cheer. It was beautiful and made the
cells bearable.

I went to get fingerprinted. I watched a girl standing in front of the 43
camera. She told the officers she was sixteen. One officer turned to the
other and said, "No wonder they are getting raped down there."

I was appalled and disgusted. I was so shocked that I couldn't say 44
anything. I finished getting my fingerprints done and walked back to
the jail cell and stayed there for a number of hours more. Eventually,
our arresting officer came to pull us out of the cells. After almost twelve
hours, I was excited to leave.

We arrived at 100 Centre Street, where we found more protesters, 45
who were all singing "99 Bottles of Beer on the Wall."

Initially, I thought singing "99 Bottles of Beer on the Wall" was fun, but after a couple verses, it got annoying. Then some of the protesters stopped singing and made an announcement: 46

"Mic Check" 47

"Mic Check" 48

"We are singing" 49

"We are singing" 50

"Because **** has a medical condition" 51

"Because **** has a medical condition 52

"and needs to use the bathroom." 53

"and needs to use the bathroom." 54

"She has been asking for over an hour" 55

"She has been asking for over an hour" 56

"So we will continue singing" 57

"So we will continue singing" 58

"Until she can use the bathroom." 59

"Until she can use the bathroom." 60

At around 21 bottles of beer on the wall, she was given the opportunity to use the bathroom. 61

At one point, we were led into a cave-like room. In the center of the room was a desk, behind which sat a TV and a number of computers. 62

The TV was, ironically, broadcasting footage of the raid. It was heartening to know that what the police did was no secret and that people on the outside were standing up for us. 63

Eventually, after thirty-six hours in jail, I was arraigned. I walked out of the jail into a cold drizzle and collapsed among a number of my fellow occupiers. 64

My outlook on the movement is that it will continue but this winter we won't see much coming out of it. Everyone is organizing for big events and actions in the spring. 65

My fellow occupiers have all had a taste of freedom, a taste of respect, and we have seen what can still be accomplished by such a small group of people. We held the attention of the world for months, and we will continue to educate and mobilize people, and the people themselves will continue to build communities. We have a power that refuses to quit. 66

VOCABULARY/USING A DICTIONARY

1. What is the formal definition of *occupy*? What are its origins? How has the word changed because of this movement?

2. What does it mean to *facilitate* (para. 12)?

3. What is the definition of *arraigned* (para. 64)?

RESPONDING TO WORDS IN CONTEXT

1. In paragraph 15, Lembitz states that "being on the finance team meant counting, by hand, thousands of dollars in cash in sketchy locations." What does she mean by the word *sketchy* here?

2. When Lembitz was on the medical team, she provided them with *report-backs* (para. 11). What is the nature of these report-backs? What else might you call these?

3. After spending the night in jail, Lembitz says, "They brought us out to be processed" (para. 41). What does the word *processed* mean in this context?

DISCUSSING MAIN POINT AND MEANING

1. Many of the scenes of the Occupy movement that the author includes have a negative tone or message. Why do you believe the author chose to include the scenes that she did?

2. What is the trigger for Lembitz's participation in Occupy Wall Street?

3. What do you think is the main purpose of this essay?

EXAMINING SENTENCES, PARAGRAPHS, AND ORGANIZATION

1. How does Lembitz choose to organize her story? Do you think this organization is effective?

2. When Lembitz describes the use of the mic check in the courthouse, everything is repeated. Why is this? Did you find this to be an effective way to illustrate the idea of the mic check?

3. In paragraph 17, Lembitz introduces her current boyfriend that she met at Occupy. What purpose do you think this introduction serves?

THINKING CRITICALLY

1. Is Lembitz's narrative the most effective way she could have relayed her story? Why or why not?

2. Does Lembitz's narrative reflect your initial impressions of the Occupy movement? Why or why not?

3. Do you think that the Occupy movement serves a positive or negative purpose? Did Lembitz's essay influence your feelings either way about the movement? How so?

WRITING ACTIVITIES

1. Using Lembitz's essay as support, write a short essay either against or in support of the Occupy movement. How does her narrative exemplify your opinion of the movement?

2. Using Lembitz's essay as a guide, write your own narrative of a time when you incited change about something important to you—whether it be at a public protest or rally, or something on a smaller scale, like standing up for a friend or speaking out about something you believe in.

3. Write a short essay that examines the difference between making a point with a narrative essay and using a more traditional essay with a thesis and support. When is narrative appropriate and effective? When is it not? Cite Lembitz's essay as an example either way.

LOOKING CLOSELY

Using Concrete Language

A sure way to make your writing vivid and memorable is to select words that convey specific and concrete meanings. Very often in the process of writing we are confronted with the choice of using either a general noun, such as *tree, bird,* or *fence,* or a more exact noun such as *maple, cardinal,* or *chain-link fence.* So it's always a good idea, especially when revising, to look closely at your word choice to avoid language that is so generalized that readers cannot visualize your images or get an exact sense of what you are attempting to convey. The terms *maple* and *cardinal* can be distinctly pictured, unlike *tree* or *bird,* and a *chain-link fence* conveys a specific type of fence we can easily picture, not just an abstract idea of one.

Observe how Breanna Lembitz, an economics major at Clark University in Worcester, Massachusetts, makes a deliberate decision throughout her narrative essay to use concrete words. She paints a clear picture that helps us better understand her experiences at the Occupy Wall Street protests in the fall of 2011. In the following paragraph from "A Taste of Freedom: What I Got at Occupy Wall Street," she vividly describes the chaotic scene as New York City policemen invade the park and arrest the protestors. Her expression conveys not only the urgency of the moment, but at the same time we find out what particular items she needs immediately from her backpack and how she is dressed. Her language draws us directly into her situation.

1
We see the contents of her backpack

2
We also see how she is dressed

We bolted upright. I grabbed my <u>backpack. Inside were two bottles of liquid antacid solution to wash pepper spray out of people's eyes, a gas mask I had borrowed from a friend, a bag of cosmetics, and a change of clothes. I ripped the bag of cosmetics out and replaced it with a purse that had books, notepads, and my cell phone charger in it</u>. (1) I slung the bag over my shoulders, pulled on my sneakers, and had the gas mask ready. I was <u>wearing jeans, a T-shirt, a sweatshirt, and the same faux leather jacket with duct-taped red crosses on it that I had been wearing practically the whole time there.</u> (2)

STUDENT WRITER AT WORK
Breanna Lembitz

R.A. What inspired you to write this essay? And submit it to the professional magazine *The Progressive*?

B.L. The editor of *The Progressive*, where I was an intern, heard about my experience at Occupy and asked me to write about it. The piece ended up being much longer than I had originally anticipated.

R.A. Who was your prime audience?

B.L. Anyone who was not living in the park!

R.A. Have you written on this topic since?

B.L. I am in the process of writing a book on my experience.

R.A. How long did it take for you to write this piece? Did you revise your work? What were your goals as you revised?

B.L. The story itself is made up of two different pieces. One was about my experience in jail, and the other was a piece describing my overall feeling about the movement. I sent *The Progressive* both of these stories and they turned them into the published version. I think I really only wrote one draft of each, and I had tried to take the time to revise, but the story was on a deadline.

R.A. What topics most interest you as a writer?

B.L. I love topics that make people think. Things that challenge the norm in a way we didn't even know was possible. I love to mix numbers and facts with anecdotes.

R.A. Are you pursuing a career in which writing will be a component?

B.L. I feel that any career requires some element of writing, but I will continue to write about my life and the lives of others, and maybe if I am in the right place at the right time again, it will be published.

R.A. What advice do you have for other student writers?

B.L. Read a chapter from someone whose style you would like to emulate before you sit down and start to write. Also, if you cannot come up with a word, write in a blank and come back later. It's better you finish the rest of the idea and lose the word than lose the idea and find the perfect word. And if you can shorten a sentence, do it.

Discussing the Unit

SUGGESTED TOPIC FOR DISCUSSION

Americans often refer to the American dream as something equally attainable for everyone. Some of the essays in this section support that idea, while others refute it, but it is only in recent years that it has really become a heated debate topic. Whether or not you believe that the American dream is alive and well, how has the landscape surrounding that dream changed, and how has the definition of the American dream evolved?

PREPARING FOR CLASS DISCUSSION

1. Compare how the 99% are portrayed in Barbara and John Ehrenreich's essay, as opposed to how they are portrayed in Breanna Lembitz's essay. Which do you think is a more accurate representation of the group, and why do you think this representation is more accurate?
2. Do all of the writers in this chapter have a similar idea of the American dream? What are the defining characteristics of this abstract idea? Use specific examples from the essays in this unit to illustrate your point.

FROM DISCUSSION TO WRITING

1. Drawing from the essays in this unit, formulate your own argument about economic mobility in America. Be sure to use quotations and specific examples to support your argument.
2. Write an essay in which you analyze the tone, organization, and genre of at least two essays in this chapter. How do their conventions affect the message, and which is the most effective?

TOPICS FOR CROSS-CULTURAL DISCUSSION

1. Despite the economic downturn, the United States still has people constantly immigrating, both legally and illegally. What do you think this says about the way the American dream is perceived abroad?
2. In the Ehrenreichs' essay, they describe the economic disparity between the white middle class and the African American middle class in the recent economic downturn. How might the idea that African Americans were more affected by the recession be applied to the other essays and ideas presented in this chapter?

This chapter continues online. Visit the e-Page at
bedfordstmartins.com/americanow/epages for an interactive graphic.

11

Can We Shrink Our Growing Prison Population?

As criminal-justice expert Joan Petersilia reports in "Beyond the Prison Bubble," U.S. prisons and jails currently house about 2.4 million inmates, or approximately one in every 100 adults, giving us the highest incarceration rate in the developed world. How did we get to this point? And what have the consequences been for the prison population and the larger society? Is it possible to reduce both the incarceration rate and the significant proportion of released prisoners who reenter the criminal-justice system?

Petersilia ties the growth of the prison population to a fivefold increase in the U.S. crime rate between 1960 and 1990, resulting in measures that incarcerated more offenders (some of whom might not have been imprisoned in the past) and lengthened sentences. While mass imprisonment has helped lower crime rates, Petersilia contends that this reduction isn't as great as many have claimed. Meanwhile, she says, expansions in prison populations have strained state budgets, disrupted low-income urban neighborhoods, and largely failed to keep those released from prison from re-offending. What, then, should be done? Petersilia argues for better and more widely applied rehabilitation programs that help prisoners while they are incarcerated and also ease their transition into the outside world once they have been released. She says,

"To avoid throwing away much of the progress we have made in reducing crime, it is more imperative than ever that we pursue alternatives to prison and new ways to ease inmates' reentry into civilian life."

But what incentives are there to reduce incarceration now that certain communities have come to rely on it? This question is implicit in Christopher Glazek's "Raise the Crime Rate." Glazek writes, "Rural communities have benefited most of all. Not only does the criminal justice sector employ 2 million people, including more than 500,000 correctional officers, most of them in rural areas, it also helps to inflate the local population of prison zones for the purposes of congressional districting and social spending."

One form of social spending being harmed by mass incarceration is funding of education. That's a key point raised by Karen Thomas, a student at American River College, in "Misplaced Priorities: It's Time to Invest in Schools, Not Prisons." Referring to California's budget in particular, Thomas argues, "Enacting a few common-sense reforms, such as paroling incarcerated non-violent drug offenders, will allow us to limit money spent on the prison system and divert those dollars to education; drug-abuse prevention, treatment, and rehabilitation; job training and employment services."

At the end of the chapter, the e-Page looks at the growth of private, for-profit prisons—businesses that are booming even in tough economic times.

Joan Petersilia

Beyond the Prison Bubble

[*Wilson Quarterly,* Winter 2011]

BEFORE YOU READ

Have you ever wondered about the effectiveness of prisons? Do they deter crimes, or must more effort be put into understanding how to rehabilitate the people we send there?

WORDS TO LEARN

punitive (para. 1): involving punishment (adj)

correlation (para. 3): equivalence (noun)

lenient (para. 4): tolerant or indulgent (adj)

mitigate (para. 4): to make less severe (verb)

outlays (para. 7): expenditures (noun)

proponent (para. 9): supporter (noun)

confinement (para. 9): restriction (noun)

subsidies (para. 12): monetary government aid (noun)

malign (para. 14): harmful, destructive (adj)

imperative (para. 17): necessary (adj)

dole (para. 17): to distribute (verb)

vocational (para. 18): relating to a particular skill or occupation (adj)

implement (para. 18): to put into effect (verb)

divert (para. 20): to turn aside (verb)

dismantle (para. 21): to take apart (verb)

akin (para. 22): similar (adj)

vitality (para. 24): exuberant force; energy (noun)

The announcement last summer that in 2009 the number of Americans behind bars had increased for the 37th year in a row provoked a fresh round of national soul-searching. With its prisons and jails now holding some 2.4 million inmates — roughly one in every 100 adults — the United States has the highest incarceration rate of any free nation. As a proportion of its population, the United States incarcerates five times more people than Britain, nine times more than Germany, and 12 times more than Japan. "No other rich country is nearly as punitive as the Land of the Free," *The Economist* has declared.

1

Joan Petersilia is the Adelbert H. Sweet Professor of Law and faculty co-director of the Stanford Criminal Justice Center at Stanford University. She is the author of eleven books on crime and public policy.

But a highly significant fact went largely unremarked amid the hub- 2
bub: The population of the nation's state prisons, which house all but a
relative handful of convicted felons, decreased by nearly 3,000. Although
the drop was slight in percentage terms, it was the first since 1972. (State
prisons held 1.4 million inmates at the end of 2009 and federal prisons more than 200,000, while the number held in local jails, mostly for
minor crimes, averaged about 770,000 over the course of the year, and
the majority had yet to face trial.) In California, which has the nation's
largest state prison system, with nearly 170,000 men and women behind
bars, the prison population fell for the first time in 38 years. The national
prison population — including those held in federal facilities — grew by
less than one percent, the slowest rate in the last decade. These changes
mean it is very likely that we are seeing the beginning of the end of America's long commitment to what some critics call "mass incarceration."

If that shift does occur, it will not be because the United States has 3
solved its crime problem. In fact, if there were a close correlation between
crime rates and incarceration, the prisons would have begun emptying
out in the late 1990s, when crime in most of its forms began to decrease.

How did we get here? Soaring crime rates, especially in the inner cit- 4
ies, are the most obvious part of the explanation. From 1960 to 1990,
the overall U.S. crime rate increased more than fivefold, the frequency of
violent crime nearly quadrupled, and the murder rate doubled. Drug use
increased. The upsurge was widely blamed on lenient punishment, particularly for violent repeat offenders. Legislatures responded by passing
"get tough" measures, including sentencing guidelines (which required
prison sentences for some offenders who in the past might have been
put on probation), so-called three-strikes-and-you're-out laws (which
mandated prison terms for repeat offenders), mandatory minimum sentences (forcing judges to impose fixed sentences regardless of mitigating
factors), and truth-in-sentencing measures (requiring inmates to serve a
greater proportion of their imposed sentence before becoming eligible
for parole). These policy changes increased both the probability of going
to prison if convicted and the length of prison terms.

Many liberal critics, pointing out that two-thirds of those impris- 5
oned in federal and state facilities are African Americans and Hispanics,
contended that "mass incarceration" is little more than a reworked form
of racial and social domination — "the new Jim Crow," as Michelle Alexander, a law professor at Ohio State University, put it in the title of her
recent book.

But virtually all those who study the matter now agree that impris- 6
onment has reached often counterproductive levels, particularly in the

case of drug possession and other nonviolent crimes. The prominent conservative scholar James Q. Wilson, whose book *Thinking About Crime* (1975) set the national crime control agenda during the 1980s, recently wrote, "This country imprisons too many people on drug charges with little observable effect." In my travels around the country I have conducted an unscientific survey of prison administrators, and nearly all of them say that 10 to 15 percent of their inmates could be safely released.

What we are seeing today is a growing recognition that our approach to dealing with convicted criminals is simply too costly. Not only is the price too high, but the benefits are too low. The states now spend an estimated $50 billion on corrections annually, and the growth of these outlays over the past 20 years has outpaced budget increases for nearly all other essential government services, including transportation, higher education, and public assistance.   7

California, where I was involved in the corrections system in various capacities under reform-minded governor Arnold Schwarzenegger, pours 10 percent of its massive state budget into correctional facilities. Between 1985 and 2005, it built 21 new prisons — more than one a year. The state's prison population surged, and so did costs: The state spent nearly $10 billion on corrections last year, or about $50,000 per prisoner. (The national average is $23,000.) Now that California is grappling with a budget crisis, it is clear that it cannot continue on this course. The evidence for the rest of the country may be less dramatic, but it is no less clear.   8

These vast sums are not buying as much as many people think. Mass imprisonment has helped reduce crime rates, but most specialists agree that the effects have been considerably smaller than proponents claim and that we are now well past the point of diminishing returns. Confinement behind bars accounted for at most about a quarter of the substantial decline in crime that occurred during the 1990s (mainly, most researchers believe, by preventing imprisoned offenders from committing fresh crimes against the general public rather than by promoting a deterrent effect).   9

More important, that decline may well be reversed if we don't do a better job of planning for the reentry of prisoners who have finished their sentences. There is a very simple and immutable "iron law" of imprisonment: Almost everyone who goes to prison ultimately returns home — about 93 percent of all offenders. (A relative handful die in jail; the rest have life sentences or are on death row.) Although the average offender now spends 2.5 years behind bars, many terms are shorter, with the result that 44 percent of all those now housed in state prisons are expected to be released within the year. This year, some 750,000 men   10 and women will go home. Many — if not most — will be no better equipped to make successful, law-abiding lives for themselves than they were before they landed in prison.

Today's offenders are different from those of the past. They are still 11 overwhelmingly male (though the female proportion of the population has climbed to nine percent), African American or Hispanic, and unskilled. But the offenders leaving prison now are more likely to have fairly long criminal records, lengthy histories of alcohol and drug abuse, significant periods of unemployment and homelessness, and a physical or mental disability. Their records are more likely to include gang activities and drug dealing. In short, the average offender today leaves prison at a greater disadvantage (and more primed for trouble) than his predecessors did. Yet fewer participate in prison rehabilitation and work programs than a decade ago. When I was cochair of California's Expert Panel on Rehabilitation in 2007, the panel found that California spent less than $3,000 per year, per inmate, on rehabilitation programs, and that 50 percent of all prisoners released the year before had not participated in a single program.

Even as the states were cutting back in-house prison programs most 12 severely, in the decade from 1985 to 1995, Congress and state legislatures were passing dozens of laws closing off many job opportunities to ex-offenders and restricting their access to welfare benefits and housing subsidies. Former inmates are now commonly barred from working in some of the economy's fastest-growing fields, including education, childcare, private security, and nursing and home health care. Such legal barriers sometimes protect us from dangerous felons, but they also make it hard for men and women who want to go straight to get their feet on the ground.

> Former inmates are now commonly barred from working in some of the economy's fastest-growing fields.

It should not come as a surprise to learn that we have a corrections 13 system that does not correct. The U.S. Bureau of Justice Statistics reports that two-thirds of released prisoners are rearrested for at least one serious new crime, and more than half are reincarcerated within three years of release. The two-thirds rearrest rate has remained virtually unchanged since the first recidivism study was conducted more than 40 years ago. Former prisoners account for an estimated 15 to 20 percent of all arrests among adults. That means that thousands of Americans are being victimized every year by criminals who have already done time without experiencing "correction."

At the same time, we are beginning to recognize that our overreliance on locking people up has an especially malign effect on poor urban neighborhoods, where up to 20 percent of the adult male population may be behind bars at any given time. Not only do the men come home with diminished prospects that hurt the whole community, but as criminologist Todd Clear shows in *Imprisoning Communities* (2007), their absence weakens the family and social networks they need when they come home and hurts those left behind. It is no accident that the sons and brothers of men who go to prison are more likely to follow the same path. These trends help cause crime rather than prevent it.   14

Prison is where some people belong, many for long periods of time. But we need policies that do not produce more crime in the long run.   15

Budget cutters may rejoice at the chance to gut corrections budgets, and liberal critics of "mass incarceration" may celebrate any policy that shrinks the prison population, but cutting corrections budgets will prove hugely counterproductive if we act without giving serious thought to how we will deal with the offenders who are released. Until recently, for example, Kansas was a model of forward-thinking prison policy. In 2007 the state legislature funded a range of programs — involving education, drug treatment, and subsidized housing — to help former inmates reintegrate. The approach appeared to work: The number of ex-offenders returning to prison dropped by 16 percent between 2007 and 2009. But then came the economic crisis and cutbacks. According to state legislator Pat Colloton, recidivism rates quickly spiked. Kansas is back where it was in 2007.   16

To avoid throwing away much of the progress we have made in reducing crime, it is more imperative than ever that we pursue alternatives to prison and new ways to ease inmates' reentry into civilian life. The good news is that after decades of false starts, researchers have finally begun to zero in on the things that can make a difference in at least some cases. The news was good enough to help persuade the conservative Bush administration to push through the $330 million Second Chance Act in 2007, giving government agencies and nonprofits the tools to get some of these efforts off the ground. The money was to be doled out over time. The bad news is that amid today's intensified financial strains, Congress may be reluctant to continue funding this effort to enhance prisoner reentry programs.   17

Rehabilitation programs reduce recidivism if they incorporate proven principles and are targeted to specific offenders. Research demonstrates that offenders who earn a high school equivalency diploma while behind bars are more likely to get jobs after release. Those who receive vocational skills training are more likely to get jobs and higher wages after release. And those who go through intensive drug treatment programs in prison   18 are less likely to relapse outside of it. If we could implement effective pro-grams, we could expect to reduce recidivism by 15 to 20 percent. To put it in concrete terms: About 495,000 of the 750,000 prisoners who will be released this year are likely to be rearrested within three years. With effective programs, we could reduce the number of repeat offenders by nearly 100,000. We could do even better if these efforts were linked to improved services in the community upon release. Such efforts would pay for themselves by reducing future criminal justice and corrections costs. Economist Mark A. Cohen and criminologist Alex Piquero found in a recent study that a high-risk youth who becomes a chronic offender costs society between $4.2 and $7.2 million, principally in police and court outlays, property losses, and medical care. We either pay now or pay later — and we pay a lot more later.

Advocates of rehabilitation constantly struggle against the wide-spread view that "nothing works." In part, this view grows out of an experience that began in the 1980s, when horrendous prison crowding in southern prisons, economic woes, and court rulings spurred some unusual experiments. When federal courts ordered states either to build new facilities or find some other way to punish offenders, the states began experimenting with alternative sanctions. Georgia, for example, developed an intensive supervision program (ISP)[1] for probationers that yielded some evidence that it reduced recidivism rates — and also appeared to save the state the cost of building two new prisons. By the mid-1990s, virtually every state had passed some kind of legislation for intermediate sanctions.   19

Probation and parole departments across the country implemented a variety of ISP programs, including boot camps, day reporting centers, and electronic monitoring. The hope was that some offenders who normally would have been bound for prison could be "diverted" from expensive prison cells to intensive community programs that could keep a closer watch on them and offer more support services. Other offenders could be released early into community programs. But as I discovered when I was co-director of the RAND Corporation's national evaluation of ISPs in the early 1990s, despite all the good intentions, most of the ISP dollars wound up being used to fund more drug testing, parole agent contacts, and electronic monitoring rather than enhanced social services. The main result was that offenders who violated court conditions by using drugs, for example, were identified more quickly and sent into custody.   20

---

[1] ISP (para 19): Intensive Supervision Program. These programs are established as alternatives to costly and ineffective prison sentences. It is an intermediate form of punishment: not a jail sentence, but requiring "intensive" participation by someone entered into it.

Within a decade, ISPs went from being "the future of American   21
corrections," as one probation officer enthused to a *Washington Post*
reporter in 1985, to what seemed to be a failed social experiment.
Most of the programs were dismantled by the late 1990s. Some advocates of the prison buildup pronounced that alternatives to prison had
been tried and did not work. But the RAND study found that in places
where efforts were actually implemented according to the original
design, they were rather effective. Offenders who participated in drug
or alcohol treatment, community service, and employment programs
had recidivism rates 10 to 20 percent below those of nonparticipating
offenders.

Today, we have even more refined knowledge of what works. The   22
most popular approach involves using something akin to a medical technique, focusing on individual cases. Called the risk-need-responsivity
(RNR) model, it uses risk assessment tools to size up each person and
match him or her to the right program. The treatment efforts are behavioral in nature (with rewards and punishments) and geared to place the
sharpest focus on higher-risk offenders. There is a heavy emphasis on
cognitive behavioral and "social learning" techniques — ranging from
anger management training to sessions devoted to weaning offenders
away from their negative and antisocial attitudes. All of these efforts use
peers and family members to reinforce their messages. And, as several
studies show, they work. Criminologist Edward J. Latessa of the University of Cincinnati studied the results of RNR efforts in Ohio's 38 halfway house programs and found that they cut the recidivism of high-risk
offenders by as much as 20 percent. Several states, including Maine, Illi-
nois, and Oregon, are now using the RNR model.

Community partnerships are another approach that hold great   23
promise. An excellent example is the Boston Reentry Initiative, a city
interagency program that brings together law enforcement, social service
agencies, and religious institutions to start working with inmates while
they are still incarcerated. On the day the prison doors swing open, a
family member or mentor is on hand to meet each released prisoner, and
social service agencies are prepared to begin working to help the former
inmate get a fresh start. The initiative focuses only on the highest-risk
offenders leaving prison. They are offered opportunities for work and
treatment, but for those who fail to take advantage of them and slip back
into crime, the program calls for swift arrest and fast-track prosecution.
In a sense, the Boston Reentry Initiative is the ISP experiment all over
again — but this time backed with treatment resources, mentorship, and
community collaboration. The results have been impressive. Harvard
researchers found that participants had a rearrest rate 30 percent lower
than that of a matched comparison group.

It is no longer justifiable to say that nothing works. There is scientific   24
evidence that prison and parole programs can reduce recidivism. It is not
easy and it is not inexpensive, but it *is* possible. To retreat now would be
to pull the rug out from under hundreds of programs that are contributing to the decades-long war against crime, which, whatever its shortcomings, has been one of the nation's great success stories, vastly improving
the lives of ordinary citizens and the vitality of cities. One of the surest
ways we know to keep crime down is to prevent those who have committed crimes in the past from doing so again.

That is not to say that criminality is a problem that can always be   25
solved. People go to prison for a reason, and in many cases there is very
little or nothing that anyone can do to change the choices they will make
in the future. Rehabilitation programs are not for every prisoner, and we
should not waste money on those who lack motivation. But it would be
foolish not to help those who wish to change. Effective rehabilitation and
reentry programs that help offenders go home to stay are good for them,
and good for the rest of us, too.

VOCABULARY/USING A DICTIONARY

1. Describe a *hubbub* (para. 2). Where does the word come from?
2. What does it mean to *quadruple* (para. 4) something? From what language is *quad* derived?
3. What is the definition of *counterproductive* (para. 6)? What other compound words do you know that begin with *counter-*?

RESPONDING TO WORDS IN CONTEXT

1. The word *relative* has more than one part of speech and has more than
   one meaning. How is it used in paragraph 2?
2. In paragraph 22, Petersilia writes that one technique employed to rehabilitate offenders is a process "devoted to weaning offenders away from
   their negative and antisocial attitudes." Under what circumstances is
   weaning usually discussed? What do you think it means in this context?
3. The word *recidivism* appears at various points throughout this essay.
   What does it mean? How might you guess its meaning from its context?

DISCUSSING MAIN POINT AND MEANING

1. Petersilia identifies two main problems with the numbers of people in
   U.S. prisons. What are they?
2. Why does Petersilia say, "It is no accident that the sons and brothers of
   men who go to prison are more likely to follow the same path" (para. 14)?
3. Does Petersilia want to rehabilitate all prisoners? What sort of changes
   does she want to see taking place?

EXAMINING SENTENCES, PARAGRAPHS, AND ORGANIZATION

1. In paragraph 13, Petersilia writes, "It should not come as a surprise to learn that we have a corrections system that does not correct." What is the effect of the echo ("corrections ... correct") in this sentence?

2. Why do you think Petersilia includes examples of approaches from different states (California, Georgia, and Massachusetts) at various points in the essay in the discussion of prison reform?

3. In this lengthy essay, there are many transitions from one train of thought in the argument to another. Find an area of transition in Petersilia's essay. How effectively does it carry the reader from one point to the next?

THINKING CRITICALLY

1. Do you believe the prison system is a deterrent to crime? Explain your answer.

2. Is it important that offenders are kept from certain types of jobs when they return from prison? What sort of jobs should they be allowed to take?

3. Do any of the programs mentioned at the end of the essay appear promising to you? Which ones? Why?

WRITING ACTIVITIES

1. Write a letter to the governor of your state explaining your position on how you'd like to see money used for the rehabilitation of prisoners. Outline some of the programs you think should receive more money, and explain what you think the government should be focusing on as people go to jail, serve time, and are released. Whether or not you choose to send the letter, re-read and revise until it is something you would feel confident mailing or e-mailing.

2. In a brief essay, describe your position on the role sentencing and prison should play in the lives of people who have committed crimes. Do you find yourself on the side of those who believe in working toward rehabilitating offenders? Toward longer sentencing and stronger punishments for offenders? For which crimes? Where do you fall on the question of juvenile crime and punishment? On capital punishment?

3. Develop a pie chart that earmarks money for various expenses in your town. Include money that goes toward prison populations. In your chart, what have you earmarked the most money for? The least? How much have you allocated for prisons? Given Petersilia's arguments about where money goes and what prisoners are offered, write an argument explaining why you have put your town's money where it is.

Christopher Glazek

Raise the Crime Rate (excerpt)

[*n+1*, Winter 2012]

BEFORE YOU READ
Is it possible for an ex-convict to go back to normal life after prison? What forces are at work to prevent reintegration into society? Who benefits from the difficulties faced by former prisoners?

WORDS TO LEARN
eligible (para. 1): qualified (adj)
vagrancy (para. 2): condition of wandering without home or employment (noun)
incarcerated (para. 3): imprisoned (adj)
prudent (para. 3): wise (adj)
lucrative (para. 4): profitable (adj)
paramilitary (para. 4): supplement to a military force (adj)

punitive (para. 4): concerned with punishment (adj)
breeds (para. 5): sorts or kinds (noun)
vacate (para. 5): to empty; to make vacant (verb)
impunity (para. 5): freedom from punishment (noun)

Once you go to prison, you never really come back. Beyond incarceration's immediate physical and mental horrors, after being convicted of a felony, your public life is functionally over. In many states, you won't be able to vote or sit on a jury. You won't be eligible for public housing or food stamps. You'll find it very difficult to attend a college, and may find it nearly impossible to get a job — like everyone else, educators and employers discriminate against ex-cons.

Finding a job is a particular problem, not only because criminals often leave prison with a large amount of debt — from court fees, conviction penalties, probation fines, and especially from child support bills, which continue to accumulate while convicts are in prison — but also because steady employment is itself often a condition of parole: a diabolical catch-22. As scholars have noted, the situation calls to mind the "vagrancy" laws

1

2

Christopher Glazek is a senior editor at n+1 *and founding director of the Yale AIDS Memorial Project. He has written for* the New Yorker *and has helped students prepare for standardized tests at Brownstone Tutors.*

passed in the South in the wake of reconstruction,[1] which made it illegal to be unemployed while black vagrants were arrested and forced back onto plantations, this time as convicts rather than slaves. An ex-con who fails to land a job may end up back in prison for violating parole. Since service-oriented occupations are usually out of the question, ex-cons are often forced to seek industrial and construction jobs far from urban centers. This puts a large number of people in the position of having to take long, expensive taxi rides to show up for low-wage jobs that don't even cover transportation costs.

The United States now spends some $200 billion on the correctional system each year, a sum that exceeds the gross domestic product of twenty-five US states and 140 foreign countries. An ever-increasing share of domestic discretionary spending, it would seem, is devoted to building and staffing earthly hells filled with able-bodied young men who have been removed from the labor force. If we added up all the money federal, state, and local governments invest in the poorest zip codes through credits and transfer payments — food stamps, Medicaid, teacher salaries, et cetera — and balanced that against all the value the government extracts from those zip codes through sin taxes, lotteries, and the incarceration complex, we might well conclude that the disinvestment outweighs the investment. Any apparent gains made in the last thirty years in narrowing the employment and education gap between African Americans and whites vanishes once you include the incarcerated population. Before asking the government to spend a fortune improving student-to-teacher ratios, it may be prudent to first ask the government to *stop* devoting public resources to ripping the heart out of inner-city economies.

> The United States now spends some $200 billion on the correctional system each year.

3

Of course, not everyone has made out badly from the country's prison-construction binge. Telephone companies run up impressive profits from prisoners forced to call collect. Defense contractors have signed lucrative contracts selling paramilitary equipment to local law enforcement agencies. Rural communities have benefited most of all. Not only does the criminal justice sector employ 2 million people, including more than 500,000 correctional officers, most of them in rural areas, it also helps to inflate the local population of prison zones for the purposes of congressional districting and social spending. Schoolchildren learn that

4

---

[1] Reconstruction (para. 2): The reorganization and reintegration of the Southern states back into the Union post–Civil War.

in 1787, slave-holding states reached a compromise with free states that allowed nonvoting slaves to count as three-fifths of a human for the purposes of apportioning congressional seats. Counting a slave as a fraction of a man seems like a vivid manifestation of the way the United States dehumanized Africans. Today, thousands of people are removed from urban districts, where public money is urgently needed, and shipped upstate, where each counts for a *full* person. In this way, prisoners bolster the voting power of rural districts, while being unable to vote themselves. Perhaps this is the reason why, as criminal justice surveys indicate, rural whites form by far the most punitive demographic.

Certain breeds of urban dwellers benefit, too. In gentrifying sections   5 of Brooklyn, for example, steep drops in crime, combined with the virtual depopulation of entire city blocks, has underwritten a real estate boom. In neighborhoods like Fort Greene and Clinton Hill, wealthy people with children have reaped the benefits of climbing land values from apartments they never would have bought had it not been for the removal of tens of thousands of locals from adjacent areas. Neighborhoods like Bedford-Stuyvesant show the population exchange in its purest form. As African American Brooklynites are exported upstate for involvement in petty drug crimes, twenty-somethings reared in prison towns migrate south and reoccupy the same areas vacated by prisoners. Often, of course, the new inhabitants proceed to consume and sell the very same drugs that got the previous tenants into trouble. Since they're white, they do so with impunity.

VOCABULARY/USING A DICTIONARY

1. What sort of crime is a *felony* (para. 1)?
2. The word *diabolical* (para. 2) closely resembles related words in Spanish and French. Do you know what words?
3. What is a *demographic* (para. 4)?

RESPONDING TO WORDS IN CONTEXT

1. *Catch-22* is the name of a famous novel by Joseph Heller. What does Glazek mean by *catch-22* in paragraph 2?
2. What is a *sin tax* (para. 3)?
3. What is a *gentrifying* section of Brooklyn (para. 5)? How can you tell what *gentrifying* means based on what follows in that paragraph?

DISCUSSING MAIN POINT AND MEANING

1. What types of discrimination do ex-convicts face when they are released from prison?
2. How have rural communities benefited from the constructions of prisons in their areas?

3. Explain what Glazek means when he says, "Once you go to prison, you never really come back" (para. 1).

EXAMINING SENTENCES, PARAGRAPHS, AND ORGANIZATION

1. What does it mean when Glazek says, " . . . we might well conclude that the *disinvestment* outweighs the *investment*" (para. 3)?
2. What does Glazek mean when he says, "Before asking the government to spend a fortune improving student-to-teacher ratios, it may be prudent to first ask the government to *stop* devoting public resources to *ripping the heart out of inner-city economies*" (para. 3)?
3. How does Glazek establish the gulf between black and white experience in paragraph 5?

THINKING CRITICALLY

1. Glazek writes that "the United States now spends some $200 billion on the correctional system each year, a sum that exceeds the gross domestic product of twenty-five U.S. states and 140 foreign countries" (para. 3). Does that surprise you? Do you think that sort of spending is extravagant or necessary? Explain your answer.
2. Why do you think so many ex-convicts end up unable to reestablish their lives post-prison or, worse, find themselves back in prison instead of reintegrating into society? Do you think anything can be done to help those who come out of prison?
3. When someone is released from prison, Glazek says he or she faces certain types of discrimination. Do you think that ex-convicts are discriminated against, or do you think that a certain amount of discrimination is expected and/or important if someone has committed a crime and spent time in prison? Why or why not?

WRITING ACTIVITIES

1. Consider that you are a real estate buyer looking for property. Why might you invest in an area that was poor but now has a vast majority of its population in prison? What benefit is there for you? Do you take into consideration the people who remain living there? Consider that you are one of the tenants left in a poor urban area, but many of your neighbors are now incarcerated or relocated. What options are available to you if prices are going up and wealthy neighbors are moving in? How will you survive? Take the position of the real estate buyer or the poor urban tenant and write an essay that describes your situation and your choices.
2. Research the vagrancy laws that came into being during the Reconstruction Era. What similarities are there between the vagrancy laws and the situation faced by many of today's ex-convicts when they look for work?

Write a brief essay that compares the two, and cite all sources (include a Works Cited page as well).

3. Is the prison problem in the United States a black vs. white problem? A rich vs. poor problem? A problem inherent in a capitalist society? Why do you think so? Argue your position in a short essay.

Karen Thomas (student essay)

Misplaced Priorities: It's Time to Invest in Schools, Not Prisons

[*American River Current*, American River College, June 2, 2011]

BEFORE YOU READ
Do you believe that nonviolent criminals should face long-term incarceration? Why or why not?

With the federal and state budgets in crisis, government spending has come under close scrutiny. Recently, the National Association for the Advancement of Colored People published a report called "Misplaced Priorities: Over Incarcerate, Under Educate." According to this report, funding for prisons has grown at a rate six times higher than funding for higher education. In addition, the Pew Center for the States analyzed state spending for the 20-year period between 1987 and 2007, and after adjusting for inflation, found that funding for higher education grew by 21 percent, while corrections funding grew by 127 percent.

The Pew study also reported that the United States is home to 5 percent of the world's population but houses 25 percent of the world's prisoners. Nearly $70 billion each year is spent on incarceration, parole, and probation functions. A quarter of the 2.3 million people behind bars have been convicted of drug-related charges, and, as a result of the "war on drugs," have been mandated prison sentences rather than drug diversion or rehabilitation.

1

2

Karen Thomas is a journalism major at American River College, where she has held various editorial and staff positions at the student newspaper where this essay first appeared.

Money from California's General Fund pays for education, health care, housing, public assistance, and prisons. It should come as no surprise that the National Association of State Budget Officers, which analyzes general fund expenditures, revealed that prison spending far surpasses elementary and secondary education spending. School budgets are being slashed time and again, teachers are being laid off, classes are being cut, and students are being turned away. Lack of educational opportunities leaves less advantaged citizens with fewer choices when it comes to feeding their families, and increases the odds these people will turn to drugs or crime to survive. **3**

It's time to stop this vicious cycle of cutting education while increasing spending on the imprisonment of non-violent offenders. Enacting a few common-sense reforms, such as paroling incarcerated non-violent drug offenders, will allow us to limit money spent on the prison system and divert those dollars to education; drug-abuse prevention, treatment, and rehabilitation; job training and employment services. **4**

> It's time to stop this vicious cycle of cutting education while increasing spending on the imprisonment of non-violent offenders.

Adequate and affordable education for all citizens should be America's priority if we hope to have a healthy and productive nation in the years to come. Instead of producing responsible, contributing members of society, our current policy will result in an ignorant, addicted, and locked-down populace that will be a costly burden on the public. **5**

VOCABULARY/USING A DICTIONARY

1. What does the word *mandated* (para. 2) mean? List at least two synonyms.
2. What part of speech is the word *costly* (para. 5), and what is the definition of the word?
3. What does the word *corrections* (para. 1) mean in this essay? What alternate definitions does the word have?

RESPONDING TO WORDS IN CONTEXT

1. In paragraph 3, Thomas writes, "School budgets are being slashed. . . ." What does the word *slashed* mean in this context?
2. Thomas refers to "less advantaged citizens" in paragraph 3. What does she mean by *less advantaged*? What other terms mean the same thing?
3. In the sentence "Enacting a few common-sense reforms . . . will allow us to limit money spent on the prison system and divert those dollars to education; drug-abuse prevention, treatment, and rehabilitation; job

training and employment services" (para. 4), what does the word *rehabilitation* specifically refer to? How do you know?

DISCUSSING MAIN POINT AND MEANING
1. Summarize Thomas's argument in one sentence.
2. According to her essay, what does Thomas believe about the war on drugs? How do you know what her stance is? Cite specific passages from the text to support your answer.
3. What solution does Thomas propose to solve the problem of overspending on incarceration?

EXAMINING SENTENCES, PARAGRAPHS, AND ORGANIZATION
1. Thomas uses many euphemisms and metaphors throughout the essay. Indicate at least two and describe their meaning.
2. What type of evidence does Thomas use to support her argument? Is this evidence effective? Why or why not?
3. How would you describe the tone of Thomas's essay? Is the tone appropriate for the subject matter? Why or why not?

THINKING CRITICALLY
1. Think back to the "Before You Read" prompt that asked you if you believe nonviolent criminals should be incarcerated. Did the statistics or ideas presented in Thomas's essay have any effect on those opinions? Why or why not?
2. Thomas argues that the money used to incarcerate drug offenders should be used for rehabilitation and drug diversion instead. Do you agree with this solution? Why or why not?
3. Thomas's argument is primarily focused on the spending gap between prisons and education, but she also makes reference to health care, housing, and public assistance as coming from the same revenue pool. Why might she have chosen to focus on education, and how do you think that affects her overall argument?

WRITING ACTIVITIES
1. Write a brief essay in which you examine one of the additional public services (health care, housing, public assistance) and compare it to the cost and benefit of incarceration.
2. In an essay, respond to Thomas's statement, "Adequate and affordable education for all citizens should be America's priority if we hope to have a healthy and productive nation in the years to come" (para. 5). Do you agree or disagree? If you agree, provide a detailed explanation why. If you disagree, explain why not and offer alternative solutions.

3. Write a short essay that analyzes the language in Thomas's essay. How does she use phrases, such as "common-sense reforms" and "it should come as no surprise" to strengthen her argument? What does this type of language indicate, and how does it affect Thomas's argument?

LOOKING CLOSELY

Effective Persuasion: Recommending a Course of Action

The primary purpose of a persuasive essay is to change someone's attitude or opinion, usually on matters of public policy. On Election Day, for example, a newspaper editorial will encourage its readers to vote for a particular candidate; in the same paper, a film review may discourage moviegoers from attending a certain film the critic finds "pointless, trivial, and profoundly dumb." And an opinion column may try to dissuade parents from buying fast food for their children. All these examples call for someone to do something, to take some course of action. In "Misplaced Priorities: It's Time to Invest in Schools, Not Prisons," Karen Thomas, a student at American River College, urges her readers to support "a few common-sense reforms" that would prioritize the state budget for schools over prisons. After clearly setting out her main point and supporting it with evidence, she then calls for the reforms that would help increase expenditures on education by enacting a better method for handling "non-violent offenders."

1 *Thomas recommends a course of action*	It's time to stop this vicious cycle of cutting education while increasing spending on the imprisonment of non-violent offenders. (1) Enacting a few common-sense reforms, such as paroling incarcerated non-violent drug offenders, will allow us to limit money spent on the prison system and divert those dollars to education; drug-abuse prevention, treatment, and rehabilitation; job training and employment services. (2)
2 *She specifies how her recommendation could be enacted*	

STUDENT WRITER AT WORK
Karen Thomas

R.A. What inspired you to write this essay? And publish it in your campus paper?

K.T. At first, my focus was on military vs. education spending at the federal level, but during my research I realized that prison spending was a more feasible comparison. I try to contribute articles that inform and bring awareness to our student body, especially on topics in which our readership has the ability to take action.

R.A. How long did it take for you to write this piece? What were your goals as you revised?

K.T. It took probably a month from first concept to final draft, including research and compiling statistics. Research and revision are the two areas in which most of my time is spent. Writing is easy; making it worth publishing (with the valuable input from my editors) is where most of the time is invested.

R.A. Do you generally show your writing to friends before submitting it? To what extent did discussion with others help you develop your point of view?

K.T. I always read my drafts aloud to a roommate, friend, or significant other, in order to hear how the piece sounds. This method helps me discover errors in my work. I do use others, especially my cohorts on the editorial board, as sounding boards. My point of view is typically pretty firm by the time a piece gets to the stage of being written. I'm a bit older than many of the students I work with, and with more years of living and experience under my belt, I try to be a leader in the topics I cover. With 'Misplaced Priorities,' I found that most people agreed with my stance, and in fact, many were astounded to learn how much more financial backing the prisons have as compared to our educational system. The outrage I feel was reflected in many of my readers.

R.A. Are you pursuing a career in which writing will be a component?

K.T. Absolutely! I don't know if my career will take the form of an online magazine (or even print), or if I will teach, tour, or write freelance, but the rest of my days here on earth will be centered on writing.

R.A. What advice do you have for other student writers?

K.T. My advice for other student writers is to find what you love and stick to it. Whether it's music, sports, or current gossip, delve into your subject and don't let detractors steer you away from that which you are passionate about. If you can't seem to find your niche, keep writing and you will create your own niche.

READ VORACIOUSLY! Read everything, especially the things that you disagree with or find abhorrent. It takes all kinds to make a world.

Use your talent to edify others, to bring valuable information to your peers, or to entertain and challenge your readers. Be honest in your efforts. We have the power to create whatever we want, so think about what it is you would like to see in the world, and create that reality through your writing. And lastly, never give up!

Discussing the Unit

SUGGESTED TOPIC FOR DISCUSSION

All of the essays in this unit question the benefit of the current prison system in light of the sheer numbers of people incarcerated and the amount of money funneled into it. Are our prisons rehabilitating anyone? What are we paying for? How can the system be made more humane and more effective?

PREPARING FOR CLASS DISCUSSION

1. Who is being sent to prison? What generalizations can be made about the U.S. prison system based on what you've read? Draw information from at least two of the essays in this chapter to support your answer.
2. What difficulties are faced by those who want to reform the prison system? Consider where the system is "broken" and needs repair.

FROM DISCUSSION TO WRITING

1. How do the writers of these essays convince you that we send too many people to prison or spend too much money on the prison system? Using their criteria, how do we know when the numbers are too much? Do you agree with their arguments? Write a brief essay that compares the viewpoint of the authors in this chapter to your own.
2. Most of the essays in this chapter describe what prisons or life after incarceration is like, in one way or other. Drawing from these descriptions, write a brief essay that imagines a different scenario or offers a suggestion that implements change.

TOPICS FOR CROSS-CULTURAL DISCUSSION

1. These essays suggest that in many ways race defines the current prison population. In the studies of prisoners and prison life offered in this chapter, how is race a factor? How do these writers explain the racial imbalance that exists in the prison system?

2. Joan Petersilia writes, "It is no accident that the sons and brothers of men who go to prison are more likely to follow the same path" (para. 14). How does one's background influence one's experience of our current incarceration system? What does this indicate about American culture?

 This chapter continues online. Visit the e-Page at
bedfordstmartins.com/americanow/epages for a video assignment.

Debating Climate Change: How Scientific Is the Evidence?

According to the National Oceanic and Atmospheric Administration (NOAA), the United States set a record for "billion-dollar weather disasters" in 2011, and in July 2012, NOAA further concluded that human-caused climate change is a likely contributor to such disasters. Although NOAA is a widely respected, nonpartisan source of climate information, its 2012 report has done little to bridge the longstanding divide between those who see a clear connection between human activity and climate change and those who question the existence of this link or believe its consequences are overstated.

What explains this divide? Can differing views on climate change be attributed to differing levels of education, or is something more complicated going on? Are global warming skeptics motivated purely by political or economic interests, or does their skepticism have real scientific value? And assuming that human activity is posing a real and serious threat to the environment, what, if anything, is the average citizen to do?

The opposing viewpoints that open this chapter—"We Can't Handle the Truth" by journalist Chris Mooney and "Unchanging Science" by editor Joseph Bottum and psychiatrist William Anderson—explore many of these questions. According to Mooney, people's opinions on climate change may have a lot more to do with their preexisting beliefs than with facts—even when facts completely contradict those beliefs. Interestingly, he writes, "[H]ead-on attempts to persuade can sometimes trigger a backfire effect, where people not only fail to change their minds when confronted with the facts—they may hold their wrong views more tenaciously than ever."

Perhaps more surprising is Mooney's conclusion that skepticism about climate change isn't necessarily tied to lower levels of education. In fact, he writes, among Republicans, who tend to be more skeptical on the subject than Democrats are, "a higher education correlated with an increased likelihood of denying the science on the issue."

For their part, Bottum and Anderson suggest that skepticism isn't purely a political, knee-jerk reaction to the climate change debate but a frame of mind essential to good science. According to the authors, the problem with climate change assertions, as presented by environmental groups, is that they are "nonfalsfiable"—that is, they do not allow for skepticism: "[T]he fact that climate change can't be falsified seems to prove, mostly, that climate change isn't science: There's no way to test for it, no way to quantify it, and no way to demonstrate it."

But what if global warming is in fact a serious threat? Does buying "green" products do anything to combat the problem? In a word, "no," says Sarah Laskow, author of "Debunking 'Green Living': Combatting Climate Change Requires Lifestyle Changes, Not Organic Products." Instead, she contends, people need to do the hard work of changing deep-seated habits.

In "Cuddly Symbols Not Cooperating in Climate Change Panic," political analyst and columnist Mona Charen shares Bottum and Anderson's doubts about global warming, or at least its seriousness. She also criticizes the "panic mongering of the global warmists."

In the final essay of the chapter, Tatevik Manucharyan, a student at Glendale Community College, shares the views of a professor who has no doubts about the seriousness of climate change and humans' role in it.

This extended chapter closes with two features that show how much awareness about climate change has grown. "America Then . . . 1985" discusses astronomer Carl Sagan's prophetic warning about global warming, which came at a time when few Americans had even heard of the problem. The e-Page feature brings us to May 5, 2012, when "people around the world volunteered, documented, educated, and protested" in efforts to address climate change.

Is Climate Change Real?

BEFORE YOU READ

Are you often persuaded by facts about a given issue or do you hold preexisting beliefs that resist those facts? Is science even able to claim facts (about climate change, for example) or should we always think of scientific data as something we can prove wrong?

Chris Mooney

We Can't Handle the Truth

[*Mother Jones*, May/June 2011]

WORDS TO LEARN

infiltrate (para. 2): to join secretly (verb)

cataclysm (para. 3): violent upheaval (noun)

asunder (para. 3): apart (adv)

refute (para. 4): to prove false (verb)

rationalization (para. 5): justification (noun)

annals (para. 7): historical records (noun)

dispassionate (para. 7): unaffected; impartial (adj)

unequivocal (para. 7): clear (adj)

uncongenial (para. 11): disagreeable (adj)

jargon (para. 12): technical language of a particular group (noun)

nuance (para. 14): a subtle distinction (noun)

stark (para. 18): absolute (adj)

deter (para. 18): to discourage (verb)

inherent (para. 19): intrinsic; inseparable (adj)

deleterious (para. 19): harmful (adj)

tenaciously (para. 20): firmly (adv)

amenable (para. 21): agreeable (adj)

dislodge (para. 22): to remove something from its place (verb)

fallacy (para. 28): false notion (noun)

gravitate (para. 30): to move toward (verb)

trove (para. 34): collection (noun)

monolithic (para. 40): having a rigid uniformity (adj)

Chris Mooney is a science and political journalist, blogger, podcaster, and author of four books. He blogs for Science Progress, *a Web site of the Center for American Progress and Center for American Progress Action Fund, and is a host of the* Point of Inquiry *podcast. His articles have appeared in* Slate, Mother Jones, *the* Washington Post, *and the* Boston Globe, *among others.*

canonical (para. 42): recognized;
   accepted (adj)
skew (para. 44): to turn off course
   (verb)

détente (para. 46): a relaxing of
   tensions (noun)

" A man with a conviction is a hard man to change. Tell him you 1
disagree and he turns away. Show him facts or figures and he
questions your sources. Appeal to logic and he fails to see your
point." So wrote the celebrated Stanford University psychologist Leon
Festinger, in a passage that might have been referring to climate change
denial — the persistent rejection, on the part of so many Americans
today, of what we know about global warming and its human causes. But
it was too early for that — this was the 1950s — and Festinger was actually describing a famous case study in psychology.

Festinger and several of his colleagues had infiltrated the Seekers, 2
a small Chicago-area cult whose members thought they were communicating with aliens — including one, "Sananda," who they believed was
the astral incarnation of Jesus Christ. The group was led by Dorothy
Martin, a Dianetics devotee who transcribed the interstellar messages
through automatic writing.

Through her, the aliens had given the precise date of an Earth-rending 3
cataclysm: December 21, 1954. Some of Martin's followers quit their jobs
and sold their property, expecting to be rescued by a flying saucer when
the continent split asunder and a new sea swallowed much of the United
States. The disciples even went so far as to remove brassieres and rip zip-
pers out of their trousers — the metal, they believed, would pose a danger
on the spacecraft.

Festinger and his team were with the cult when the prophecy failed. 4
First, the "boys upstairs" (as the aliens were sometimes called) did not
show up and rescue the Seekers. Then December 21 arrived without
incident. It was the moment Festinger had been waiting for: How would
people so emotionally invested in a belief system react, now that it had
been soundly refuted?

At first, the group struggled for an explanation. But then ratio- 5
nalization set in. A new message arrived, announcing that they'd all
been spared at the last minute. Festinger summarized the extraterres-
trials' new pronouncement: "The little group, sitting all night long, had
spread so much light that God had saved the world from destruction."
Their willingness to believe in the prophecy had saved Earth from the
prophecy!

From that day forward, the Seekers, previously shy of the press and 6
indifferent toward evangelizing, began to proselytize. "Their sense of

urgency was enormous," wrote Festinger. The devastation of all they had believed had made them even more certain of their beliefs.

In the annals of denial, it doesn't get much more extreme than the Seekers. They lost their jobs, the press mocked them, and there were efforts to keep them away from impressionable young minds. But while Martin's space cult might lie at the far end of the spectrum of human self-delusion, there's plenty to go around. And since Festinger's day, an array of new discoveries in psychology and neuroscience has further demonstrated how our preexisting beliefs, far more than any new facts, can skew our thoughts and even color what we consider our most dispassionate and logical conclusions. This tendency toward so-called "motivated reasoning" helps explain why we find groups so polarized over matters where the evidence is so unequivocal: climate change, vaccines, "death panels," the birthplace and religion of the president, and much else. It would seem that expecting people to be convinced by the facts flies in the face of, you know, the facts.

The theory of motivated reasoning builds on a key insight of modern neuroscience: Reasoning is actually suffused with emotion (or what researchers often call "affect"). Not only are the two inseparable, but our positive or negative feelings about people, things, and ideas arise much more rapidly than our conscious thoughts, in a matter of milliseconds — fast enough to detect with an EEG[1] device, but long before we're aware of it. That shouldn't be surprising: Evolution required us to react very quickly to stimuli in our environment. It's a "basic human survival skill," explains political scientist Arthur Lupia of the University of Michigan. We push threatening information away; we pull friendly information close. We apply fight-or-flight reflexes not only to predators, but to data itself.

We're not driven only by emotions, of course — we also reason, deliberate. But reasoning comes later, works slower — and even then, it doesn't take place in an emotional vacuum. Rather, our quick-fire emotions can set us on a course of thinking that's highly biased, especially on topics we care a great deal about.

Consider a person who has heard about a scientific discovery that deeply challenges her belief in divine creation — a new hominid, say, that confirms our evolutionary origins. What happens next, explains political scientist Charles Taber of Stony Brook University, is a subconscious negative response to the new information — and that response, in turn, guides the type of memories and associations formed in the conscious mind. "They retrieve thoughts that are consistent with their previous

7

8

9

10

---

[1] EEG (para. 8): Short for electroenchephalogram, a diagnositic tool that measures electrical activity in the brain.

beliefs," says Taber, "and that will lead them to build an argument and challenge what they're hearing."

In other words, when we think we're reasoning, we may instead   11 be rationalizing. Or to use an analogy offered by University of Virginia psychologist Jonathan Haidt: We may think we're being scientists, but we're actually being lawyers. Our "reasoning" is a means to a predetermined end — winning our "case" — and is shot through with biases. They include "confirmation bias," in which we give greater heed to evidence and arguments that bolster our beliefs, and "disconfirmation bias," in which we expend disproportionate energy trying to debunk or refute views and arguments that we find uncongenial.

That's a lot of jargon, but we all understand these mechanisms   12 when it comes to interpersonal relationships. If I don't want to believe that my spouse is being unfaithful, or that my child is a bully, I can go to great lengths to explain away behavior that seems obvious to everybody else — everybody who isn't too emotionally invested to accept it, anyway. That's not to suggest that we aren't also motivated to perceive the world accurately — we are. Or that we never change our minds — we do. It's just that we have other important goals besides accuracy — including identity affirmation and protecting one's sense of self — and often those make us highly resistant to changing our beliefs when the facts say we should.

Modern science originated from an attempt to weed out such sub-   13 jective lapses — what that great seventeenth century theorist of the scientific method, Francis Bacon, dubbed the "idols of the mind." Even if individual researchers are prone to falling in love with their own theories, the broader processes of peer review and institutionalized skepticism are designed to ensure that, eventually, the best ideas prevail.

Our individual responses to the conclusions that science reaches,   14 however, are quite another matter. Ironically, in part because researchers employ so much nuance and strive to disclose all remaining sources of uncertainty, scientific evidence is highly susceptible to selective reading and misinterpretation. Giving ideologues or partisans scientific data that's relevant to their beliefs is like unleashing them in the motivated-reasoning equivalent of a candy store.

Sure enough, a large number of psychological studies have shown   15 that people respond to scientific or technical evidence in ways that justify their preexisting beliefs. In a classic 1979 experiment, pro- and anti-death penalty advocates were exposed to descriptions of two fake scientific studies: one supporting and one undermining the notion that capital punishment deters violent crime and, in particular, murder. They were also shown detailed methodological critiques of the fake studies — and in a scientific sense, neither study was stronger than the other. Yet in each case, advocates more heavily criticized the study whose conclusions disagreed with their own, while describing the study that was more ideologically congenial as more "convincing."

Since then, similar results have been found for how people respond to "evidence" about affirmative action, gun control, the accuracy of gay stereotypes, and much else. Even when study subjects are explicitly instructed to be unbiased and even-handed about the evidence, they often fail.   16

And it's not just that people twist or selectively read scientific evidence to support their preexisting views. According to research by Yale Law School professor Dan Kahan and his colleagues, people's deep-seated views about morality, and about the way society should be ordered, strongly predict whom they consider to be a legitimate scientific expert in the first place — and thus where they consider "scientific consensus" to lie on contested issues.   17

In Kahan's research, individuals are classified, based on their cultural values, as either "individualists" or "communitarians," and as either "hierarchical" or "egalitarian" in outlook. (Somewhat oversimplifying, you can think of hierarchical individualists as akin to conservative Republicans, and egalitarian communitarians as liberal Democrats.) In one study, subjects in the different groups were asked to help a close friend determine the risks associated with climate change, sequestering nuclear waste, or concealed carry laws: "The friend tells you that he or she is planning to read a book about the issue but would like to get your opinion on whether the author seems like a knowledgeable and trustworthy expert." A subject was then presented with the résumé of a fake expert "depicted as a member of the National Academy of Sciences who had earned a Ph.D. in a pertinent field from one elite university and who was now on the faculty of another." The subject was then shown a book excerpt by that "expert," in which the risk of the issue at hand was portrayed as high or low, well-founded or speculative. The results were stark: When the scientist's position stated that global warming is real and human-caused, for instance, only 23 percent of hierarchical individualists agreed the person was a "trustworthy and knowledgeable expert." Yet 88 percent of egalitarian communitarians accepted the same scientist's expertise. Similar divides were observed on whether nuclear waste can be safely stored underground and whether letting people carry guns deters crime. (The alliances did not always hold. In another study, hierarchs and communitarians were in favor of laws that would compel the mentally ill to accept treatment, whereas individualists and egalitarians were opposed.)   18

In other words, people rejected the validity of a scientific source because its conclusion contradicted their deeply held views — and thus   19 the relative risks inherent in each scenario. A hierarchal individualist finds it difficult to believe that the things he prizes (commerce, industry, a man's freedom to possess a gun to defend his family) could lead to outcomes deleterious to society. Whereas egalitarian communitarians tend to think that the free market causes harm, that patriarchal families mess up kids, and that people can't handle their guns. The study subjects weren't "anti-science" — not in their own minds, anyway. It's just that "science" was whatever they wanted it to be. "We've come to a misadventure, a bad situation where diverse citizens, who rely on diverse systems of cultural certification, are in conflict," says Kahan.

And that undercuts the standard notion that the way to persuade people is via evidence and argument. In fact, head-on attempts to persuade can sometimes trigger a backfire effect, where people not only fail to change their minds when confronted with the facts — they may hold their wrong views more tenaciously than ever. 20

> Head-on attempts to persuade can sometimes trigger a backfire effect.

Take, for instance, the question of whether Saddam Hussein possessed hidden weapons of mass destruction just before the U.S. invasion of Iraq in 2003. When political scientists Brendan Nyhan and Jason Reifler showed subjects fake newspaper articles in which this was first suggested (in a 2004 quote from President Bush) and then refuted (with the findings of the Bush-commissioned Iraq Survey Group report, which found no evidence of active WMD programs in pre-invasion Iraq), they found that conservatives were more likely than before to believe the claim. (The researchers also tested how liberals responded when shown that Bush did not actually "ban" embryonic stem-cell research. Liberals weren't particularly amenable to persuasion, either, but no backfire effect was observed.) 21

Another study gives some inkling of what may be going through people's minds when they resist persuasion. Northwestern University sociologist Monica Prasad and her colleagues wanted to test whether they could dislodge the notion that Saddam Hussein and Al Qaeda were secretly collaborating among those most likely to believe it — Republican partisans from highly GOP-friendly counties. So the researchers set up a study in which they discussed the topic with some of these Republicans in person. They would cite the findings of the 9/11 Commission, as well as a statement in which George W. Bush himself denied his administration had "said the 9/11 attacks were orchestrated between Saddam and Al Qaeda." 22

As it turned out, not even Bush's own words could change the minds of these Bush voters — just 1 of the 49 partisans who originally believed the Iraq-Al Qaeda claim changed his or her mind. Far more common was 23 resisting the correction in a variety of ways, either by coming up with counterarguments or by simply being unmovable:

Interviewer: [T]he September 11 Commission found no link 24 between Saddam and 9/11, and this is what President Bush said. Do you have any comments on either of those?

Respondent: Well, I bet they say that the Commission didn't have 25 any proof of it but I guess we still can have our opinions and feel that way even though they say that.

The same types of responses are already being documented on 26 divisive topics facing the current administration. Take the "Ground Zero mosque." Using information from the political myth-busting site FactCheck.org, a team at Ohio State presented subjects with a detailed rebuttal to the claim that "Feisal Abdul Rauf, the Imam backing the proposed Islamic cultural center and mosque, is a terrorist-sympathizer." Yet among those who were aware of the rumor and believed it, fewer than a third changed their minds.

A key question — and one that's difficult to answer — is how "irra- 27 tional" all this is. On the one hand, it doesn't make sense to discard an entire belief system, built up over a lifetime, because of some new snippet of information. "It is quite possible to say, 'I reached this pro-capital-punishment decision based on real information that I arrived at over my life,'" explains Stanford social psychologist Jon Krosnick. Indeed, there's a sense in which science denial could be considered keenly "rational." In certain conservative communities, explains Yale's Kahan, "People who say, 'I think there's something to climate change,' that's going to mark them out as a certain kind of person, and their life is going to go less well."

This may help explain a curious pattern Nyhan and his colleagues found 28 when they tried to test the fallacy that President Obama is a Muslim. When a nonwhite researcher was administering their study, research subjects were amenable to changing their minds about the president's religion and updating incorrect views. But when only white researchers were present, GOP survey subjects in particular were more likely to believe the Obama Muslim myth than before. The subjects were using "social desirabililty" to tailor their beliefs (or stated beliefs, anyway) to whoever was listening.

Which leads us to the media. When people grow polarized over a 29 body of evidence, or a resolvable matter of fact, the cause may be some form of biased reasoning, but they could also be receiving skewed information to begin with — or a complicated combination of both. In the Ground Zero mosque case, for instance, a follow-up study showed that survey respondents who watched Fox News were more likely to believe the Rauf rumor and three related ones — and they believed them more strongly than non-Fox watchers.

Okay, so people gravitate toward information that confirms what   30
they believe, and they select sources that deliver it. Same as it ever was,
right? Maybe, but the problem is arguably growing more acute, given
the way we now consume information — through the Facebook links of
friends, or tweets that lack nuance or context, or "narrowcast" and often
highly ideological media that have relatively small, like-minded audiences. Those basic human survival skills of ours, says Michigan's Arthur
Lupia, are "not well-adapted to our information age."

If you wanted to show how and why fact is ditched in favor of motivated   31
reasoning, you could find no better test case than climate change. After all, it's
an issue where you have highly technical information on one hand and very
strong beliefs on the other. And sure enough, one key predictor of whether
you accept the science of global warming is whether you're a Republican or
a Democrat. The two groups have been growing more divided in their views
about the topic, even as the science becomes more unequivocal.

So perhaps it should come as no surprise that more education   32
doesn't budge Republican views. On the contrary: In a 2008 Pew survey,
for instance, only 19 percent of college-educated Republicans agreed
that the planet is warming due to human actions, versus 31 percent of
non-college-educated Republicans. In other words, a higher education
correlated with an increased likelihood of denying the science on the
issue. Meanwhile, among Democrats and independents, more education
correlated with greater acceptance of the science.

Other studies have shown a similar effect: Republicans who think   33
they understand the global warming issue best are least concerned about
it; and among Republicans and those with higher levels of distrust of
science in general, learning more about the issue doesn't increase one's
concern about it. What's going on here? Well, according to Charles Taber
and Milton Lodge of Stony Brook, one insidious aspect of motivated reasoning is that political sophisticates are prone to be more biased than
those who know less about the issues. "People who have a dislike of some
policy — for example, abortion — if they're unsophisticated they can
just reject it out of hand," says Lodge. "But if they're sophisticated, they
can go one step further and start coming up with counterarguments."
These individuals are just as emotionally driven and biased as the rest of
us, but they're able to generate more and better reasons to explain why
they're right — and so their minds become harder to change.

That may be why the selectively quoted emails of Climategate[2] were   34
so quickly and easily seized upon by partisans as evidence of scandal.

---

[2] Climategate (para. 34): Hacked e-mails from University of East Anglia that
raise questions about the details of climate change and how the issue has been
presented to the public.

Cherry-picking is precisely the sort of behavior you would expect motivated reasoners to engage in to bolster their views — and whatever you
may think about Climategate, the emails were a rich trove of new information upon which to impose one's ideology.

Climategate had a substantial impact on public opinion, according   35
to Anthony Leiserowitz, director of the Yale Project on Climate Change
Communication. It contributed to an overall drop in public concern
about climate change and a significant loss of trust in scientists. But — as
we should expect by now — these declines were concentrated among
particular groups of Americans: Republicans, conservatives, and those
with "individualistic" values. Liberals and those with "egalitarian" values didn't lose much trust in climate science or scientists at all. "In some
ways, Climategate was like a Rorschach test,[3]" Leiserowitz says, "with
different groups interpreting ambiguous facts in very different ways."

So is there a case study of science denial that largely occupies the   36
political left? Yes: the claim that childhood vaccines are causing an epidemic of autism. Its most famous proponents are an environmentalist
(Robert F. Kennedy Jr.) and numerous Hollywood celebrities (most
notably Jenny McCarthy and Jim Carrey). The *Huffington Post* gives a
very large megaphone to denialists. And Seth Mnookin, author of the
new book *The Panic Virus*, notes that if you want to find vaccine deniers,
all you need to do is go hang out at Whole Foods.

Vaccine denial has all the hallmarks of a belief system that's not ame-   37
nable to refutation. Over the past decade, the assertion that childhood
vaccines are driving autism rates has been undermined by multiple epide-
miological studies — as well as the simple fact that autism rates continue
to rise, even though the alleged offending agent in vaccines (a mercury-
based preservative called thimerosal) has long since been removed.

Yet the true believers persist — critiquing each new study that chal-   38
lenges their views, and even rallying to the defense of vaccine-autism
researcher Andrew Wakefield, after his 1998 *Lancet* paper — which originated the current vaccine scare — was retracted and he subsequently lost
his license to practice medicine. But then, why should we be surprised?
Vaccine deniers created their own partisan media, such as the website Age
of Autism, that instantly blast out critiques and counterarguments whenever any new development casts further doubt on anti-vaccine views.

It all raises the question: Do left and right differ in any meaning-   39
ful way when it comes to biases in processing information, or are we all
equally susceptible?

---

[3] Rorschach test (para. 35): A still popular psychological test dating back to the
1920s and used to evaluate personality based on the perception and interpretation of what various inkblot shapes resemble.

There are some clear differences. Science denial today is considerably   40
more prominent on the political right — once you survey climate and
related environmental issues, anti-evolutionism, attacks on reproductive health science by the Christian right, and stem-cell and biomedical
matters. More tellingly, anti-vaccine positions are virtually nonexistent
among Democratic officeholders today — whereas anti-climate-science
views are becoming monolithic among Republican elected officials.

Some researchers have suggested that there are psychological differ-   41
ences between the left and the right that might impact responses to new
information — that conservatives are more rigid and authoritarian, and
liberals more tolerant of ambiguity. Psychologist John Jost of New York
University has further argued that conservatives are "system justifiers":
They engage in motivated reasoning to defend the status quo.

This is a contested area, however, because as soon as one tries to psy-   42
choanalyze inherent political differences, a battery of counterarguments
emerges: What about dogmatic and militant communists? What about how
the parties have differed through history? After all, the most canonical case
of ideologically driven science denial is probably the rejection of genetics in
the Soviet Union, where researchers disagreeing with the anti-Mendelian
scientist (and Stalin stooge) Trofim Lysenko were executed, and genetics
itself was denounced as a "bourgeois" science and officially banned.

The upshot: All we can currently bank on is the fact that we all have   43
blinders in some situations. The question then becomes: What can be
done to counteract human nature itself?

Given the power of our prior beliefs to skew how we respond to new   44
information, one thing is becoming clear: If you want someone to accept
new evidence, make sure to present it to them in a context that doesn't
trigger a defensive, emotional reaction.

This theory is gaining traction in part because of Kahan's work at   45
Yale. In one study, he and his colleagues packaged the basic science of
climate change into fake newspaper articles bearing two very different
headlines — "Scientific Panel Recommends Anti-Pollution Solution to
Global Warming" and "Scientific Panel Recommends Nuclear Solution
to Global Warming" — and then tested how citizens with different values responded. Sure enough, the latter framing made hierarchical individualists much more open to accepting the fact that humans are causing
global warming. Kahan infers that the effect occurred because the science had been written into an alternative narrative that appealed to their
pro-industry worldview.

You can follow the logic to its conclusion: Conservatives are more   46
likely to embrace climate science if it comes to them via a business or religious leader, who can set the issue in the context of different values than

In retrospect, we probably should have paid more attention when, around 2005, activists shifted their primary vocabulary from *global warming* to *climate change* to describe the impact of human beings on this biosphere we call the Earth. Both phrases had been around for a while, of course. *Global warming* got its modern start back in 1975, when the journal *Science* published a feature asking, "Are We on the Brink of a Pronounced Global Warming?" In one form or another, *climate change* has been in use since the physicist Joseph Fourier wrote of the greenhouse effect in the 1820s.

For that matter, both are unexceptionable meteorological terms with reasonably clear meanings: global warming a particular species or instantiation of general changes in the globe's climate. The public purpose of those words, however — the political intent: That was a different thing altogether. For decades, *global warming* seemed a powerful, dynamic term to use — an apocalyptic phrase that summoned a grim vision of the eschaton, our world reduced to a lifeless wasteland. The only trouble was that it required the world to be, you know, *warming.* Constantly. A cold winter, and people started to wonder. A chilly spring, and people started to doubt.

Recent news reports have been dominated by squabbles between Berkeley's Richard Muller and Georgia Tech's Judith Curry, both involved in research that led to the release of data in October from the Berkeley Earth Surface Temperatures study. Muller claims that the fact of global warming now leaves "little room for doubt," while Curry tells the *Daily Mail* that there exists "no scientific basis for saying that warming hasn't stopped." And yet, even in the midst of touting the study, Muller admits that the Berkeley data show that temperatures have not risen over the last decade.

Which confirms, more or less, what seems to be emerging as the feeling of the general public: These recent winters have been *cold*, and the summers themselves not so hot. That, in turn, creates a problem, for no sense of impending apocalypse survives widespread disbelief. And so — right around the point where it all started to seem a little hard to swallow — the phrase *climate change*, more generic if less picturesque, began to slip into public pronouncements, supplanting the old, falsifiable term *global warming.* A bitter January in the Midwest could well be a sign of climate change. Hurricanes in the Caribbean, mudslides in Latin America, floods in Australia. Earthquakes, even. Everything and anything, the whole wild uncertainty of the world, proved that we were right to feel under the gun — faced with an eschatological doom of our own creation.

The more the term embraced, however, the less it explained. That's not as contradictory as it may seem. There's a simple epistemological process by which, as we move up the genus-species tree, we arrive at ideas that cover more cases but convey less information: Lots more mammals exist in general than marmosets in particular, but *mammal* doesn't tell us as much about the beast in question as *marmoset* does. Move up high enough into the linguistic arbor, and you arrive at terms that refer to all but mean none: *thing,* for example, or *being.*

Or *climate change,* as far as that goes. The great emotional gain of the 6
shift from *global warming* to *climate change* was that the name had become so generic that nothing imaginable could prove it wrong. Every shift in weather is a confirming instance. The only problem left was the pesky little scientific one that, well, *nothing imaginable could prove it wrong.* In its public use, in the mouths of activists and the titles of organizations such as the United Nations Framework Convention on Climate Change, the phrase had come to describe something nonfalsifiable.

This is what was in the background when Ivar Giaever, a Nobel 7
laureate in physics, resigned recently from the American Physical Society — in protest over the society's loudly declared position that evidence of human-caused climate change is "incontrovertible." Giaever is not some committed global warming skeptic, but he decided that he just couldn't stomach the claim that *anything* in science is incontrovertible. If you can't imagine conditions under which it might be controverted, then you're no longer doing science.

It was back in the 1930s that Karl Popper popularized the idea of fal- 8
sifiability as a necessary property of a scientific proposition. Several of the intellectual currents of the era combined to make Popper's work seem a major breakthrough. The mechanisms of inductive logic had become a crisis point in philosophy, for example, and the commonly used "fact-value distinction" lacked clarity.

None of these philosophical problems seem particularly pressing 9
these days, but the concept of falsifiability still grants some insight into the vagaries of modern environmentalism. In politics, the notion that climate change can't be falsified — everything only serves to confirm it, nothing imaginable can contradict it — has been a marvelous boon. In science, the fact that climate change can't be falsified seems to prove, mostly, that climate change isn't science: There's no way to test for it, no way to quantify it, and no way to demonstrate it.

If politics is the human activity by which collective decisions are 10
made, then (whatever the structure of the regime, from the most coercive authoritarianism to the most radical democracy) all government depends on some kind of agreement. Our political instincts have developed over many millennia, but the essential commonality is that we are most comfortable when we shape our opinions to the consensus of our group. As a general matter, we'd rather be wrong in a group than right but alone.

Science, on the other hand, is a methodological tool by which we 11
coordinate observation, logic, and experiment to attempt to discover

facts. Science doesn't deal in either certainty or consensus. Every well-formed theory contains a set of testable hypotheses. When these hypotheses fail confirmation by repeated experiment, the theory has to change. Thus the progress of science is halting and erratic, ultimately convergent on, but never achieving, final explanations of our world.

Naturally, that means confusion reigns when scientists dabble in   12
politics and politicians attempt to explain science — as when we are confronted by such oxymorons as "settled science." And, unfortunately, in the worlds of climate change, such confusions seem to be happening a lot — from the United Nations agency that got caught taking an environmental activist group's unsupported (and mistaken) word that Himalayan glaciers would all be melted away by 2035, to the *Times Atlas* that recently decided global warming would be more striking if 15 percent of the Greenland ice cap were arbitrarily erased from the map. To say nothing of the 2009 case in which bizarre emails between influential scientists and activists, hacked from a server at the University of East Anglia (which is climate-change central, keeper of international temperature records), were released to the public.

Professional scientists are people, of course, and thus participants in   13
the rough and tumble of political debate. Professional politicians are also people, of a sort, and they're always eager to use the prestige of science to claim support for their political goals. Most of the time, these cross-over category errors stay relatively minor. Occasionally, however, conflations of politics and science snowball into disasters for both politics and science — and the debate over climate change is as clear an example as we've had since stem cells rolled into public view.

An hour's poking around on the Internet reveals that no scientific   14
consensus on massive human-caused climate change actually exists. Those afflicted with what economists call "perverse incentives," however, *want* scientific consensus to exist, and they try, hard, to pull that consensus into being. Naturally, the debate is skewed toward the faction which controls the most political and economic resources — particularly the United Nations, on the commanding heights of resource allocation for activists through the mechanism of its various interlocking directorates of committees and NGOs.[1]

> No scientific consensus on massive human-caused climate change actually exists.

The result is an astonishing tangle of mostly ad hominem arguments.   15
Proponents of catastrophic global warming claim that their opponents

---

[1] NGO (para.14): Non-Governmental Organization.

are in denial and corrupted by corporate funding. Skeptics counter that these alarmists are corrupted by government funding and political pressure. The result has been good for neither politicians nor scientists, with every new poll betraying smaller numbers of those who trust either government or science to speak the truth — much less to fix our strange and broken world.

As far as the actual facts go, they go quickly, the first casualties in the   16
battles at the crossroads of science and politics. We do know that there have been periodic ice ages for the past million or so years, and that the period of those ice ages is on the order of 100,000 years. About 10 percent of discernible history is made up of warm periods (such as our current climate), and the rest much colder, with large portions of the earth covered with thick ice.

The cause of this periodicity is not well understood. Human activity   17
may have contributed to some of it recently, but clearly not to changes occurring over millions of years. Variations in solar irradiance, changes in atmospheric gases, variable ocean currents, and cosmic rays have been hypothesized, each the bearer of a much greater burden than human activity could be. We now appear, on the basis of prior history, to be in the last stages of a warm period which has existed, with some variations, for about 10,000 years.

Within each era, variances of climate occur, as warmer and colder   18
periods of several hundred years come and go. The causes of these changes are similarly uncertain. Is there an ideal global average temperature? If so, what is it? And how do we measure it? Can our species influence these changes? If so, should we? In which direction? What are the costs, risks, and benefits? These questions are not, to say the least, in any realm of settled science.

Enter the climate scientists. The research enterprise in the modern   19
world is a large-scale activity. Difficult questions are raised, and hypotheses are generated to move toward an answer. This requires hiring staff, recruiting experts and consultants, purchasing equipment, and putting all of it in a building, preferably on a university campus. Most of all, what's needed for this kind of research is oceans of money. And where money is the driver, politics is the unavoidable road down which the scientist has to race. Grant-making authorities, whether in government, industries, or foundations, tend to have a preferred perspective on the process and outcome of research. These preferences are not lost on the applicant researchers.

A few research centers have dominated the study of climate change,   20
and these are typically funded by national governments, with the approval of U.N. agencies and the transnational perspective that U.N. agencies

represent. What has emerged, in other words, is a *political* consensus that emphasizes the claim of ongoing climate change which (1) tends toward warming, (2) is caused by human activity, and (3) threatens to be apocalyptic. Groupthink then emerges as the dominant social response, with ostracism of skeptics and excommunication of apostates.

As the grant-achieving scientists congealed their opinions around 21 the hypothesis (and now doctrine) of catastrophic anthropogenic global warming — warmed, themselves, by their presumptive guardianship of truth and virtue — some have succumbed to the temptation to cut corners. Dissenting investigators have been marginalized, their research papers viewed with prejudice by academic journals. The principle of free availability of raw data has been ignored. Peer review has degenerated into pal review. Cases of data destruction and tampering have been documented.

Through all this, public opinion has remained bemused, and only 22 mildly interested, with polls suggesting a small decrease in concern over catastrophic manmade climate change and a gradual increase in disbelief about the whole thing. Which has to concern the people whose livelihood depends on predicting catastrophe. Prophecy demands belief.

Perhaps the greatest reason for any of us to feel skepticism about climate 23 change, however, is the unchanging politics of those who employed it to advance their agendas. Are we wrong to suspect that most global warming activists are merely using global warming as the latest in a long series of tools with which to demand fundamental changes in Western civilization?

Think of it this way: The premise of catastrophe produces the conclusion 24 that the political and economic underpinnings of Western civilization must be discarded. Governments must take control of economies. Capitalism must give way. All decisions must be made by our scientific and political elite, for only they can save us from doom.

Now, in a purely logical world, the rejection of the premise would 25 mean that we don't have to accept the conclusion. *If A, then B* and *not A* together produce nothing. But the people who've been lecturing us for more than a decade now about global warming and climate change didn't start by holding *A*. They began by holding *B* — the conclusion, the proposition that Western civilization must change. And it is, literally, a nonfalsifiable proposition: If global warming and climate change help lead to it, then hurray for global warming and climate change. If not, well, then, they'll find something else.

Yet facts remain stubborn things, and the thesis of climate change, 26 at least, is clearly in decline. The once-proud carbontrading market in Chicago is now defunct. Similar European schemes have collapsed in confusion and fraud. Alternative scientific theory is beginning to find its footing. Flawed methods have been exposed. Leaked emails indicate a corrupted scientific process. Most of all, public opinion has not been stampeded, in spite of intense climate-change advocacy in the media.

Skepticism, the prime scientific virtue, still lives, in other words. If nothing else, Ivar Giaever may yet be able to rejoin the American Physical Society.   27

VOCABULARY/USING A DICTIONARY

1. What scientific terms did you find in these two essays? List as many as you can, with definitions.
2. Break the word *transcribe* (Mooney, para. 2) into prefix and root. From what language are those parts derived?
3. If a substance is *congealed*, what does it look like? With that in mind, what does the verb *congeal* (Bottum/Anderson, para. 21) mean?

RESPONDING TO WORDS IN CONTEXT

1. In paragraph 2 (Mooney), how do you understand what is meant by *automatic writing*?
2. Why does Mooney use words like *disciples* (para. 3), *prophecy* (para. 4), *evangelizing* (para. 6), and *proselytize* (para. 6) in his essay? What do these words mean and in what context are they usually used?
3. Bottum and Anderson refer to *proponents* and *opponents* of catastrophic global warming in paragraph 15. What is the position of a proponent or opponent on that issue?
4. Define *linguistic*. Define *arbor*. What do you think Bottum and Anderson mean by a "linguistic arbor" in paragraph 5?

DISCUSSING MAIN POINT AND MEANING

1. According to Mooney, when do individuals and groups have difficulty accepting factual information?
2. How are scientists and politicians interconnected, according to Bottum and Anderson?
3. What types of individuals, presented by Yale professor Dan Kahan in his research on predicting responses to scientific evidence, does Mooney isolate as typical decision makers? How do their different belief systems affect their positions on topics like global warming?
4. Why, according to Bottum and Anderson, was the term *global warming* changed to *climate change*?

EXAMINING SENTENCES, PARAGRAPHS, AND ORGANIZATION

1. What figure of speech is Mooney using in the following sentence to illustrate his argument: "Giving ideologues or partisans scientific data that's

relevant to their beliefs is like unleashing them in the motivated-reasoning equivalent of a candy store" (para. 14)? What is its effect?

2. Consider Bottum and Anderson's statement in paragraph 24: "Think of it this way: The premise of catastrophe produces the conclusion that the political and economic underpinnings of Western civilization must be discarded. Governments must take control of economies. Capitalism must give way. All decisions must be made by our scientific and political elite, for only they can save us from doom." Do you think they mean that this will happen? Why or why not?

3. Can you determine the authors' position on climate change in "Unchanging Science"? What about in "We Can't Handle the Truth"? How can you tell?

THINKING CRITICALLY

1. Where do the essays in this debate seem to be talking about a human condition, and where do they feel slanted toward a particular agenda? Why?

2. Is it possible, as Mooney suggests, to lead from the perspective of values in a conversation about a charged topic in order to "give the facts a fighting chance"? What might that sort of conversation look like?

3. Do you agree with Bottum and Anderson that "the thesis of climate change, at least, is clearly in decline"? Why or why not?

WRITING ACTIVITIES

1. An organization technique used in Mooney's long essay is to provide an example in one paragraph and then to summarize its meaning in the topic sentence of the next paragraph. For instance, in paragraph 18, an example of how various people divide on issues based on previously held beliefs is followed in paragraph 19 with the sentence, "In other words, people rejected the validity of a scientific source because its conclusion contradicted their deeply held beliefs." Following this example, write a paragraph about how you responded to either essay in this debate. Describe your reaction in detail and then write the summary that explains the description: "In other words . . ." Does the retelling clarify the example? Does it add anything to what you've written?

2. Research the topic of climate change, focusing on any details from the essays that you feel is important. Once you've gathered your research, write a brief essay arguing your position on the topic.

3. Do you agree with Mooney's categorization of people? Does "who we are" affect our understanding and acceptance of current political and scientific issues? How does who you are affect your responses to issues he brings up in his essay?

Sarah Laskow

Debunking "Green Living": Combatting Climate Change Requires Lifestyle Changes, Not Organic Products

[*GOOD*, May 12, 2012]

BEFORE YOU READ

Do you buy products that claim to promote "green living"? What are some of the more important things we can do to combat climate change?

WORDS TO LEARN

ecstatic (para. 1): rapturous; extremely happy (adj)

conundrum (para. 1): something puzzling (noun)

pantheon (para. 5): collection (noun)

organic (para. 5): a substance of animal or vegetable origin (untainted by

chemically formulated fertilizers, pesticides, etc.) (adj)

livelihood (para. 5): a means of support (noun)

retrofit (para. 6): replacing old materials or equipment with newer ones (noun)

When I first heard that the Union of Concerned Scientists was creating a research-based guide to green living, I was ecstatic. How brilliant, I thought, to finally have the answer to the question of which of the seemingly infinite "green" actions make the most difference. Should I obsess about turning the lights off before I leave the house? Was composting worth the effort after all? UCS, which has a well-deserved reputation for accuracy and fact-based advocacy, seemed equipped to answer these conundrums once and for all. 1

Cooler Smarter: Practical Steps for Low-Carbon Living came out this week. And true to its promise, it uses research to determine which green actions make the most difference. I'm disappointed in the answers they 2

Sarah Laskow is a freelance editor, reporter, and writer living in New York City—focusing on sustainability, the environment, and politics. Her work has appeared in Salon, Capital, Newsweek, GOOD, The Nation, *and* The American Prospect.

came up with, though — not because they're wrong or overly complicated, but because they're not.

> The most important strategies for reducing a person's carbon footprint are to change what and how you drive, the energy you use at home, and what you eat.

After two years of research, UCS found 3 that the most important strategies for reducing a person's carbon footprint are to change "what and how you drive, the energy you use at home, and what you eat."

Those are answers we already knew. The 4 vast majority of the green advice you'll read? It's irrelevant. There are four primary activities that dump carbon into the atmosphere: traveling from place to place, keeping buildings at pleasant temperatures, creating electricity, and raising animals for meat.

The rest of the green living pantheon — bamboo utensils, composting, 5 eating local, reclaimed wood tables, organic cotton sheets — are nice gestures. And they often have other benefits: they might keep chemicals out of the water or provide a livelihood for local farmers. Many are also better than the alternatives they're replacing. But when it comes to tackling climate change — not only the most dangerous environmental issue the world faces, but also a looming human rights problem — choosing these green products can only make a tiny difference.

If we already know how to live without creating so much carbon, 6 that raises a more disturbing question: Why aren't we *doing it*? There is any number of excuses: Fixing buildings requires investing a chunk of cash up front, and deciding on the right retrofits is a complicated process. Meat is too good to give up. Clean energy is more expensive. If Congress had only passed cap-and-trade,[1] we wouldn't need to be making these choices, because more carbon-intensive products would cost more and fewer people would buy them.

But we're going to need to figure out how to make those choices. 7 Researchers who study behavior change and climate have found that even if the world did agree to cap carbon emissions, people would still need to change their habits if the planet is to avoid the worst consequences a changing climate will bring. So now they're experimenting with systems that can nudge people in the right direction. California is running a challenge, for instance, in which cities compete against each other to take smart green actions. At this point, we know the right steps to take. Now we just need to convince people to live more responsibly.

---

[1] Cap-and-trade (para. 6): Environmental policy tool, also known as emissions trading, that would provide economic incentives or reward a company that reduces its emissions and controls its pollution output.

VOCABULARY/USING A DICTIONARY

1. What is a *strategy* (para. 3)?
2. What does it mean if something is *irrelevant* (para. 4)? What does it mean if it's *relevant*?
3. What is an *emission* (para. 7)? What part of speech is it? What does it mean to *emit* something?

RESPONDING TO WORDS IN CONTEXT

1. How is "green living" (para. 1) different from other ways of living?
2. Laskow comments that a research-based guide to green living sounds *brilliant* (para. 1). What do you think she means? What other meanings does *brilliant* have?
3. Explain what is meant by the term *carbon footprint* (para. 3).

DISCUSSING MAIN POINT AND MEANING

1. What, according to Laskow, are the four main ways we create carbon emissions?
2. How does the author suggest we start fixing the problem of our carbon emissions?
3. According to Laskow, what are the benefits of buying organic sheets and eating food grown locally?

EXAMINING SENTENCES, PARAGRAPHS, AND ORGANIZATION

1. Laskow writes that researchers are "experimenting with systems that can nudge people in the right direction" to change their behaviors. Based on the information included in the paragraph, why do you think "nudge" is the right word to describe what the researchers are doing?
2. Where might Laskow have included more data to support the position of the UCS scientists? What might that data have looked like?
3. Laskow lists a number of "excuses" in paragraph 6 to explain why we aren't simply changing our behaviors to avoid climate change. What do these answers reveal about the problems of changing behavior and about our own attitudes?

THINKING CRITICALLY

1. Are you surprised by Laskow's reaction to the answers provided in *Cooler Smarter: Practical Steps for Low-Carbon Living*? Why or why not?
2. Have you given thought to the effect on the environment of products you use? Why or why not? What products do you use that support greener living? In what way might they be part of the "green living pantheon," as Laskow calls it?
3. Laskow ends her essay by saying, "Now we just need to convince people to live more responsibly." What do you think she means? What does living responsibly mean to you?

WRITING ACTIVITIES

1. Go to the supermarket. Look at the cleaning products, the food aisles, the hardware section, the packaging on products of all kinds. Take notes on what you see. After doing your research, write a short essay on the ways products and packaging are represented as "green" or as being better somehow for the environment. In your essay, consider Laskow's points about what really reduces a carbon footprint and comment on whether or not any of these products are truly helping to combat climate change. If they are not, discuss any benefit or truth linked to the way they're being marketed.

2. If Laskow and the UCS are right, there are four basic ways to reduce one's carbon footprint. In a brief narrative essay, write about how your lifestyle helps or hurts the environment. If the way in which you live seems to hurt the environment, consider what you would need to do to change your behavior.

Mona Charen

Cuddly Symbols Not Cooperating in Climate Change Panic

[Townhall.com, June 14, 2012]

BEFORE YOU READ

Is an argument more likely to be more troubling if it centers around an idea or image or if it provides numbers and statistics? Are you often swayed by the emotional impact of an argument before you research its facts thoroughly?

WORDS TO LEARN

manipulation (para. 1): the act of adapting or doctoring something to suit one's needs (noun)
potent (para. 2): powerful (adj)

iconic (para. 2): emblematic (adj)
winsome (para. 3): innocently charming (adj)
aerial (para. 5): in the air (adj)

Mona Charen is a political analyst and former White House staff member whose syndicated column appears in more than two hundred newspapers. She is a former CNN commentator, Pulitzer Prize judge, and the author of bestsellers Useful Idiots: How Liberals Got It Wrong in the Cold War and Still Blame America First *(2003) and* Do-Gooders: How Liberals Harm Those They Claim to Help—and the Rest of Us *(2005).*

symbolic (para. 7): representative of something (adj)

undermine (para. 11): to weaken or destroy in imperceptible stages (verb)

prestige (para. 11): importance through reputation (noun)

In a better world, debates about science — and nearly everything else — would be conducted without resort to demagoguery, sentimentality, cynical manipulation, or hysteria. In the world we inhabit, those tactics are dismayingly routine. Still, the great weakness of overwrought predictions of doom is that they can be checked.

The past year has not been kind to the most potent symbols of climate change hysteria. Consider the polar bears. Among the most moving images of the warmists' warnings was the solitary polar bear, supposedly marooned on an ice floe. The image became iconic after it was published in *Science Magazine*. Among the most memorable moments in Al Gore's film, *An Inconvenient Truth,* was an animated clip depicting struggling polar bears.

> The past year has not been kind to the most potent symbols of climate change hysteria.

You don't hear stories, as you do with dolphins, of polar bears rescuing drowning humans. But polar bears, especially cubs, have a different claim on our sympathy — they're adorable. We shudder to see winsome, furry mammals drifting off to sea on ice floes — all because we couldn't part with our SUVs. A children's book prepared by the United Nations put it just that way.

Well, according to WattsUpWithThat.com, the picture of that "stranded" polar bear has been lampooned as "ursus bogus." Experts on those creatures always found the warmists' interpretation of that photo odd, since polar bears can swim for hundreds of miles at a time. The longest recorded polar bear swim, according to *National Geographic,* was 426 miles straight (though *National Geographic* is all in on climate change). Since polar bears swim for a living, they're probably pretty good at gauging where land and ice floes are.

A new study from Canada, based on aerial surveys along the western shore of the Hudson Bay — a region considered a bellwether for bear numbers in the Arctic generally — found that the polar bear population was 66 percent higher than expected. Drikus Gissing, director of wildlife management for the Nunavut region, told the *Globe* and *Mail,* "The bear population is not in crisis as people believed. There is no doom and gloom." Oh, and the scientist for the Department of the Interior whose 2004 work on drowning polar bears inspired Al Gore and others has been placed on administrative leave for unspecified wrongdoing.

On the other side of the globe, a new survey using satellite technology has found that there are twice as many emperor penguins in Antarctica as previously thought. *Science Daily* reports, "Using a technique known as pan-sharpening to increase the resolution of the satellite imagery, the science teams were able to differentiate between birds, ice, shadow, and penguin poo or guano. They then used ground counts and aerial photography to calibrate the analysis." The results: 595,000 birds dressed in black tie, almost double the previous estimates.   6

Less beguiling, but no less important for symbolic value, are the melting glaciers. The U.N. Intergovernmental Panel on Climate Change (co-winner of the Nobel Peace Prize with Gore) predicted in 2007 that "Glaciers in the Himalayas are receding faster than in any other part of the world and if the present rate continues, the likelihood of their disappearing by the year 2035 and perhaps sooner is very high if the Earth keeps warming at the current rate." The melting glaciers, we were told, would "devastate" the lives of more than a billion people living in Asia and eventually, swamp Manhattan and other coastal cities.   7

In 2010, the IPCC admitted that the melting Himalayas prediction was not based on science but on a 1999 media interview given by one scientist. They said they regretted the error.   8

Now, a study in *Nature*, based on satellite imagery, has shown that some melting of lower altitude glaciers is taking place but that higher glaciers have been adding ice. The range called Karakorum, which includes the K2 peak, has been adding mass over the past decade, while other regions have lost mass. None of the glaciologists knows why.   9

Nature reports that the loss of ice from the Himalayas, once estimated at 50 gigatons per year, was actually measured at only 4 gigatons per year between 2003 and 2010. That's quite a difference.   10

That the climate is warming is not, if you ask most scientists, in question, though it hasn't warmed much — if at all — in the past decade. But the panic mongering of the global warmists has not just undermined their own cause — it has diminished the prestige of science generally, and that is a serious loss.   11

VOCABULARY/USING A DICTIONARY

1. What is *demagoguery* (para. 1)? What is a *demagogue*?
2. Describe the original meaning of *bellwether* (para. 5).
3. The melting glaciers are apparently less *beguiling* (para. 7) than animals in the argument about climate change. What does that mean? What is the definition of *guile*?

RESPONDING TO WORDS IN CONTEXT

1. In paragraph 1, Charen says that debates about science sometimes resort to *sentimentality* in their arguments. What does it mean to be sentimental? Why might a polar bear be a sentimental figure to include in a debate?

2. Charen says the image of the stranded polar bear has been "lampooned as 'ursus bogus'" (para. 3). What does it mean to *lampoon* something? How might you guess what the word means from what follows in the sentence?

3. What part of speech is the word *swamp* in paragraph 7? What does it mean? What other parts of speech and definitions of the word do you know?

DISCUSSING MAIN POINT AND MEANING

1. Why are people moved by the idea of polar bears in trouble?

2. Give one example of "panic mongering" in this essay.

3. What is taking place in the Himalayas that is baffling the scientists who have been watching the region? What does their information suggest about the effect of climate change?

EXAMINING SENTENCES, PARAGRAPHS, AND ORGANIZATION

1. Why might Charen use the word "warmists" in paragraph 4? What is the effect of that particular moniker?

2. Charen begins her essay by saying that "overwrought predictions of doom . . . can be checked" (para. 1). Do "checks" allay fears about the polar bears and glaciers? How is her information presented?

3. Why does Charen include references to *An Inconvenient Truth* and other contemporary books, Web sites, and media? Do her references add to the article overall? Explain.

THINKING CRITICALLY

1. Do you think the story of polar bears drowning is a good example of science "resort[ing] to demagoguery, sentimentality, cynical manipulation, or hysteria" (para. 1)? Why or why not?

2. What should the role and tone of science be, especially around topics like climate change? Does your opinion differ from Charen's view or do you agree?

3. Can scientific accounts about an issue differ? How might that happen? If there are two different accounts about the same issue, whom do you believe and why?

WRITING ACTIVITIES

1. Explore the Web site WattsUpWithThat.com that is mentioned in paragraph 4. Write a short review of the site: what is found there, the subject and tone of the articles, the frequency of the posts, and the intended

audience. Would you expect to find the information on the polar bear that Charen mentions on this site? Why or why not?

2. Charen states that "*National Geographic* is all in on climate change" (para. 4). Do some online or library research on *National Geographic* — skim old issues, and identify the overall mission and tone of the magazine. What do you think Charen means by her statement? Explain.

3. Write a brief essay about the use of "cuddly symbols" in scientific argument. You may discuss other "cuddly symbols" besides penguins and polar bears that come up in discussions of climate change, or you may write about a different scientific debate. Also consider symbols that are not so cuddly and examine why one symbol might be used at one time and another is chosen in a different argument.

Tatevik Manucharyan (student essay)

Professor Lectures on Dangers of Climate Change

[*El Vaquero*, Glendale Community College, April 4, 2012]

BEFORE YOU READ

How do you view the potential impact of climate change? Does it matter whether or not it is due to natural processes or man-made activity? If it is a coming reality, how do you think people might combat it effectively?

WORDS TO LEARN

comprehensive (para. 2): having a large scope (adj)

implication (para. 9): something suggested indirectly (noun)

vital (para. 11): forceful or necessary (adj)

excessive (para. 14): extravagant; characterized by excess (adj)

foreseeable (para. 15): able to be anticipated (adj)

Tatevik Manucharyan graduated in 2011 from the University of California– Berkeley with a degree in political science. She authored this essay, among others for the newspaper, while taking a journalism course at Glendale Community College.

In his lecture, "Three Questions About Climate Change," Glendale Community College Professor Poorna Pal tackled one of the hottest topics of the century — is the planet undergoing global warming, and if so, who is to be blamed and what can be done?

After providing a comprehensive overview of the latest research and drawing on data from such authoritative sources as NASA and the U.S. Environmental Protection Agency, Pal presented the findings of the scientific community showing that there is, indeed, a rise in the temperature of the planet. "Yes, global warming is taking place, no questions about that," he said.

Standing in front of a mixed audience of students, faculty, and elderly people, Pal engaged everyone in a fast-paced debate. He addressed the present and future state of the planet by sprinkling humor over highly alarming data.

"Is global warming really bad? Well, why should we only think of penguins and polar bears?" Pal said, " . . . you can grow apples in Alaska! They've already started doing that . . . You can grow bananas in Kansas! Global warming is not bad."

"How many of you guys would like Glendale college on a beach?" Pal asked, bringing the issue of a worldwide rise in sea levels closer to home.

But then there were cases, when the outlook on climate change took a turn for the serious. "You have just another 25 years to go and visit Maldives[1] — beautiful islands" said the professor, "Why only 25 years? Then Maldives will be under water."

The central question of the lecture was not whether or not climate change is a reality. The key issue was whether global warming is due to human activity or natural processes.

> The key issue was whether global warming is due to human activity or natural processes.

After going over research establishing the link between increased carbon dioxide levels in the atmosphere and the rise in global temperatures, Pal said that scientists would be only too happy to find a reason other than "human industrial activity" to explain the "shoot up in carbon dioxide." However, to this day, no other explanation has been found, he added.

According to Pal, while there is not much to be done if global warming is the result of natural processes, the implications that human activity is responsible for climate change are far more serious, calling for action

---

[1] Maldives (para. 6): Islands considered to be threatened by global warming, located southwest of India and Sri Lanka.

on our part. Yet, taking action may be impossible given certain economic and political realities.

On one of his lecture slides, he pointed out that "Economic prosperity and energy consumption are closely correlated and so are economic prosperity and carbon emissions." Showing the close correlation between economic growth and carbon-based energy use, Pal warned against the environmental impact of the economic rise of BRIC countries — Brazil, Russia, India, and China — referring to them as "the most significant sources of future carbon emissions." 10

At the same time, Pal underlined the impossibility of stopping the growth of these countries, considering their vital role in the global economy. He discussed the use of nuclear energy, as a more realistic alternative to trying to stop the growth of BRIC countries, but this option, too, was problematic. 11

"The problem is that energy pollutes, whatever source we look at. That's why . . . nuclear energy would have been a good alternative," said Pal, "but you see, after that Japanese tsunami and that disaster at the nuclear plant, everybody's worried about it, everybody's afraid of it." 12

Unlike the rest of the lecture, the ending of the talk was far from cheerful. 13

"I keep trying to see if we can find some reason for excessive carbon dioxide in the atmosphere," Pal said. 14

" . . . Otherwise it is a reality and I don't see how we are going to change it in the foreseeable future without seeking to stop the growth of India, to stop the growth of China . . . and that means that the alternative is to sit down and cry. Sorry I wish I had better news for you," concluded the professor with a bitter smile on his face. 15

VOCABULARY/USING A DICTIONARY

1. Define *authoritative* (para. 2). What does it mean to be an *authority* on something?
2. What part of speech is *correlated* (para. 10)? What about *correlation* (para. 10)?
3. What is a *tsunami* (para. 12)? From what language is it derived?

RESPONDING TO WORDS IN CONTEXT

1. Manucharyan writes that Pal *underlined* (para. 11) the impossibility of stopping industrial growth in Brazil, Russia, India, and China. What does that verb mean in this context?
2. What do you think Pal is referring to when he mentions "certain economic and political realities" (para. 9) that get in the way of our action to reduce the increase in our carbon dioxide levels?

3. What does the "bitter smile" (para. 15) on Pal's face tell you about how he feels about global warming?

DISCUSSING MAIN POINT AND MEANING

1. Why does Pal indicate that stopping man-made global warming may be impossible?

2. What are the three questions about climate change that Pal sets out to discuss in his lecture?

3. What, according to Manucharyan, is the main question talked about in the lecture?

EXAMINING SENTENCES, PARAGRAPHS, AND ORGANIZATION

1. Manucharyan opens the essay with the statement, "In his lecture, 'Three Questions About Climate Change,' Glendale Community College Professor Poorna Pal tackled one of the hottest topics of the century—is the planet undergoing global warming, and if so, who is to be blamed and what can be done?" How does this opening reflect the humorous tone Pal assumes at the beginning of the lecture?

2. Describe Manucharyan's approach in writing this essay. How does this essay differ from others in this chapter?

3. What is the effect of including quotations in the essay? What do they add to the essay?

THINKING CRITICALLY

1. What do you think of how Pal approaches his material in his lecture? Would you be interested in hearing him lecture? Why or why not?

2. How does the ending of the essay influence your feelings about climate change and what can be done to stop it? If you believe that climate change is a reality, is the essay's ending likely to call you to action or leave you feeling defeated? If you do not believe in climate change, write an essay supporting your views. Cite readings from this chapter to bolster your argument.

3. Is it impossible to reduce human industrial activity? Why or why not?

WRITING ACTIVITIES

1. Interview a professor or fellow student on a subject you feel he or she is knowledgeable about, taking detailed notes during the discussion. Then write a brief article that describes the interview, focusing on your subject. Edit out any references to your own input in the conversation. After looking over the article, take notes on how your subject comes across in the essay: Does he or she seem notably somber, humorous, silly, or animated based on what he or she has said? Consider how the style of your essay mimics the style of Manucharyan's description of Pal's lecture.

2. Research explanations for climate change due to natural processes. Do you believe that climate change due to natural processes is a sufficient explanation? Why or why not?
3. Research the "Japanese tsunami and the disaster at the nuclear plant." In a brief essay, discuss what, if any, impact that event has made on your opinion of using nuclear power.

Integrating Quotations

Two types of quotations are routinely used in nonfiction. One type, more common in essays and criticism, is the use of a famous or previously published remark. For example, a writer might begin an essay: "As Franklin Delano Roosevelt once said, 'We have nothing to fear but fear itself.'" A book like *Bartlett's Familiar Quotations* is a rich source of memorable quotes and has been used by several generations of writers, artists, celebrities, and political figures. Many well-known quotations and their sources can easily be found online.

More commonly seen in journalism, however, are quotations gathered from live interviews, speeches, or lectures. In writing news or feature stories, the journalist usually needs to collect interviews from several people or cite the various remarks from one speaker in the course of a speech. But whether the writer is relying on multiple interviews or the comments of a single speaker, the gathered remarks are only one part of the writing process. The writer also needs to integrate the quotations so that they work effectively within the body of the essay.

In "Professor Lectures on Dangers of Climate Change," Tatevik Manucharyan effectively covers an event at Glendale Community College that deals with what she calls (pun intended) "one of the hottest topics of the century — is the planet undergoing global warming . . . ?" The purpose of the coverage was not to provide students with a full transcript of Professor Poorna Pal's lecture but to report briefly on his most salient points. To do this, Manucharyan cites Pal throughout the essay; in fact, his comments are the main source of information. Note how quotations compose practically the entire body of the essay. Yet, to string one quotation after another would be monotonous, so Manucharyan at times paraphrases the lecturer and adds her own commentary detailing the audience and style of the lecturer. By selecting only certain key remarks that are then effectively integrated into the body of the essay, the author is able to cover the professor's main points without an over-citation that would be monotonous.

After providing a comprehensive overview of the latest research and drawing on data from such authoritative sources as NASA and the U.S. Environmental Protection Agency, <u>Pal presented the findings of the scientific community showing that there is, indeed, a rise in the temperature of the planet. "Yes, global warming is taking place, no questions about that," he said.</u> (1)

1
First quotation summarizes key point

<u>Standing in front of a mixed audience of students, faculty, and elderly people, Pal engaged everyone in a fast-paced debate.</u> (2) He addressed the present and future state of the planet by sprinkling humor over highly alarming data.

2
Comments on audience and style of lecture

<u>"Is global warming really bad? Well, why should we only think of penguins and polar bears?" Pal said, " . . . you can grow apples in Alaska! They've already started doing that . . . You can grow bananas in Kansas! Global warming is not bad."</u> (3)

3
Next quotation shows humor and supports main point

STUDENT WRITER AT WORK
Tatevik Manucharyan

R.A. What inspired you to write this essay? And publish it in your campus paper?

T.M. I wanted to cover an on-campus event. The topic of climate change sounded interesting to me, so I decided to attend the lecture and write about it. By writing this article and publishing it in the college newspaper, I wanted to inform the student body about the issue of climate change and all the problems associated with it.

R.A. How long did it take for you to write this piece? Did you revise your work? What were your goals as you revised?

T.M. It took me several hours to write the article as I'm the type of writer who likes to get it right the first time. Then I reviewed that initial draft, checking for accuracy of information and quotes.

R.A. Do you generally show your writing to friends before submitting it? Do you collaborate or bounce your ideas off others?

T.M. Generally, I ask one or two people to read my work after I write it. Since this was a news article, I did not express my point of view on this topic.

R.A. What do you like to read?

T.M. I like reading fiction — mostly from the nineteenth and twentieth centuries. I also read the *New York Times*, the *Los Angeles Times*, and the local daily newspaper.

R.A. What topics most interest you as a writer?

T.M. I'm most interested in issues of social and cultural nature, also the human psyche, interactions, and relationships.

R.A. Do you plan to continue writing for publication?

T.M. Definitely!

R.A. Are you pursuing a career in which writing will be a component?

T.M. I plan to become a researcher and/or journalist, so writing will certainly be a big part of my career.

R.A. What advice do you have for other student writers?

T.M. I think the secret to being a good writer is reading voraciously and analyzing the writing style of one's favorite authors. When it comes to journalism, accuracy and fact-checking are also very important. You don't want to misinform your readers.

The Warming of the World

In a famous short poem in 1920, Robert Frost wondered whether the earth would end in fire or ice — melted by overheating or turned completely into a frozen wasteland. At the time, it appeared that the future climate of the earth could go in either direction. Many doomsday scenarios, in fact, pictured another Ice Age, with the earth becoming uninhabitable as glaciers expanded and rivers and seas froze over. In the mid-1970s, such predictions grew popular, and they found scientific support in 1981 when a prominent British astronomer, Sir Frederick Hoyle, published his forecast of a new ice age, *Ice: The Ultimate Human Catastrophe.*

But by this time, many scientists were also gathering evidence for an opposing worst-case scenario: The earth was seriously overheating as a result of what was called a "greenhouse effect." The crisis was man-made and attributable to the ever-increasing use of fossil fuels (coal, gas, and oil). In 1985, one of America's leading scientists and a prolific scientific writer, Carl Sagan, published a warning in the popular Sunday

© Tony Korody/Sygma/Corbis.

Astronomer Carl Sagan, 1981. Carl Sagan (1934–1996) was for years one of America's best-known scientists, largely because of such popular books as *The Dragons of Eden: Speculations on the Evolution of Human Intelligence* (1977), *Broca's Brain: Reflections on the Romance of Science* (1979), and the enormously successful TV series he hosted, *Cosmos.* Part of his popularity can be attributed to his respect for the general public he was writing for and speaking to. He once said, "The public is a lot brighter and more interested in science than they're given credit for . . . . They're not numbskulls. Thinking scientifically is as natural as breathing."

magazine *Parade*. In "The Warming of the World," Sagan — like Hoyle, an astronomer — explained to his readers how fossil fuels produced dangerous levels of carbon dioxide (CO_2) that were "irreversible." Since the industrial revolution, Sagan wrote, the amount of CO_2 in the atmosphere has been steadily increasing and, unless nothing changes, the surface temperature of the earth will also increase.

One of the earliest proponents of global warming (a term that was first used in 1969), Sagan asked in his *Parade* essay the key questions: At our present rate of fuel consumption, how long will it take before our climate becomes dangerously warmer? And what would be the consequences of a perceptibly warmer earth? But despite the alarming evidence even then, Sagan never sounded panic-stricken and he was optimistic that solutions would be discovered in time. Had this great scientist lived into his late seventies, it would be interesting to see what his attitude towards climate change would be today.

Discussing the Unit

SUGGESTED TOPIC FOR DISCUSSION

In this unit, the essays tackle issues of skepticism, conviction about a topic vs. evidence, and misinformation as related to the topic of climate change. When should we accept fact as fact and ignore our preexisting beliefs? Is it even possible to do so? Should we believe something just because an "expert" tells us it is true?

PREPARING FOR CLASS DISCUSSION

1. Describe what you think the political views are of these essayists based on what you find in their writing. Can you identify each one individually as liberal or conservative? What evidence backs up your assumptions?
2. Do the writers of these essays believe in climate change or do they not? How can you tell?

FROM DISCUSSION TO WRITING

1. Compare the analysis of how we form ideas about issues discussed by Mooney in "We Can't Handle the Truth" with the arguments presented by Charen and Bottum and Anderson in their essays. Are Charen and Bottum and Anderson confirming what they already believe in their essays, or are they writing without bias? Use examples from these essays to support your answer.

2. Do you hold strong beliefs about particular issues such as climate change? Have you ever changed your mind about such an issue? What, according to the essayists in this chapter, affects your stance on issues such as these, and what would it take to change your mind? Write a brief essay that explains your answer.

TOPIC FOR CROSS-CULTURAL DISCUSSION
Do Americans view issues such as climate change differently from people in other parts of the world? If yes, why might this be so? If no, why would there be no cultural difference?

This chapter continues online. Visit the e-Page at **bedfordstmartins.com/americanow/epages** for a Web selection.

Continued from page iv

Armendariz, Rebecca, "Chat History" from *GOOD*, September 14, 2011, http://www.good.is/post /chat-history/. Copyright © 2011 by GOOD Worldwide, LLC. Reprinted with permission. All rights reserved.

Bissinger, Buzz, "Why College Football Should be Banned" from the *Wall Street Journal*, May 8, 2012. Copyright © 2012 by Dow Jones & Company, Inc. Reprinted with permission of Dow Jones & Company, Inc. License number 2978411060100. All rights reserved worldwide.

Bottum, Joseph, and William Anderson, "Unchanging Science" from *The Weekly Standard*, November 28, 2011. Copyright © 2011 by Joseph Bottum and William Anderson. Reprinted with permission of *The Weekly Standard*. All rights reserved.

Brottman, Mikita, "Spelling Matters" from *The Chronicile of Higher Education*, January 15, 2012. Copyright © 2012 by Mikita Brottman. Reprinted with permission of the author. All rights reserved.

Charen, Mona, "Cuddly Symbols Not Cooperating in Climate Change Panic" from Townhall.com, June 14, 2012. Copyright © 2012 by Mona Charen. Reprinted with permission with Creators Syndicate. All rights reserved.

Delbanco, Andrew, "3 Reasons College Still Matters" from *College*, published by Princeton University Press, as appeared in *The Boston Globe Magazine*, March 4, 2012. Copyright © 2012 by Andrew Delbarco. Reprinted with permission of Princeton University Press.

Diamond, Shayna, "Words Are What We Make of Them," Ka Leo, University of Hawai'i, February 5, 2012. Reprinted by permission of the author.

Dimera, Maria, "A College Degree Is a Worthy Achievement" from the *Corsair*, October 8, 2011. Copyright © 2011 by Maria Dimera. Reprinted with permission of the author.

Ehrenreich, Barbara, and John Ehrenreich, "The Making of the 99%" from *The Nation*, December 14, 2011. Copyright © by Barbara Ehrenreich and John Ehrenreich. Reprinted with permission from *The Nation*. All rights reserved. For subscription information, call 1-800-333-8536. Portions of each week's *Nation* magazine can be accessed at http://www.thenation.com.

Ewing, Jacob. "Steven Pinker and the Question of Violence," Ashland University, June 17, 2012. Reprinted by permission of the author.

Gabel, Aja, "The Marriage Crisis" from the *University of Virginia Magazine*, summer 2012. Copyright © 2012 by UVA Alumni Association. Reprinted with permission. All rights reserved.

Ghuman, Shawn, "Technology Hurts Social Bonds," *Collegiate Times*, Virginia Tech, February 22, 2012. Reprinted by permission of the author.

Glazek, Christopher, excerpts from "Raise the Crime Rate" from *n + 1*, winter 2012. Copyright © 2012 by Christopher Glazek. Reprinted with permission of the author. All rights reserved.

Greenwell, Megan, "Do College Sports Affect Students' Grades? A Defense of the NCAA," from *GOOD*, January 3, 2012, http://www.good.is/post/do-college-sports-affect-students-grades-a -defense-of-the-ncaa/. Copyright © 2012 by GOOD Worldwide, LLC. Reprinted with permission. All rights reserved.

Iyer, Pico, "The Terminal Check" from *Granta*, No. 116, summer 2011. Copyright © 2011 by Pico Iyer. Reprinted with permission of the author. All rights reserved.

John-Hall, Annette, "Using Video Games to Reduce Violence" from *The Philadelphia Inquirer*, February 3, 2012. Copyright © 2012 by *The Philadelphia Inquirer*. Reprinted with permission of The YGS Group. All rights reserved.

Kotlowitz, Alex, "Defusing Violence" from *The Rotarian*, February 2012. Copyright © 2012 by Alex Kotlowitz. Reprinted with permission of the author. All rights reserved.

Kutcher, Ashton, "Has Texting Killed Romance?" from *Harper's Bazaar*, January 2011. Copyright © 2011 by Ashton Kutcher. Reprinted with permission of the author. All rights reserved.

Laskow, Sarah, "Debunking 'Green Living': Combating Climate Change Requires Lifestyle Changes, Not Organic Products" from *GOOD*, May 17, 2012, http://www/good.is/post/debunking

Smith, Lauren, "No, The Holiday Season Just Brings Out the Giver in Us All" from *The Glacier*,
December 9, 2011. Copyright © 2011 by Lauren Smith. Reprinted with permission of *The
Glacier*, Moraine Valley Community College. All rights reserved.

Sukel, Kayt, "Rethinking Monogamy" from *Big Think*, June 3, 2012. Copyright © 2012 by The Big
Think, Inc. Reprinted with permission. All rights reserved.

Tabarrok, Alex, "Tuning In to Dropping Out" from *The Chronicle of Higher Education*, March 9, 2012.
Copyright © 2012 by Alex Tabarrok. Reprinted with permission of the author. All rights reserved.

Thomas, Karen. "Misplaced Priorities: It's Time to Invest in Schools, Not Prisons," *American River
Current*, American River College, June 2, 2011. Reprinted by permission of the author.

Trubek, Anne, "Use Your Own Words" from *Wired*, February 2012. Copyright © 2012 by Anne
Trubek/*Wired* Magazine/Conde Nast. Reprinted with permission. All rights reserved.

Venegas, Maria, "The Devil's Spine" originally published in *Ploughshares*, spring 2012. Copyright
© 2012 by Maria Venegas. Reprinted with permission of the Wylie Agency, LLC. All rights
reserved.

Williams, Thomas Chatterton, "As Black as We Wish To Be" from *The New York Times*, March 18,
2012. Copyright © 2012 by *The New York Times*. All rights reserved. Used by permission and
protected by the Copyright Laws of the United States. The printing, copying, redistribution, or
retransmission of this Content without expressed, written permission is prohibited. http://www
.nytimes.com/

e-Pages Acknowledgments

Chapter 1: The Baby Name Voyager: BabyNameWizard.com

Chapter 2: The Interactive Singles Map of the United States: http://www.xoxosoma.com/singles/

Chapter 3: Hashtag Humblebrag: © Humblebrag

Chapter 4: Project Implicit: © Project Implicit

Chapter 5: The Living Room Candidate: Dwight D. Eisenhower Presidential Library/NARA

Chapter 6: Should College Football Be Banned?: Excerpt from the debate: "Ban college football?"
Courtesy of Intelligence Squared U.S. Debates, May 18, 2012, www.iq2us.org

Chapter 7: Test Your Gun Law IQ (Brady Campaign): Brady Campaign to Prevent Gun Violence

Chapter 8: On the Web, Do Spelling and Grammar Matter?: Google.com

Chapter 9: Khan Academy "172,799,250 Lessons Delivered": Khan Academy

Chapter 10: What's Your Economic Outlook?: From *The New York Times*, 10/10/2011. *The New York
Times*. All rights reserved. Used by permission and protected by the copyright laws of the United
States. The printing, copying, redistribution or retransmission of this Content without express
written permission is prohibited.

Chapter 11: The Private Prison Problem (ACLU): RT TV/YouTube

Chapter 12: Connect the Dots: 350.org

Index of Authors and Titles

ACLU, *The Man on the Left* [advertisement], 42

Ahmad, Meher, *My Homeland Security Journey* [student essay], 124

Ajmani, Tim, *Compensation for College Athletes?* [student essay], 177

American Indian College Fund, *Think Indian* [advertisement], 137

American Mobility, 271

Anderson, William, *Unchanging Science*, 333

Armendariz, Rebecca, *Chat History*, 103

As Black as We Wish to Be, 132

Atwan, Robert, *Can the State Prohibit the Sale of Violent Video Games to Minors?*, 211

Beyond the Prison Bubble, 301

Bissinger, Buzz, *Why College Football Should Be Banned*, 169

Bottum, Joseph, and William Anderson, *Unchanging Science*, 333

Brottman, Mikita, *Spelling Matters*, 217

Can the State Prohibit the Sale of Violent Video Games to Minors?, 211

Charen, Mona, *Cuddly Symbols Not Cooperating in Climate Change Panic*, 344

Chat History, 102

College Degree is a Worthy Achievement, A, [student essay], 258

Compensation for College Athletes? [student essay], 177

Could Temporary Marriages Reduce the Alarming Rate of Divorce? [student essay], 80

Cuddly Symbols Not Cooperating in Climate Change Panic, 344

Debunking "Green Living": Combatting Climate Change Requires Lifestyle Changes, Not Organic Products, 341

Defusing Violence, 202

Delbanco, Andrew, *Three Reasons College Still Matters*, 243

Devil's Spine, The, 54

Diamond, Shayna, *Words Are What We Make of Them* [student essay], 229

Diaz, Alan, *Elián González* [photograph], 34

Dimera, Maria, *A College Degree is a Worthy Achievement* [student essay], 258

Do College Sports Affect Students' Grades? A Defense of the NCAA, 173

Easily Pronounced Names May Make People More Likable, 49
Ehrenreich, Barbara, and John Ehrenreich, *The Making of the 99%,* 279
Electronic Intimacy, 91
Elián González [photograph], 34
Ewing, Jacob, *Steven Pinker and the Question of Violence* [student essay], 195

Fischer, Ed, *It's Only until We End Terrorism* [cartoon], 39
Flag Raising at Iwo Jima [photograph], 32
Franklin, Thomas E., *Three Firefighters Raising the Flag* [photograph], 33

Gabel, Aja, *The Marriage Crisis,* 71
Ghuman, Shawn, *Is Technology Destroying Social Bonds?* [student essay], 110
Glazek, Christopher, *Raise the Crime Rate,* 310
Greenwell, Megan, *Do College Sports Affect Students' Grades? A Defense of the NCAA,* 173

Has Texting Killed Romance?, 99
How to Approach a Different Culture? [student essay], 27

Is Technology Destroying Social Bonds? [student essay], 110
Is the Holiday Season Too Materialistic? NO [student essay], 158
Is the Holiday Season Too Materialistic? YES [student essay], 157
It's Only until We End Terrorism [cartoon], 39
Iyer, Pico, *The Terminal Check,* 119

John-Hall, Annette, *Using Video Games to Reduce Violence,* 208

Kosic, Milos, *How to Approach a Different Culture?* [student essay], 27
Kotlowitz, Alex, *Defusing Violence,* 202
Kutcher, Ashton, *Has Texting Killed Romance?,* 99

Laskow, Sarah, *Debunking "Green Living": Combatting Climate Change Requires Lifestyle Changes, Not Organic Products,* 341
Lembitz, Breanna, *A Taste of Freedom: What I Got at Occupy Wall Street* [student essay], 287

Livingston, James, *Why Thou Should Shop and Spend for the Planet*, 153

Making of the 99%, The, 279
Man on the Left, The [advertisement], 42
Manucharyan, Tatevik, *Professor Lectures on Dangers of Climate Change* [student essay], 348
Many Paths to Success — With or Without a College Education, The [student essay], 17
Marche, Stephen, *We Are Not All Created Equal*, 267
Marlette, Doug, *When It's Too Late to Warn Iran* [cartoon], 37
Marriage Crisis, The, 71
Mather, Kati, *The Many Paths to Success — With or Without a College Education* [student essay], 17
Meyer, Bruce D., and James X. Sullivan, *American Mobility*, 271
Misplaced Priorities: It's Time to Invest in Schools, Not Prisons [student essay], 314
Mooney, Chris, *We Can't Handle the Truth*, 323
Mosher, Dave, *Easily Pronounced Names May Make People More Likable*, 49
Muther, Christopher, *We Get the Point!*, 224
My Homeland Security Journey [student essay], 124

Nasif, Greg, *Washington, Yea! Redskins, Boo!* [student essay], 58
Not All College Majors Are Created Equal, 254
Not-So-Great Expectations [student essay], 22

Ophir, Alexander G., Steven M. Phelps, Anna Bess Sorin, and Jerry O. Wolff, *Social but Not Genetic Monogamy Is Associated with Greater Breeding Success in Prairie Voles*, 79

Petersilia, Joan, *Beyond the Prison Bubble*, 301
Pinker, Steven, *Violence Vanquished*, 187
Professor Lectures on Dangers of Climate Change [student essay], 348

Raise the Crime Rate, 310
Rardon, Candace Rose, *Not-So-Great Expectations* [student essay], 22
Rethinking Monogamy, 78
Rivera, Natalie, *Could Temporary Marriages Reduce the Alarming Rate of Divorce?* [student essay], 80

Rosen, Christine, *Electronic Intimacy*, 91
Rosenthal, Joe, *Flag Raising at Iwo Jima* [photograph], 32

Saleh, Amel, *Is the Holiday Season is Too Materialistic? YES*
    [student essay], 157
Sandel, Michael J., *What Isn't For Sale?*, 145
Singletary, Michelle, *Not All College Majors Are Created Equal*, 254
Smith, Lauren, *Is the Holiday Season Too Materialistic? NO*
    [student essay], 158
Social but Not Genetic Monogamy Is Associated with Greater Breeding Success in
    Prairie Voles, 79
Spelling Matters, 217
Stem Cells [cartoon], 40
Steven Pinker and the Question of Violence [student essay], 195
Sukel, Kayt, *Rethinking Monogamy*, 78
Sullivan, James X., *American Mobility*, 271

Tabarrok, Alex, *Tuning In to Dropping Out*, 249
Taste of Freedom: What I Got at Occupy Wall Street, A, [student essay], 287
Terminal Check, The, 119
Think Indian [advertisement], 137
Thomas, Karen, *Misplaced Priorities: It's Time to Invest in Schools, Not Prisons*
    [student essay], 314
Three Firefighters Raising the Flag [photograph], 33
Three Reasons College Still Matters, 243
Trubek, Anne, *Use Your Own Words*, 220
Tuning In to Dropping Out, 249

Unchanging Science, 333
Use Your Own Words, 220
Using Video Games to Reduce Violence, 208

Venegas, Maria, *The Devil's Spine*, 54
Violence Vanquished, 187

Washington, Yea! Redskins, Boo! [student essay], 58
We Are Not All Created Equal, 267
We Can't Handle the Truth, 323
We Get the Point!, 224

What Isn't For Sale?, 145
When It's Too Late to Warn Iran [cartoon], 37
Why College Football Should Be Banned, 169
Why Thou Should Shop and Spend for the Planet, 153
Williams, Thomas Chatterton, *As Black as We Wish to Be*, 132
Words Are What We Make of Them [student essay], 229

Ziegler, Jack, *Stem Cells* [cartoon], 40

Missing something? To access the e-Pages that accompany this text, visit **bedfordstmartins.com/americanow/epages**. Students who do not buy a new book can purchase access to e-Pages at this site.

Inside the e-Pages for *America Now*

The Baby Name Voyager [interactive graphic]

The Interactive Singles Map of the United States [interactive graphic]

Hashtag Humblebrag [image]

Project Implicit [interactive quiz]

The Living Room Candidate [videos]

Should College Football Be Banned? [video]

Test Your Gun Law IQ [interactive quiz]

On the Web, Do Spelling and Grammar Matter? [video]

Khan Academy: "172,799,250 Lessons Delivered" [video]

What's Your Economic Outlook? [interactive graphic]

The Private Prison Problem [video]

Connect the Dots [image]